STUDIES IN
EARLY
CHRISTIANITY

A Collection of Scholarly Essays

edited by
Everett Ferguson
ABILENE CHRISTIAN UNIVERSITY

with
David M. Scholer
NORTH PARK COLLEGE AND THEOLOGICAL SEMINARY

and
Paul Corby Finney
CENTER OF THEOLOGICAL INQUIRY

A Garland Series

CONTENTS OF SERIES

VOLUME IX

Doctrines of
God and Christ
in the Early Church

edited with introductions by

Everett Ferguson

Garland Publishing, Inc.
New York & London
1993

Library of Congress Cataloging-in-Publication Data

Doctrines of God and Christ in the early church / edited by Everett
Ferguson.
    p.   cm. — (Studies in early Christianity ; v. 9)
    Includes bibliographical references.
    ISBN 0–8153–1069–2 (alk. paper)
    1. God—History of doctrines—Early church, ca. 30–600.
2. Jesus Christ—History of doctrines—Early church, ca. 30–600.
I. Ferguson, Everett, 1933-   . II. Series.
BT98. D56   1993
231'.09'015—dc20   92–41865
                                       CIP

Printed on acid-free, 250-year-life paper
Manufactured in the United States of America

Contents

Series Introduction

Christianity has been the formative influence on Western civilization and has maintained a significant presence as well in the Near East and, through its missions, in Africa and Asia. No one can understand Western civilization and the world today, much less religious history, without an understanding of the early history of Christianity.

The first six hundred years after the birth of Jesus were the formative period of Christian history. The theology, liturgy, and organization of the church assumed their definitive shape during this period. Since biblical studies form a separate, distinctive discipline, this series confines itself to sources outside the biblical canon, except as these sources were concerned with the interpretation and use of the biblical books. During the period covered in this series the distinctive characteristics of the Roman Catholic and Eastern Orthodox Churches emerged.

The study of early Christian literature, traditionally known as Patristics (for the church fathers), has experienced a resurgence in the late twentieth century. Evidences of this are the flourishing of a new professional society, the North American Patristics Society, a little over twenty years old; the growing number of teachers and course offerings at major universities and seminaries; the number of graduate students studying and choosing to write their dissertations in this area; the volume of books published in the field; and attendance at the quadrennial International Conferences on Patristic Studies at Oxford as well as at many smaller specialized conferences. This collection of articles reflects this recent growing interest and is intended to encourage further study. The papers at the International Conferences on Patristic Studies from the first conference in 1951 to the present have been published in the series *Studia Patristica,* and interested readers are referred to these volumes for more extensive treatment of the topics considered in this series of reprints and many other matters as well.

The volumes in this series are arranged topically to cover biography, literature, doctrines, practices, institutions, worship, missions, and daily life. Archaeology and art as well as writings are drawn on in order to give reality to the Christian movement in its early centuries. Ample attention is also given to the relation of Christianity to pagan thought and life, to the Roman state, to Judaism, and to doctrines and practices that came to be judged as heretical or schismatic. Introductions to each volume will attempt to tie the articles together so that an integrated understanding of the history will result.

The aim of the collection is to give balanced and comprehensive coverage. Early on I had to give up the idealism and admit the arrogance of attempting to select the "best" article on each topic. Criteria applied in the selection included the following: original and excellent research and writing, subject matter of use to teachers and students, groundbreaking importance for the history of research, foundational information for introducing issues and options. Preference was given to articles in English where available. Occasional French and German titles are included as a reminder of the international nature of scholarship.

The *Encyclopedia of Early Christianity* (New York: Garland, 1990) provides a comprehensive survey of the field written in a manner accessible to the average reader, yet containing information useful to the specialist. This series of reprints of Studies in Early Christianity is designed to supplement the encyclopedia and to be used with it.

The articles were chosen with the needs of teachers and students of early church history in mind with the hope that teachers will send students to these volumes to acquaint them with issues and scholarship in early Christian history. The volumes will fill the need of many libraries that do not have all the journals in the field or do not have complete holdings of those to which they subscribe. The series will provide an overview of the issues in the study of early Christianity and the resources for that study.

Understanding the development of early Christianity and its impact on Western history and thought provides indispensable insight into the modern world and the present situation of Christianity. It also provides perspective on comparable developments in other periods of history and insight into human nature in its religious dimension. Christians of all denominations may continue to learn from the preaching, writing, thinking, and working of the early church.

Introduction

The principal doctrinal achievements that resulted from the fusion of biblical faith and Greek philosophy studied in Volume VIII were the definitions of the Trinity and Christology arrived at in the doctrinal controversies of the fourth and fifth centuries. These classic theological positions—still adhered to by Catholic, Orthodox, and Protestant churches—were agreed to in the four ecumenical councils between 325 and 451. The Trinitarian doctrine set forth in the Nicene Creed has held sway throughout Christian history since the fourth century, but, in contrast, the Christological controversies of the fifth and sixth centuries resulted in separated churches in the countries of the Near and Middle East and their diaspora: the so-called Nestorians, claiming the heritage of the Antiochian school of thought, and the so-called Monophysites, claiming the theological heritage of Cyril of Alexandria, represented in the Coptic, Syrian Orthodox, Armenian, and Ethiopian churches. The later iconoclastic controversies were largely fought in terms of Christological doctrine. The articles in this volume primarily study the doctrines themselves and the philosophical concepts and terminology with which they were expressed. Also included are articles dealing with the thought of some of the principal actors in these controversies: Athanasius, Arius, Eusebius, Nestorius, Cyril of Alexandria, Justinian, and others.

The first two ecumenical councils of the church (Nicaea in 325 and Constantinople in 381) dealt with the Godhead, and the next two (Ephesus in 431 and Chalcedon in 451) dealt with the nature of Christ. A somewhat oversimplified schematization of these councils would say that the first ecumenical council (Nicaea) affirmed the oneness of God (Christ is *homoousios*, "of the same substance," with God), and the second (Constantinople) balanced this by approving the threeness of God (three *hypostases* and one *ousia*). The third ecumenical council (Ephesus) emphasized the oneness of Christ (condemning Nestorius on the grounds of teaching that he was two persons), and the fourth (Chalcedon) balanced this by confessing two natures, fully divine and fully human (one person or *hypostasis* in two natures).

The articles in this collection relevant to the Trinitarian controversy are bracketed (because of a chronological arrangement) by two studies on other aspects of the doctrine of God. William Schoedel examines a frequently repeated concept in the Christian definition of God—that he encompasses all things but is himself encompassed by nothing. The honoree of Schoedel's article, Robert M. Grant, has written two books on the early Christian doctrine of God.[1] The problem of theodicy, the existence of evil in a world created by a good God, has been a persistent question in philosophy for Christian theism. The views of the Greek Fathers on this subject are discussed by Frances Young.

Trinitarian doctrine was heavily influenced by the philosophical thought of the time, as the word studies by Stead show.[2] Athanasius was the single most significant individual in the triumph of the Nicene creed in the fourth-century Trinitarian debates. His persistence, his preaching, and his publications eventually carried the day. Questions were raised about his administration of the see of Alexandria and his character, but none can question his statesmanship and the vigor of his thought.

Two articles are devoted to the theology of Athanasius, one by Charles Kannengiesser, the foremost contemporary student of Athanasius, on his Christology, which anticipated the subsequent debates on this subject, and one by Christou, treating two of the fundamental distinctions involved in the Trinitarian controversy.

The fourth-century debates about the Trinity began in Alexandria between the presbyter Arius and his bishop Alexander. The subsequent controversies are still called the Arian controversy, and all the opponents of the creed of Nicaea are called "Arians," although the issues soon became broader than and different from those raised by Arius, even when they were developments from his premises. There has been considerable contemporary study of "Arianism" and the controversies it provoked, including efforts to rehabilitate the religious strengths of the Arian views and to clarify the historical and theological developments.[3] C. Kannengiesser and J. Lienhard introduce some of the issues involved in these discussions. Two of those sympathetic to Arius and opposed to Athanasius were both named Eusebius, bishops of Caesarea and of Nicomedia. Stead's second article in this collection argues that the two Eusebii were not as far apart as they are often portrayed to have been.

The Trinitarian and Christological controversies were principally fought in the Greek east, so this volume is limited to the Greek discussions. The definitive statement of Trinitarian doctrine for the Latin church was provided by Augustine's *De Trinitate*, a work building on the results achieved by Greek theologians but going beyond them in many ways.[4]

The article by Robert Wilken is particularly important for understanding the Christological controversies of the fourth and fifth centuries. It shows the importance of the exegesis of scripture in the debates.[5] Wilken further explains why the Arian controversy kept coming up in the Christological debates. It was not simply the usual tendency in religious polemics to paint one's opponent with the colors of an already condemned heresy. There was genuine concern by the schools of thought in Antioch and Alexandria that the other had sold out the argument against Arianism by its approach to the Gospel texts about Christ. A consequence of the different exegetical approaches was that the classical argument from a uniform apostolic tradition no longer held true— regional traditions had been laid on top. It is characteristic of religious positions that proponents of a given position are unable to distinguish a viewpoint and what is really at stake in it from the arguments used to support it. When someone rejects those arguments or does not recognize and use them, they are thought to have abandoned the position those arguments were designed to defend.

Richard Norris has made a similarly significant contribution to understanding the arguments and exegesis of Alexandria.[6] He clarifies the importance of John 1:14 and the linguistic model of subject and predicate to the Christology of Cyril of Alexandria, who led the opposition to the teaching of Nestorius in Constantinople. The background to Alexandrian Christology is found in its thought about the human soul of Jesus, which is the subject of Frances Young's study.

It is generally recognized that the classic Antiochian and Nestorian theology derived from Diodore of Tarsus. His views are studied by Rowan Greer, who is also a major interpreter of the leading theologian of the Antiochian school, Theodore of Mopsuestia.[7] There has been a considerable effort in this century at the rehabilitation of Nestorius, exemplified in this volume by Milton Anastos.[8] Nestorius's teaching was a failure in terminology and concepts to express adequately the unity of the divine-human person, but not "heresy." His fault was more of personality and will than of intention. His teaching continued in the Syriac-speaking "Church of the East."

The strength of the Alexandrian Christology in the east and dissatisfaction with the council of Chalcedon meant that imperial policy for the next two centuries had to try to find a means of reconciling the competing Christologies. Justinian sought to appease those who claimed the heritage of Cyril of Alexandria by condemning the teachings of three theologians associated with the Antiochian school—Theodore of Mopsuestia, Theodoret of Cyrus, and Ibas of Edessa (Constantelos). Such compromises failed and the result was the formation of independent churches called Monophysite by their opponents (a terminology they do not prefer) in Egypt, Ethiopia, and Armenia, as well as in Syria and Mesopotamia (Vööbus).

Christ carried the burden of Trinitarian discussion in the early church. The Holy Spirit did not receive much separate attention until the last phase of the "Arian" conflict. The Charismatic revivals and Neopentecostalism of the twentieth century have brought the Holy Spirit once more to prominence, but the concerns raised by scholars sympathetic to these movements have had more to do with the gifts of the Spirit and the Spirit in the life of the individual or the church and less to do with his place in the Godhead.

The iconoclastic controversy of the eighth and ninth centuries was argued in terms of Christology and may be seen as an extension of the Christological controversies. The tradition of the Fathers loomed as large or larger than the scriptural considerations in the argument. The articles included here trace the tradition of opposition to the icons up to the iconoclastic controversy (Baynes) and the concepts used in the Trinitarian and Christological debates that were then applied to the question of the images (Ladner). There was a tradition of the devotional use of icons before they became the focus of controversy.[9]

Notes

1. *The Early Christian Doctrine of God* (Charlottesville: U of Virginia P, 1966); *Gods and the One God* (Philadelphia: Westminster, 1986).

2. G.C. Stead, "The Significance of the *Homoousios*," *Studia Patristica* 3 (1961): 397–412. See also his book *Divine Substance* (Oxford: Oxford UP, 1977).

3. R. C. Gregg and D. E. Groh, *Early Arianism: A View of Salvation* (Philadelphia: Fortress, 1981); R. C. Gregg, ed., *Arianism: Historical and Theological Reassessments* (Cambridge, Mass.: Philadelphia Patristic Foundation, 1985); R. Williams, *Arius: Heresy and Tradition* (London: Darton, Longman and Todd, 1987); R. P. C. Hanson, *The Search for the Christian Doctrine of God: The Arian Controversy 318–381* (Edinburgh: T. and T. Clark, 1988); idem, "The Centrality of Soteriology in Early Arianism," *Studia Patristica* 15 (1984):305–16.

4. R. D. Crouse, "St. Augustine's *De Trinitate*: Philosophical Method," *Studia Patristica* 16 (1985):501–510.

5. For the Trinitarian controversy, see T. E. Pollard, "The Exegesis of Scripture and the Arian Controversy," *Bulletin of the John Rylands Library* 41 (1958–59):414–429; for the Christological controversy, R. A. Greer, "The Use of Scripture in the Nestorian Controversy," *Scottish Journal of Theology* 20 (1967):413–422.

6. Richard A. Norris, "Christological Models in Cyril of Alexandria," *Studia Patristica* 13 (1975): 255–268.

7. R. A. Greer, *Theodore of Mopsuestia, Exegete and Theologian* (London: Faith, 1961); idem, "The Analogy of Grace in Theodore of Mopsuestia's Christology," *Journal of Theological Studies* n.s. 34 (1983):82–98; see also F. A. Sullivan, *The Christology of Theodore of Mopsuestia* (Rome: Pontifical Gregorian UP, 1956); J. L. McKenzie, "Annotations on the Christology of Theodore of Mopsuestia," *Theological Studies* 19 (1958):345–373; F. A. Sullivan, "Further Notes on Theodore of Mopsuestia: A Reply to Father McKenzie," *Theological Studies* 20 (1959):264–279; R. A. Norris, *Manhood and Christ: A Study in the Christology of Theodore of Mopsuestia* (Oxford: Clarendon, 1963).

8. See also J. F. Bethune-Baker, *Nestorius and His Teaching* (Cambridge: Cambridge UP, 1908); H. E. W. Turner, "Nestorius Reconsidered," *Studia Patristica* 13 (1975):306–321, who concludes that Nestorius's intentions did not match his achievements; Roberta C. Chesnut, "The Two Prosopa in Nestorius' *Bazaar of Heracleides*," *Journal of Theological Studies* n.s. 29 (1978):392–409.

9. E. Kitzinger, "The Cult of Images in the Age Before Iconoclasm," *Dumbarton Oaks Papers* 8 (1954):83–150; for the west note R. A. Markus, "The Cult of Icons in Sixth-Century Gaul," *Journal of Theological Studies* n.s. 29 (1978):151–157.

WILLIAM R. SCHOEDEL

ENCLOSING, NOT ENCLOSED :
THE EARLY CHRISTIAN DOCTRINE OF GOD

One of the baffling philosophical issues that sends Lucian's hero, Menippus, on his flight to heaven for answers is whether the universe is finite or infinite, whether the All is circumscribed or not *(Icaromenippus* 7). It is generally conceded that the Greek intellectual tradition indentified the intelligible with the limited and found it difficult therefore to associate the unlimited with the divine. Yet it was in this same tradition that Philo and the church fathers found resources for a new doctrine of God that ultimately resulted in a reversal of the Greek evaluation of the infinite. The importance of the development can hardly be exaggerated. On one reading of the evidence, it may even be said that the conception of God's infinity served, after many transformations, as a presupposition in the emergence of the modern physical sciences[1]. It was one of the merits of Robert M. Grant's book on the early Christian doctrine of God to have uncovered some of the complex sources of the new teaching[2]. It is our intention here to extend the range of considerations that have a bearing on this issue.

The debate in the early church came to a focus in the formula "enclosing, not enclosed" and related expressions. The use here of the verb "to enclose" (περιέχειν) seems to have two main sources: (a) the pre-Socratic description of the originative substance as divine and enclosing all things[3], (b) Aristotle's discussion of the infinite *(Phys.* 3.4-8, 202b' 30), of place (4.1-5, 208a 27), and of the void (4.6-9,

---

1. Ivor LECLERC, *The Nature of Physical Existence* (London, 1972).
2. *The Early Christian Doctrine of God* (Charlottesville, 1966) 105-10.
3. Cf. ARISTOTLE. *Phys.* 3.4, 203b 7; *De caelo* 3.5, 503b 10; *Metaph.* 12.8, 1074a 38.

1

213a 12). The antithesis, "enclosing, not enclosed", first gains currency in Philo as a description of God and seems to owe its striking formulation to an impulse to go beyond the Greek tradition in emphasizing the divine transcendence[4].

To say that God encloses all things and is not enclosed means for Philo (a) that God is immaterial and not in a place[5], (b) that he is unknowable in his essence[6], and (c) that he is creator of all things (*Migr. Abr.* 183; cf. *Leg. alleg.* 3.51). Such themes presuppose a God who transcends the cosmos and is not simply (as in Greek philosophy) a factor in the totality of things. To be sure, the emphasis on God's immateriality reflects, as an isolated theme, Plato more than the Bible. But it points here in a new direction. For ultimately, it was to provide a context within which the infinite "could be detached from the concept of the corporeal, with which it had been essentially united in Greek thought"[7]. An indication of the novelty of Philo's thought in this connection is the emphasis, perhaps for the first time, on the idea that the essence of God is unknowable[8].

Philo, however, has an ambivalent attitude toward the infinite as such[9]. Once he goes so far as to say that it is not right to think that God is in contact with "infinite and confused matter" (*Spec. leg.* 1.329). In such sentiments the influence of the Greek philosophical tradition is strong. To be sure, that tradition was itself changing, but the very restricted application of the term "infinite" to the divine hypostases by Plotinus illustrates how even the most mystical of the Greek philosophers drew back from a positive evaluation of the unlimited[10]. One reason that the church fathers went farther than Philo in this regard is

---

4. Cf. Harry A. WOLFSON,*Philo* (2 vols.; Cambridge, 1947) 1. 247-51, 317-22. Wolfson connects the formula with the Rabbinic teaching that God "is the place of the world, but the world is not his place" (*Gen. R.* 68.9).

5. *Migr. Abr.* 182; 192-93; *Somn.* 1.63; 1.185; *Sobr.* 63; *Post. Cain.* 15; 18.

6. *Somn.* 1.184; *Conf. ling.* 138; *Post. Cain.* 15; 18.

7. LECLERC, *Physical Existence*, 65. Leclerc is speaking of Origen, but the comment is equally relevant to Philo.

8. WOLFSON, *Philo*, 2.94-164. But see now John M. Dillon (*The Middle Plaionists* (London, 1977) 155) who suggests that Philo was dependant on Platonism for his view of God as incomprehensible.

9. A.M. J. FESTUGIÈRE, *La révélation d'Hermès Trismégiste*, Vol. IV: *Le Dieu inconnu et la gnose* (Études Bibliques; Paris, 1954) 109.

10. Hilary ARMSTRONG, "Plotinus's Doctrine of the Infinite and Its Significance for Christian Thought", *Downside Review* 73 (1955) 47-58.

that (largely because of the conflict with Gnosticism) they looked more deeply into Greek sources and found there arguments that linked the Oneness of Being with its infinity.

1. IRENAEUS AND THE GNOSTICS

That God "contains (χωρῶν) all things and is alone uncontained (ἀχώρητos)" was given a position of central importance in Christian thought by Hermas (*Man.* 1.1; cf. *Sim.* 9.14.5). The verb χωρεῖν expresses fundamentally the same idea as the verb περιέχειν[11], and the two come to be used side by side[12]. The close relation between place (τόπos) and space (χώρα) in Stoicism may account for the appearance of the new term[13]. In any event, the epithet "uncontained" had one advantage over the expression "not enclosed": it suggested more readily that God cannot be grasped with the mind[14].

In Hermas the reference is to God as the creator. In other early sources such language is used (as in Philo) to attack polytheism or to explain away Biblical anthropomorphisms[15]. The development of the theme in Theophilus (*Ad Aut.* 1.5; 2.3) and *Teach. Silv.* (99.31-100.4) strongly suggests the continued influence of Hellenistic Jewish ideas[16].

But Valentinian Gnostics also knew that God was "uncontained" (Irenaeus, *Adv. haer.* 1.1.1) and applied the formula "enclosing, not enclosed" to him (Epiphanius, *Pan.* 31.5.3). Moreover, there is associated with this language an emphasis on divine transcendence including (somewhat vaguely) God's infinity and ineffability[17]. The fre-

---

11. In a saying attributed to Thales (Diogenes Laertes 1.35) we are told that "place (τοπos) is the greatest thing, for it contains (χωρεῖ) all things".

12. Cf. HIPPOLYTUS, *Pasch.* 3; CLEMENT, *Strom.* 2.2, 6.1-3; DIDYMUS, *De trinit.* 2.6.2; GREGORY OF NYSSA. *Contra Eun.* 2.67-70, PG 45. 932C; MAXIMUS. *Ambigu. lb.*, PG 91. 1184B.

13. Cf. SEXTUS EMPIRICUS. *Pyrrh. hyp.* 3.124; *Aetii plac.* 1.20.1-2; PHILO. *Somn.* 1.63-64; 1.185; *Conf. ling.* 136.

14. G.W.H. LAMPE. *A Patristic Greek Lexicon* (Oxford, 1961-68) 280-81.

15. *Kerygma Petri*, in CLEMENT. *Strom.* 6.5, 39.3; ARISTIDES. *Apol.* 1.4-5 (Syriac); JUSTIN. *Dial.* 127.2; ATHENAGORAS. *Leg.* 10.1.

16. William R. SCHOEDEL. "Topological Theology and some Monistic Trends in Gnosticism", *Essays on the Nag Hammadi Texts in Honour of Alexander Böhlig* (ed. Martin Krause; Nad Hammadi Studies 3; Leiden, 1972) 88-108.

17. Cf. Ekkehard MÜHLENBERG. *Die Unendlichkeit Gottes bei Gregory von Nyssa* (Göttingen, 1966) 178-83.

quency of the view in the *Corpus Hermeticum* that the cosmos or God encloses all things (11.18-20; 16.12; Exc. 6.3; 14.1; 15.1; 23.7, 48; Frg. 26) suggests the inevitability of its appeal to Gnostics.

The problem that this language raised for dualistic Gnosticism is. obvious, and it was exploited to the full by Irenaeus in the second book of his work *Adversus haereses*. Irenaeus, who strongly advocates the formula "enclosing, not enclosed" (the verb is *continere* or *circumcontinere* — that is, περιέχειν)[18], first attacks Gnostic theology on the assumption that its two gods are outside each other. The main points are as follows: (1) If there is more than one Fulness or God, he is no longer the Fulness: he will lack what is beyond him; morever he will have "beginning, middle, and end" with respect to those beyond him and will be limited and enclosed by them (2.1.2; cf. 2.1.5). (2) Again, if there is something outside the Fulness, either (a) the Fulness will enclose it (apparently by definition) yet be enclosed by it (since there is a Fulness outside the first Fulness), or (b) if they are separated by an immense distance, there will be a third kind of thing that separates them and encloses them; moreover, if it is assumed that this third thing is itself limited, the process will go on *ad infinitum* (2.1.3-4).

This argumentation shows the influence of a stream of ideas reflected most clearly in the Pseudo-Aristotelian, *De Melisso, Xenophane, Gorgia* (first century A.D. according to Diels) where the thought of Xenophanes and the Eleatic philosophers are inextricably mixed. First, it should be observed that Irenaeus is leading up to a description of the divine being (*Adv. haer.* 2.13.3; 2.13.8) modelled on Xenophanes' "One" of whom it is said, "All of him sees, all thinks, and all hears" (Frg. 24; cf. *De Melisso* 3, 977a 36; Diogenes Laertes 9.19) — that is, he is undifferentiated throughout[19]. The ancient opponent of polytheism

---

18. Bruno REYNDERS, *Lexique comparé du texte Grec et des versions Latine, Arménienne et Syriaque de l'Adversus Haereses de Saint Irénée* (Corpus Scriptorum Christianorum Orientalium 141-42; Louvain, 1954) 1.87; 2.52, 68.

19. The formulation is not unknown elsewhere in the early church. In *Orac. Sib.* 8.284-285 it is applied to God as the creator. More complex and interesting for our purposes is the connection between it and the description of God as enclosing everything (cf.CLEMENT, *Strom.* 7.2, 5.5; *Eugnostos* 73.6-11; HILARY, *De Trinit.* 2.6; *Tract. super psalm.* 118.19.8; 129.3; AMBROSE, *De fide* 1.16.106). JUSTIN (*Dial.* 127.2) and THEOPHILUS (*Ad Aut.* 2.3) offer what look like Biblicized versions of the same thought (God sees and hears all things) — though a similar modification in *Orac. Sib.* 8.282 finds its best parallel in *Orph. Hymn.* 64.8. Pagan interest in the formula is exemplified by PLINY, *Nat. hist.* 2.5.14 (against polytheism).

is pressed into service against Gnostic dualists who, as Irenaeus sees it, are led into error by thinking too anthropomorphically (2.13.3-4)[20]. Irenaeus' description of God as "altogether like himself" *(totus ipse sibimet similis)* also reflects language especially characterictic of the Eleatic theology[21].

Second, the argumentation itself reflects features of the Eleatic rejection of the many. Xenophanes (like Irenaeus) begins by ruling out the possibility of two or more gods by definition: God, to be God, must "rule and not be ruled" (3, 977a 27) — observe that this is a reasonably close parallel to the formula "enclosing, not enclosed"[22] — which leaves no room for more than one. "For if there were two or more, he would no longer be mightiest and best of all" (3, 977a 24)[23]. Again, both Melissus (1, 974a 11) and Xenophanes (3, 977b 6) were understood to argue that if the One is thus supreme (or infinite, in the case of Melissus) another existent would set limits to it (περαινεῖν εἰς or πρός or some such expression bulks large in the discussion) and thus negate its supremacy (cf. Melissus, Frgs. 5-6). Moreover, having beginning, middle, end is regarded as the mark of something finite in this context (3, 977b 4; see also Melissus, Frgs. 2-4, where reference is made to beginning and end and where these temporal categories acquire spacial significance)[24].

Irenaeus' second set of arguments reflects the same atmosphere. The contradiction involved in the first alternative of thinking of a being which both encloses and is enclosed reflects the mental habits of one exposed to an argument like that of Xenophanes according to which if God were not everywhere alike, the parts of God would both rule and be ruled by one another, "which is impossible" (3, 977a 38). The second

---

20. Philo probably harks back to Xenophanes too when he says (against Stoic and Epicurean views of divinity) that God is "like (ὅμοιον) nothing of things in creation" *(Somn.* 1.184-185; cf. XENOPHANES. Frg. 23; DIOGENES LAERTES 9.19). Otherwise Philo shows no special interest in this pre-Socratic philosopher.

21. PARMENIDES. Frg. 8.22; Melissus, in *De Melisso* 1, 974a 13; 974a 15; 974b 8; DIOGENES LAERTES 9.24; XENOPHANES. in *De Melisso* 3, 977a 37; 977b 1.

22. For the close relation between περιέχειν and κρατεῖν in relevant contexts see PHILO. *Aet. mund.* 106; 114; ATHENAGORAS. *Leg.* 8.5; THEOPHILUS. *Ad Aut.* 1.4; ADAMANTIUS. *Dial.* 3.12.

23. Tertullian *(Adv. Marc.* 1.3) also argues against Marcionite dualism from the definition of God as supreme.

24. Cf. G.S. KIRK and J.E. RAVEN. *The Presocratic Philosophers* (Cambridge, 1957) 301.

alternative takes us farther afield. One feature of Melissus' argument for the sole existence of the One is that the many would have to be separated by the void (a possibility which he rejects)[25]; Zeno's paradox (Frg. 3) that a plurality would have to be both limited and unlimited relies in part on the point that there would always have to be something "between" the entities and so on *ad infinitum* (cf. Frg. 1); and elsewhere Zeno argued that "if everything real is in a place, then there will be a place of the place and so an *ad infinitum*" (Aristotle, *Phys.* 4.1, 209a 23)[26]. The parallels with Irenaeus are not exact here but they are close enough to leave little doubt about the tradition at work. Irenaeus' use of such arguments shows that he is nearer the conclusions of Melissus (that the One is infinite) than of Parmenides and Zeno (that the One is a limited sphere surrounded by absolutely nothing) or of Xenophanes (that the One is neither infinite nor limited: *De Melisso* 3, 977b 3; cf. Clement, *Strom.* 2.2, 6.1-3; *Allogenes* 67.1-4). Thus a teaching, more or less heretical in the classical tradition, enters the mainstream of theological thought.

Irenaeus' Gnostic opponents were not unaffected by such arguments. Some, we learn from Irenaeus, were prepared to grant that God contains all; and they went on to argue that talk of things within and without the Fulness have only to do with knowledge of God or the lack of it and that the (evil) creation is within the All like a center in a circle or a spot in a garment[27]. Irenaeus wonders how in that event defect and error can be within God *(Adv. haer.* 2.4.3; 2.5.3; 2.8.2) or how things in God can be ignorant of his existence — though Irenaeus himself takes it for granted (like Philo) that creatures cannot know God's essence[28].

The Gnosticizing *Teachings of Silvanus* gives us some clues as to how Gnostic monism presented its case[29]. The *Gospel of Truth*, however, is

25. Leon ROBIN. *Greek Thought* (tr. M.R. Dobie: New York, 1928) 96-7. Cf. MELISSUS, Frg. 7.7. (reflected in *De Melisso* 1, 947a 15); ARISTOTLE, *De gen. et corr.* 1.8, 325a 2.

26. Aristotle (*Phys.* 3.4, 203b20) gives as a fourth argument advanced by some in favor of the infinite that "there cannot be a limit if one thing must always set limits to another (περαινεῖν …ἕτερον πρὸς ἕτερον) ". An *ad infinitum* argument seems implied. Aristotle is probably thinking of Melissus.

27. *Adv. haer.* 2.2.2-3; 2.4.2; 2.5.1-3; 2.8.2-3; 2.13.6; 2.31.1. Note especially 2.5.2 where Irenaeus explicitly says that "certain of them" advance this line of argument.

28. *Adv. haer* 2.6.1; cf. Philo, *Spec. leg.* 1.32; *Post. Cain.* 168-169.

29. See note 16.

probably an even more direct witness to such a theology. To be sure, "the All" which is said to be in the Father yet ignorant of him consists of the Aeons[30]. And the *maeit* (τοποι, places?) mentioned in connection with "Him who encloses every place, whereas there is nothing that encloses him", seem connected in some way with the aeons[31]. Yet the line between Aeons and human beings is fluid in our gospel. Gnostics, in fact, appear to be regarded as fallen Aeons[32]. And statements about the restoration of the All or the Aeons merge imperceptibly with remarks that have a direct bearing on life in this world (cf. 18.29-19.27; 20.14-23.18; 23.33-24.28). No doubt a literal understanding of what it would mean for a spiritual being to exist in the Father would be inappropriate. Yet there is scant evidence that even matter, after it had been produced from the anguish of the All and the labor of Error (17.10-21) was in any sense expelled. In one passage, the redeemed Aeons and/or Gnostics who are in the Father are in turn said to devour matter in themselves (25.15-16). In short, it seems likely that the reformulation of Valentinian doctrine in our gospel reflects the monistic interpretation of the Gnostic myth mentioned by Irenaeus. We are not surprised to find, then, that cosmological language frequently takes on marked epistemological significance (18.7-11; 22.27-29; 24.29-32; 25.10-25; 27.22-23)[33]. It also coheres with this interpretation that two figures of great importance in the dualistic mythology of Valentinianism — Sophia and the Demiurge — have disappeared from the scene[34]. On any reading of the *Gospel of Truth*, the Father emerges in an unexpectedly impressive way as the ground of existence of all things[35].

II. TRANSCENDENCE

Echoes of Irenaeus' critique of Gnostic cosmology continue to be heard in the early church. Methodius' debate with Valentinianism about

---

30. Sasagu ARAI. *Die Christologie des Evangelium Veritatis* (Leiden, 1964) 46. Cf. EPIPHANIUS. *Pan*. 31.5.3.
31. 22.25-27; cf. 20.22, 35; 22.22; 25.10; 26.15; 27.10, 25; 28.11; 42.8.
32. ARAI. *Christologie*, 52, 57, 59.
33. ARAI. *Christologie*, 60.
34. ARAI. *Christologie*, 34, 53-4.
35. ARAI. *Christologie*, 61.

God and matter covers a somewhat different range of alternatives, but especially with his argument against two unoriginated substances (God and matter, if separated, require something that separates them... and so on *ad infinitum*) we are on familiar ground (*De autexous.* 5.1-5)[36]. Adamantius' attack on the existence of two unoriginated substances "of infinite greatness" first points out the contradiction involved in positing two substances that must be everywhere and then argues that if they are separated, they must be limited and have a beginning and end (*Dial.* 2.1; 3.13)[37]. In another passage he takes up (in the manner of Irenaeus) the unfortunate implications of the admission of his Gnostic opponent that God contains everything (*Dial.* 3.12). Mani, on the other hand, is made to insist in the *Acta Archelai* 16 (14) that God cannot fill everything and to reject the idea that there is no "place" outside of him. John of Damascus still makes much of the fact that Mani's theology implies not only that God is "in a place" and "enclosed", but also that the enclosing place is itself circumscribed (*Disp. cum Man.* 2, PG 96. 1321C).

A much earlier passage — Athenagoras, *Leg.* 8 (directed against polytheism rather than Gnosticism) — apparently has somewhat different affinities. The apologist argues that "if there are two or more gods", they are either (a) in one and the same category and (i) similar (but in that event, says Athenagoras, they would have to be individuals derived from a model) or (ii) dissimilar (forming a composite unity); or (b) they are distinct beings who, however, (i) cannot be in or around our world (which is ruled by the creator) or (ii) in or around another world (among other things because the second god would have little power and no place to stand since the creator "fills" everything). Now the arguments of Xenophanes in *De Melisso* (3, 977a 24) can be schematized as follows: "if there are two or more" (gods), either (a) each is supreme, or (b) they are superior to one another in different respects, or (c) they are equal. And the first two of these could plausibly be seen as answering to Athenagoras' arguments (a) (i) and (ii). Moreover, Athenagoras' point (b) depends heavily on Xenophanes' argument by defini-

---

36. Cf. ATHANASIUS *(Contra gentes* 7) who also refers to the third thing that must be invoked to separate the two gods of Marcion.
37. Cf. GREGORY OF NAZIANZUS, *Theol. or.* 4.18; Being is limited "neither by that before it nor that after it".

8

tion which we have already discussed[38]. But there is a complication. Proclus in his commentary on Plato's *Timaeus* argues in favor of the one Animal of *Timaeus* 31A (the world of Ideas) on the grounds that if there were more than one, either (a) each would have all things, or (b) one would have all, one not all ("so that one would be a part, the other a whole"), or (c) neither would have all. That is so close to the three alternatives in Xenophanes that there must be a connection between the two traditions. The point to be made here, however, is that Athenagoras echoes the Platonic criticism of the first alternative (both Plato and Proclus argue that there would have to be a prototype for two like entities) and seems closer to Proclus also on the second alternative.

Another important passage — this time from Gregory of Nazianzus, *Theol. or.* 2.10 — is too complex to analyze here. It shows acquaintance with many of the arguments about place already encountered. Its novelty is that not only does it profess to spell out the significance of God's immateriality, but also that it exempts from difficulties none of the traditional language about God enclosing all things. This is taken by Gregory as an illustration of God's unknowability — a point which is upheld here against Eunomius who can make a case for Arian Christology only if words like generate and ingenerate can be taken to reveal the nature of God and Christ. Gregory feels compelled to improve on Plato and to say that it is impossible — not simply difficult — to know God as he is (2.4). And in a line of thought that goes back through Clement (*Strom.* 2.2, 6.1-3) to Philo (*Post. Cain.* 13-16) and on to Gregory of Nyssa (*Vit. Mos.* 86.12 Musurillo; *PG* 44. 376D), he asserts that all we can know of God is his unknowability — or more precisely, his ἀπειρία or infinity (*Or.* 45.3).

It was Gregory of Nyssa who gave such thoughts their definitive expression in Greek theology[39]. In his hands, the discussion of God's place became associated with the clearest statement of the distinction between the creator and his creatures, the unknowability of God in his essence [40], and the precedence of faith over knowledge (*Contra Eun.* 2.92-93, *PG* 45. 941B). Such themes are associated in Gregory not only

---

38 Cf. ATHANASIUS *(Contra gentes* 6) who also appeals (against Marcionite dualism) to the single fact that God "fills" everything as he embraces heaven and earth.

39. MÜHLENBERG. *Die Unendlichkeit Gottes.*

40. *Contra Eun.* 2.67-70, *PG* 45. 932C; cf. *Contra Eun.* 1.168-171, *PG* 45. 301C; *Vit. Mos.* 4.3 Musurillo, *PG* 44. 301A.

with a rejection of Eunomian rationalism but also with his effort to avoid difficulties inherited from Origenism. In particular, God's infinity has as its corollary the strictly endless ascent of man to God — a doctrine which avoids the Origenistic teaching of the fall of pure spirits through "satiety" and all the questionable consequences that flow from it[41]. Origen's interpretation of the formula "containing, not contained" and his thoroughly Hellenic delimitation of God's power (*De princ*. 2.9.1: 4.4.8) is decisively overcome.

It appears that Gregory's proof of God's illimitability looks to yet a different philosophical model. His teaching (*Vit. Mos.* 115.9 Musurillo; *PG* 44. 404BC) that "if the divine is conceived of in any limit, then that after the limit must be thought of along with it" and that what is limited must come to rest in something of a different kind (εἰς ἑτερογενὲς καταλήγειν) like fish in water or birds in air (with a surface, ἐπιφανεία between) — all this and more is derived from arguments made by Stoics such as Cleomedes against Aristotle's denial of the existence of a void outside the cosmos (Cleomedes, *De motu* 1.1.5-8). Cleomedes uses precisely such terms in defending the Stoic teaching that there is an infinite void beyond the world and enclosing it[42]. Cleomedes holds that the void has a certain substantial existence even though he regards the conception of it as "most simple" and insists that the void has no materiality whatever (1.1.4). What Gregory has done is to apply arguments about the infinite void to God himself. It would seem that the Stoic view had the advantage of permitting more clearly than previously a distinction between the finite cosmos and the infinite God.

It was left to Maximus the Confessor in Greek theology to return directly to Aristotle's discussion of place, to reexamine it, and to show (at least to his satisfaction) that it is precisely the uncircumscribed and the infinite that is unmoved and that creation out of nothing is the corollary of such infinity (*Ambig. lib., PG* 91. 1180B-1188B).

---

41. Ronald E. Heine. *Perfection in the Virtuous Life* (Patristic Monograph Series 2; Philadelphia, 1975).

42. According to Cleomedes, the cosmos itself is limited and encloses all bodies within it (1.1.1).

III. IMMANENCE

From the earliest period, the term "enclosing" served to express not only transcendence but also immanence. Philo more than once couples "enclosing" with "filling" or "pervading" in his description of God's relation to the world (*Conf. ling.* 136; *Leg. alleg.* 1.44; *Post. Cain. 14*). In this connection he introduces the important distinction between God as transcendent (that is, enclosing all, in the proper sense of the term) according to his nature or essence and God as immanent according to his power and goodness (*Migr. Abr.* 182). Such themes were later taken over into Christian theology [43] and were naturally extended to include the theme of incarnation. The idea that the One Containing became the One Contained was obviously more sharply paradoxical than anything found in Philo. And, as is to be expected, it expressed itself with least reservations in the naiver theologies and in modalism[44]. Elsewhere various qualifications were made, and one observes a tendency to treat the incarnation as the supreme instance of the presence of God in the world[45]. However qualified, the theme of incarnation powerfully reinforced the unwillingness of Christian theologians to permit a doctrine of God's transcendence to negate the possibility of revelation and the manifestation of the divine in time and space[46].

---

43. Cf. ATHANASIUS. *Ep. de decret. Nic.* 11; EPIPHANIUS. *Pan.* 70.7; GREGORY OF NAZIANZUS. *Theol. or.* 5.29; DIDYMUS. *De trinit.* 2.6.2; THEODORET. *In Ezech.* 3:12; CYRIL OF ALEXANDRIA. *In Jo. comm.* 11.9 (17.13); PSEUDO-MACARIUS. *Elevat. ment. 8*.

44. Cf. MELITO. Frg. 13; *Pasch. hom.* 5.37-38; HIPPOLYTUS or PSEUDO-HIPPOLYTUS. *Pasch.* 3; HIPPOLYTUS. *Ref.* 9.10.9-10; ATHANASIUS. *De synod.* 26.7.

45. EUSEBIUS. *Dem. evang.* 4.6; *De eccl. theol.* 2.17.128; ATHANASIUS. *De incarnat. verb.* 17; GREGORY OF NYSSA. *Orat. catech.* 10; 14; *In Christ. ascens.*, PG 46. 693A.

46. Augustine's use of the formula "containing, not contained" deserves separate treatment and can only be touched on here. Among the important passages devoted to the theme is the opening discussion of God's being in the *Confession* (1.2.2-1.3.3; cf. 1.6.7; 1.18.28; 3.7.12; 5.2.2; 5.10.20; 6.3.4; 6.4.5; 7.1.1-2; 7.5.7; 7.15.21; 7.20.26; 10.26.26; 12.7.7; 12.27.37; 13.11.12). One of the noteworthy features of Augustine's discussion is the enrichment of the "enclosing, not enclosed" formula with the teaching that God is "present everywhere in his totality (*totus ubique*)". R.J. O'Connell ("Ennead VI. 4 and 5 in the Works of St. Augustine", *Revue des études augustiniennes*, 9 (1963) 1-39) has argued persuasively for a Plotinian source for this complex of motifs. At the same time, Augustine's discussion may also have been reinforced by the development of the "enclosing, not enclosed" formula in the church, especially as it was used against the dualism of the Gnostics (cf. *Conf.* 5.10.20). There may also have been some connection between Xenophanes' view of the One as "like every way" (πάντη ὅμοιον, or, as Irenaeus has it, *totus ipse sibimet similis*; see note 21) and Plotinus' more sophisticated

We may well ask, then, whether the Biblical model of God as actor was not more alive in the development that we have sketched than may appear at first sight. We have noted the tendency to interpret the polarity of finite and infinite in terms of creatures and creator. Moreover, it was the Gnostics more than any others who exploited the mystical possibilities of talk of God's infinity and ineffability. The Hellenistic Jewish view, developed by the church fathers, that God though unknowable in his essence communicates himself through his works, may well depend on an awareness that "interpersonal knowledge depends on the *other's acts* and not simply our observation, that is, on something intrinsically inacessible to us, something that we cannot at will make accessible"[47].

teaching that the One is *totus ubique*. It is particularly intriguing to find that Hilary uses a form of the *totus ubique* formula in contexts closely related to those with which we have been dealing: Semper extra locum, quia non continetur Deus autem et ubique *et totus ubicumque* est *(De Trinit.* 2.6); Non corporalibus locis Deus continetur... Adest *ubique et totus ubicumque* est *(Tract. super Psalm.* 118.19.8); Deus autem, qui et *ubique* et in omnibus est, totus audit, totus videt, totus, efficit, totus incedit... Deus ergo *ubique* est *et ubicumque* adest, audit, videt, efficit *(Tract. super Psalm.* 129.3; note also the clear echo in this last passage of Xenophanes' insistance that the One hears and sees and acts in his totality).

47. Gordon D. KAUFMAN. *God the Problem* (Cambridge, 1972) 74. Cf. G.L. PRESTIGE. *God in Patristic Thought* (London, 1936) 1-24.

SOME REFLECTIONS ON THE ORIGINS OF THE DOCTRINE OF THE TRINITY

'THE doctrine of the Trinity is the product of rational reflection on those particular manifestations of the divine activity which centre in the birth, ministry, crucifixion, resurrection and ascension of Jesus Christ and the gift of the Holy Spirit to the Church... it could not have been discovered without the occurrence of those events, which drove human reason to see that they required a trinitarian God for their cause.'[1] This statement of Dr. Hodgson about the source of the doctrine of the Trinity would, I imagine, be accorded widespread assent today, together with its negative corollary that it is a fair criticism of particular theologies of the Trinity to say that their thought is based on 'the acceptance of the Bible as giving revelation in the form of propositions concerning the inner mysteries of the Godhead'.[2] Dr. Hodgson's approach, it is generally assumed, will still provide us with an essential rather than an economic doctrine of the Trinity. The purpose of this article is to question whether the full implications of his approach to this subject have been recognized.

Dr. Bethune-Baker asserts that 'Sabellianism, in recognizing only a Trinity in human experience, disregards the fact that such a Trinity of revelation is only possible if the very being of the Godhead, which is thus revealed, is itself a Trinity'.[3] The validity of this assertion does not need to come up for question here. But, on Dr. Hodgson's thesis, the corollary of this must also be true. There can be no knowledge of an essential Trinity, except through a Trinity of revelation. Do we, in fact, find such an unmistakable Trinity of revelation in God's dealings with mankind?

The most obvious distinction to which the concept of God's self-revelation gives rise is the distinction between God in himself and God active in the world, accommodating himself to the needs of men. This was a distinction which both Greek thought and post-exilic Jewish thought about God naturally suggested at the outset of the Christian era. It did, in fact, play its part in determining the ascription of particular acts of God to particular persons of the Trinity. Thus Irenaeus writes:

It was not the Father of all, who is not seen by the world, the Maker of all who said 'Heaven is my throne, and earth is my footstool: what house will ye build me or what is the place of my rest?' and who 'comprehendeth the earth with his hand and with his span the heaven'—it was not He that

---

[1] L. Hodgson, *Doctrine of the Trinity* (1944), p. 25.   [2] Ibid., p. 229.
[3] *Introduction to the Early History of Christian Doctrine* (5th ed. 1933), p. 106.

[Journal of Theological Studies, N.S., Vol. VIII, Pt. i, April 1957]

came and stood in a very small space and spake with Abraham; but the Word of God, who was ever with mankind, and made known beforehand what should come to pass in the future, and taught men the things of God.[1]

The same argument in relation to the anthropomorphisms of the Old Testament is developed more fully by Novatian. God is infinite and contains all things; yet the scripture speaks of God descending to the tower of Babel. The selfsame author within scripture declares on the one hand that 'no man can see God and live' and on the other that 'God was seen of Abraham'. From these apparent contradictions he concludes: 'So it may be understood that it was not the Father who was seen . . . but the Son who has both been accustomed to descend and to be seen because He has descended.'[2] Tertullian applies the same argument to the text of the New Testament. St. John declares emphatically that 'no man hath seen God at any time', and yet the same writer testifies that he and his fellow apostles had both seen and handled Christ. So he concludes: 'The Father acts by mind and thought, whilst the Son, who is in the Father's mind and thought, gives form to what he sees.'[3] But this line of argument would have led to a binitarian rather than to a trinitarian form of theology, as is clearly shown by the conclusion of the passage quoted from Irenaeus: 'So then the Father is God and the Son is God; for that which is begotten of God is God.'[4] In the Christian doctrine of the Trinity all three persons are involved both in the eternal and essential life of God and also in his activity and self-revelation to the world. Our Trinity of revelation must therefore be sought not in a distinction between God in himself and God active, but in the threefold character of the activity of God in the world.

As we come to this stage in our investigation, it is important to remember just what it is that we are doing. We are not starting with the assumption of a revealed trinitarian doctrine of God and then looking at the manner of God's self-revealing activity in the world to see if it can appropriately be understood in a way which corresponds to the already known trinitarian nature of God. We are, on the contrary, seeking to look at the activity of God to see if it is of such unquestionably threefold character that we are forced, in order to explain it rationally, to postulate a threefold character in God himself. The Anglican Catechism certainly suggests that there is such a threefold activity, when it speaks of 'God the Father, who made me and all the world, God the Son, who hath redeemed me and all mankind and God the Holy Ghost, who sanctifieth me and all the elect people of God.' This, it should be noted, is not really one but a combination of two different threefold analyses of

[1] Irenaeus, *Demonstratio*, 45.
[2] Novatian, *De Trin.* 17, 18.
[3] Tertullian, *Adv. Prax.* 15.
[4] Irenaeus, op. cit. 47.

the activity of God. The first is a division based on the type of activity-creation, redemption and sanctification being ascribed respectively to Father, Son, and Holy Ghost. The second is a division based on the range of activity—all creation, rational life, spiritual life. Does either or both of these represent such a threefold division of revelation as we are looking for? At first sight it might appear that they do. But when we consider them more carefully it is not at all clear that they do correspond to the divisions of the Trinity. Thus while the first division—creation, redemption, sanctification—is probably the one that springs most naturally to the modern mind, it is doubtful whether it is to be found at all in the New Testament or in the earliest period, when trinitarian doctrine was first being worked out. The New Testament most explicitly associates the second person of the Trinity with the work of creation,[1] and this concept of the creative activity of the Logos is a dominant theme throughout the early patristic period. The second division—that by range of activity—has at least one exact counterpart in the earliest period. According to Origen, the Father is concerned with all life, the Son with all rational beings, and the Holy Spirit with specifically Christian life.[2] But this is not an unvarying or generally accepted principle. Rufinus 'corrects' the theology of Origen in the passage just quoted so as to make it more in accord with the normal view by classing Father and Son together as equally concerned with the whole range of creation. Nor is the restriction of the Spirit to spiritual life in the narrower sense of the words one that is consistently maintained. Irenaeus and others regularly associate the Spirit with the work of creation.[3] It is evident from the general tenor of fourth-century teaching that the description of the Spirit as life-giver in the Constantinopolitan creed was not intended to be understood in any restricted sense.[4] It seems absurd to claim that we are aware of the trinitarian nature of God through the threefold character of revelation, and at the same time to maintain that that threefold character of revelation does not precisely correspond to the three persons of the Trinity. Yet this dilemma faces us whatever

[1] John i. 2; Col. i. 16.
[2] *De Princ.* i. 3. 5 (Greek text preserved in Justinian, *Ep. ad Mennam,* Mansi, ix. 524).
[3] For examples see p. 98 below. The famous saying 'where the Church is, there is the Spirit of God, and where the Spirit of God is, there is the Church and all grace' (*Adv. Haer.* iii. 24. 1) appears to make Irenaeus' view agree closely with that of Origen. The context, however, makes it quite clear that it is not intended as a complete description of the sphere of the Spirit's activity, but simply to deny his operation in heretical bodies.
[4] Cp., for example, Gregory of Nyssa: 'The Holy Spirit, from whom all the supply of good things for the creation has its source' (printed among the letters of Basil as *Ep.* 38. 4).

threefold division we choose to make. God has revealed himself in three stages—Old Testament dispensation, the Incarnation, New Testament dispensation; but if we try and fit this division to the persons of the Trinity, we find that it fits some of the facts (e.g. John vii. 39: 'The Spirit was not yet given because Jesus was not yet glorified') but not others (e.g. 'who spake by the prophets'),[1] and this particular division has been rightly seen to lead to dangerous heresy.

In his essay 'On the evolution of the Doctrine of the Trinity',[2] Dr. Kirk sees the problem in very much the same terms as it is posed in this article. He believes that the required differentia in experience can be found in three different kinds of relationship which exist between God and man. There is the 'King-servant' relation which points to the Father, a relation of personal 'communion' which points to the Son, and a relation which is still personal but to which he gives the name 'possession', which points to the Spirit. This is certainly an acute and suggestive analysis, but it is questionable whether it fulfils all that is required of it. Dr. Kirk claims that these 'three modes of intercourse . . . point to three distinguishable termini within the Godhead, of each of which hypostatic character must, and can, be predicated without impairing the divine unity'.[3] But he produces very little evidence to substantiate the claim and has to admit that the differentia is by no means absolute. 'It would be impossible', he writes, 'to analyse the New Testament or the Fathers and show that all the passages which refer to this kind of divine action [sc. possession] are associated with the Spirit, and none of them with the name of the Son.'[4] But such an analysis is surely required if his case is to be accepted, and I do not believe that it could be made.

The impossibility of finding such a clear-cut threefold division of activity is perhaps most clearly shown by the uncertainty throughout the early period as to what activities in many of the primary spheres of God's self-revelation ought to be attributed to the Son and what to the Spirit. This can be illustrated from the spheres of incarnation, inspiration, and creation.

Luke i. 35 had declared explicitly that the conception of Christ was effected by the coming of Holy Spirit upon the Virgin Mary. Later orthodoxy, as expressed in the Apostles' creed, has therefore attributed this crucial act, by which the incarnation was effected, to the third person of the Trinity. The majority of early writers, however, were led by the

[1] Cp. Novatian, *De Trin.* 29: 'The Holy Spirit is not new in the Gospel, nor yet even newly given, for it was He Himself who accused the people in the prophets.'

[2] In *Essays on the Trinity and the Incarnation* (1928), edited by A. E. J. Rawlinson. [3] Op. cit., p. 227.

[4] Ibid., p. 234.

17

logic of their thought to identify Holy Spirit in this context with the
Logos, and so to attribute the conception to the second person of the
Trinity. This is done explicitly by Justin and Tertullian.[1] Other writers
are less explicit in the identification of Spirit and Logos in their treatment of the passage, but their language seems normally to imply the
same interpretation.[2] Irenaeus' view of the matter is particularly
difficult to determine with clarity but according to the considered
judgement of J. Armitage Robinson, 'he seems to prefer to think of a
co-operation of the Word of God and the Wisdom of God—the two
Hands of God to whom the creation of the first-formed man was due'.[3]
This general uncertainty about the efficient agent in the work of incarnation is paralleled by an uncertainty about the efficient agent of consecration in the Eucharist to whom the prayer of Epiklesis should be
addressed.[4]

Both scripture and the Nicene creed have accustomed us to think of
the inspiration of the Old Testament prophets as the particular function of the Holy Spirit. This indeed represents also the general mind
of the early Fathers. In fact Justin and Irenaeus even speak in such a way
as to imply that the inspiration of the prophets was the primary and
distinctive characteristic of the Spirit. Thus Justin speaks of worshipping
the Father, the Son, and the prophetic Spirit,[5] and of the use in baptism
of the name of the Father Lord God of the universe, and of Jesus
Christ, who was crucified under Pontius Pilate, and of the Holy Spirit,
who through the prophets announced the things relating to Jesus.[6] And
Irenaeus says that heretics either 'despise the Father, or do not accept
the Son, that is speak against the dispensation of His incarnation, or do
not accept the Spirit, that is, reject prophecy',[7] and in a positive exposition of the faith of the Apostles he speaks of belief in 'one God the
Father almighty, Who made the heaven and the earth and the seas and
all the things in them; and in one Christ Jesus, the Son of God, who was
made flesh for our salvation, and in the Holy Spirit, Who through the
prophets proclaimed the saving dispensations . . .'[8] Yet to many of the
early writers (including Justin and Irenaeus) it seemed reasonable to
associate this work of inspiration also with the divine Logos. Thus
Justin, in developing the argument from prophecy in the *First Apology*,

[1] Justin, *Ap.* i. 33; Tertullian, *Adv. Prax.* 26; *De Carne Christi*, 14.
[2] e.g. Hippolytus, *Con. Noet.* 4; Lactantius, *Div. Inst.* iv. 12.
[3] J. Armitage Robinson, *St. Irenaeus: Demonstratio* (1920), p. 67. (Cp.
Irenaeus, *Adv. Haer.* iii. 21. 4; v. 1. 3; *Dem.* 40, 71.)
[4] Cp. G. Dix, *The Shape of the Liturgy* (1944), p. 276; G. Kretschmar, *Studien
zur frühchristlichen Trinitätstheologie* (1956), pp. 190, 191.
[5] Justin, *Ap.* i. 6, 13.   [6] Ibid. 61.
[7] Irenaeus, *Demonstratio*, 100.   [8] *Adv. Haer.* i. 10. 1.

attributes the utterances of the prophets to 'the prophetic spirit' and to 'the Holy Spirit of prophecy', and yet in the selfsame passage declares the prophets to be 'inspired by the divine word who moves them'.[1] Irenaeus in a single chapter of the *Adversus Haereses* speaks first of the prophets 'receiving their prophetic gift from the Word' and of 'the Word of God foretelling from the beginning that God should be seen by men', and a little later on of the same prophets as acting 'according to the suggestions of the Spirit' and of 'the Spirit of God as pointing out things to come by them'.[2] Similarly Hippolytus writes: 'One God gave the law and the prophets; and in giving them, He made them speak by the Holy Ghost, in order that being gifted with the inspiration of the Father's power, they might declare the Father's counsel and will. Acting then in these prophets, the Word spoke of Himself. For already He became His own herald.'[3] Thus none of these writers finds any incongruity in ascribing the work of inspiration both to the Holy Spirit and the Logos. In fact Lietzmann declares of Justin that, 'according to his theory, the Son, as the Logos, is identical with the Spirit which revealed itself in the prophets';[4] Swete states that Clement of Alexandria 'connects the Word and the Spirit, when he speaks of the inspiration of the prophets, ascribing this to either person almost indiscriminately';[5] and Lawson asserts that for Irenaeus the Son and the Spirit are 'equal and interchangeable in function', explicitly in the matter of inspiration and implicitly in the matter of revelation.[6] This last judgement requires some slight qualification in view of the fact that Irenaeus once again seems to think of the inspiration of scripture as the joint activity of the Word and the Spirit,[7] and even attempts to draw a distinction between their respective roles. The Word is the source of revelation about himself, the Spirit the agent. In revelation of the Father, the Word is also agent.[8] None the less, the conclusion is evident that the inspiration of scripture is not an activity which points directly to or which can be associated exclusively with one particular person of the Trinity.

It is in the third selected sphere, that of the work of creation, that this uncertainty is most widespread. Modern thought is most inclined to attribute this kind of activity either directly to the Father or in its more immanentist aspects to the Spirit. But the early Fathers ascribe the

---

[1] Justin, *Ap.* i. 31, 44 and 36.   [2] Irenaeus, *Adv. Haer.* iv. 20. 4, 8.
[3] Hippolytus, *Con. Noet.* 11, 12.
[4] H. Lietzmann, *Geschichte der alten Kirche*, ii (1936), p. 184 (Eng. trans. *Founding of the Church Universal* (2nd ed. 1950), p. 184).
[5] H. B. Swete, article 'Holy Ghost' in Smith and Wace, *Dictionary of Christian Biography*, iii (1882), p. 118.
[6] J. Lawson, *Biblical Theology of St. Irenaeus* (1948), p. 127.
[7] Irenaeus, *Adv. Haer.* ii. 28. 2; iv. 20. 6.   [8] *Dem.* 5–7.

work of creation either to the Logos alone, or else to the Logos and the Spirit together. Eusebius describes how the Logos by his divine prerogative

always continuously pervades the whole matter of the elements and of actual bodies; and, as being creator-word of God, stamps on it the principles of the wisdom derived from Him. He impresses life on what is lifeless and form on what is itself formless and indeterminate, reproducing in the qualities of the bodies the values and the unembodied forms inherent in Him; He sets into an all-wise and all-harmonious motion things that are on their own account lifeless and immobile—earth, water, air and fire; He orders everything out of disorder, giving development and completion; with the actual power of deity and logos, He all but forces all things; He pervades all things and grasps all things; yet contracts no injury from any nor is sullied in Himself.[1]

More frequently, especially under the influence of Ps. xxxiii. 6, this kind of thing is ascribed to the Son and the Spirit together. Thus Athenagoras speaks of God 'framing all things by the Logos and holding them in being by His Spirit'.[2] Irenaeus frequently speaks in this kind of way. He speaks of God 'producing creatures by His Word and fashioning everything by His Spirit',[3] 'establishing all things by His word and binding them together by His wisdom',[4] 'making things by His word and adorning them by His wisdom',[5] or again of 'the Son executing and fabricating', while 'the Spirit nourishes and increases'.[6] Similarly Hippolytus says that 'God created all things by the Logos and arranged them by the Wisdom'.[7] Dr. Prestige defines the distinction between the roles of the Logos and the Spirit here as a 'connection of the universal scheme and fundamental principles of the creation, regarding creation not as a finished product but as a continuous process, with the Logos, and that of its living growth and progress with the Spirit of Life'.[8] Irenaeus is the one early writer who makes a similar attempt to show that the distinction is a logical and significant one. 'Since the word', he says, 'establishes, that is to say, gives body and grants the reality of being, and the Spirit gives order and form to the diversity of powers, rightly and fittingly is the Word called the Son, and the Spirit the Wisdom of God'.[9] No doubt some such distinction can be drawn, but it is hardly one that *requires* us to think of different persons within the Godhead. Nor, as we have seen, was it consistently maintained. Even Ps. xxxiii. 6 with its reference to 'word' and 'breath' was not always interpreted as implying the second and third persons of the Trinity. Tertullian interprets both

[1] Eusebius, *Dem. Ev.* iv. 13. 2, 3 (cp. Irenaeus, *Adv. Haer.* ii. 2. 4, 5).
[2] Athenagoras, *Suppl.* vi. 3.   [3] Irenaeus, *Dem.* 5.   [4] *Adv. Haer.* iii. 24. 2.
[5] Ibid. iv. 20. 2.   [6] Ibid. iv. 38. 3.   [7] Hippolytus, *Con. Noet.* 10.
[8] G. L. Prestige, *God in Patristic Thought* (1936), p. 36.
[9] Irenaeus, *Dem.* 5.

parts of the verse as referring to the Word, so that, whereas the verse suggested to Irenaeus the picture of the Son and the Spirit as the two hands of God, for Tertullian the Word is in Himself both the hands of God.[1] All this kind of thinking is consciously based upon the concept of Wisdom to be found in the Old Testament. Its ascription to the second or third person of the Trinity therefore depended on whether Wisdom was to be identified with the Son or with the Spirit. Theophilus, in the earliest example of the word τρίας in this context, speaks of the 'triad, God and His Word and His Wisdom'.[2] Irenaeus also makes explicit identification of Wisdom and the Holy Spirit.[3] But the majority of writers, partly under the influence of 1 Cor. i. 24 and partly motivated by the obvious similarity of idea between Sophia and Logos, preferred to identify Wisdom with the second person of the Trinity.[4]

'Later theology', wrote E. F. Scott, 'has been unable to define the threefold nature in such a way as to preserve a real distinction between the Spirit and Christ.'[5] And while this may be an over-statement when applied to the whole historical development of theology, it seems at least to be true of the ante-Nicene period. The thought of the earliest Fathers about God was not so unfailingly threefold in character that they were forced to think in trinitarian terms. Their thought about God was at least as much binitarian as trinitarian. Why, then, should Christian thought about God have taken so clear a trinitarian form, if its content was as much binitarian as trinitarian? The answer appears to be that the threefold form was a basic datum for Christian thought from the very beginning. If not emphasized, it was at least present in scripture. From a comparatively early time it seems to have provided the framework for semi-credal confessions, summaries of the faith, and baptismal practice. We have seen that many of the writers of the first three centuries were far from clear about the distinctions between the three persons of the Godhead. Many of the passages in which they speak most clearly in a threefold trinitarian fashion about God are passages in which there are definite allusions to baptism or which read like stereotyped summaries of the faith along lines given in catechetical instruction. Thus Justin Martyr has an explicit reference to baptism in the trinitarian passage already quoted.[6] Irenaeus sums up his most explicitly trinitarian summary of the faith with the words: 'Therefore the baptism of our rebirth

---

[1] Tertullian, *Adv. Herm.* 45 (cp. also *Adv. Prax.* 7, 19).

[2] Theophilus, *Ad Aut.* ii. 15; (cp. also ibid. i. 7; ii. 10).

[3] Irenaeus, *Adv. Haer.* iv. 7. 4; iv. 20. 3; *Dem.* 5, 10.

[4] Athenagoras, *Suppl.* xxiv. 1; Tertullian, *Adv. Prax.* 6, 19; Origen, *De Princ.* i. 2. 3; i. 2. 10; ii. 9. 4; *Com. Jn.* i. 19.

[5] *The Spirit in the New Testament* (1923), p. 232.   [6] See p. 96 above.

comes through these three articles, granting us rebirth unto God the Father, through His Son, by the Holy Spirit.'[1] Origen describes how 'when we come to the grace of baptism, renouncing all other gods and lords, we confess only God the Father and Son and Holy Spirit'.[2] Tertullian, in arguing for the distinct personality of the Son, refers to the dominical command to baptize into the Father and the Son and the Holy Ghost, and adds: 'For not once but thrice are we baptised into each several person at each several name.'[3] Origen uses a similar argument in support of the true dignity of the person of the Spirit.[4] Similarly, numerous examples could be given of expositions of 'the rule of faith', which fall into a clear trinitarian form. We have already quoted one such passage from Irenaeus.[5] Origen makes it quite clear that faith in God and Jesus Christ and the Holy Spirit is the heart of apostolic teaching.[6] Tertullian's summaries of the faith are not so clearly trinitarian in character, although they tend in that direction.[7] If these trinitarian forms were a later evolutionary development from an earlier universal practice of simple Christological confessions or binitarian creeds, then they would have to be regarded more as a result than a cause of the adoption of a threefold scheme in thought about God. But this is not the case. In his *Early Christian Creeds* Dr. Kelly has shown that this conception of the development of trinitarian credal forms was an unproved axiom of certain scholars. He has shown that the trinitarian pattern in stylized expressions of faith is present from the very beginning.[8] It is true that it is present alongside simpler Christological and binitarian forms, but that is quite sufficient for the purposes of our argument. If trinitarian forms were in existence at all from the beginning, it is highly probable that they would exercise considerable effect upon later thought. It was easier for binitarian forms to be expanded, than for existing trinitarian forms to be truncated. Where argument, going beyond the simple appeal to established belief, is employed, the appeal is not so much to the threefold character of God's revelation as experienced but rather to the letter of scripture. Thus Origen bases his clear distinction of the three persons constituting the one Trinity on the wording of the gospels in which Jesus speaks of the Father as ἄλλος from himself, and of the Spirit as ἄλλος παράκλητος.[9]

---

[1] Irenaeus, *Dem.* 6, 7.   [2] Origen, *Hom. Ex.* viii. 4.
[3] Tertullian, *Adv. Prax.* 26 (cp. also Hippolytus, *Con. Noet.* 14).
[4] Origen, *De Princ.* i. 3. 2.
[5] See p. 96 above (cp. also *Adv. Haer.* iv. 33. 7).
[6] Origen, *De Princ.* praef. 2, 4 (cp. also *Matt. Comm. Ser.* 33; *Com. Jn.* xxxii. 16; *Hom. Jer.* v. 13; *1 Cor. Frag.* 4, in *J.T.S.* ix (1908), p. 234).
[7] Tertullian, *Adv. Prax.* 2; *De Praescr.* 13.
[8] See especially pp. 23–29, 94.   [9] Origen, *Hom. Num.* xii. 1.

We are therefore bound to conclude that the ante-Nicene Fathers did not adopt a trinitarian scheme of thought about God because they found themselves compelled to do so as the only rational means of explanation of their experience of God in Christ. Rather they came to accept a trinitarian form, because it was the already accepted pattern of expression, even though they often found it difficult to interpret their experience of God in this particular threefold way.

By the fourth century, however, the issues at stake had changed. The threefold pattern was fully and firmly established. The main efforts of the catholic theologians were directed against the 'semi-Arian' tradition, with its radical division of the three hypostases within the Godhead, and the Macedonian tendency to deny the full divinity of the Spirit. For this purpose the difficulty of making any clear division between the three persons of the Trinity, which had been something of an embarrassment at the earlier stage of development, was a fact of incomparable value for the establishment and defence of orthodoxy. Time and again, in arguing for the identity of substance between the three persons of the Trinity, they base their case upon the identity of their operations. This perhaps finds its clearest expression in the words of Gregory of Nyssa:

If we recognise that the operation of the Father, the Son and the Holy Spirit is one, with no point of difference or variation, then we are forced to infer from the identity of their operation the unity of their natures. Sanctification, life-giving illumination and consolation and all similar gifts are the work alike of the Father, the Son and the Holy Spirit. And no one should attribute the power of sanctification in the especial sense to the Spirit, when he hears the Saviour in the Gospel saying to the Father regarding the disciples: 'Father, sanctify them in Thy name'. So too all the other gifts, which are produced in the lives of those deserving them, come equally from the Father, the Son and the Holy Spirit. And the same is true of every grace or virtue—guidance, life, consolation, translation to immortality, passing into freedom—in fact it is true of any boon there may be, which comes down to us. . . . Thus the identity of operation in Father, Son and Holy Spirit shows clearly the indistinguishable character of their nature.[1]

In one form or another, the same argument is repeated by all the main writers of the fourth century.[2] The various gifts of God are not the gifts of one particular member of the Trinity; every gift comes from the

---

[1] Printed among the letters of Basil as *Ep.* 189. 6, 7.

[2] e.g. Athanasius, *Ad Ser.* i. 14, 20; Basil, *De Spir. Sanct.* 19; ps.-Basil (probably Didymus), *Adv. Eun.* iv. 1. (*P.G.* 29: 676A); Gregory of Nyssa, *Con. Eun.* ii (*P.G.* 45: 564A, B); Didymus, *De Spir. Sanct.* 16; Cyril Alex., *Com. Jn.* in vi. 45 (*P.G.* 73: 556), in xiv. 14 (*P.G.* 74: 249C–252B), in xv. 1 (*P.G.* 74: 333D–337D).

Father through the Son in or with the Holy Spirit.[1] This was naturally worked out with reference to the spheres of incarnation, inspiration, and creation, where as we have seen the attachment of the activity to one particular member of the Trinity had been hesitant and vacillating from the beginning. Rufinus finds mention of all three persons of the Trinity in the actual text of Luke i. 35—the Holy Spirit, the Power, and the Most High.[2] Cyril of Alexandria interprets the text itself as referring only to the Holy Spirit, but quotes alongside it two other texts to prove the equal participation of the first and second members of the Trinity in the work of incarnation.[3] The different formulae to be found in scripture describing the inspiration of the prophets show that it also may be ascribed to any of the members of the Trinity; this too is evidence for unity of substance.[4] The work of creation is the work of all three members of the Trinity. The Father creates all things through the Word in the Spirit, the Word being the actual agent of creation, the Spirit being the source of the power to continue in existence.[5] The Father originates, commands, or conceives, the Son creates, and the Spirit perfects.[6] The association of the Spirit with the work of creation is of particular importance, because the exclusion of the Spirit from that sphere of the divine activity was an argument being used both by Eunomius and the Macedonians against his full Godhead.[7] Didymus actually contrives to interpret a single text from the creation story as having reference to all three members of the Trinity—God the Son made man in the image of God the Father, and God the Spirit saw that it was good and blessed them.[8] Thus in these three spheres the idea of the joint activity of the persons of the Trinity, already suggested by Irenaeus, finds its full development.

Even so this does not represent the highest point in thought about the unity of the operations of the Trinity. Not merely is it heretical to exclude the Spirit from the work of creation. Any kind of division of function within the Trinity is evidence of heresy. Even the basic formula

[1] Cyril, *Catecheses*, xvi. 24; Athanasius, *Ad Ser.* i. 28, 31; Gregory of Nyssa, *Quod non sint tres dei* (*P.G.* 45: 125C); Cyril Alex., *Com. Jn.* in vi. 57 (*P.G.* 73: 588A).
[2] Rufinus, *Com. in Symb. Ap.* 10 (cp. Athanasius, *Ad Ser.* iii. 6).
[3] Cyril Alex., *Com. Jn.* in vi. 57. (*P.G.* 73: 585D–588A).
[4] Athanasius, *Ad Ser.* i. 31, iii. 5; Didymus, *De Spir. Sanct.* 29, *De Trin.* ii (*P.G.* 39: 500); Cyril Alex., *De Trin.* vii (*P.G.* 75: 1093C–1096A).
[5] Athanasius, *Ad Ser.* iii. 5.
[6] Basil, *De Spir. Sanct.* 38; Gregory Nazianzen, *Or.* xxxviii. 9 (cp. Gregory of Nyssa, *Adv. Mac.* 13).
[7] Basil, *Adv. Eun.* iii. 5; Eunomius, *Apology*, 27; Gregory of Nyssa, *Adv. Mac.* 11; ps.-Athanasius, *De Trin.* iii. 16–19.
[8] Didymus, *De Trin.* ii (*P G.* 39: 565C).

'from the Father through the Son in the Holy Spirit' must not be regarded as an invariable description of the activity of God. If it were so, it would imply the existence of a difference between the persons, which is in danger of constituting a difference of essence.[1] Thus for the Cappadocians there is no difference whatever between the persons of the Trinity in their relation to the world; the only difference is to be found in their internal relations to one another. Basil describes the distinguishing characteristics as πατρότης, υἱότης, and ἁγιασμός or ἁγιαστικὴ δύναμις.[2] Gregory of Nazianzus has the most clear-cut scheme in terms of ἀγεννησία, γέννησις, and ἐκπόρευσις, or their equivalents.[3] Gregory of Nyssa uses the terms ἀγέννητος and μονογενής for the first two persons, but then has to speak of the ἴδια γνωρίσματα of the Spirit, which he can only express negatively and periphrastically.[4] But despite these differences in terminology, they are united and emphatic about the central fact—namely that it is in this sphere of their mutual relations alone that any distinction between the persons of the Trinity is to be found.[5] As an answer to the challenge of their opponents their work represents a great achievement. In the East it was developed in terms of the doctrine of περιχώρησις; in the West it underlies the work of Augustine and his repeated insistence on the inseparability of the operations of the three persons.[6] Thus it has remained and still remains fundamental to the full orthodox doctrine of the Trinity.

None the less, it is evident that a serious difficulty remains. If there is no distinction whatever in the activity of the Trinity towards us, how can we have any knowledge of the distinctions at all? It is logically impossible, if we accept the full Cappadocian doctrine, to claim that they are known to us as a result of 'rational reflection on those particular manifestations of the divine activity which centre in the birth, ministry, crucifixion, resurrection, and ascension of Jesus Christ and the gift of the Holy Spirit to the Church'. This difficulty is not often dealt with by the fourth-century writers themselves, because for them the same

[1] Basil, De Spir. Sanct. v. 7–12; Gregory Nazianzen, Or. xxxi. 20, xxxix. 12.
[2] Basil, Ep. 214. 4; 236. 6.
[3] Gregory Nazianzen, Or. xxxi. 8 (a large number of examples are listed in K. Holl, Amphilochius von Ikonium (1904), pp. 167–8).
[4] Gregory of Nyssa, Con. Eun. i (P.G. 45: 336B–D); cp. also Adv. Mac. 2.
[5] This is most forcefully expressed by Gregory of Nyssa, De Com. Not. (P.G. 45: 180C); Adv. Mac. 14; De Fide (P.G. 45: 144A, B). Cp. also Gregory Nazianzen, Or. xxix. 16, xxxi. 9. It should be noticed that even the division of the activity of the Trinity in the work of creation already quoted (see p. 102 above) is really inconsistent with this insistence on the complete identity of their operations. There is no doubt that it is the latter which is their main teaching. (Cp. K. Holl, op. cit., pp. 146–7.)
[6] e.g. Augustine, De Trin. iv. 30.

epistemological difficulty did not arise. Athanasius admits that judging solely from the facts of prophecy and of creation, one might well be led to identify the Son and the Spirit. The only reason why we must not draw that conclusion is the written form of revelation and the traditions of the faith, especially the formula of baptism.[1] In the case of the Cappadocians the problem is still more acute. Not only is there no difference in the operations, through which we might come to know of the different persons of the Trinity, but we are not even given any idea of the difference in meaning between the relationships of 'generation' and 'procession'—the only difference which is admitted to exist. It is quite clear, however, that their belief in the three persons has the same basis as that of Athanasius, with an even greater emphasis upon the baptismal formula.[2] It is therefore evident that Dr. Hodgson's approach will not carry us the whole way to the fully articulated doctrine of the Trinity. The Cappadocian construction was built upon and logically requires the foundation belief that the threefold form of the Godhead is a datum of revelation given in clear propositional form.

In the light of this evidence, we seem forced to choose between three possibilities:

either (1) we do after all know about the Trinity through a revelation in the form of propositions concerning the inner mysteries of the Godhead;

or (2) there is an inherent threefoldness about every act of God's revelation, which requires us to think in trinitarian terms of the nature of God, even though we cannot speak of the different persons of the Trinity being responsible for specific facets of God's revelation;

or (3) our Trinity of revelation is an arbitrary analysis of the activity of God, which though of value in Christian thought and devotion is not of essential significance.

Of these three possibilities (1) and (2) are much more closely in accord with the general tradition of Christendom than (3), and yet both have serious difficulties. Of (1) one must simply say that it appears to conflict with the whole idea of the nature of revelation to which biblical criticism has led us. (2) is a view upheld by Karl Barth. Barth adheres strictly to the classical 'rule for theologising on the Trinity, *opera trinitatis ad extra sunt indivisa*' and affirms that 'there is no attribute, no act of God which would not in like manner be the attribute, the act of the Father, the Son and the Spirit'.[3] He finds the root of the

---

[1] Athanasius, *Ad Ser.* iv. 3–6.

[2] Gregory Nazianzen, *Or.* xxix. 16, xxxi. 9; Basil, *De Spir. Sanct.* 24–28.

[3] K. Barth, *Kirchliche Dogmatik* 1/1 (1932), pp. 395, 381–2 (Eng. trans. *Doctrine of the Word of God* (1936), pp. 430, 415); C. R. Welch, *The Trinity in Contemporary Theology* (1953), pp. 192–3.

doctrine of the Trinity in the statement that God reveals himself as the Lord. The meaning of this statement is to be analysed in terms of the three concepts, Revealer, Revelation, and Revealedness. The doctrine is a theoretical formulation, but one which is immediately and directly required by the statement about revelation itself.[1] Barth says: 'If we have rejected the possibility of reading off the distinction between the three modes of existence from the varieties of content in the thought of God contained in the concept of revelation, because in the last resort we cannot speak of such things, so now we should and must assert that the formal individual characteristics of the three modes of existence can quite well be read off from the concept of revelation—what actually constitutes them modes of existence—namely, the characteristics due to their relation to one another.'[2] This view of the source of the doctrine would not take us the whole way to the fullest Cappadocian doctrine in that by admitting a threefold distinction in the structure of every divine act it conflicts with the Cappadocian insistence that not even the 'from whom', 'through whom', and 'in whom' of the trinitarian formula belong exclusively to the different persons.[3] None the less, if it could be accepted, it would certainly establish an orthodox and essential doctrine of the Trinity. But for all the advocacy of Karl Barth, it seems impossible seriously to maintain that the statement about revelation is something that *requires* a trinitarian explanation. The whole argument sounds suspiciously like a later rationalization to support a doctrine really based on (1) and now in search of a new foundation.

(3) is admittedly revolutionary, but no more so than the break-away from the idea of propositional revelation of which it appears to be the logical conclusion. Even in the patristic and medieval periods, there is a very occasional pointer to the possibility of a more than threefold analysis of the Godhead. Two very different examples may be given. The first comes from the ante-Nicene period when the idea of the Trinity is still closely linked with the variety of divine activity. In one passage Hippolytus gives a number of the customary formulations—the Father willed, the Son performed, and the Spirit manifested; the Father commands, the Son obeys, the Holy Spirit gives understanding; the Father is above all, the Son through all, and the Holy Spirit in all. But together with these stands another which seems to cry out for completion as a quaternity—the Father decrees, the Word executes, the Son is revealed.[4] The second is from Thomas Aquinas. Thomas is

---

[1] Welch, op. cit., pp. 168–71 (cp. also L. Hodgson's criticism of the view in *J.T.S.*, N.S., v (1954), p. 50).

[2] Barth, op. cit., pp. 382–3 (Eng. trans., pp. 416–17).

[3] Welch, op. cit., p. 223.   [4] Hippolytus, *Con. Noet.* 14.

emphatic that the only distinctions within the Trinity are distinctions
of internal relation, and quite rightly insists (as we have been insisting)
that for that very reason it is logically impossible for the doctrine to be
known in any other way than by authoritative revelation.[1] Yet the logic
of his thought forces him to postulate five notions or properties—
innascibility, paternity, filiation, common *spiratio*, and procession—in
God.[2] Naturally he argues that only three of these are 'personal properties'.[3] But the existence of such a discussion is sufficient evidence that
even within the concept of the internal relations of the Godhead there
are factors which might tend to push us beyond the number three. It
is not, however, upon the validity of such admittedly tentative pre-
figurements that our case rests. The heart of the matter is much
simpler. The 'threeness' of the completed orthodox doctrine of the
Trinity can logically be known only on the basis of a propositional
revelation about the inner mysteries of the Godhead or through some
other kind of specific authoritative revelation. If that basis be removed,
then the necessity (though not necessarily the desirability or the value)
of trinitarian thought is removed. So D. M. Edwards, starting from the
premise that 'the ultimate basis on which the doctrine [sc. of the Trinity]
was built is, of course, found in the New Testament, in the experience
of the divine quality and potency of the historic Jesus as mediated by
His living and abiding Spirit', is led on to the conclusion that 'the
modern mind . . . cannot see any necessity of thought for fixing on the
number three, neither less nor more' and that 'no convincing reason can
be given why, in view of the rich manifoldness of divine functions and
activities, the number of the hypostases may not be increased inde-
finitely'.[4]

It might appear that the purpose of this article is entirely negative and
destructive. I do not believe that that is the case. If its thesis is refuted,
the refutation would necessarily involve a valuable examination of the
concept of the Trinity in the light of recent epistemological ideas.
If its thesis is accepted, it would represent a signal warning of the need
for caution in the making of dogmatic statements about the inner life of
God. In either event, there would be great positive gain.

                                                MAURICE WILES

[1] Thomas Aquinas, *Summa Theol.* i, Q. 32. 1.
[2] Ibid., Q. 32. 3.
[3] Ibid., Q. 40. 1.
[4] D. M. Edwards, *Christianity and Philosophy* (1932), pp. 339, 354, 355.

Vigiliae Christianae 29, 1–14; © *North-Holland Publishing Company* 1975

THE CONCEPT OF DIVINE SUBSTANCE

BY

G. CHRISTOPHER STEAD

The concept of substance has been a focus for some of the most obscure problems of logic and metaphysics; and if one wishes to apply it to theology, and speak of divine substance,[1] one has to come to a judgement also on some of the most strenuously debated questions of theology. I have tried to investigate two problems in particular: the lexical and philosophical background of the Nicene term *homoousios*, and the significance of the term *ousia* itself, especially when it refers to divine being. In the first case, I am particularly concerned with the Doctrine of the Trinity; in the second, I have had to consider some larger questions about the whole Christian doctrine of God, and the value or disvalue of Greek metaphysics in interpreting it; a question which has been much discussed by biblical theologians, but has also been treated from the patristic side by G. L. Prestige in England, and again by Wolfhart Pannenberg in Germany.[2] But the core of the problem is of course the analysis of the term *ousia* itself; and here I am amazed how little work has been done by qualified patristic scholars. There have been some brief general studies (e.g. that of R. Hirzel, *Philologus* 72, 1913); the Latin word *substantia* has been discussed in some detail by C. Arpe (*Philologus* 94, 1940) and others, not to mention the excellent work of René Braun on Tertullian's theological vocabulary, *Deus Christianorum* (Paris 1962). There have also been several instructive essays on the use of *ousia* in Greek philosophy, especially in Plato and Aristotle.[3] But for a survey of

---

[1] My forthcoming book *Divine Substance* (Oxford 1975–6) deals with: the concept of being; universals and particulars; being and activity; the concept of absolute unity and the doctrine of the Trinity; *ousia* in Greek philosophy and in the Fathers; the term *homoousios*; and some concluding reflections. This paper is the English version of a lecture delivered in German at Göttingen in 1971.

[2] G. L. Prestige, *God in Patristic Thought* (London ²1952); W. Pannenberg, Der philosophische Gottesbegriff in frühchristlicher Theologie, *ZKG* 70 (1959) 1–45.

[3] See also the recent work of Charles H. Kahn, *The Verb "Be" in Ancient Greek*, ed. by J. W. M. Verhaar (Dordrecht 1973).

ousia in the Christian fathers one has to go back to two articles in the *Journal of Theological Studies* 1901–2, by T. B. Strong, later Bishop of Oxford.

In this respect there has been a striking contrast between the words *ousia* and *hypostasis*; on *hypostasis*, besides the work of Prestige, one has the outstandingly valuable surveys of R. E. Witt and especially of Heinrich Dörrie; and its use in later theology has been thoroughly investigated by Marcel Richard.[4] If one asks, why has the word *ousia*, in comparison with *hypostasis*, been so much neglected, one answer may be the following: the word *hypostasis* has a complex and fascinating variety of meanings which lie outside the sphere of philosophy; it can mean sediment, a basis, a buttress, resources, or confidence, as well as matter, reality, and individual thing. But the different senses of *ousia* lie almost entirely within the sphere of philosophy, were constantly confused by ancient writers, and are much harder to distinguish even by modern critics, who need some acquaintance with semantics, logic and metaphysics; and these are aptitudes that not many patristic scholars have the opportunity to cultivate.

2. I will briefly set out the method which I have tried to follow. I desire *both* to describe what these ancient writers have said, *and* to appreciate their achievements and explain their mistakes. Two consequences follow. First, we must determine a standpoint *from which* criticisms can be made; in fact we have to determine, in the light of our whole philosophical tradition, what *ought* to be said about substance; and therefore also, what *ought* to be said about being; and also about unity; and also (as I shall explain) about the individual and the universal – in fact all the central problems of classical metaphysics! I shall return to this point in a moment. But secondly, we must distinguish very carefully between exposition and criticism; and that means, that we must consider "the meaning of meaning". We patristic scholars often say, "X means so-and-so"; but do we ourselves consider the meaning of this very phrase, "X means so-and-so"? Too often it is used to introduce a mildly idealized version of X's opinion, which is neither honest description or acknowl-

---

[4] R. E. Witt, Hypostasis, in *Amicitiae Corolla* (Festschr. J. R. Harris), ed. H. G. Wood (London 1933) 319–43; H. Dörrie, Hypostasis, Wort- und Bedeutungsgeschichte, *Nachr. Göttingen, phil.-hist. Klasse* 1955, 3, 35–93; M. Richard, L'introduction du mot hypostase dans la théologie de l'Incarnation, *Mel. Sc. Rel.* 2 (1945) 5–32, 243–70.

edged correction. Here, I think, we must choose; and if we say, "X means so-and-so", we must *either* offer an interpretative paraphrase, remaining within the writer's circle of ideas; *or* a corrective paraphrase, introducing modern critical refinements. Both these tasks are legitimate and useful, but they must be kept distinct. But note further: the same principal applies when it comes to saying that a *word* has different meanings. Here again we must choose. Are we going to point out distinctions of meaning which were recognized by ancient writers themselves, or are we going to point out distinctions of meaning which we ourselves detect? Here again, both tasks are useful and important, but they must be kept distinct. Ancient writers "knew the meanings" of the words they used, *in the sense that* they could use them freely and naturally, conforming without difficulty to current usage; at times, also, they made use of traditional distinctions of meanings; but they certainly did not study their own usage, as we can, in the light of exact philology and semantics. Hence their opinions about their own usage are frequently misleading. Let us take a very simple example. Athanasius tells us that *ousia* and *hypostasis* are synonymous (*Ad Afros* 4). Do we believe him? Of course we do not! In its context, no doubt, Athanasius' equation of the two terms is intelligible and justifiable enough;[5] but it gives no reliable information about current usage; and this does *not* of course mean that Athanasius ought to have distinguished them along the lines which Basil was just then exploring. The situation is completely different. No doubt the two words often mean the same; but there are numerous passages, even in Athanasius himself, in which *hypostasis* cannot be substituted for *ousia*. Thus *ousia* quite naturally refers to the category of substance; it naturally stands in contrast with *poiotēs*, or with *metousia*, and so on. *Hypostasis* does neither. It may be that Athanasius believed what he said; or it may be that he said what he said merely because it suited his argument; but in any case he is not correctly reporting his own usage, let alone that of other Greek theologians.

We therefore have the right to establish distinctions in the meanings of words which were not recognized by their users. To say this is merely to say that the science of lexicography can make progress. A quite different task, equally important, is to study the contemporaneous understanding

---

[5]   Prof. Dörrie very justly pointed out the importance of Athanasius' situation and purpose in writing what he did. But his pronouncement has been very frequently quoted out of context as simple report of his own usage.

of important words, and the different senses which their *users* recognized. I merely insist that these tasks must be kept distinct. There is, of course, a place for an exegetical approach to patristics; but if one attempts to clarify, develop and correct the thought of an ancient writer, it should be remembered that this interpretation of his work is a modern production; it cannot, as such, have played any part in the development of ancient thought.

I now return to my former point: despite all difficulties, we have to determine a philosophical point of departure; we have to determine what *ought* to be said about substance, about being, and so on.

Questions about being and substance have been discussed in at least three distinct philosophical idioms. The first, which we may call *traditionalist*, passes from Aristotle to Aquinas and his modern interpreters, and some other present-day sympathizers. This method has the great advantage of a stable and continuous tradition, and has been followed by some modern scholars of great distinction. But, as I shall argue, it is out of touch with modern logic; and since it aims at presenting a synthesized body of doctrine, it cannot easily take account of historical scholarship, as for instance the work of Werner Jaeger on Aristotle. Secondly there is existentialism, which I think has more influence on the continent of Europe than in English-speaking countries. This indeed arose as a reaction against the rationalism, particularly, of Hegel; and it professes to attach importance to the concrete particularity of the individual in the circumstances of his life. Yet its manner of speaking often seems strange, uncontrolled and speculative; it can be theologically suggestive, but I myself would class it with prophecy or poetry rather than with philosophy. This is not necessarily disrespectful; perhaps the Church has learnt more from prophets and poets than from philosophers. But it can hardly be congenial to sober, practical historical scholars like ourselves.

Thirdly there is the method which I have tried to interpret, namely logical empiricism. This originally stems from the German-speaking area, in fact from Austria, from the Logical Positivism of the so-called "Wiener Kreis" in the 1920's. Established at Cambridge by Ludwig Wittgenstein (whose lectures I once attended) and since then widely disseminated, it has by degrees divested itself of much of the crudity of its early positivistic phase, which was often hostile both to metaphysics and to theology. What now prevails, in Oxford and elsewhere, is a much more flexible and realistic appraisal of the functions of our language, which can be combined with a sound critical and philological approach to ancient writers. Properly interpreted, its sober, disciplined analysis can be made attractive to historical thologians.

There is one particular feature of this method which I desire to point out. Traditionalist logic tends to be governed by a principle of *isomorphy*; it assumes that the structure of our thinking, and of our language, corresponds to the structure of reality; therefore words like "being" and "substance" are each of them names for things which exist *in rerum natura*. Empiricist logic, on the other hand, emphasizes the flexibility of our language, which can often express the same facts in quite different alternative linguistic forms. (In principle, of course, this goes back to Aristotle, who observed that it makes no difference whether we say βαδίζει or βαδίζων ἐστί, *Metaphysics* Δ 7). But if two quite differently-formed expressions are equally appropriate, there is no longer any need to think that either of them corresponds formally to the state of affairs to which they refer. Again, we need no longer assume that each single term, like "being" or "substance", stands as a name for just one complex fact about the real universe. On the contrary, we shall now suppose that we use these terms in different senses and in different connections to deal with a variety of problems which have been associated largely by accident in the course of the history of philosophy. And these problems can be discussed more lucidly and, if I may say so, more reverently, if we cease we assume that the structure of reality must conform – as Kant said – to the structure of our minds. For are not rationalist philosophers like the tower-builders of Babel? – supposing that they can build a structure of human concepts which will bring the heavenly realities into clear view? Yet if this is clearly seen to be presumptuous, then it is pointless to indulge in the rhetorical gestures and renunciations of anti-rationalism.

3. Let us now apply these general principles to theology. I ask the question: is it possible to talk without contradiction, (a) about the being of God, and (b) about one God in three persons? I assume that we should make every effort to avoid contradiction, and do so without artificially contracting our traditional faith. I allow, indeed I declare, that the mystery of the Godhead surpasses rational apprehension; and it may be that in the end it will have to be represented by a contradiction. But it is essential that this should happen only when all our rational resources are at an end. It is ludicrous if we represent divine mysteries by *avoidable* contradictions, by muddles, which more disciplined thinking would

enable us to dispel. And it is idolatrous if we cultivate paradox for the sake of paradox, when we could speak clearly.

I think, then, that the traditionalist method does lead to contradictions which, at least in part, are avoidable. Let me try to outline some of the consequences of its isomorphy, namely those which follow if we take the word "being" as the name for a unified complex of thought.

First, we sometimes use the word "to be" in order to assert that something really exists. From this it is often inferred that existence itself is a predicate; and conversely, that whenever we make a statement of the form "S is P", we assert the existence of S. It follows, further, that if our statement is a theological one, and qualifies S as a pure and powerful being, then *a fortiori* it qualifies him as existing. This does not, of course, entail that theological statements cannot be false – no one, I take it, could possibly accept that conclusion! – but it does entail, I think, that we cannot make statements about (for instance) the deities of other cults without professing belief in their existence; but this is manifestly false, and proves the falsity of the premises from which it follows. Again, it entails that if we can settle our questions about the nature of God, then no further questions need be asked about his reality; which introduces the well-known difficulties of the ontological argument. It is unrealistic to think that important conclusions can be won so easily; and here at least I think that the existentialists have made a valid point against what they describe as "essentialism". But to carry the matter further, I have tried to examine the quite different account of existential statements given by the logical empiricists. These assert that such propositions primarily refer to the name itself, rather than to the object named. This, I think, has manifest advantages on the side of logic; in particular, it enables us to give a fully analogous explanation of the proposition that something does *not* exist. Such a proposition asserts that the name does *not* refer to anything. We need not then assume that sea-serpents and the like have some kind of "logical" existence, in order that they may truly be characterized as fictitious.

However, this solution of the problem necessarily assumes that the verb "to exist" has a precise and distinctive logic, and that it is in no way comparable with other verbs, such as "to live" and "to act". But in fact such verbs seem to convey at least a strong presumption that their subject is to be taken as real; it is possible, but it is certainly not usual, to say that X did so-and-so without suggesting that X really exists (one might, for instance, refer to the mythical acts of Zeus, even using the unqualified phrase "Zeus did so-and-so"). I think, then, that we should distinguish several different functions of such statements; first, they specify the act, the subject, etc.; then, they indicate the time and manner of action, etc.; then, they say whether the ostensible subject has or has not done it; lastly, they intimate that this whole proposition is to be regarded as true to fact. The verb "to do", being extremely general, gives no indication of the *kind* of action which is in view; but it generally, though not invariably, serves to intimate that the subject is real. The verb "to exist", which is still more general, commonly gives no indication of the manner in which something exists; it is then used exclusively to assert (or question, or deny) the reality of its subject. However, the two words have a logic which is comparable; and this gives us the possibility of acknowledging occasional variations in the meaning of the word "to exist" without running into the logical difficulties which I have mentioned. And this can be an advantage in theology. I wish to avoid the fallacy of "subreption"; but I also wish to assert that God exists in a manner appropriate to his splendour and glory.

Secondly: we sometimes use the verb "to be" in order to assert an identity. From this it is often inferred that in every case the verb "to be" has an identifying force; it asserts the unity of subject and predicate. From this and some other arguments it seems to follow that a *perfect* being must be an absolute undifferentiated unity. But this conclusion seems to exclude both a plurality of divine attributes and also a Trinity of divine persons. I cannot see that classical orthodoxy has ever offered a satisfying solution, on the conceptual level, of this problem of unity and multiplicity in the Godhead. It is sometimes argued, no doubt, that the divine attributes are only differentiated *quoad nos*; because we ourselves are different, and have variable moods and circumstances, the one un-changing divine life manifests itself towards us in different guises. But no orthodox theologian could apply this solution to the Persons of the Trinity.

Thirdly: somewhat similar problems arise from the classical descrip-tions of God as "pure form" and "pure act". Aristotle identified being with form, and form with universality; he regarded matter as the "principle of individuation", which explains the existence of several individuals who have the same form. This line of argument suggests that God, who stands in extreme contrast with the world of matter, must be γενικώτατος; he must be, or be comparable to, the most inclusive of all universals; he must be pure being; or if not, then at least he must be described as pure being; in this way theologians sought to express the view that we can know nothing about God, save the fact that He Is. I need not say that this metaphysical presentation of God is hardly compatible with the divine being as disclosed in the Bible, as one who acts in human history and cares for human souls.

In principle, however, the former conclusion can be avoided if we take note that "matter" can have a quite general sense, and conversely "*a form*" *can refer to something irreducibly particular*, such that no examples of it can be produced or conceived. Aristotle himself sometimes uses "this matter" to denote "this kind of matter" (for the τέτταρες ὕλαι of *De caelo* IV 5 are not four *objects*!); and conversely "this form" (or an analogous expression) quite commonly means "this particular example of this form" (cf. *Metaph.* H 3, 1043 a 29); for instance, "the letters on this wax tablet" (*ibid.* Z 10, 1035 a 16). If an individual thing can be called "a sphere", using a form-denoting word, there is no reason why it should not be called, more generally, "a form". Aristotle therefore misleads us when he says that a form is not a "this" but a "such" (*ibid.* Z 7, 1032 b 32). But of course this criticism will have to be developed in my book.

Fourthly, however: the term "pure being" is sometimes applied to God in, as it seems, a directly contrary sense; we mean now, life, power, activity, which is "pure" in the sense that it is exempt from the limitations and compromises which attach to our human life. Now I do not question the theological value of this conception; but I am puzzled about its basis in logic. Why sould the term "being" be used in two such widely differing senses, first as "mere being", which is shared by all realities whatsoever, but secondly as "unqualified being", which belongs to God alone? I ask myself, is this amphiboly, this double usage, a feature which belongs uniquely to the concept of being, or is it a general fact which applies to other universal terms? I am inclined to think that the latter is the case. Thus in certain contexts the word "man" means no more than "member of the human race"; but in other contexts it can suggest all the varieties and all the achievements of human life. Of course the contrast between the "abstract" and the "concrete" uses of the concept of *being* is exceptionally sharp; though this has not prevented their being confusingly assimilated, as by Aristotle, who is admitted to have drawn no clear distinction between "metaphysica generalis" and "metaphysica specialis", which roughly correspond to "categorial theory" and "theology".[6] But in principle the logical peculiarities of the concept of being are comparable

---

[6]   Cf. P. Merlan, *From Platonism to Neoplatonism* (The Hague ²1960).

with those of other concepts; so that this concept need no longer be mysterious. This will not mean, of course, that there are no mysteries; but it may mean that it is no longer appropriate to refer to them as "pure being".

Fifthly: there are distinctive problems which arise from the more technical term "substance", which can either reproduce the very various meanings of the Greek word *ousià* or refer in particular to the category of substance. This category has been called in question by many modern philosophers, partly I think because of a misunderstanding of Aristotle's doctrine. Aristotle saw this category represented primarily by the individual thing, which possesses predicates, some of which are invariable (its genus, its *differentia*, its *propria*) and others contingent (the *accidentia*). But his analysis also suggested the notion of substance as a mere counterpart to predicates, i.e. as a mere subject – a concept which cannot be anything more than an abstraction or ideal limit. However in late antiquity these two notions were often confused, as if something could actually exist without possessing qualities, etc. I cannot yet trace the origins of this confusion; it may be that Aristotle's theory was contaminated by the Stoic concept of unqualified matter (ἄποιος ὕλη = ἄποιος οὐσία); on the other hand it was transmitted by text-books, which commonly divided the categories into *substantia* and *accidentia*, as if all possible predicates of a substance were contingent and removable; and this misunderstanding developed the more easily since there were quite different, theological grounds for representing God himself as ἄποιος, as exempt from qualifications.

This misunderstanding can I think be avoided by careful analysis; but one may still question the usefulness of the term "substance" in theology. I think perhaps the case may be put in Kantian terms. If, as I believe, the so-called concept of substance must be analysed into a number of separate problems and solutions, it can no longer have any *constitutive* value in this field; it cannot claim to provide a uniquely appropriate designation for God. But it may still have some *regulative* value; it can guide our thinking and perhaps inform our understanding of divine revelation, provided other terms derived from the Bible and Christian tradition are retained as a corrective.

4. Let us now return to patristics, and try to understand what actually was said or assumed about substance by early Christian theologians; how did they actually use the term substance, and more particularly the actual word *ousià*?

It may be convenient to begin by recalling the accounts which are commonly given. First, it is commonly supposed that their usage is dominated by the distinction drawn in Aristotle's *Categories* between πρώτη οὐσία and δευτέρα οὐσία, between the individual on the one hand and the genus or species on the other. This was assumed by the medieval commentators, by Petavius and Bull, and by older historians of dogma like Zahn and Harnack. A sophisticated variant was offered by Loofs in his analysis of *homoousios* in the Müller Festschrift of 1922;[7] he distinguishes two main senses, "singularisch" and "generisch", but subdivides the latter into four, the "purely generic", the "generic-generative" (e.g. parent-offspring), the "generic-partitative" (e.g. fire-sparks) and the "generic-commutative" (indicating spiritual interchange or participation). A rather similar general picture is presented by those scholars who interpret the early use of *ousia* in the light of the Cappadocian distinction between *ousia* and *hypostasis*; one frequently reads such a comment as, "in this sentence *ousia* is used in the sense of substance", or "... of person"; this again implies that there are just two possibilities. As a critical comment, this is usually valueless, in my opinion; it merely indicates what verbal modifications would be needed to bring the sentence into line with post-Cappadocian orthodoxy.

Secondly: a rather different scheme is used by the aforementioned T. B. Strong, who derived it from the excellent work of Dr. Edwin Hatch, *The Influence of Greek Ideas ... upon the Christian Church* (London 1890); it has since been used by Dr. J. N. D. Kelly in his well-known history of doctrine. Hatch's treatment has the great merit that it partly glimpses the complexity of the problem; he writes "*Ousia* is used in at least three distinct senses" (p. 269), and he refers these back to Aristotle, *Metaph.* Z 10, 1035 a, οὐσία ἥ τε ὕλη καὶ τὸ εἶδος καὶ τὸ ἐκ τούτων, a text whose importance was recognized in antiquity at least by the neo-Platonists. In this account, therefore, *ousia* can mean *either* matter *or* form *or* the composite object, τὸ σύνθετον, which results when they are combined; and this last certainly looks like, and was soon identified with, the πρώτη οὐσία of the *Categories*.

I wish now to suggest that, even if these two schemes give us some clue to the thoughts of philosophers in our period, they are wholly misleading if they are taken as a description of actual common usage. In particular, it is quite false to suggest that any writer who used *ousia* would decide

---

[7] *Festgabe für K. Müller*, ed. O. Scheel (Tübingen 1922).

for, and would select, *either* the individual *or* the generic sense. First, the *Categories* was not very widely followed, and its distinction of πρώτη/δευτέρα οὐσία was embarrassing to Platonists, who disliked the suggestion that individual, and therefore perceptible, things should be called by the dignified name of "first substance". Hippolytus is, I think, the only "pre-Cappadocian" Christian writer to refer to *Categories*, c. 5. Secondly, when Platonists thought of *ousia*, the distinction that came readily to them was that of οὐσία αἰσθητή/νοητή; but this by no means corresponds to the logical distinction of individuals/species; rather, both these phrases are general terms which can refer either to individuals or to classes. Thirdly, the distinction between individuals and species was commonly expressed by phrases which do not involve *ousia*, such as τὰ καθόλου/τὰ κατὰ μέρος; note also that the Stoics drew this distinction in the category of *poiotēs*, not of *ousia*; with them the species is τὸ κοινῶς ποιόν, the individual is τὸ ἰδίως ποιόν. Fourthly, where the phrases πρώτη οὐσία, δευτέρα οὐσία *are* used, they are not used as technical terms, but exhibit a free variation of senses. I demonstrate this in detail in my book, both from Christian writers and from philosophers such as Porphyry.

If then we seek to explore the actual pattern of usage, we must begin again from the beginning; and here my method has been to try to establish a very precise set of distinctions for critical purposes; but also to make it clear that *ousia* was *not* always used with a precise sense by the ancient writers. I have, so to speak, drawn a diagram with a great many different squares or boxes; but I do not assume that in any given instance the use of *ousia* falls neatly into any one of them. In effect, the critic has to ask himself two questions, not one; first, where on the diagram is this usage to be located? and secondly, how precisely can it be located?

Let me now describe my diagram. It is a rectangle, and so is extended in two dimensions, in length and in breadth.

In some important respects, the use of the noun *ousia* reflects that of the verb *einai*. This verb, as we know, can be used either with a predicate or without. Used without a predicate, it can express either the existence of a person or thing, or the truth of a notion: existence, as when one asks, εἰ θεοὶ εἶσι; truth, as when one says, ἔστι ταῦτα. Used with a predicate, it can identify a subject, or it can describe it in various respects. On this basis, I have tried to show that *ousia* conveys not less than *seven* basic notions: first, mere existence; second, kind or category, when one uses it to formulate the most general possible questions about the nature of a thing; thirdly, substance, as defined by Aristotle and others – a possible answer to the foregoing questions; fourthly, stuff or matter; fifthly, form or species; sixthly, the definition of a thing; and seventhly, truth.

I have thus established the length of my diagram. It has seven lines or rows. Let me now establish its breadth.

I said that οὐσία reflects the verb εἶναι; but in what manner? Sometimes the noun οὐσία can be paraphrased with the infinitive τὸ εἶναι; thus Origen speaks of atheists τὴν οὐσίαν τοῦ θεοῦ ἀρνούμενοι, *Orat.* 5. οὐσία here I think means "existence". In other cases, however, οὐσία corresponds, not with τὸ εἶναι but with τὸ ὄν; for example, ἡ οὐσία can mean "the universe", understood as "all that exists". But further, the expression τὸ ὄν itself can stand either for the subject of a sentence in which εἶναι is used, or for its predicate; so, in Greek, one can distinguish by the accent between ὅ ἔστι and ὅ ἐστὶ; ὅ ἔστι means, "das, was *ist*", and ὅ ἐστὶ means, "das, *was* etwas ist". Now these two need not be identical. A good instance is a passage in Clement where he discusses the theory that milk is formed out of blood.[8] He says that milk has blood as its οὐσία, its basic material; this implies that blood is its ὅ ἐστὶ, "das, was Milch *ist*". Yet a little before, he speaks of ἡ τοῦ γάλακτος ζωοτρόφος οὐσία, "the life-giving substance of milk"; and here the context shows that ἡ τοῦ γάλακτος οὐσία does not refer to blood, but to milk itself; milk is itself a stuff, it is something ὅ ἔστι, "etwas, das *ist*", and therefore it is called an οὐσία. So a thing can be identified with its οὐσία, as the ancients sometimes claim; but it can also be distinguished therefrom.

Finally, it is at this point that one has to introduce the distinction between referring to things individually and referring to them in general terms. I have tried to show that this matter is more complicated than is suggested by Aristotle's theories of individual, species and genus, or of πρώτη οὐσία and δευτέρα οὐσία. But I cannot incorporate all these complexities in my diagram without making it unwieldy; so for practical purposes I recognize only four cases: (A) the verbal sense, equivalent to τὸ εἶναι; (B) the predicative sense; (C) and (D), substantival senses, distinguished as general and particular. In the case from Clement which I have just discussed, he uses *ousia* in the *fourth* of my basic senses, namely "stuff", and we have just illustrated the difference between sense 4 B, where "the *ousia* of milk" refers to blood, its stuff or basic material, and sense 4 C, where it denotes milk itself, considered as a stuff. Since the

---

[8]   *Paed.* I 39,5, cf. *ibid.* 35,3.

reference to milk is fairly general, I classify it as 4 C; 4 D might refer to a particular drop or draught of milk. 4 A would be used if we were simply stating the fact that milk has this composition. Similar considerations will apply at other levels in the diagram; so that in theory – but only in theory – I shall recognize twenty-eight different possible senses of *ousia*.

5. Now obviously, I cannot hope to justify my classification in a single lecture, or even render it plausible; I must refer you to my book. But you will want to know how this logical analysis affects our thinking about divine substance, and our criticism of what was said in antiquity about ἡ οὐσία τοῦ θεοῦ.

If my analysis is correct, I think it follows that, even if one simply asks the question, "What is the *ousia* of God?", the word *ousia* can be used in very different ways. It is used, though not very commonly, to express the fact of God's existence (sense 1); and again, to pose or answer extremely general questions about God's nature (sense 2); to place him in the category of substance (sense 3); to suggest that he has something comparable to a constituent material (sense 4); or to pose a verbal definition (sense 6). Some writers, of course, doubted whether God has an *ousia*, often appealing to the Platonic phrase ἐπέκεινα νοῦ καὶ οὐσίας; but this phrase also is applied to *exclude* several quite distinct possibilities. It goes without saying that ancient writers were not in a position to criticize their own usage in the manner which I have proposed. They simply observed that the traditional statements about God's *ousia* were full of contradictions; or rather, perhaps, they did not always even observe this fact, but became accustomed to tolerate contradictions in theology, assuming that they spring necessarily from the inability of the human mind to comprehend the divine. As I have said, I myself accept the argument that if God really is God as Christians have described him, he must be beyond the reach of human apprehension. But if one believes this, then it is a pity to become nervous and try to restrict the quite proper desire for accurate thinking, for fear I suppose that God should be captured after all! No, I say! God is a fox; and he likes fox-cubs.

When it comes to Trinitarian problems, I think the concept of *ousia* becomes relevant in the following way. Some writers used it to describe God in metaphysical terms; it seems to follow from the mere concept of a supreme being that he must have certain attributes; he must be eternal, unlimited, and so on; and therefore cannot be denied the title of a possessor of attributes, i.e. a substance. Others, however, offered what

41

we may call an empirical concept; as where God is described as light, or more particularly spirit. I still think this difference is related to a contrast within the Platonic tradition, between a strict rationalistic Platonism and a Stoicizing Platonism. But it has the result that some thinkers see no difficulty in the notion that the *ousia* of God the Father can be communicated to the Son, regarded as another. This is true of the Stoicizing concept, and of some aspects of the metaphysical concept, such as eternity. But the metaphysical concept contains other aspects, such as uniqueness and undifferentiated unity, which had been absorbed by Christian tradition, and yet were fundamentally irreconcilable with Trinitarian orthodoxy.

As regards the Nicene formula itself, I have not been able to formulate my conclusions in anything like final form. I do believe that the Council was influenced by genuine theological tensions, even though the issues were poorly understood and questions of ecclesiastical politics also played some part. On the basis of my present study, I am not much disposed to sympathize with the Arians, so far as these expressed themselves in terms of confident rationalism; but I am much interested in those thinkers who sensed the difficulties of applying the test phrases ὁμοούσιος and ἐκ τῆς οὐσίας to the Logos or Son. I have convinced myself that Athanasius, even when he is at his most sympathetic and conciliatory, has not appreciated the real value of their position; and that although, on the plane of Christian confession, he strongly asserts the incomprehensibility of the divine *ousia*, yet when it comes to theological persuasion, he sometimes resorts to easy and fallacious arguments which should long ago have been exploded.[9] I should be much happier if I knew whether he fully identified himself with these arguments, or whether he was consciously playing a rhetorical game, so that "by all means he could save some" (I Cor. 9,22). Could he say with St. Paul (as I try to say for myself), "We are fools for Christ's sake" ... "It is you who have forced my hand"?

Ely, Cambs., The Black Hostelry, The College

---

[9] Note e.g. the contradiction between *De syn.* 41 (κασσίτερος ὅμοιός ἐστι ... τῷ ἀργυρίῳ) and *ibid.* 53 (ἐπι τῶν οὐσιῶν οὐχ ὁμοιότης, ἀλλὰ ταυτότης ἂν λεχθείη ... ἄνθρωπος κυνὶ οὐκ »ἀνόμοιος« λέγεται, ἀλλ' »ἑτεροφυής«. Both claims are at fault, the first by needlessly restricting the use of "like"; there is no valid objection to saying that one dog is like another, or that dogs are like wolves, and unlike men.

NOTES

ATHANASIUS OF ALEXANDRIA AND THE FOUNDATION OF TRADITIONAL CHRISTOLOGY

About 150 years ago the prestigious personality of Athanasius, bishop of Alexandria from 328 to 373, was suddenly given much popularity with the publication of Johann Adam Möhler's *Athanasius der Grosse und die Kirche seiner Zeit* (1827) and J. H. Newman's *The Arians of the Fourth Century* (1883). Independently and in different contexts these two authors worked out a somewhat romantic typology. They denounced the sclerosis of theology and the deficiencies of the Church characteristic of their times and suggested that the nineteenth century was renewing certain errors committed by the Arians in the fourth century. Therefore, they were presenting Athanasius as the invincible promotor of theological truth and the savior of the institutional Church. But after the wave of *Dogmengeschichte* manuals to the end of the last century, with Dorner, Baur, Harnack, and Loofs, all of whom attributed to Athanasius a decisive role in the history of Christian doctrine, the twentieth century down to our own day has known but one first-rate Athanasian scholar. That is Eduard Schwartz, the historian of Göttingen, also well known for his monumental edition of *Acta conciliorum*. But Schwartz was above all interested in Athanasius as a politician and did not spare him criticisms inspired by his own particularly bellicose spirit. One of Schwartz's students, H. G. Opitz, published some remarkable preparatory works for a critical edition of Athanasius' works before the Second World War, and he succeeded in bringing out the first fascicles of this edition. But Nazism and the war interrupted this enterprise; it has not been resumed and completed, despite the efforts of Wilhelm Schneemelcher of Bonn. A treatise of Athanasius, *On the Incarnation of the Word*, has occasioned much textual-critical literature in the last fifty years or so because of the difficult problem of a double recension. An edition of this treatise was published in 1971 by R. W. Thomson in the *Oxford Early Christian Texts*. I judge it a provisional edition for two reasons: (1) my own edition of this text is due to appear early in 1973; (2) the author of this Oxford edition is a scholar in the Armenian language and does not pretend to be a specialist in the text of Athanasius.

It is not surprising if the actual output of work on Athanasius appears meager. Despite an impressive development of patristic studies and a sufficiently abundant publication of patristic writings in the last fifty years, theologians on the whole have not exhibited a very lively interest in these studies. Because of the problems raised by historical criticism

103

in the past half century or more, the primary task of research has centered on determining the sense of the New Testament or of the Bible as a whole. But the crisis of civilization which affects our ecclesiastical institutions today invites us to a similar effort to determine the content and sense of the Christian tradition as a whole. From this point of view a critical reflection on the origin and function of this tradition takes on a new importance for us.

We see easily enough in what traditional Christology consists. But we know also that we look at this Christology from the outside, from the perspective of a mental attitude, hermeneutical need, and faith-understanding which have become foreign to the tradition on which this Christology depends. We have not yet fully replaced the traditional structure of the Christological dogma with a different tradition, but we know that this is now being done and that it must be done if we wish to take seriously the fact of our being believers. That is what enables us to have a quite genuine and timely interest in the origin of Christology's traditional dogma.

Möhler and Newman were living in a denominational Christianity whose very divisions appeared traditional. Their return to the past of the Church did not alienate them much from their own milieu. They foresaw the future of the churches as a realization of certain institutions typical of the early Church. It appears to me that a return to such an early Church would produce an alienation from our own present-day life, all the more felt the more we realize the extent to which the theological structures about which we are concerned have remained fundamentally the same to our day. The institutions typical of the early Church are precisely those that we can no longer accept, such as its idea of divine revelation, its principle of authority founded on this idea of revelation, its understanding of man with his reason, his moral conscience, and his social organization. So many things that were obvious to the early Church are justified by an interpretation of the Bible whose principles are unacceptable to us. For us, therefore, the question is not at all that of Möhler or Newman: How does understanding of the early Church show us who we are and what we ought to do in our present-day churches? It would rather be: How does knowledge of the early Church help us to know why we need new theological and ecclesiological structures? In other words: Why should we not continue to do what has been done till now in the name of that early Church? That is why we wish to know precisely what was being done in that early Church. It is a question no longer of typology but of new hermeneutics, which questions the Christian tradition across all the clearly highlighted differences in order to prepare for a future which ought not to result solely from this tradition.

It might appear paradoxical to introduce Athanasius in this context. The fierce defender of Nicene orthodoxy illustrated rather a dogmatic immobility. But this precise facet is of little importance to us. Besides, I do not believe that in speaking thus of him we have said everything about him. My one purpose is to analyze the original contributions which made Athanasius the greatest leader of the Church in his times, specifically his contribution in the domain of Christology. I note also this singular fact, which has become unusual in the Church of modern times: a leader of the Church playing a creative role in Christology.

However, this role should not be exaggerated. Athanasius did not invent a Christology. Before him there had been the Semitic meditation of the Judeo-Christians, with their representation of a Christ sometimes apocalyptic, sometimes angelic, often confused with the Holy Spirit. Others like Justin in Rome, Tertullian in Africa, Clement in Alexandria, and above all Origen had tried their hand at it. Among the older contemporaries of Athanasius mention can be made of Eusebius of Caesarea, who summarized the Christological tradition of the Apologists in rigorizing their subordinationism and placed Origen's ingenious but sometimes equivocal formulas at the reach of everybody— perhaps of too many.

Athanasius came to know of this tradition little by little and doubtless never in a methodical manner. In his panegyric on Athanasius, Gregory of Nazianzus had already remarked that Athanasius cannot be called a great "scholar" educated in the famous universities as he himself had been. I believe that Athanasius, born in 295, was first trained by some monks under whom he took shelter during the anti-Christian persecutions which raged in the region of Alexandria till 313. Next he must have attended the school of Bishop Alexander, his predecessor and his "father" as he calls him. But this is only a supposition. As a student, then as a deacon, Athanasius knew intimately the theological teachings of Alexander which provoked the protestations and the schism of Arius in the heart of the Christian community of Alexandria. Elected bishop in 328 to succeed Alexander, whom he had helped as secretary in the great Synod of Nicaea (May 325), Athanasius composed all his works in theology and unleashed the force of his personality in the time between Nicaea and the eruption of the first properly Christological crisis in the modern sense, the one provoked by Bishop Apollinaris of Laodicea, a friend dangerously faithful to Athanasius. Therefore, if I speak of a relation between Athanasius and "the foundation of traditional Christology," by "foundation" I understand primarily the great controversy over the divinity and humanity of Jesus Christ which lasted through the fourth century. It was a controversy led by the bishops and their theologians in a political background created by the interests of each

Christian metropolitan in the boundaries of the Roman Empire. It was also complicated by the growing nationalism under a religious guise in Egypt and in the whole of the Roman Orient. Such a controversy must have resulted in political decisions inspired by the imperial government. What we call the "ecumenical councils," in particular Nicaea, Ephesus, and Chalcedon, are of special interest here. The traditional Christology transmitted in its canonical formulation down to our own times is the fruit of the politics of Constantine, of Princesses Arcadia and Macrina, of Empress Pulcheria of Spanish blood and her docile husband Marcion. These women of the imperial court exerted a formidable impact on the fixing of the official Christian dogma. These nonreligious and political factors operative in the origin of traditional Christology remain inseparable from the theological venture and from the mystical convictions of the intellectual bishops of this epoch. In any case, it was not the sublime and lofty reflections of Origen, nor the dialectic of a Gregory of Nyssa, nor the popular piety of the faithful masses of those times which created by themselves the canonical structure of Christology transmitted for a millennium and a half in both East and West. For that a supreme decision on the political plane was necessary. What, then, was the particular role of Athanasius in relation to this decision embodied in the first three ecumenical councils of the imperial Christianity of the fourth and fifth centuries?

I see the role of Athanasius in the formation of a traditional and canonical Christology on three levels:

1) Athanasius introduces into the perception of the mystery of faith concerning the person of Christ *an original concept of man*, altogether consonant with the spontaneous anthropology of his contemporaries but rethought by him with reference to Christology. This first characteristic initiative of Athanasius precedes the others chronologically as well as ontologically. In the chronological order it is in fact a part of Athanasius' first known writing, his Christological treatise *On the Incarnation of the Word*, which explicates more precisely the new anthropology on which his theological framework is based. Ontologically it is clearly always a definite idea of man which enables Christians to explain the Christ of their faith.

2) On the second level of his doctrinal work, Athanasius develops his Christological originality in terms of *a new manner of interpreting Scripture*. Since the beginning of the twentieth century, writers have been so obsessed by the political and denominational aspect of Athanasius' work that they have completely overlooked another characteristic, his frequent recourse to the Bible. Though writers constantly repeat that Athanasius was a man of the Bible, no one has ever tried to study him seriously under this aspect. I emphasize this because it is im-

portant for our contemporary critical interest in early Christology that
the initiative of Athanasius in this domain would never have taken on
lasting historical significance if it had not benefited from his very original method of having recourse to the Bible as a theologian.

3) On the third level, which presupposes the first two, Athanasius
was the first bishop and theologian of the early Church who attempted
to *organize all Christian doctrine concerning the incarnation of God*.
This contribution of systematic order directly influenced the *Great
Catechism* of Gregory of Nyssa; it influenced Ambrose of Milan and
Cyril of Alexandria. This third aspect of Athanasius' theology has
never caught the attention of the critics, for the simple reason that
no one has ever tried to discover the logical plan of the three discourses
Against the Arians, where the Christocentricism of his theology appears most clearly. I will return to each of these three levels to examine the sense and scope of Athanasian Christology.

A fourth level would perhaps be that of political expediency, at
least in the framework of the ecclesiastical politics of the great metropolis of Alexandria against that of Antioch or of Constantinople, in a
setting in which Cyril of Alexandria would become a redoubtable
champion two generations after Athanasius, to the extent of imposing
on us the dogmatic definition of Ephesus solely to affirm the supremacy
of the Alexandrian Church as a "great power." But let us leave aside
this fourth level. It is more agreeable to work with the other three. And
let us see exactly what Athanasius did on the first of these three levels,
where he introduced the anthropology of his times into his Christological contribution.

AN ORIGINAL CONCEPT OF MAN

Let us start with the citation of a passage, perhaps a little too long,
from the second chapter of the treatise *Contra gentes*, which constitutes with *De incarnatione Verbi* the first theological work of Athanasius. I have tried to prove elsewhere, above all in the case of *De incarnatione Verbi*, that this work was composed by Athanasius not when
he was just eighteen or twenty-two years old, as was thought since
Bernard de Montfaucon, the renowned Maurist (1655–1741), but between 335 and 337, when Athanasius was about forty years old and
already a bishop for about seven years, at the time when he was
exiled by the personal efforts of Constantine, the first of his numerous
exiles, the one he spent in the far west of the Roman Empire, at Trier,
the northern capital of Gaul. Here is the passage (tr. Thomson, p. 7):

For God, the creator of the universe and king of all, who is beyond all being and
human thought, since he is good and bountiful, has made mankind in his own
image through his own Word, our Saviour Jesus Christ; and he also made man

perceptive and understanding of reality through his similarity to him, giving him also a conception and knowledge of his own eternity, so that as long as he kept this likeness he might never abandon his concept of God or leave the company of saints, but retaining the grace of him who bestowed it on him and also the special power given him by the Father's Word, he might rejoice and converse with God, living an idyllic and truly blessed and immortal life. For having no obstacle to the knowledge of the divine, he continuously contemplates by his purity the image of the Father, God the Word, in whose image he was made, and is filled with admiration when he grasps his providence towards the universe. He is superior to sensual things and all bodily impressions, and by the power of his mind clings to the divine and intelligible realities in heaven.

We find in this passage all the elements we need to answer our question about the anthropology of Athanasius:

1) First, there is the ideal state of Adam, the Creator's work still intact. He is a contemplative, an ascetic, who is unconscious of his own self, spontaneously turned away from his body and from the sensible world, and ecstatically turned towards the divine Logos, the Image of the Father. This Adam idealized in Platonic terms was not unknown to the Alexandrian tradition. One could show how this text echoes Philo, Clement, and Origen and through them Neoplatonism or the other more ancient currents of Greek mysticism. It is of capital importance for the interpretation of Athanasius to discover that this ideal Adam is found right in the beginning of the theological development both in *Contra gentes* and *De incarnatione*, but from then on disappears altogether from the Athanasian scene. Although Athanasius recapitulates a long tradition of this Platonized Adam now Christianized, he disassociates himself at once from such a concept.

2) In fact, a point which has not been very much discussed until now is that the ideal Adam of Athanasius has no soul (*psychē*) as long as he remains immersed in the contemplation of the divine Logos. In the whole of chapter 2 and also in chapter 3 in the same context Athanasius speaks only of "(Adam's) *mind* fixed on God" (*ton noun eschēkenai pros ton theon*), of the "power of his *mind*" (*tē dynamei tou nou*), the "power which they had received from the beginning" (*tēs ecks archēs autōn para theou dynameōs*). He does not speak of the soul of Adam and Eve, or rather, according to his favorite expression, of the soul of the original "men" (*hoi anthrōpoi*) except from the moment when "they turned their mind from intelligible reality" (*tōn men noētōn apestēsan heautōn ton noun*) and when in consequence "they imprisoned their souls in the pleasures of the body" (*synekleisan heautōn tēn psychēn*).

3) This is because for Athanasius it is not the soul that is "in the image" (*kat' eikona*) of the divine Word, but the *mind*, the *nous*, the superior pole and the principal director of the human soul. Precisely for this reason we do not find in Athanasius the famous distinction current since Origen between *kat' eikona* and *kath' homoiōsin* drawn from the words of the Creator in Gn 1:26: "Let us make man in our image, after our likeness." Origen attributed the *kat' eikona* to the *psychē* but reserved the *homoiōsis* to the final stage of the spiritual progress of the soul, where it finds again its quality of *nous* which it had possessed before its entrance into the terrestrial and corporeal existence. Nothing of that sort is found in Athanasius, and he is the only one in the whole Origenist tradition who did not make such a distinction. Another originality of Athanasius in this regard is that he never calls the human *nous* an *eikōn* of God or of the divine Logos, as Philo, Clement of Alexandria, and Origen had done before him, and Eusebius repeated in his times. The only *eikōn tou theou* known to Athanasius is the *logos tou theou*, and the human *nous* will always be defined by him in its created quality as *kat' eikona*.

These precisions of vocabulary are not just bits of curiosity for the erudite; they lead us directly into the heart of Athanasius' theological anthropology. For him, the myth of Adam as the model of Christian perfection belongs to the past. Origen had developed an admirable doctrine of the progress of the soul which made man pass from the state of *eikōn tou diabolou* to that of *eikōn tou Christou* until he reached the eschatological *homoiōsis tou theou* where he finds himself completely spiritualized and in the ecstasy of total union with the divine *logos*. In this grandiose perspective the incarnation of God does not appear to have been a decisive and central event. Gregory of Nyssa will take up this same perspective but will explicate more fully the irreplaceable role of the Word incarnate; for Gregory knew the Athanasian Christology well. In fact, Athanasius had frankly reacted against the intellectualism of the Origenian gnosis. With a taste for clarity and systematic precision which would characterize the entire Greek theology of the fourth century, and above all the great Cappadocians, Athanasius had at first reserved the quality of the divine *kat' eikona* only to the human *nous*. Later he had the divine *eikōn* itself, in the act of becoming incarnate in a human body, assume all the original functions of the *nous* of Adam. The result is that the salvation of men henceforth takes place not through purification and spiritualization according to Origen's model, but through their personal encounter with the *eikōn* of God who has become a man. This man makes use of his body as an instrument (*organon*) to show that he is also the temple

of the Logos of God. The Logos shines everywhere, by vivifying and instructing all other men who are attracted by this being who has become
similar to them. Thus men become capable of union with God again
by the mediation of the incarnate Logos as they had been in the beginning by the mediation of their *nous* in ecstasy in the Logos. Henceforth Christ takes the place of that which was the Logos nonincarnate
for Adam. But because Christ is the Logos in the body, there is no
longer a question of mimicking the angels as the Platonized Adam had
done without great success or, as according to Origen, the "perfect"
Christians had tried to do. It is a question of man realizing all his
personal perfection even now in body, in social life, in the community
of the Church, and in the present experience of faith. Thus a spiritualistic anthropology rethought in an original manner led Athanasius
to center his existence in faith on the divine reality of the incarnate
Logos. He would never change this position in his later writings dis-
tributed over the more than thirty remaining years of his life.

A NEW METHOD OF BIBLE INTERPRETATION

I now wish to examine the originality of Athanasius on the second level
of his Christological contribution. He is the inventor of what one can
call the "dogmatic exegesis" which became one of the principal forms
of biblical interpretation throughout the great controversies of the
fourth and fifth centuries. On the level of his anthropology Athanasius
had respected all the essential elements of his tradition, marked by
the genius of Origen. But with these elements he composed a new concept of man and his salvation, expressed in Christian terms. His insistence on the corporeal condition makes one think of a definite influence from Irenaeus of Lyons. Still, fundamentally he remains an
Origenist in his teachings on the nature and significance of the Bible.
But he presents the spiritual experience of Antony the Hermit in his
Vita Antonii in such an original manner that the reading of Scripture
seen according to the principles of Origen leads him to a result which
is no longer Origenian. This leads him to prefer the actual moment of
faith, in the immediate and corporeal condition, to all other possible
forms of gnosis. We are reminded of his anthropology. On the level of
the theory of interpretation this Athanasius, who would never be an
anti-Origenian as other bishops of Alexandria had been before him,
completely stops using the allegorism characteristic of Origen. He
preserves a moderate typology in his exegesis, but he always remains
at the antipodes of the allegorizing Origenism of a Didymus the Blind,
on whom however he confers an eminent teaching position in his own
Alexandrian church.

Whereas in the order of practical experience he took as a model Antony, the father of monasticism, in the order of intellectual experience Athanasius imagines an approach to Scripture which none has ever practiced before him. He constructs the train of his arguments directly from the scriptural texts which he intends to defend against the Arians. More than Origen, he maintains a balance between the arguments which are purely dialectical and those supported by the biblical quotations. His first *Treatise against the Arians* centers on the divinity of the Son. His second work *Contra Arianos* is devoted to the missions of the Son. His third treatise develops the question more directly linked with the dogma of the Son's incarnation. It shows again how this concept has become central in the Athanasian vision of Christianity. We could analyze the theological vocabulary of Athanasius and observe that it remains always inspired by the Bible. Astonishingly, the great defender of Nicaea uses the technical word of the Synod, the famous *homoousios*, only once or twice in all his writings. He prefers to keep to expressions and images which are more biblical, in this in agreement with his adversaries, the most tenacious among the Arians. One could also examine what texts of the Bible Athanasius prefers, or how he has taken the trouble to balance his recourse to the Gospel of John with the letters of Paul, how he develops the arguments drawn from the Old Testament in making them agree with the quotations from the New. But his essential and too little recognized originality in Christology will always be that he developed his exposition on the basis of a new interpretive technique geared to the needs of the controversy with the Arians and to the genius of his epoch. Nobody doubts that in this regard he has even been somewhat influenced by the very exegesis of the Arians. But I would now like to end with a few remarks on the third level, where in my opinion the special contribution of Athanasius to traditional Christology lies.

THE ATHANASIAN CHRISTOCENTRISM

Doubtlessly the questions posed to Athanasius the theologian and leader concerning the formulation of the dogma of the Incarnation changed between 328 and 373. To a keen observer his theological language offers some interesting contrasts. Thus, the titles which he gives to God the Father or the Son remain the same; his notions of anthropology do not change; his exegetical vocabulary has a remarkable stability. On the other hand, in his Christology, in several instances, he changed profoundly both his terminology and his approach to the problems. Some have insinuated that *De incarnatione* is not by Athanasius because it presents a Christological terminology different from that of *Contra Arianos*. But this is altogether painful to the ears of one who has devoted many years of his life precisely to *De incarnatione*. And certainly this is to misunderstand Athanasius. For in the last great period of his life, in his sixties, therefore about twenty years after the composition of *Contra Arianos*, one sees him once again modifying his points of view and his formulations in Christology. This time it is be-cause he finds himself confronted by a new kind of dispute whose arguments are closed to him now that he has become old, and which announces the crises of Apollinarism. Therefore, we should not be surprised if he again changes his Christological language in the same manner as he did the first time he undertook to refute the Arian theses.

It would be useful to show on the basis of which Arian documents and by what systematic analyses of these documents Athanasius com-posed his great *Treatises* against the Arians. In any case, the funda-mental intuition of Athanasius over which no doubt could be enter-tained and which motivates his entire refutation of Arianism is essentially Christological. More than anything else, through all sorts of arguments whose weaknesses are sometimes evident and whose de-velopment may appear quite clumsy, Athanasius insists that the Arians are mistaken in their concept of theology, because they believe they are able to form a Christian idea of God by first developing in isolation the theory of the divinity of the Father and the Son, without taking into consideration right from the start the mystery of the incarnation of the Son. Although Athanasius changed his technical terminology several times, he remained faithful throughout his life to this fundamental intuition: that which is first in the exposition of the Christian faith is not God as such, nor the universe in its divine origin, but the historical event of salvation accomplished in Christ.

I would not like to anticipate in Athanasius a Karl Barth or a Pan-nenberg, but Athanasian Christocentrism remains an astonishing innovation in the context of the ancient theological tradition of Alex-andria. This is because the fundamental intuition of Athanasian theology was directed against Eusebius as well as against Origen himself, that is to say, against all religious cosmology posited before the exposition of faith, according to a pattern inherited from Gnostic theology and more generally according to classical Hellenism.

What does Athanasius say? In *Contra Arianos* 1 he first treats of the divinity of the Son according to the *Thaleia* of Arius whom he refutes; he does not cease to explain that it is useless to argue a priori about the divinity of the Son, as a mere supposition of reason, instead of en-quiring into Scripture and seeing how it teaches us to discover the divinity of the Son starting from the concrete economy of salvation. In

Contra Arianos 2, where he exposes the doctrine of the missions of the Son, he centers the whole work on the exegesis of Prv 8:22: "The Lord created me at the beginning of his ways," a versicle which he applies in a well-known manner, as Manlio Simonetti has clearly pointed out, to the mystery of the incarnation of the Son. It is needless to multiply these examples. The lesson of Athanasius will never be forgotten. He was the first Christian writer to publish a treatise "On the Incarnation of the Word." Likewise in his singular way, which happens to be more intuitive than speculative and a generation before Gregory of Nyssa, he disassociates himself from the systematization of Christian theology received from Origen. This innovation, which shook the foundation of the traditional structures but respected the language and authority of the tradition, was in the last analysis more oriented toward the future than the disrespectful and flashy but basically very traditionalist argument of the Arians.

But who was the Christ of Athanasius? How did he formulate Christ's mystery in his so-called Christological contribution? Did Athanasius really miss the point by being the theologian of the human soul of Christ, as has been repeated time and again since the period of *Dogmengeschichte*? Was he a precursor of Apollinarism? Was he influenced by the very early theologians of the West, since he perhaps knew Latin and spent long years in exile in Gaul and certainly in Rome? Did his entire dogmatic work on Scripture really constitute a biblical Christology? There will be so many questions to be asked by those who would like to write books on Athanasius in 1973, the year of the sixteenth centenary of his death, which will be celebrated in Paris in September with an International Session of Athanasian Studies. I intended only to point out in what spirit and according to what type of initiative Athanasius set himself to be the defender of the "orthodox" faith, at first in his local church and then on the scale of the Empire. He restored Christology to what it is in the first place, a source of renewal for the Christian concept of man. It is for this reason that he elaborated a new idea of man and developed it in his Christology. He corroborated this innovation by an assiduous study of Scripture, and for his goal he discovered a new interpretation of the Bible. He was above all the man of a single battle: he refused a systematic Christology which he did not consider sufficiently inspired by Scripture. Was he right or wrong? In any case, he presents us with a serious challenge for our own innovations in Christology.

Institut Catholique, Paris   CHARLES KANNENGIESSER, S.J.

Uncreated and Created, Unbegotten and Begotten in the Theology of Athanasius of Alexandria

It is a common fallacy that the entire contrast between Orthodoxy and Arianism in the fourth century, and the theology resulting from it, revolve around the terms, ὁμοιούσιος, ὁμοούσιος, ὅμοιος and ἀνόμοιος.

That this impression is not substantiated by the facts is demonstrated as much by the lack of consistency in the use of these terms, as by the fact that Athanasius wavers between the first two of them. In fact, so as not to provoke opposition, instead of the term ὁμοούσιος, which seemed to divide Christians, he at first preferred the term ὁμοιούσιος and only when he perceived that the sense given it by the semi-Arians was different[1] did he choose the term ὁμοούσιος with the aim of later declaring finally that both terms are acceptable.

This indicates that these terms did not have quite the importance we attribute to them today. They were simply watchwords in a battle which nevertheless certainly expressed definite theological ideas, since they also occupied a position in the creeds drawn up in the councils that met during that period.

The extent to which Athanasius attributed little significance to these words is apparent in his letters on the Holy Ghost, where he writes : " It is enough to know that the Spirit is not a creature " [2]. This indicates where the basis of theological disagreement is to be found between the rival parties. What is the Spirit, a creature, or a non-created being ? What is the Son, a creature, or a non-created being ? Upon the answer hangs all else.

Athanasius bases his theological work in general upon polemic against the tenets of Arius " out of non-being ", " there

---

[1] Cf. I. KALOGIROU, " Τό τριαδολογικόν δόγμα κατά τόν δ' αἰῶνα ", Ἐπετηρὶς Θεολογικῆς Σχολῆς Πανεπιστημίου Θεσσαλονίκης 13 (1968), 299.
[2] *Letters to Serapion* I, 17.

was when he was not " " of a changeable nature ", and " creature " ³, which are clearly all connected with creation.

The two opposing poles in the universe are the imperishaɔle and the perishable, the ἄφθαρτον and the φθαρτόν, which correspond to the two forms of existence, the ἄκτιστον, uncreated, and the κτιστόν, created. This dinstinction has a direct connection with the creative energy of God which connects the uncreated with the created. This is fundamental to the Christian understanding of the universe. Christians directly link the idea of God with that of the Creator.

Although the same does not happen with the Greek philosophers, it is impossible to refrain from mentioning here the misinterpretation which has so often slipped into this question. The usual assertion that the Greek position is diametrically opposed to the Christian is based on an oversimplification of the facts, because the Greeks had the concept of both the uncreated, as Athanasius himself recognizes ⁴, and of the Creator. For nearly all the Greek philosophical systems there is a distinction between the one and the many, between the unchangeable ὄντως ὄν, and the things which are changeable, even if the idea of a creator, was not always included and when it was it did not perform the same rôle that it did in Christianity.

Thus, to confine ourselves to the two principal representatives of Greek thought, Plato draws a distinction between the uncreated which is eternally the same, and the created, which is liable to corruption ⁵, and then adds a third element, that of space, or rather of room, which could be identified with what Aristotle calls matter, formless matter, upon which God acts.

According to Aristotle, matter represents the element of genesis and of corruption, which is extended to one point only,

---

³ " « ἐξ οὐκ ὄντων " " ἦν ποτε ὅτε οὐκ ἦν " " τρεπτῆς φύσεως " " κτίσμα " " ποίημα ". Cf. I. KARMIRIS, Τά δογματικά καί συμβολικά μνημεῖα τῆς Ὀρθοδόξου Καθολικῆς Ἐκκλησίας, V. I² Athens 1960, pp. 57 ff.

⁴ Contra Arianos I, 34 " Τό ἀγένητον παρ᾽ Ἑλλήνων εἴρηται, τῶν μή γινωσκόντων Θεόν ". Because they do not know God, they are not able to speak about a Father and speak about an unoriginated Being.

⁵ Timaeus 52a, " Ἕν μέν εἶναι τό κατά ταυτά εἶδος ἔχον, ἀγένητον καί ἀνώλεθρον ... τό δέ ... δεύτερον αἰσθητόν, γενητόν ... γιγνόμενόν τε ἔν τινι τόπῳ καί πάλιν ἀπολλύμενον ". 27 ᵈ, " τί τό ὄν ἀεί, γένεσιν δέ οὐκ ἔχον, καί τό γιγνόμενον μέν ἀεί, ὄν δέ οὐδέποτε ". Cf. Phaedruos 245 ᵈ, on the world soul, " " ἐπειδή ἀγένητόν ἐστι καί ἀδιάφθορον ἀνάγκη εἶναι ".

beyond which exists the world of the unchangeable — pure energy. The pure energy is the prime mover that is not itself moved, God, through whose operation matter is transformed, and the world of perishable beings is created.

Consequently the idea of the creator is found in both Plato and Aristotle, but in both writers creation appears as having been carried out upon pre-existent matter. Matter certainly in their thought approximates to non-being, since it is neither a quality, nor any of those things by which being is defined [6]. Creation, therefore, could be seen as formed, in the view of these two philosophers, from non-being, if matter were merely non-being, nothing. Yet it is not merely a negative element ; it is also a positive one, because it has within itself a tendency to acquire a form, it is capable of becoming something, it has the potential. This is the essential difference between these philosophical positions and the Christian doctrine, which teaches that creation was constructed from absolutely nothing.

The Greek Philosophers, therefore, when speaking about God, did not, from necessity, immediately reach the Creator, and they did not give creation the character it has in Christianity. It is reasonable, then, that instead of the terms characterizing the uncreatedness of God, and the createdness of the world, they used terms that indicated that God is unoriginated and the world originated, that is to say they used the words, ἀγένητος and γενητός, instead of ἄκτιστος and κτιστός.

In spite of all this, the notions of the uncreated and the created, with all their particular aspects, exist in both systems, the Greek philosophical and the Christian, and this is what interests us in our inquiry.

Because of the place of creation in the Christian theological system, Athanasius prefers for God the terms δημιουργός and κτίστης, to ἀγένητος which is a negative term not capable of portraying the creative energy of God. He does not, however, reject the word completely, but uses it occasionally (with reservations), in that it had certainly become a by-word on the lips of the Arians to distinguish the uncreated God from the created Son [7]. Athanasius rarely uses it without reservation. He always

---

[6] " Λέγω δ' ὕλην ἣ καθ' ἑαυτὴν μήτε τὶ μήτε ποσόν, μήτε ἄλλο μηδὲν λέγεται, οἷς ὥρισται τό ὄν ", ARISTOTLE, *Metaphys.* XXIII 1029 a.

[7] *Contra Arianos* I, 30-33.

sounds a warning against using it to distinguish between the Father and the Son, as it merely distinguishes between creator and creatures. Therefore, he says, the term ἀγένητος signifies a distinction of the Father not from the Son, but from the things made through the Son ; and correctly so, for God is not like created things [8]. These terms indicate a gulf between God and the world, and the impossibility of comprehending the former. God, who exists beyond all originated nature, is incomprehensible to man, who is made from non-being, while God is unoriginated, " and what communion, or what identity can there be between creature and creator ? " [9]

Given this distinction, God is described by Athanasius with the terminology of Plato as for ever unchangeable [10], while created things are subject to change [11], because they derive from non-being via an initial radical change. The creatures bear no essential resemblance to the creator [12], and have a predisposition towards corruption, a tendency towards non-being. Since they came from non-being, they tend to return to non-being. This return is accomplished through corruption [13]. This is an innate inclination in man, although he is equipped with a bestowed likeness to God, by means of which, if he kept it intact, he would blunt the corruptible which is his by nature, and would become imperishable.

Arius particularly exalted the concept of creation, having as a model the second century Apologists, the Dynamic Monarchians, and above all Origen. It is uncertain whether the Apologists could clearly distinguish between the categories of divine essence and divine revelation, but it is quite clear that they inseparably linked the Logos with the work of creation.

---

[8] " Τὸ ἀγένητον ἄρα οὐ διὰ τὸν Υἱὸν ἀλλὰ διὰ τὰ δι 'Υἱοῦ γενόμενα σημαίνεται · καὶ καλῶς, ὅτι οὐκ ἔστιν ὡς τὰ γενητὰ ὁ Θεός ", Contra Arianos I, 33.

[9] Letters to Serapion I, 9.

[10] Contra Arianos I, 35, " ἄτρεπτος καὶ ἀναλλοίωτος καὶ ἀεὶ ὡσαύτως ἔχει ".

[11] Ibid, I, 36.

[12] Ibid, I, 20.

[13] De Incarnatione 4, " ἡ γὰρ παράβασις τῆς ἐντολῆς εἰς τό κατὰ φύσιν αὐτοὺς ἐπέστρεψεν ", " ἔστι μέν κατὰ φύσιν ἄνθρωπος θνητός, ἅτε δὴ ἐξ οὐκ ὄντων γεγονός ".

[14] Ibid, 4, " διὰ δέ τήν πρός τά ὄντα ὁμοιότητα, ἥν εἰ ἐφύλαττε διὰ τῆς πρός αὐτόν κατανοήσεως, ἤμβλυκεν ἄν τὴν κατὰ φύσιν φθορὰν καὶ ἔμεινεν ἄφθαρτος ".

So also did Origen explicitly connect the begetting of the Son with the origin of the world.

Origen, following the general line of Christian theology, could not conceive God without being led immediately on to the creator. But he was mistaken in his precise evaluation of things, apparently because he wanted to give excessive emphasis to the concept of the identity of God and creator, against the Gnostic assertions that they were separate. From the principle that the creator was certainly God, he arrived at the conclusion that God was certainly a creator. This, however, means that he was always a creator, and that creation is an eternal product of God, in a kind of projection. Naturally the Logos existed before the ages, and its existence is linked to creation.

Of course, since he realized the danger of Christian Theology concluding from this idea that the world existed before the ages, just like God, he ascribed the creation before the ages to the will of God. He was then led on to a further absurdity ; because of the close connection, in his understanding, between the Logos and the world, he understood the Logos also to have been begotten from the will of the Father [15]. He rejects the opinion that the Logos was begotten ἐκ τῆς οὐσίας τοῦ Πατρός, out of the essence of the Father, because he saw it as leading to the Gnostic world view, not realizing that he thus removed the Son from the Godhead.

Arius'theory had a cosmological starting point, as he was not interested in other properties of God than the creative ones. Instead, however, of relegating creation to eternity, as did Origen, Arius debases the Logos by placing it within time. The fact however that he sometimes places the existence of the Logos " before time and before the ages " [16] is made of no effect by his use of all those other expressions that define the Logos as a creature. " All things are brought about from non-being, and all that have been brought into being are creatures and works. So also the Logos of God was brought about from non-being, and there was when he was not, and he was not before he was brought about, but he as well had a beginning

---

[15] " 'Εκ τοῦ θελήματος τοῦ Πατρός ἐγεννήθη ", MANSI, Sanct. Concil. Coll., IX, 525 as quoted by Justinian.

[16] " « Πρό τῶν χρόνων καί πρό τῶν αἰώνων ", Letter to Eusebius of Nicomedia, EPIPHANIUS, Panarion, LXIX, 6, and THEODORETUS, Hist. Eccl. I, 4, 63.

of being created "[17]. Consequently the phrase "before time and before the ages" has a completely typical sense since, through the genesis, that is the creation, of the Logos, a certain change occurs, which can only be perceived within time. The difference is that his genesis was realized before the other beings came into existence, for the sake of creating the other beings, as he was a necessary intermediary.

Thus, as Arius believed, the unique quality of God's being uncreated was preserved. This, following an extension of the Aristotelian view, is a characteristic only of the Prime Mover. Only God the Father is uncreated, unoriginated, and eternal. He placed the dividing line, not between God and the creatures, but between God and the Logos which was linked with the creatures. The Logos as a creature is unlike the Father, and was finite, mutable, subject to change. His divinity, however, is authentic [18].

The Orthodox line of thought differs from this Arian one by giving a fuller picture of God in depth. God is creator, but not merely this, because he also exists apart from his creative activity. The other thing inherent in God's existence is his nature. God, that is, is nature and will together, and the former certainly dominates the latter : nature is above will [19]. He is therefore being and energy, which in the theological terminology that later prevailed are essence and energy. There is, therefore, an essential distinction — not merely a nominal one — in God's existence [20].

In these two categories of the God-head, essence and will, there are corresponding and analogous distinctions. In the essence, to start with, there are the distinctions of existence or otherwise of the Triadic hypostases, which belong within the God-head, while on the other hand, in the will there are the distinctions of the creative relations which belong outside.

---

[17] " Πάντων γενομένων ἐξ οὐκ ὄντων καί πάντων ὄντων κτισμάτων καί ποιημάτων γενομένων, καί αὐτός ὁ τοῦ Θεοῦ Λόγος ἐξ οὐκ ὄντων γέγονε καί ἦν ποτε ὅτε οὐκ ἦν καί οὐκ ἦν πρίν γένηται ἀλλ' ἀρχήν τοῦ κτίζεσθαι ἔσχε καί αὐτός ", Contra Arianos I, 5.

[18] Cf. I. Kalogirou, " Τό τριαδολογικόν δόγμα κατά τόν δ' αἰῶνα ", pp. 287 ff.

[19] " ὑπεραναβέβηκε τῆς βουλήσεως τό πεφυκέναι ", Contra Arianos, II, 2.

[20] G. Florovsky, " The Concept of Creation in St. Athanasius ", Studia Patristica V (1961), 56 ff.

Within the Godhead there is γέννησις (birth) ; without, γένεσις (genesis) pertains. Hence God is at once Father and Creator. Whereas he is Father by nature, he is creator by will. Consequently he might not to be a creator, and the created world might not have existed. The dividing line, in Orthodox Christianity, lies between God and creatures, between the uncreated and the created.

The origin of the Logos is a process which belongs within the category of nature or essence. The creatures, as products of a will, at one time were non-existent ; God " wills " to create them. He did not, however, " pre-will " his Logos, which was begotten from his own nature [21]. Nor is the existence of the Logos directly linked to creation. If he is a creator, this occurs not because this is his function, as if he were brought about specifically to create, as an instrument, especially since God does not need an intermediary, but rather as the perfect image of God [22].

" The Logos of God," Athanasius writes, " did not come about because of us, but rather we came about because of him, and in him were all things created. And he, being powerful was not, because of our weakness, brought into being by the Father alone, so that the latter might create us as through an instrument. Certainly this is not the case. And even if it were glory to God not to have made, the Logos would nevertheless be in no way diminished before God, and the Father would nevertheless be within him. Nevertheless, the creatures were unable to come into being without the Logos. Thus they came into being and were created through him " [23].

As the Logos had this origin, it is not possible to connect him with creation, from which he is separated by a wide gulf.

---

[21] Contra Arianos III, 61, " τά μέν γάρ μή ὄντα ποτέ, ἀλλ' ἔξωθεν ἐπιγινόμενα ὁ δημιουργός βουλεύεται ποιῆσαι · τόν δέ ἴδιον Λόγον ἐξ αὐτοῦ φύσει γεννώμενον οὐ προβουλεύεται ",

[22] G. FLOROVSKY, " The Concept of Creation in St. Athanasius ", p. 47.

[23] " Ὁ τοῦ Θεοῦ Λόγος οὐ δι' ἡμᾶς γέγονεν, ἀλλά μᾶλλον ἡμεῖς δι' αὐτοῦ γεγόναμεν καί ἐν αὐτῷ ἐκτίσθη τά πάντα · οὐδέ διά τήν ἡμῶν ἀσθένειαν οὗτος, ὤν δυνατός, ὑπό μόνου τοῦ Πατρός γέγονεν, ἵν' ἡμᾶς δι' αὐτοῦ ὡς δι' ὀργάνου δημιουργήσῃ, μή γένοιτο, οὐκ ἔστιν οὕτω. Καί γάρ, εἰ καί δόξαν ἦν τῷ Θεῷ μή ποιῆσαι τά γενητά, ἀλλ' ἦν οὐδέν ἧττον ὁ Λόγος πρός τόν Θεόν καί ἐν αὐτῷ ἦν ὁ Πατήρ. Τά μέντοι γενητά ἀδύνατον ἦν χωρίς τοῦ Λόγου γενέσθαι · οὕτω γάρ καί γέγονεν δι' αὐτοῦ καί ἐκτίσθη ".

He is within creation, but only through his operation. He holds creation together, and stops it returning to non-being [24]. But in his essence he is outside creation [25].

As uncreated and begotten of the Father, the Logos has all the properties of the Father, who is unoriginated, unchangeable, imperishable, immortal, and he is ὁμοούσιος with the Father, inasmuch as it is not possible for several uncreated being that are of different essence (that is in effect several uncreated essences) to exist. Ontologically, multiplicity implies temporality and change, while unity entails eternity and unchangeability, according to a basic tenet of Greek philosophy. That the Spirit does not belong to the many indicates, according to Athanasius, that it is uncreated and ὁμοούσιος with the Father, as is also the Son [26].

By his teaching, Athanasius himself changed the direction of theology from the genesis of the Son (as, of course, also of the Spirit) to the begetting ; from γένεσις to γέννησις. Since creation is a category outside the sphere of the divine, ἀγένητος and γενητός, uncreated and created, are used for describing the relation between God and creation, while the terms ἀγέννη-τος and γεννητός, unbegotten and begotten, are more frequently used for describing the relations within the Trinity ; these are the same words, but written with two ν's, and certainly having a different meaning and etymology. Upon these Last two words (ἀγέννητος γεννητός) the Anomoeans constructed their whole theory, adopting them so as to emerge from the deadlock with their far-fetched interpretation. The two words are distinguished by the wide gap indicated by the prefix α-. Two persons are consequently distinguished which belong to two completely different worlds. The first in the eternal and unchangeable ; the second in the temporal and changeable.

" If he is unbegotten, he is not Son, if he is Son, he is not unbegotten " [27], taught Eunomius. The Logos, if he is Son, is necessarily *begotten*.

---

[24] *Contra Gentes* 41.

[25] *De Incarnatione* 17, ἐκτός μέν ἔστι τοῦ παντός κατ' οὐσίαν, ἐν πᾶσι δέ ἐστι ταῖς ἑαυτοῦ δυνάμεσιν ".

[26] *Letters to Serapion* I, 27, " καί οὐκ ἄδηλον, ὅτι οὐκ ἔστι τῶν πολλῶν τό Πνεῦμα, ἀλλ' οὐδέ ἄγγελος, ἀλλ' ἕν ὄν, μᾶλλον δέ τοῦ Λόγου ἑνός ὄντος ἴδιον, καί τοῦ Θεοῦ, ἑνός ὄντος, καί ὁμοούσιόν ἐστι ".

[27] " "Αν τε γάρ ἀγέννητος, οὐχ Υἱός, ἄν τε Υἱός, οὐχ ἀγέννητος ", Eu-NOMIOS, *Apologia II*.

It can be said that the Anomoeans returned to the original doctrine of Arius, using the term ἀγέννητος with the sense of ἀγένητος or ἄκτιστος and the term γεννητός with the sense of γενητός or κτιστός ; the term unbegotten, that is, in the sense of uncreated, and begotten in the sense of created. Consequently the change of terminology, which Athanasius' arguments against the Son's having been created imposed, did not in any way change the opinions of the Arians.

The semi-Arians accepted the new terminology much more readily. The Synod held in Ancyra in 358 under Basil, bishop of that city, clearly emphasized the distinction between ἀγένητος as being uncreated, and ἀγέννητος as not begotten, but begetting.

" Creator and creature are one thing ; Father and Son are quite another " [28]. Both categories of divine existence are to be found here ; that of the will through which God creates and is creator, and that of the essence through which he begets by nature, and is Father. So for them, the change of terminology meant almost full alignment with Athanasius on this question.

This alignment, however, only covered half the area. Even though the semi-Arians abandoned the term and concept of the Son's having been created, they did not abandon it for the Spirit, which they persisted in seeing as of another essence, ἑτερούσιον [29], and as an angelic creation, ἀγγελοειδὲς κτίσμα [30]. Athanasius sharply refuted their views on the Spirit, and was not able to accept even a simple conjecture on its being a creature. He attributes to its procession the idea of birth, because it also proceeds from the essence of God, even though he does not specifically use this word ; even though he does not specifically call him God, or ὁμοούσιον with the Father. The reserve is due exclusively to the desire to avoid any new pretext for conflict, and to find means of making a rapprochement with the semi-Arians.

What is said, however, about the Spirit covers the full extent of its divinity. If it is unique and united with the Father, it is unquestionably divine and if it is uncreated it is true God.

---

[28] " Ἄλλο κτίστης καὶ κτίσμα, ἄλλο Πατὴρ καὶ Υἱός ", EPIPHANIUS, *Panarion*, 7, 3.

[29] The Tropicists in Egypt, cf. ATHANASIUS, *Letters to Serapion* I, 2.

[30] Macedonius, SOCRATES, *Hist. Eccles.* II, 45.

4

To say that the Spirit is uncreated is to say everything about it, because anything that is uncreated is essentialy God. On the other hand, when something is named God, it is not necessarily uncreated, because the word god is also used to describe the possession of divinity by participation, and in other cases as well [31]. Consequently it is a more exalted description to call the Spirit uncreated than to call him god.

This terminology of Athanasius is connected on the one hand with the Trinitarian doctrine, and on the other with the religious practice of Christians.

The Trinitarian doctrine is a concept of the divine that is innate in Christianity, because right from its first emergence it was based on faith in a triad of divine persons. Certainly, ever since, attempts have been made to interpret the Trinity as an imaginary state, but in the fourth century, when Monarchianism of the Sabellian kind had been fully superceded, Christian Theologians generally wrote along the lines of Trinitarian theology, as moreover did the Neo-Platonic theologians at exactly this time, by way of imitation.

Yet while the Trinitarian doctrine based on Logos-Christology included an element of subordination, which was the basis of the doctrine of Arianism, Athanasius left this stage behind, although he did not abandon the world *Logos*. He did not accept identity of the Divine Persons, but identity of the essence of the Persons. Each of them as uncreated possesses the entirety of the divine nature, and is God, but as far as the *internal* relations are concerned, Athanasius preserves the divided state within the Trinity. On the other hand he did not accept diversity of nature. Internally, the Trinity is not unlike, or of diverse nature [32], but is composed of uncreated beings identical in nature and essence. It is therefore not possible to accept the divinity of the Father and to regard the Son and the Spirit as creatures, nor can one accept the divinity of the Father and the Son, and regard the Spirit as a creature. Within the Trinity, nothing alien is mingled with its essence. " Οὐ γὰρ ἀλλότριον ἐπιμίγνυται τῇ Τριάδι " [33]. If the Logos and the Spirit were

---

[31] *Letters to Serapion* II, 4, " εἰ δέ καί θεοί τινες ἐκλήθησαν, οὐ τῇ φύσει ἀλλά τῇ μετανοίᾳ τοῦ Υἱοῦ ".

[32] *Ibid* I, 20.

[33] *Ibid* I, 17.

creatures, they would be subject to time, and if they were not without beginning, the Triad would depend upon time, it would be an economic Trinity [34].

Further, the redemption and rebirth of mankind generally, and of each person individually is caused by the Trinity acting as a whole, but also by the persons of the Trinity acting individually. How would man be made divine if the Logos were not God, if mankind had been linked, by the incarnation of the Logos, to the creature? How would man be brought to the Father, if the one that put on a body were not himself the true Son by nature? [35] How should we become communicants in the Divine Nature, with the sharing in the Spirit, if the latter were a created nature, and not God? [36] Baptism, pronounced in the name not only of the Father, but also of the Son and the Spirit, would have no value if it were given in the name of creatures. It would be a worship of creatures ; to wit, idolatry.

It was these pragmatic considerations, far more than any reflections which led Athanasius to impart a polemical tone to his theology.

Panachiotis Christou
Università di Salonicco

---

[34] I. Kalogirou, " Τό Τριαδολογικόν δόγμα κατά τόν δ' αἰῶνα ", p. 298.

[35] *Contra Arianos* II, 70 " Οὐκ ἂν δὲ πάλιν ἐθεοποιήθη κτίσματι συναφθεὶς ὁ ἄνθρωπος, εἰ μὴ Θεὸς ἦν ὁ Υἱὸς, καὶ οὐκ ἂν πάρεστη τῷ Πατρὶ ὁ ἄνθρωπος, εἰ μὴ φύσει ἀληθινὸς ἦν αὐτοῦ ὁ Λόγος ὁ ἐνδυσάμενος τὸ σῶμα ".

[36] *Letters to Serapion* I, 24 " Εἰ δὲ τῇ τοῦ Πνεύματος μετουσία γινόμεθα κοινωνοὶ θείας φύσεως, μαίνοιτ' ἄν τις λέγων τὸ Πνεῦμα τῆς κτιστῆς φύσεως κοὶ μὴ τῆς τοῦ Θεοῦ. Διὰ τοῦτο γὰρ καὶ ἐν οἷς γίνεται, οὗτοι θεοποιοῦνται · εἰ δὲ θεοποιεῖ, οὐκ ἀμφίβολον ὅτι ἡ τούτου φύσις Θεοῦ ἐστιν ",

Theological Studies
44 (1983)

CURRENT THEOLOGY

ARIUS AND THE ARIANS

CHARLES KANNENGIESSER, S.J.

University of Notre Dame

"Surveying the publications on Arianism in the past ten years, it becomes clear that the questions are far from settled. A revision of older views, especially those formulated by the German historians of dogma early in the twentieth century, is under way."[1] Joseph T. Lienhard's judicious remark concludes a recent survey of nine books published from 1971 to 1982.[2] My intention is not to duplicate the critical analysis of these books, already well done by Lienhard, even if most of his observation are fairly short.[3] It would be helpful to reflect on the suggested orientation of the contemporary inquiries about Arianism, as a revision of German views from the early decades of this century. In fact, to know how far patristic research in the 80's is actually "oriented" by its dependence on a former generation of scholars, or marked at all by new methodological criteria or by a new sort of ideology, is a task beyond the limits of the present bulletin. Such an important question is a task for a colloquy.

In the present instance I ask only *why* "the questions are far from settled" in any contemporary attempt to interpret Arius and the so-called Arian crisis of the fourth century. In trying to clarify the reasons for what seems to be a fatal uncertainty in these matters, I shall add further bibliography to Lienhard's data. My main purpose, however, is to examine the motives and the achievements in today's studies on Arianism; I hope to pinpoint a few critical sources of this "unsettlement" on which all who are engaged in these studies may agree.

Perhaps it is best to enumerate bluntly, at the start, the sources of this

[1] Joseph T. Lienhard, "Recent Studies in Arianism," *Religious Studies Review* 8 (1982) 331–37, at 337.

[2] The nine works under scrutiny are: E. Bellini, ed., *Alessandro e Ario: Un esempio di conflitto tra fe e ideologia. Documenti della prima controversia ariana* (Milan, 1974); R. A. Norris, Jr., tr. and ed., *The Christological Controversy* (Philadelphia, 1980); W. G. Rusch, tr. and ed. *The Trinitarian Controversy* (Philadelphia, 1980); R. Klein, *Constantius II. und die christliche Kirche* (Darmstadt, 1977); M. Simonetti, *La crisi ariana nel IV secolo* (Rome, 1975); T. A. Kopeček, *A History of Neo-Arianism* (Cambridge, Mass., 1979); E. Boularand, *L'Hérésie d'Arius et la "foi" de Nicée* (Paris, 1971); R. Lorenz, *Arius judaïzans? Untersuchungen zur dogmengeschichtlichen Einordnung des Arius* (Göttingen, 1979); R. G. Gregg and D. E. Groh, *Early Arianism: A View of Salvation* (Philadelphia, 1981).

[3] A full discussion of Gregg and Groh, Lorenz, and Kopeček, can be found in *RechScR* 70 (1982) 600–607.

456

malaise: (1) a too limited knowledge of the *primary sources*; (2) a lack of appropriate *methodology* in the treatment of these sources; (3) a one-sided consideration of *the social and political setting* of Arianism; (4) a reluctance to accept what *theology* meant for Arius and the so-called Arians. These four limitations are not designed as a veiled attack on my colleagues who share my own project of trying to reach a clearer under-standing in Arian matters. Limitations are imposed more or less directly on all of us, and this for very different reasons. It is the hermeneutical state of today's research which is questioned here, not so much the individual contributions of the interpreters, even if they illustrate (some-times quite unwittingly) the limits of scholarship on which I insist.

PRIMARY SOURCES

The primary sources on the Arian controversy are in poor condition. A general agreement on this point is often accompanied by a fairly general disinterest on the needed remedies. It is not a question of new sources of that kind. The historical recovery of the Christian heritage on the Arian issue, as well as in many similar areas, demands not so much a hunt for unknown witnesses from the past as a more accurate herme-neutical practice with witnesses well known. Yet such discoveries occur. The most spectacular is that of a young Austrian scholar, Johannes Divjak, who recently identified in the codex Lat. 16861, Bibliothèque Nationale, Paris, and in codex 203 of the public library of Marseille, a set of twenty-eight letters written by the older Augustine, with two others sent to him, and a last one from Jerome to Aurelius, bishop of Carthage.[4]

In the Arian and anti-Arian literature (or among its poor remains after the dogmatic struggles of the times of the Constantinian empire) special mention should be made of H. Nordberg's *Athanasiana* (Helsinki, 1962), first critical edition of the significant pseudepigraphic "Five Homilies," "Expositio Fidei," and "Sermo Maior," and of M. Richard's *Asterii Sophistae Commentariorum in Psalmos quae supersunt* (Oslo, 1956). In both cases invaluable primary textual evidences became available. They are still waiting, after twenty or thirty years, for their doctrinal explo-ration on a doctoral level or in a monograph. Other sources, like the fascinating Arian series of homilies called *Opus imperfectum in Mat-thaeum* (PG 56) among the Pseudo-Chrysostomiana, have not yet ap-peared in a critical edition, or even attracted the attention needed for their thorough analysis. Like many Arian texts, the *Opus imperfectum* is known thanks to the historians and philologists who worked on it at the beginning of this century. Unfortunately, its message remains sealed and sterile for today's hermeneutics applied to Arianism.

[4] *Epistulae ex duobus codicibus nuper in lucem prolatae* (CSEL 88; Vienna, 1981).

The benefit of a systematic, rigorous study of isolated, even badly damaged, primary Arian sources for a better understanding of Arianism as a whole, in all its political and religious complexities, has been shown recently by Roger Gryson's masterful publications concerning the synod of Aquileia in September 381.[5] The dramatic showdown between Ambrose of Milan and the last Arian bishops in the west of the Roman Empire is now convincingly illuminated thanks to the paleographic and lexicographic accomplishments of Gryson, a professor at Louvain-la-Neuve, Belgium. The "Arian collection from Verona," *Veronensis LI*, 157 folios, probably a local product from Verona itself under the reign of the Gothic ruler Theodoric (493–526), is unique in being the only complete Arian book we possess today.[6]

But all the older or most recent critical editions of primary sources on Arius and the Arians are still dominated by the *Urkunden zum arianischen Streite* (*Athanasius Werke* 3) published by H.-G. Opitz in 1934. After half a century it would be worth submitting the whole collection of thirty-four documents to an updated analysis which could lead to more than one interesting discovery. The letters of Constantine are quoted or translated or paraphased by recent historians, like Paul Keresztes or Timothy D. Barnes (see below). The letters of Alexander of Alexandria are translated and very briefly commented upon by Enzo Bellini, as noted by Lienhard.[7] But in both cases the emperor's and the Alexandrian bishop's writings deserved a genuine study, on the linguistic level, in regard to their style and content.

Urkunde 18, transmitted in Syriac, but retrotranslated into Greek by E. Schwartz, is a letter from the Antiochene synod of the winter 324–25. It was scrutinized by E. Abramowski in an article in the *Zeitschrift für Kirchengeschichte* (86 [1975] 1), "Die Synod von Antiochien 324/25 und ihr Symbol," which gives not only illuminating advice for a better Greek text but helps to locate the synod in its Origenian tradition.

Urkunden 1, 6, and 30, being written, or at least signed, by Arius, lead to most difficult and vital challenges for scholars interested today in Arian primary sources. On one side, they need to be interpreted themselves in the light of precise circumstances, about which we lack most of the needed information. On the other side, their real significance can only be elucidated with the help of what we may learn about Arius thanks

---

[5] *Scolies ariennes sur le concile d'Aquilée* (SC 267; Paris, 1980); *Le recueil arien de Vérone* (Instrumenta patristica 13; The Hague–Steenbrugge, 1982).

[6] Gryson, *Le recueil arien de Vérone* 70.

[7] "Recent Studies" 331. The translation into English, with an extensive philological, historical, and theological commentary, of Alexander of Alexandria's letters and other remains, to the extent that such remains are identifiable, would be a fine topic for a doctoral dissertation.

to Athanasius. Since P. Nautin made a few stylistic observations on *Urkunde* 1, with a speculative conjecture about two anti-Arian interpolations in it,[8] no one has tried to evaluate these rare documents, proper to Arius, with new interpretative techniques. But they have been carefully checked, and compared with other testimonies from Arius, by R. Lorenz in his book *Arius judaïzans?* cited above.[9] Their comparison with the Arian quotations in Athanasius introduces some urgent methodological remarks about the correct treatment of that sort of sources.

METHODOLOGY

A methodical use of Arian quotations transmitted through the writings of the anti-Arian leader par excellence, Athanasius of Alexandria, rests on a first set of criteria unanimously recognized: (a) Arius is cited by Athanasius for a strictly polemical purpose; (b) most of the quotations are fragmentary; (c) they are transmitted out of context, and exposed to arbitrary changes at the convenience of their citer. As early as 1926, Gustave Bardy popularized his conviction that the Athanasian quotations from Arius' *Thalia* are careless.[10] John Henry Newman had already suggested the same opinion, reinforced in printed form by A. Robertson.[11] The traditional view inclined scholars to give less credit to Athanasius when he quoted his worst enemies in the heat of a bitter and long-lasting fight. Even if this a priori distrust seems reasonable, it should have engaged the critics (and G. Bardy among the first) in analysis of the techniques of citing in Athanasius.

But there is a whole set of other criteria, linked with the aims of literary criticism, which never became effective enough, it seems to me, in the way scholars handled Arius as quoted by the Alexandrian bishop: (a) Being quotations, the passages from the *Thalia* and the other Arian extracts belong, first of all, to the works in which they are located. (b) The use of the Arian quotations by modern scholars for their historical and theological purposes is always, and necessarily, combined with a simultaneous use of the Athanasian writings which transmit to us these quotations. To use a critical eye on the quotations, with an uncritical

[8] P. Nautin, "Deux interpolations orthodoxes dans une lettre d'Arius," *Analecta Bollandiana* 67 (1949) 137–41.

[9] See also G. C. Stead, "The *Thalia* of Arius and the Testimony of Athanasius," *JTS*, n.s. 29 (1978) 20–38.

[10] "Saint Alexandre d'Alexandrie a-t-il connu la Thalie d'Arius?," *RevScRel* 7 (1926) 527–32; more explicit, *Recherches sur saint Lucien d'Antioche et son école* (Paris: Beauchesne, 1936) 247: "L'évêque d'Alexandrie indique très inexactement ses sources.... Saint Athanase abrège, résume, bouleverse les textes qu'il cite."

[11] In A. Robertson's edition of the Athanasian *Discourses against the Arians* (NPNF, 2d series, 4 [1891] 308 f.) only the "commencement of Arius' Thalia" is printed as a trustworthy quotation, the rest being printed as if it were Athanasius' text.

69

view on their immediate literary setting, is itself uncritical. (c) Athanasius as a citer of Arius justifies his quotations. He introduces them, divides them, concludes them, and usually adds to the distinct parts of the quoted texts some short comments. The Arian texts in the status of quotations need then to be understood in regard to their Athanasian frames. (d) If the same quotations are recurrent, any interpretation of their repeated wordings in different works of Athanasius rests on the chronology fixed for these works. It would seem hazardous to decide anything about the repeated phrases, and especially about their possible variations, before having cleared up the foundations of the fixed chronology. (e) The practice of polemic quotations in late antiquity presents a certain flexibility. Even careful authors, like Eusebius of Caesarea, may put their own mark on their citations. In dogmatic polemics it is not always easy to detect where a quotation stands or ends, or if its text has only been paraphrased. Before being charged as untrustworthy or negligent, these authors deserve to be recognized as following the practices of quotation customary in their time.

The list of literary criteria required for the appropriate treatment of Arian quotations in Athanasius would sound tedious if continued in the same abstract way. One certitude supports them in any case: *we reach the essential Arius through Athanasius,* and in no other way. The historian who writes on Arius without the needed concern for the Athanasian literary mediation can easily miss the point, as soon as he[12] or she[13] characterizes Arius' thought and position with the help of quoted extracts, which must be understood in the light of the writer who transmits them to us. There still exists a broad disagreement among experts about the value of Arian quotations, of Arian documents, found in the literary heritage of Athanasius. One of the main sources of uncertainty in this matter results very often from a lack of appropriate forms of literary criticism.

THE SOCIAL AND POLITICAL SETTING

Four books may exemplify the limitation of contemporary scholarship focusing on Arianism in regard to its social and political setting. Paul Keresztes, who teaches classics and history at the University of Waterloo, Ontario, has produced a somewhat anachronistic *laus,* in the old classical fashion, of *Constantine: A Great Christian Monarch and Apostle* (Amsterdam: J. C. Gieben, 1981; 218 pp.). He offers readable, even elegant, English translations of all the writings of Constantine faced with the so-

[12] See below, the instances of Klein and Barnes, but most of all the book on Arius' doctrine of salvation by Gregg and Groh.

[13] See Lienhard's review, n. 1 above, or, among many other negative reviews, K. M. Girardet, *Historische Zeitschrift* 231 (1980) 141–43.

called Arian crisis. Quoted at full length, these writings are now available for teachers and students.

Unknown to Keresztes, the volume of Richard Klein, *Constantius II. und die christliche Kirche* (Darmstadt: Wissenschaftliche Buchgesellschaft, 1977; 321 pp.), follows a similar path of historical apologetics, with less politeness, more pugnacity, and an almost partisan viewpoint. Klein devotes the second half of his book (160–269) to Constantius' *Aussenpolitik*, his warfare and politics with Armenia, Persia, and the Goths. This horizon should not be overlooked in a consideration of the religious turmoil spread over the east and the west of the Roman Empire under the rule of Constantine's younger son, even if one concludes with Lienhard that "Constantius' religious dealings with nations outside the Roman Empire are not of any great significance" ("Recent Studies" 333).

A History of Neo-Arianism, by Thomas A. Kopeček,[14] covers the last years of Constantius' reign and follows the neo-Arian party in its "transformation from a party to a sect" down to 377 and until its extinction around 395. The critical, well-balanced, and perfectly documented presentation of both neo-Arian leaders, Aetius and Eunomius, confers on Kopeček's whole study a refreshing quality of sound objectivity. This is a helpful work for experts as well as for students. One of its best features throughout the two volumes is the stress on the social setting of each initiative taken by Aetius or Eunomius, or by the bishops who opposed them.

One of the main failures of this research[15] belongs to a certain lack of criticism in regard to the Athanasian writings. A more recent compilation of modern scholarship, alert and richly documented, on *Constantine and Eusebius*, by Timothy D. Barnes,[16] will elicit some other comments in the next issue of this bulletin, which will be dedicated to Athanasius. Here, Part 1 on Constantine, 2 on Eusebius, and 3 on the Christian Empire are only considered in reference to Arius and to the notion of Arianism, as investigated and developed by Barnes. As a general appraisal of this valuable study, one must agree with its own advertising: "Mr. Barnes gives the fullest available [add: in English] narrative history of the reigns of Diocletian and Constantine." More than half the volume is occupied by the notes, bibliography, and indexes—a substantial harvest of historical erudition, introducing patristic scholars into less familiar primary sources and into the most qualified contemporary expertise in classics and late Roman history at once. The field covered by Barnes is immense; the institutional and social contexts are well rendered in all

---

[14] Patristic Monograph Series 8 (2 vols.; Cambridge, Mass.: Philadelphia Patristic Foundation, 1979; 553 pp.).

[15] L. R. Wickham mentions also some defective translations: *JTS*, n.s. 33/2 (1982) 572.

[16] Cambridge, Mass.: Harvard University, 1981; 458 pp.

their complexities. One becomes more aware of the deep reciprocal implications of the Christian religion and the imperial politics in what may be called the genius of Constantine.

A limitation of scholarship common to these four books for very different reasons concerns precisely Arius and the Arians. Keresztes poses his imperial hero filled with "the fervour of the novice," as a "sincere neophyte, or rather catechumen," offended in his pure soul by "the humanistic, materialistic, and down-to-earth logic of the Alexandrian priest" (117). Old hagiographic clichés are thus combined with what seems to derive from a misunderstanding of the traditional portrait of Arius as a follower of Lucian of Antioch in his biblical exegesis. The literary and prosopographic presentation of Constantine reveals no real concern for the genuine political and social setting of Arius himself or of the earliest Arians. A one-sided description of the imperial scene misses the local, Alexandrian scene, decisive for any balanced approach to the historical encounter between the Western liberator of the Eastern Empire, after his final victory over Licinius, and the Libyan priest, settled in Alexandria and excommunicated by his local bishop. More than that, Keresztes, writing on Constantine, has in common with Boularand, writing on Arius and Nicaea (see my notes 2–3), a prejudiced dogmatistic attitude which allows him to judge the heresiarch in the light of what he believes to be the true orthodoxy, more than in the line of his capacity as a historian.

Richard Klein's "impulse" in the study of Arius intends to establish the thesis of the Emperor Constantius as totally free from pro-Arian feelings. The imperial politics were in this case twisted unwillingly and finally biased in the common historiography, thanks to "the propagandistic arguments of Athanasius" (29). In the early 40's, an "inclination of the emperor as well as of the Oriental bishops toward the Arian doctrine is excluded" (45). In 357, at the time of the pro-Arian synod of Sirmium, and of the "blasphemy" of Sirmium as the pro-Nicaeans called it, a provisory political turn to Arianism from the side of Constantius must be conceded, but "there is no question about an inner conviction in assuming Arian formulae and doctrines" (64). Even if there is some small truth in such statements (the religious personality of this Augustus being sufficiently complicated to allow several contrasting judgments), Klein's partisan conclusions lead him to lay the sole charge on the "Athanasian polemic" (101) for diffusing the image of a Constantius inclined to Arianism. Klein comes to speak in a paradoxical way of "the Arian propaganda of Athanasius" (113, 116), meaning by it the calumnious abuse of the denomination "Arian" by Athanasius in indicting his political foes. Klein's genuine contribution consists only in dramatizing a very common view, and I would easily agree with a less polemic analysis of the analogical and rhetorical value of the controverted epithet in Athanasius' writings. But such an agreement would need to rest on a certain familiarity with the writings. Klein offers such a one-sided picture of the emperor's politics in religious matters that he neglects to wonder what Arius' proper doctrine actually meant for his contemporaries. In the study of Arius it seems hard to find the right equilibrium between a precise evaluation of theological motives and a balanced appreciation of the political realities.

Thomas A. Kopeček is not liable to this sort of criticism in his *History of Neo-Arianism*. But the very success of this task illustrates for me another limitation of contemporary scholarship when devoted to Arius and to the Arians. The crisis of the Christian Church in the fourth century was more activated by Constantine's sovereign patronage and its consequences than by anything else. It is therefore of primary importance, when one outlines the later phases of the theological controversy, to keep in mind the very first steps of "Arianism" when it became a political issue under Constantine. In the earlier decades of the twentieth century, A. Harnack, J. Gummerus, L. Duchesne, and a few others had developed the panoramic views of the successive stages and struggles of the so-called Arian crisis. E. Schwartz completed their work with a sharper, much more documented exposition of the political crisis in Church and state at the time of Athanasius. The *Urkunden* edited by Opitz are among the most durable fruits of the powerful revival in the studies on Arianism for which Schwartz has to be credited. Now Kopeček shows, I would suggest, the inevitable difficulty faced by a younger generation after several decades of more and more specialized researches in patristics in general, and in the historiography of the Constantinian era in particular.[17] It is certainly not hypercriticism if, as more and more problems of chronology and authenticity wait for new solutions, the more rigorous scholarship exercises its normal right in regard to Arius and the Arians. But in the case of Kopeček's dissertation, neo-Arianism fails to identify itself as neo, the needed counterexpertise on the first and genuine Arianism, that especially of Arius himself, being omitted in this work. Therefore the historical perspective, which would help to underscore the original significance of Aetius and Eunomius, is more or less obliterated. But, given the obscure data on Arius, who gave his name to the main dogmatic fight of his century, and given the limits of a dissertation, how could Kopeček have concentrated in a few chapters the needed critical information? In studying carefully the *last* phase of the so-called Arian crisis, he demonstrates *e contrario* the obvious need of a similar, reshaped, and deepened study of its *first* phase. He is not blinded by dogmatistic

[17] On this situation see the comments of Robert Wilken in "Diversity and Unity in Early Christianity," *The Second Century* 1 (1981) 101–10.

prejudice or fanatical apologetics; his view becomes limited only by the lack of a global perception of what Arius and Arianism represent on the turbulent scene of the fourth century.

One could hardly address this same complaint against T. D. Barnes in his approach to *Constantine and Eusebius*. Barnes multiplies with delight the entrees into the heart of the matter, in devoting substantial chapters to Diocletian and Galerius before starting with Constantine, or a less vivid but extensive summary to Origen of Alexandria before describing Eusebius as a biblical scholar,[18] a historian, and an apologist. He also introduces the reader to the manifold disciplines of contemporary historical criticism, including papyrology, chronography, text criticism, classics, hagiography, numismatics, philosophy, "and even theology," as Goethe's Dr. Faust would have observed. This welcome multidisciplinary practice does not exclude personal preferences for critical redating, which gives a more spicy flavor to his vigorous style. For all these admitted qualities, the figure of Arius seems, so to say, evanescent in Barnes's recent book. We are brought to an extreme opposite to that of Klein. In Barnes's view, almost everyone around Constantius and Constantine himself, not to speak of Constantius II, became "Arian." In particular, Eusebius of Caesarea without any doubt, and the Oriental bishops as a whole, were true "Arians." After having read this book, it is impossible to see how and why Arius was a special source of trouble, or why soon after his death he was anathematized and his memory damned by these same "Arian" bishops celebrated by Barnes.

The Constantine whom Eusebius quotes speaks of a first God and a second God who are 'two substances with one perfection,' and he asserts that the substance of the second God derives its existence from the first. In 338 or 339, such views were unmistakably Arian. It is hard to believe that Eusebius did not intend his readers to infer that Constantine shared his own Arian views (271).

Who knows, after all? One suspects, however, that the author who comes to such a conclusion omitted to elaborate specific views about the Arian theology. Why not claim that the common Middle Platonic doctrine of the Godhead is somehow Arian?

This powerful investment in the narrative history of the political and institutional transformation of the Roman Empire during the fourth century, though useful and illuminating after the works of giants like A. H. M. Jones and E. Schwartz among many others, even if enriched by the meticulous checking of all sorts of primary sources, just does not

---

[18] An occasional small slip is added to a few too hasty comments on P. Nautin's recent *Origène*, p. 170, where Barnes claims that Eusebius spoke about Hosea 5:14, in his *Prophetic Extracts*, with a statement "taken over from Didymus of Alexandria," not yet born at that time.

supply the indispensable analysis of the Arian documents considered in their own social, political, and theological setting. A one-sided approach prevents Barnes from identifying the real historical figure of Arius. It misleads him completely—like R. Klein, as it seems to me—in his negative evaluation of Athanasius, and this to the point of letting him apparently ignore the fact that the Alexandrian bishop was also a Christian theologian and a spiritual leader acclaimed by his people for a record period of forty-five years in office.

THEOLOGY

Finally, it is theology that builds up the essential issue as soon as Arius and the Arians become the subject of scholarly inquiry. What makes Arian sources rare is the militant theology of the fourth-century Church which destroyed them. And what makes their remains obscure is the difficulty contemporary scholars have interpreting their theology comprehensively enough. It is also theology which overshadows the appropriate literary treatment of the Arian sources. Since F. C. Baur, historical theology was often reduced to a form of history of ideas, the latter being of course formulated by the historian himself, the interpreter of the past, in command of the primary sources. The most striking effect of this strategy was to produce histories of Christian dogma claiming to recover the true doctrinal meaning of sources never considered for themselves. *Literary* testimonies, however, are supposed to be treated first by *literary* criticism, even if they transmit sublime truths. This principle should be equally admitted for the Koran, the Talmud, or the Jewish-Christian Scriptures. The same holds true of the vast amount of documentation witnessing to the Christian tradition in its founding stage and in its later historical journey through the cultures of East and West.

In the case of Arius, no consensus of opinion among modern theologians dispenses from the arduous philological and doctrinal recovery of his devastated heritage. Textbook theology used to obliterate the needed process of acute discernment, and apologetic routines led to superficial solutions. A strict form of literary criticism applied to the sources giving access to Arius' thought calls for, and presupposes at the same time, a renewed theological availability in order to interpret without a fixed set of patristic commonplaces the thought of this singular theologian of the past. And when the stress of the studies on Arius and the Arians is laid on their social and political contexts, a new *theological* awareness of their significance is even more necessary. As the battle in which they were engaged was ultimately a theological one, all the necessary contextual detours, imposed by the need we recognize for more realistic approaches to their situation, achieve the goal of introducing us to Arius and the Arians themselves—only at the price of a stronger theological comprehension. Otherwise we would confuse the Oriental moderate forms of Origenism in the east of the fourth-century Empire with the radical theory proper to Arius, or we would blur the distinctive features of this peculiar theory in its genuine distance from neo-Arianism, and so on.

The last and most demanding step, in reviewing here the hermeneutical status of contemporary studies on Arius and the Arians, should then be opened by asking: Why are the questions about Arian theology far from settled today?

The Identification of Arian Sources

I shall limit my observations to the Arian sources transmitted by Athanasius which are quoted and alluded to most commonly in recent critical literature. Following the general outline fixed by G. Bardy,[19] G. C. Stead undertook a scrutiny of Arius' fragments located in Athanasian writings. This task had been neglected by E. Schwartz and his followers, mainly because the critical edition of the *Athanasius Werke* in the collection of the Berlin Academy did not yet include the dogmatic writings, but only most of the apologies. As this edition could not be completed after World War II, many decisions about the textual data in Athanasius are still somehow provisory.[20] Happily, among the apologies published by H.-G. Opitz[21] one finds *De synodis* with its full quotation of the "Blasphemies of Arius."[22] This remarkable piece, introduced by Athanasius as being the *Thalia* of Arius, is one of the key texts in the access to the heresiarch provided for many centuries by his opponent. In "The *Thalia* of Arius and the Testimony of Arius,"[23] Stead noted a misprint in Opitz' text of the *Blasphemies* (243, 17, read *exichniasai*, not *-sei*); otherwise their original wording seems to be warranted.[24] It is Stead's distinguished merit to have drawn the attention of critics to the many doctrinal observations made possible thanks to a precise analysis of *De synodis* 15, and thanks to its comparative study with other quotations from the Arian *Thalia* given by Athanasius. In his other publications, e.g., in "The Platonism of Arius,"[25] "Rhetorical Method in Athanasius,"[26] or *Divine Substance*,[27] Stead quotes the *Thalia* indistinctly in

[19] Main publication in this matter: *Recherches sur s. Lucien d'Antioche et son école* (Paris, 1936).
[20] The editor, H.-G. Opitz, was killed at the Front in 1943. My own collations of *C. Ar.* show no substantial change in the text edited by Montfaucon and reprinted in PG 26.
[21] *Athanasius Werke* 2/1 (1934–37).
[22] Chap. 15 (Opitz 242–43).
[23] *JTS*, n.s. 21 (1978) 20–52.
[24] The other textual improvements of the *Blasphemies*, suggested by Stead (50–51) for metrical reasons, are only hypothetical and not to be considered here.
[25] *JTS*, n.s. 15 (1964) 16–31.
[26] *VC* 30 (1976) 121–37, at 130, n. 12.
[27] Oxford: Clarendon, 1977, 241; my review, *RechScR* 70 (1982) 599–600.

Syn. 15 and in *Contra Arianos* 1, 5–6.[28]

This lack of differentiation, inaugurated by Bardy in a detailed text analysis, was already admitted by editors and scholars in the nineteenth century and earlier. What is new is the contemporary attempt to catch Arius' genuine creativity as a theologian and as a literary witness of his own theology from a more critical perception of his statements in the *Thalia*. Here I deal first with this perception itself, which supposes a positive identification of the sources in question. We will see later the theological models deduced from these sources, or invented for what was supposed to be a better understanding of them. The need for clarifying the common perception of the Arian *Thalia* is obvious. It is also of basic importance, for the whole interpretation of Arianism, to know if Arius, as quoted by Athanasius, has really been correctly identified. We will observe in the next section how R. C. Gregg and D. E. Groh (see n. 2 above) use parts of the Arian text quoted as the *Thalia* in *C. Ar.* 1, 5 for the central argument of their "view of salvation" in Arian terms, with a strong claim of being supported by *Syn.* 15. R. Lorenz (n. 2 above) repeats Stead's practice in his synoptic presentation of the fragments of Arius preserved in Athanasian works, as well as in their theological discussion.[29] M. Simonetti, in what may be considered the best general study on Arianism available today (n. 2 above), fixes with authority the same textual practice and stresses its importance:

> Veri e propri frammenti di quest'opera [*Thalia*] due soltanto sono giunti a noi ad opera di Atanasio: l'inizio (*frag.* 1) *apud* Athan., *CA* 1,5; e un lungo passa di 42 versi (*frag.* 2) *apud* Athan. *Synod.* 15, che ha l'aria di essere un aggregato di brevi passi non continui fra loro: *questo frammenta è dottrinalmente molto importante.*[30]

I mentioned for the first time my doubts about Arius as the author of the *Blasphemies* put under his name in *Syn.* 15 at the Oxford Patristic Conference in September 1979,[31] and I gave a more explicit comment on the *Blasphemies* in a colloquy organized at the Center for Hermeneutical Studies in Berkeley, California, in December 1981.[32] Simonetti noted that the so-called *Thalia* fragment in *Syn.* 15 "looked like an aggregate of small passages without continuity among them," but he did not

---

[28] PG 26.

[29] Chap. 2 and 3: 37–66.

[30] P. 44; the last italics are mine.

[31] *Studia patristica* 18, in three parts, ed. Elizabeth A. Livingstone (Oxford and New York: Pergamon, 1982) 989.

[32] *Holy Scripture and Hellenistic Hermeneutics in Alexandrian Christology: The Arian Crisis* (Berkeley: G.T.U. and U.C., 1982) 14–15. For a full analysis, see my forthcoming book *Athanase d'Alexandrie évêque et écrivain: Une recherche sur les traités Contre les Ariens* (Paris: Beauchesne, 1983).

investigate the matter. A closer examination would have had to start with a literary analysis of this long citation. When Christopher Stead noted in 1978, at the start of his own remarks on *Thalia* in *Syn.* 15, "the general impression given is distasteful to orthodox sentiment ... the quotations are only a hostile selection from a larger whole," [33] he projected over *Syn.* 15, as Bardy and many other critics have done, what could have been said more evidently about the *Thalia* in *C. Ar.* 1, 5–6. As a matter of fact, it is completely wrong to identify "a hostile selection" of extracts from Arius in *Syn.* 15. The quotation in *Syn.* 15 of that "selection" is hostile, not the "selection" itself. And there is no "selection" at all, as Stead and probably Simonetti supposed it, always arguing in conformity with the model of quoting applied for the *Thalia* produced in *C. Ar.* 1, 5–6. The "aggregate," or "selection," of *Syn.* 15 does not show the marks of an anti-Arian citer intending to condense in such a digest the perversity of the heresy he denounces. On the contrary, the whole quotation of *Syn.* 15 reveals the careful thought and the dialectical ability of an author eager to express his own theological concern through the paraphrase of the *Thalia* he elaborates. Not only are the sentences "selected" truly Arian, but so is the actual collection constituted by them. All the grammatical and lexical means used to put the "selected" sentences together tend only to one purpose, which is to stress the logical value of the different propositions and their coherency as a whole. In other words, we cannot speak of a "selection," even of a friendly one, or better an Arian one, the whole text being deliberately construed around the thesis announced in the first proposition, and evolved from sentence to sentence in order to explicitate the theological content of that initial proposition. What may have suggested a "hostile selection" is the interesting fact that the anonymous author tries to integrate in his commentary several characteristics taken over from the *Thalia* quoted in *C. Ar.* 1, 5.

No need for more details about this literary find; they have been given elsewhere.[34] But I hope I have indicated clearly enough that the usual hermeneutical practice with the main sources of Arius' own theology is not always as free from misleading routines as it should be.

A similar clarification should be attempted in *C. Ar.* 1, 5 about the two Arian fragments inserted by Athanasius into his first and genuine citation of the *Thalia* (PG 26, 21b9-d1). They were bluntly declared parcels of

[33] "The *Thalia*" (n. 23 above) 24.

[34] See the publications mentioned in n. 32 above. In his responses to my Berkeley paper, Kopeček agreed with the analysis of *Syn.* 15 epitomized here (*Holy Scripture and Hellenistic Hermeneutics* 53). But Stead, in what he called "some provisional comments," concluded with "I stand by my judgment of 1978" (ibid. 73–74.) The discussion obviously needs to be continued in the same serene and stimulating way.

the *Thalia* itself by Bardy.[35] Stead still does not examine their provenance and their function in *C. Ar.* 1–2. However, they could help greatly to identify the structure of the *Thalia* in *C. Ar.* 1, 5–6, and they deserve to be linked with the other quotations of Asterius in *C. Ar.* 1–2. Then only would their real nature and significance as another Arian source become available.[36]

I should also stress the need for further work on Arian exegesis, in order to state what sort of primary information we may receive through the *Contra Arianos* and other Athanasian writings.[37]

The Theological Interpretation of Arian Sources

The doctrinal figure of Arius is polymorphic indeed in contemporary scholarship, according to the different erudite foundations on which the critics build their portrayals. The Alexandrian heresiarch does not look the same (1) if he is pictured on the strict basis of his own sayings, as available through the ancient sources; (2) if he is approached according to the anti-Arian reaction of the fourth century, in which case the presence of Athanasius is overwhelmingly predominant; (3) if he is encountered only on the non-Alexandrian and nontheological scene of imperial politics at the time of Constantine and his sons. I need add here only a few comments about Arius as recognized in his theological position on the ground of the sources mentioned above.

These sources being fragmentary, and manipulated by their known or unknown transmitters, the doctrinal image of Arius which they project is necessarily fragmentary as well, and quite often biased by uncontrolled manipulations. We face on this point one of the most unsurmountable limits of any possible knowledge based on scientific grounds about Arius and Arianism. In the best of cases the figure of the Alexandrian priest remains enigmatic. But in regard to the primary sources this figure becomes more confused, if not contradictory, as soon as contemporary criticism fails to identify those sources correctly. The supplementary difficulty created by an eclectic or confusing analysis of the fragments of Arius may explain how one comes to conclusions which sound unexpect-

---

[35] Noted by Stead, "The *Thalia*" 27.

[36] In "The *Thalia*" Stead seems to follow Bardy, who attributed the Asterius fragment to Arius: "The concluding sentences of *C. Ar.* I, 5, which charge Arius. . . .The *de Synodis* extract of the *Thalia* provides no evidence on this point. . . ." For a partial and incidental mention of the questions raised about these fragments, see *Holy Scripture and Hellenistic Hermeneutics* 14. More will come in *Athanase d'Alexandrie évêque et écrivain*.

[37] T. E. Pollard, "The Exegesis of Scripture and the Arian Controversy," *BJRL* 41 (1959) 414 ff; *Johannine Christology and the Early Church* (Cambridge: University Press, 1970) chaps. 4–7.

edly trivial.[38] Finally, it is not surprising that most of the recent attempts to outline Arius' theological profile are, in fact, managed on other levels than on the circumscribed and problematic basis offered by the poor remains of his writings.

Two Contemporary Views on Arius

Early Arianism: A View of Salvation, by Robert C. Gregg and Dennis E. Groh, deals explicitly with Arius himself and projects a very peculiar image of his doctrinal position. According to this image, "the Arian Christ was a 'creature' or a 'work' of God and the Creator who had been promoted to the rank of a divine son and redeemer" (1). The authors imply that such a notion of Christ "does not mean that cosmology or the doctrine of God was their [the Arians'] early starting point, as almost all modern scholars have contended" (2). Surprisingly enough, a few lines further on they add: "the early Arians seem to have proceeded from their exegesis of the scriptures to the conclusion that even the preexistent Christ was, and had to be, a creature, no matter how exalted were the results of his creaturehood" (ibid.). It seems rather paradoxical to let the first Arians conclude in this way, by eliminating the doctrine of God from their "starting point." But the authors do not care about this; they see only how they can develop, from there on, the "view of salvation" which they attribute to Arius and to his earliest "companions," Asterius and Eusebius of Nicomedia.

Two observations seem indispensable here. In their first chapter the authors do not wonder how such a reductionist idea of Christ could have been accepted in a Christian church of the fourth century. Secondly, neither here nor elsewhere in the next chapters do Gregg and Groh ask what it means to emphasize so strongly the most severe accusations of Arius' episcopal censors, Alexander and Athanasius of Alexandria. Hoping to avoid metaphysics about the Arian notion of God and of Christ, as well as the biased polemics in the anti-Arian allegations of the Alexandrian bishops, they limit Arius' central concern to "the existential and psychological aspects of creaturely existence in the ministry of Jesus" (3). Where they find the episcopal opponents denouncing Arius for stressing evangelical data in order to deny the true divinity of Jesus, Gregg and Groh observe that "to the physical limitations of the body the Arians added the full range of psychological and spiritual limitations of a creature" (4), and that their central Christological motivation was "the desire to chronicle the savior's creaturely characteristics for a positive soteriology" (12). They undertake to develop the "'constructive' elements

[38] For instance: "Arius ..., though sharing the traditional inconsistency of language, remains much more nearly within the logical limits of a doctrine of three hypostases" (Stead, "The *Thalia*" 39).

of Arian Christology," in pointing out that the "positive christological concern" of Arius and of his first followers "goes almost entirely unnoticed in the scholarly and popular literature on Arianism" (ibid.).

On one side, Gregg and Groh declare that the theory of the Logos and the cosmo-theological frame of the nascent Arianism was arbitrarily imposed in its evaluation by Alexander and Athanasius, and they are no longer interested in it. On the other side, they interpret exclusively in an "existential and psychological" viewpoint tesserae from the New Testament which the Alexandrian bishops considered as having been abused by the earliest Arians against the dogma of the equality of Father and Son. Thereby they claim frankly: "We are not interested in the orthodox opposition except insofar as it transmits the Arian position" (25).

In other terms, Gregg and Groh present a view on Arius dependent on one limited part of the canonical dossier elaborated by Alexander and Athanasius for his excommunication and for the refutation of his doctrine. Admittedly, any view of Arius depends in some way on the "orthodox" reaction of these two bishops. But in the case of Gregg and Groh this dependence looks very curious if its references are examined more precisely. From p. 3 on ("Athanasius introduces a series of Gospel texts used by the Arians ...") , and without interruption in the whole book, the basic view on Arius stressed by the authors derives from the third treatise *C. Arianos* in the Athanasian corpus, and it is intimately combined with the testimony of the so-called *Thalia* in *Syn.* 15.[39] The Arian "view of salvation," reconstructed in the different chapters of Gregg and Groh, is exactly the view in opposition to which the author of *C. Ar.* 3 hoped to establish his own anti-Arian doctrine. In a debate ideologically overladen as was the Arian debate in Alexandria during the first quarter of the fourth century—after all, in any debate of that sort—"position" and "opposition" are correlated and convertible terms. I cannot see how one is consistent with historical logic in arguing on the ground of a "position" defined by the correlate "opposition," without focusing as critically as possible on this "opposition." The case of Gregg and Groh's "Arius" becomes even more untenable, should their main source of information, *C. Ar.* 3, be considered uncertain in its Athanasian authenticity, as their second primary source, the so-called *Thalia* of *Syn.* 15, must be excluded for other reasons from direct access to Arius' thought.[40]

Rudolf Lorenz' *Arius judaizans?* is a very strange book. Why the title does not ask "Arius Origenistic?" remains obscure. Lorenz starts with a first chapter, mentioned above, where he enumerates in a synoptic form

[39] I stressed this one-sidedness in the compromising support given to Gregg and Groh by "Athanasius" in *RSR* 70 (1982) 604 f. An unpublished paper by S. G. Hall on the same issue is mentioned in *JTS*, n.s. 34 (1983) 74, n. 93.

[40] See my Oxford paper from 1979, quoted in n. 31 above.

all the fragments of "Arius" transmitted by Alexander (Encyclical *Henos Sōmatos*) and Athanasius (*C. Ar.* 1, 5–6, 9; *Ep. ad episc. Aeg. et Libyae* 12; *De decr. Nic. syn.* 6, 1–2; *Syn.* 15). He presents a "provisory determination of Arius' theological starting point" (title of chap. 3) which is not only "provisory" but as problematic as the similar analysis provided by Stead, *Syn.* 15 being constantly mixed up with the other testimonies of Arius' thought. In such a study the method of the traditional *Dogmengeschichte*, being a "theological" one, seems to consider it superfluous to submit to the needed *literary* criticism of the *literary* witnesses on which it depends. In fact, the immediate sources of Arius' doctrine are treated in this analysis from a contextual point of view. It helps to understand why in the following chapters, where different possible contexts are examined in regard to the fragments of Arius, the latter are never treated in their own right, but atomized and reduced to a dust of dispersed thoughts, illuminated by heterogeneous parallels from Origen, Philo, the Gnostics, the adoptionists, and late Judaism with its different sects. Only in his ninth and final chapter does Lorenz go back to a direct consideration of Arius' doctrine, this time comparing it with the teaching of Eusebius of Nicomedia, Asterius, and Lucian of Antioch, or in its credal form with the creed of Nicaea, the second creed of Antioch, and the creed of Eusebius of Caesarea.

The main conclusions of this synoptic analysis must be welcomed: *Arius distances himself from the Collucianists as well as from Origen, even if he reveals many of their views. He cannot be explained as just a more radical subordinationist in the line of the traditional Origenian theology.* This conclusion of Lorenz should be considered decisive and durable. It gives its value to the whole book, even if the last section of the last chapter, "Vergleich der origenistischen Christologie im engeren Sinne (Lehre von der Menschwerdung) mit Arius" (211–24), devalues in fact all the earlier chapters. In this last step, Lorenz thinks he has established that the pre-existent Origenistic soul of Jesus was confused by Arius with the incarnate Logos. I have shown elsewhere why this solution seems highly speculative and inconsistent.[41]

These two antagonistic views on Arius complement each other in their reciprocal failure. Gregg and Groh insist on the "nonmetaphysical" doctrine of salvation, according to which Arius would have aimed at a pastoral and pietistic revival in his church, with Jesus, "the obedient Logos," as "one of many brothers" "*a representative creature*" (29–30, italics in text). They modernize the oldest data of the Arian controversy, in adapting to our contemporary language the anthropology they find expressed in these data. Lorenz antiquates Arius in his own time, in

[41] *Holy Scripture and Hellenistic Hermeneutics* 30–31; see also Lienhard, "Recent Studies" 334 f.

imagining him trapped and confined in the most problematic corner of Origenistic metaphysics. His paradoxical approach frees Arius from the patristic commonplace which used to keep him bound to Origenian subordinationism in the philosophical realm of Middle Platonism; but at the same time it leads him to a sophisticated Origenistic metaphysician whose alter ego would be, two generations later, Evagrius Ponticus. In reviewing such extreme interpretations, the most positive remarks may stress their obvious freshness in the attempt to liberate Arius' doctrinal position from desiccated textbook patrology. A more reserved appraisal is due to the deficient critical foundation of these attempts, as soon as the primary sources giving access to Arius have to be considered. There still exists a vital need for such consideration, and a constant one, which must be urged again and again.

"The Logic of Arianism"

An excellent article has been published under this title by R. D. Williams in the last issue of the *Journal of Theological Studies*.[42] The author examines the logical features of Arius' earliest and most striking theses: his negation of the Son "proper to the Father's substance," his rejection of the Son as a "consubstantial portion" of the Father, his opposition to the doctrine of "two unbegotten." He shows convincingly that the position of Arius, authenticated by many declarations of Arius and others, needs to be interpreted as a philosophical one, and he undertakes "to suggest what kind of philosophical assumptions Arius brings to his theology" (58). For the use of "proper" (*idios*), Williams claims that the best context of Arius' argument is given by Porphyry.

It is well to recall that in 333 Constantine ordered the destruction of Arius' writings and those of his supporters, calling them "Porphyrians." "Perhaps it reflects a recognition that echoes of Porphyrian logic could indeed be caught in Arius' work" (60). Williams points to the discussion of the meaning of *idios* developed in Porphyry's *Isagoge*. "Whether or not Arius has Porphyry directly in mind, it is clear at least that he knows what he means by *idios* and knows that it cannot be applied to a *hypostasis* but only to the defining properties, the eternal and essential attributes, of God" (62).

For the notion of a "consubstantial portion," the best philosophical parallel is also Neoplatonic: "It is worth noting that *meros homoousion* for a component part of a *synthetos* substance is partly paralleled in an important passage of Iamblichus' *de mysteriis*" (III, 21.150.9, p. 128 E. des Places).[64] Cautiously Williams adds: "There is no way of telling whether or not Arius knew Iamblichus' work" (ibid.), but he stresses firm affinities between Arius' notion of "consubstantial" and the Iamblichian

---

[42] *JTS*, n.s. 34 (1983) 56–81.

doctrine (65 f.). A longer analysis devoted to the Arian refusal of *duo agennēta* explicitates a complete and coherent set of other philosophical teachings belonging to the line of theology developed by Arius. His final conclusion, if critical and well balanced, is sympathetic to the Alexandrian priest: "above all, by relentlessly pressing home the logic of treating 'God' as the name of a unique subsistent, he stirred an intellectually careless Church into a ferment of conceptual reconstruction. . . . Theology continues to need its Ariuses" (81).

Thanks to Williams, we have finally encountered in this bulletin the real Arius; at least, we are afforded a glimpse of him. I call him "real" because he is treated seriously in his own way: the way of a scholarly trained philosopher who speaks and writes in a technical language, who presents in his lexical data and his style the rigor of a systematic thinker, who belongs to a definite school of thought. It was the same Arius I had in mind when I communicated in 1981 a few observations about "the logic of the *Thalia* and the *Ennead V.*" [43] Later on I found a signal in the same direction given by R. M. Huebner, *Der Gott der Kirchenväter und der Gott der Bibel: Zur Frage der Hellenisierung des Christentums* (Munich, 1979). Huebner's conjecture and my interpretation of the logical structure of the *Thalia* in the light of Plotinus, and with special mention of Iamblichus, needed more evidence from the philosophical milieu echoed by Arius. Williams' article is an important contribution to such evidence.

On two points this contribution could be easily improved. (1) If Williams would agree with my statement about the *Blasphemies* transmitted in *Syn.* 15 (not from Arius, but from a neo-Arian in the second half of the fourth century), he could observe on pp. 60, 61, 62, 66, 67, 77, and 78 of his article how the quotations from *Syn.* 15 regularly interfere with what he concludes from *C. Ar.* 1, 5–6 or from other early writings of Arius: the phrases and termini read in the *Blasphemies* deepen and strengthen what is said in the other writings, or they introduce a new term, a new image, which needs a special justification. A better knowledge of Arius' immediate philosophical context underlines the need for a stricter determination of Arius' own proposition. (2) The author, especially pp. 73 and 76–77, has a few interesting comments on Athanasius' refutation of Arius and of the early Arians. He succeeds in showing that, in contrast to Arius, the Alexandrian bishop adopts a nontechnical language. He also gives us to understand that behind the preference for a nontechnical style of argumentation Athanasius can nevertheless be aware of the philosophical techniques engaged in the dispute. It would be illuminating, for a more precise comprehension of both Arius and

[43] *Holy Scripture and Hellenistic Hermeneutics* 35–40.

Athanasius, to examine further the logic of the Athanasian *Contra Arianos*.[44]

[44] One of the goals aimed in my forthcoming *Athanase d'Alexandrie évêque et écrivain* is to prepare the way toward a logical analysis of *C. Ar* on the basis of their thematic, lexical and theological analysis.—Let me add here some recent work on Arius and the Arians. Kurt Aland, in *Aufstieg und Niedergang der römischen Welt* (= ANRW 23/1 [1979] 60–241), published the equivalent of a book on the relations between Church and state from the New Testament to the era of Constantine. This study is ignored by Keresztes and Barnes. Aland offers useful insights into what can be reconstructed about Constantine's conversion. See also A. M. Ritter, "Arianismus," *TRE* 3 (1978) 692–719, and A. Solignac, "Marius Victorinus," *DSpir* 10 (1980) 616–23. *Luciferi Calaritani opera quae supersunt*, ed. G. F. Diercks in *CC ser. lat.* 8 (Turnhout: Brepols, 1978; 565 pp.), and *Luciferi Calaritani De regibus apostaticis et Moriendum esse pro Dei Filio*, ed. V. Ugenti in *Studi e testi Latini e Greci* 1 (Lecce: Milella, 1980; 215 pp.), give a completely renewed access to the writings of the most vibrant pro-Nicene resister to Constantius II. The *index verborum* in Diercks counts 180 pages; in Ugenti, 52.

Theological Studies
48 (1987)

THE "ARIAN" CONTROVERSY: SOME CATEGORIES RECONSIDERED

JOSEPH T. LIENHARD, S.J.

Marquette University

E LEMENTARY TEXTBOOKS often paint a clear and dramatic picture of the "Arian" controversy, more or less as follows. Shortly before 318, in Alexandria, Arius began to preach that the Son of God is a creature. In 318 a synod convoked by the bishop, Alexander of Alexandria, condemned Arius' teaching. Arius then withdrew to Asia Minor, where he won many converts to his doctrines, especially from among the *Sylloukianistai*, his fellow pupils of the martyr Lucian of Antioch. In 325 the Council of Nicaea decisively rejected Arianism and proclaimed the orthodox doctrine in its creed and particularly in the renowned word *homoousion*. But the majority of Eastern bishops continued to adhere to the Arian heresy in subtler and subtler forms; and Arianizing emperors, especially Constantius, conspired with these bishops to force Arius' heresy on the whole Church. At first, resistance to Arianism came almost singlehandedly from Athanasius of Alexandria, who, despite persecution and exile, indefatigably defended Nicene orthodoxy. The year 360 marked the nadir: "The whole world groaned and marveled that it was Arian," wrote Jerome.[1] Constantius' death in 361 was a turning point. The three Cappadocian Fathers received the baton of orthodoxy from Athanasius and continued the defense of the Nicene doctrine. The ascendancy of Arianism was definitively ended by the Council of Constantinople in 381, and orthodoxy triumphed.

But in order to present so clear a picture, several problems and inconsistencies must be glossed over. It is hard, for example, to explain how Arius could have found such quick and enthusiastic acceptance in Syria and Asia Minor if his doctrine were new and strange. And then, the Eastern bishops refused, in fact, to be called "Arians" and in their creeds regularly anathematized typically "Arian" doctrines such as that the Son was created out of nothing, or that he is from a different

---

EDITOR'S NOTE.—This article is based on a *Habilitationsschrift* entitled *Contra Marcellum: The Influence of Marcellus of Ancyra on Fourth-Century Greek Theology* accepted by the Faculty of Theology of the University of Freiburg i. Br. in 1986. Much of the research was done in Freiburg in 1984 under a fellowship from the Alexander von Humboldt-Stiftung, Bonn.

[1] Jerome, *Altercatio Luciferiani et orthodoxi* 19 (PL 23 [1883] 181B): "Ingemuit totus orbis, et Arianum se esse miratus est."

415

hypostasis than the Father, or that there was a time or an age when he did not exist. And finally, for 30 or more years after 325, the Council of Nicaea is hardly mentioned and the word *homoousion* rarely used.[2]

Some of these problems and inconsistencies can be explained by the fact that older research depended heavily on Athanasius as its source. The 19th century lionized Athanasius and made his career appear even more glorious than it was.[3] This prejudice is understandable. Athanasius' works supply the fullest documentation available for the history of the controversy but—not surprisingly—are written from his point of view. When the controversy is seen from another point of view—Marcellus of Ancyra's, for example, or that of other bishops and theologians in Asia Minor, Syria, or Palestine—a distinctly different picture develops. In particular, Athanasius characterizes almost all his opponents as "Arians." But this category may well be a poor starting point for understanding the era and the issues at stake.

The choice of categories to designate the two opposing sides in the fourth-century theological controversy is crucially important, for the categories color the whole interpretation of the controversy. Some of the categories used in the past are less than satisfactory. The pair "Arian" and "Nicene" is anachronistic, and perhaps too dogmatic. "Antiochene" and "Alexandrian" are misleading. "Eusebian" for one side is, historically, fairly accurate, but lacks a usable counterpart. After examining these categories more closely, I will suggest a pair of more strictly theological categories.

INADEQUATE CATEGORIES

Perhaps the commonest categories for the two conflicting parties in the controversy are "Arian" and "Nicene." There is hardly any other name in use for the fourth-century theological conflict than "the Arian controversy." But Adolf Martin Ritter, in a recent article on Arianism,[4] draws some conclusions from modern studies of the early fourth century

---

[2] These points are documented below.

[3] See, e.g., J. A. Möhler, *Athanasius der Grosse* (Mainz: Kupferberg, 1827), and J. H. Newman, *Arians of the Fourth Century* (London: Rivington, 1833). A reaction set in in the 20th century; it is especially clear in the work of Eduard Schwartz (collected in his *Gesammelte Schriften* 3: *Zur Geschichte des Athanasius* [Berlin: de Gruyter, 1959]), who saw Athanasius primarily as a self-interested political operative, and more recently in R. Klein (*Constantius II. und die christliche Kirche* [Darmstadt: Wissenschaftliche Buchgesellschaft, 1977]), who tried to portray Constantius II as a wise and patient monarch and Athanasius as a scoundrel.

[4] A. M. Ritter, "Arianismus," *TRE* 3 (1978) 692–719, at 693. See also the articles and useful bibliography in R. C. Gregg, ed., *Arianism: Historical and Theological Reassessments* (Cambridge, Mass.: Philadelphia Patristic Foundation, 1985), e.g. J. N. Steenson, "Basil of Ancyra on the Meaning of Homoousios," ibid. 267–79, esp. 277 n. 2.

and says that the theology usually called "Arian" should continue to be called that only under three conditions. One must recognize, he writes, firstly, that Arius' own role in the "Arian controversies" was comparatively small; secondly, that fourth-century polemicists made vastly excessive use of the name "Arian" without doing justice to the motives and intentions of those so labeled; and thirdly, that "Arianism" was not merely a conceptual category; it can be understood only in its historical situation.

The term "Arian" seems to have been Athanasius' own coinage and his favored appellation for his opponents (unless he could call them "Ariomaniacs"). Apparently it was only in 341, however, that the Eastern bishops learned that they were being called "Arians." In that year Julius of Rome sent the Eastern bishops a letter that is crucial for understanding how the two opposing parties were formed and defined, and for understanding that the opponents became aware of themselves as parties only around 341 and not earlier.[5]

In 340 a deputation from the East went to Rome to explain the Easterners' case against Athanasius, Marcellus of Ancyra, and others and to urge Julius to recognize Pistus as the legitimate bishop of Alexandria. Marcellus, Athanasius, and Asclepas of Gaza, all of them deposed, also traveled to Rome, presumably hoping for vindication. Julius took the occasion to summon a synod that would retry the cases of Athanasius and Marcellus and wrote to the Eastern bishops inviting them to attend. The Eastern bishops refused to come, on the ground that the decisions of one council (Tyre, in 335, which had deposed Athanasius) could not be reversed by another. Julius, however, persisted in holding a synod, which upheld the orthodoxy and innocence of Athanasius, Marcellus, and others; and Julius received them into communion. He then wrote the letter already mentioned to the Easterners to explain these actions. In the course of his letter Julius defined and clearly named two opposing parties: they were "the Eusebians" (*hoi peri Eusebion*) and "the Athanasians" (*hoi peri Athanasion*). ("Eusebius" was Eusebius of Nicomedia; Eusebius of Caesarea was already dead.) Further, Julius portentously identified the Eusebians as "Arians," and he linked Athanasius' name with Marcellus of Ancyra's, thus implying that there were two opposing parties. The source of Julius' knowledge of the Easterners' dispute was undoubtedly Athanasius and Marcellus. His reason for calling the Eastern bishops Arians, however, was not their doctrine but the fact that

[5] Athanasius preserved the letter in his *Apologia contra Arianos* 21–35 (Engl. tr. in NPNF 2/4, 111–19). The letter describes the course of events here summarized. L. W. Barnard's analysis ("Pope Julius, Marcellus of Ancyra and the Council of Sardica: A Reconsideration," *RTAM* 38 [1971] 69–79) is unsatisfactory.

they favored Pistus, who had been excommunicated by Alexander of Alexandria and then been ordained by a bishop favorable to Arius.

The Eastern bishops reacted with shock and indignation at being called "Arians." Meeting in council in the summer of 341 for the dedication of a church in Antioch, they answered Julius' letter. The so-called "First Creed of Antioch" is an excerpt from the letter that the Eastern bishops sent to Julius as an example of the "faith handed down from the beginning." In the sentence that introduces the creed, they express their indignation:

We have not been followers of Arius. For how could we, as bishops, follow a presbyter? Nor did we receive any other faith except the one handed down from the beginning. We ourselves were the testers and examiners of his [i.e., Arius'] faith. We admitted him; we did not follow him.[6]

Julius' accusation clearly surprised the Eusebians and cut them to the quick, all the more so because they had decided in Jerusalem in 335 to receive Arius back into communion, and would have done so in Constantinople in 336 had he not died shortly before.[7]

Similarly, the theology of those who opposed the "Arians" (to retain the term for the moment) was not explicitly Nicene. The Council of Nicaea did not enjoy any unique authority until several decades after it was held. Writers in the two or three decades after Nicaea make no appeal to its creed as uniquely authoritative or to the term *homoousion* as a touchstone of orthodoxy.[8] Its greatest influence, curiously, was apparently a negative one: more than a few creeds and authors accepted its anathemas as an adequate definition of the heresy to be rejected and

[6] Text in A. Hahn, *Bibliothek der Symbole und Glaubensregeln der alten Kirche* (3rd ed.; Breslau: Morgenstern, 1897; repr. Hildesheim: Olms, 1962) #153. Eduard Schwartz recognized the provenance of the "First Creed"; see his *Gesammelte Schriften* 3, 311–12, and J. N. D. Kelly, *Early Christian Creeds* (3rd ed.; London, Longman, 1972) 264–66.

[7] On the last days of Arius, see Athanasius, *De synodis* 21, 2–7; Socrates, *Hist. eccl.* 1, 28; Sozomen, *Hist. eccl.* 2, 27; 13–14; Theodoret, *Hist. eccl.* 1, 13; Epiphanius, *Panarion* 68, 7; Gregory of Nazianzus, *Oration* 21, 13.

[8] See H.-J. Sieben, *Die Konzilsidee der alten Kirche* (Paderborn: Schöningh, 1979). E.g., when Athansius mentioned the Council of Nicaea in *Orationes contra Arianos* 1, 6, which Sieben dates in 339, the Council was not, for Athanasius, an authority in the sense of a positive norm for faith (p. 29). Athanasius first defended the word *homoousion* in *De decretis* 20, composed between 345 and 355 (p. 37). In *De synodis*, written in 359, the authority is not a fixed formula but the acceptance of a tradition as such, i.e. the Fathers together (pp. 51–52). Only in the *Epistula ad Iouianum imperatorem* (363) is Nicaea correct for Athanasius not only because it is apostolic but also because it is the universal, ecumenical faith and hence the divine faith of the Church catholic (p. 53).

regularly quote them as an assurance of their own orthodoxy.[9]

Other authors have tried to explain the conflict with the categories "Alexandrian" and "Antiochene." It is true that some of the "Arians" were, or may have been, pupils of Lucian of Antioch,[10] and that some of its adherents lived in Syria. But these terms risk implying an intellectual bridge between Lucian of Antioch and his disciples on the one hand, and the later Christology of Diodore of Tarsus, Theodore of Mopsuestia, and Nestorius on the other.[11] The roots of dyoprosopic Christology are not in Lucian and the circle around the two Eusebii; if anything, this Christology is foreshadowed in Eustathius of Antioch and Marcellus of Ancyra. Cyril of Alexandria, for the other side, wanted to believe that he drew his terms from Athanasius; but, as is well known, one of his key formulas came from Apollinaris of Laodicea.[12] The relationship between theological speculation in the early fourth century and the Christological controversy of the fifth century is complex and unclear; and to try to interpret the first period by later categories does neither a service.

As a historical phenomenon, it would be most accurate to call the "Arian" theology "Eusebian," understood as a way of thought shared and fostered by Eusebius of Caesarea and Eusebius of Nicomedia, among others. Marcellus of Ancyra, for example, traces his opponent Asterius' intellectual lineage through Paulinus of Tyre back to Eusebius of Nico-

[9] See, e.g., Eusebius of Caesarea, *De ecclesiastica theologia* 1, 9, 6; the anathemas of the second and fourth creeds of Antioch (341; Hahn, *Bibliothek* #154, 156; and Kelly, *Creeds* 268–73); the *Ekthesis makrostichos* or Creed of the Long Lines (344; Hahn, *Bibliothek* #159); the first creed of Sirmium, 351 (ibid. #160, and Kelly, *Creeds* 281–82); and Ps.-Athanasius, *Fourth Oration against the Arians* 25.

[10] The famous word *Sylloukianistai* is used only once, in a letter that Arius wrote to Eusebius of Nicomedia ca. 318; text in Athanasius, *Werke* 3: *Urkunden zur Geschichte des arianischen Streites, 318–328*, ed. H.-G. Opitz (Berlin: de Gruyter, 1935), Urkunde 1.

[11] Robert Grant, in a review of D. S. Wallace-Hadrill's *Christian Antioch: A Study of Early Christian Thought in the East* (Cambridge, 1982), quotes a sentence in which Wallace-Hadrill says that one of the strongest branches of Alexandrian Origenism was associated with Antioch. At that point Grant asks: "Does the traditional geographical classification need revision or even rejection?" Grant seems to think it may need rejection; "It may be," he writes, "that the basic scheme arises out of classifications helpful only to partisans, students, and teachers." The review is in *Church History* 52 (1983) 494–95. A. M. Ritter, in an excellent survey ("Dogma und Lehre in der alten Kirche," in *Handbuch der Dogmen- und Theologiegeschichte* 1: *Die Lehrentwicklung im Rahmen der Katholizität*, ed. C. Andersen et al. [Göttingen: Vandenhoeck & Ruprecht, 1982] 99–283, at 146), also rejects the categories "Alexandrian" and "Antiochene" as historically inaccurate and misleading. But Ritter uses the term "Origenist" a little too freely.

[12] The phrase is *mia physis tou theou logou sesarkōmenē*; see A. Grillmeier, *Christ in Christian Tradition* 1 (2nd ed.; Atlanta: John Knox, 1975) 473–83, especially 481–82. On dyoprosopic Christology see also A. L. Pettersen, "The Questioning Jesus in Athanasius' Contra Arianos 3," in Gregg, *Arianism* 243–55.

media.[13] All of the elements of this theology are already present in
Eusebius of Caesarea's two great apologetic works, the *Praeparatio euangelica* and the *Demonstratio euangelica*. The Eusebian theology has
been called "Origenist." There is some truth in this, but it may obscure
Origen's broad and deep influence on all of Eastern theology. Finally,
there is no usable counterpart to the category "Eusebian"; "Athanasian"
would be anachronistic.

TWO THEOLOGICAL TRADITIONS

The conflict in the fourth century was one between two theological
traditions, both of which were well established by the beginning of the
century, but neither of which proved adequate to answer the theological
problems raised in the second and third decades of that century.

The crisis of 318 was part of a larger movement: a movement from the
rule of faith to theology, from the language of confession to the language
of reflection, from belief to speculation on what was believed. The rule
of faith and the *lex orandi* were clear and accepted by all. For centuries
Christians had believed in one God, the Father, and in His Son Jesus
Christ, and in the Holy Spirit. They had prayed to God the Father
through His Son Jesus Christ, their Lord. And they had baptized in the
name of the Father, and of the Son, and of the Holy Spirit. Christians
of the early fourth century looked at the Christ of the Gospels and saw
one who was so much more than a man, and yet not identical with God
the Father. Characteristically, the Fathers of the early fourth century
can readily quote credal statements, but cannot so readily explain them.
Since Origen, no great theologian had come along to explain the faith in
the language of reflection and speculation. Furthermore, Christians in
the first two decades of the fourth century had had to concern themselves
first of all with survival, in the face of what was perhaps the only
systematic attempt ever, on the part of the Roman government, to destroy
the Christian Church. In many ways the questions brought suddenly to
the fore in 318 caught the Church unawares.

There was general agreement on some fundamental theological principles. All Christians were monotheists: there was, and could be, only
one God. All Christians rejected psilanthropism: to say that Jesus the
Christ was simply a human being, and only a human being, in no way
adequately explained him or came close to exhausting his meaning. All
Christians agreed that Christ had brought salvation to the human race,

---

[13] Eusebius of Nicomedia, Marcellus says, was Paulinus of Tyre's teacher, and Paulinus
was Asterius' patron. See Marcellus, frag. 87, in Eusebius of Caesarea, *Gegen Marcell. Über
die kirchliche Theologie. Die Fragmente Marcells*, ed. E. Klostermann, 2nd ed. by G. C.
Hansen (GCS Eusebius 4; Berlin: Akademie, 1972).

although they hardly agreed on how that salvation had taken place. Finally, all Christians agreed on the authority of the Scriptures, which were God's word; read rightly, they revealed all that Christians needed to know about God and His relation to the world.

Disagreement came when theologians tried to express, in the language of speculation, how Christian monotheism and the doctrine of Christ's deity could be reconciled. Specifically, they had to search for a way of expressing what was singular and what was plural in God.

Greek-speaking theologians of the early fourth century had three words for something that really exists, and exists in itself, as distinguished from an accident or a quality. The words are *ousia*, *hypostasis*, and *hyparxis*; the corresponding verbs are *einai*, *hyphistasthai* and *hyparchein*. Despite the complex, later development of a distinction between *ousia* and *hypostasis*, the two words were, in the early fourth century, first and foremost synonyms.[14] Nevertheless, subtle distinctions began to emerge. *Hyparxis* never achieved the status of a technical term. Before 325 Eusebius of Caesarea and Narcissus of Neronias were willing to speak of two *ousiai* in the Godhead. After 325 this usage disappears. The Eusebians' most characteristic phrase for what is plural in God is "two *hypostaseis*."

Athanasius, Marcellus, and the Westerners insisted just as vigorously that the divine *hypostasis*, the reality of God, is singular. As the fourth century progressed, *hypostasis* became, more and more, the one term that was the center of controversy. The Creed of Nicaea anathematized anyone who said that the Son of God is "of a different *hypostasis* or substance (*ousia*) than the Father." The Second Creed of Antioch, promulgated in 341 by the Easterners at the Dedication Council after they had received Julius of Rome's letter, insisted belligerently that Father, Son, and Holy Spirit are "three in *hypostasis*, one in agreement (*symphōnia*)."[15] The doctrinal statement of the Western Council of Sardica (342 or 343), in which Athanasius and Marcellus participated, insisted even more belligerently that "We have received and been taught, and we hold this catholic and apostolic tradition and faith and confession: there is one *hypostasis* (which is termed "essence" [*ousia*] by the heretics) of the Father, the Son, and the Holy Spirit."[16] In 362 a synod that

[14] See further G. L. Prestige, *God in Patristic Thought* (2nd ed.; London: S.P.C.K., 1952) esp. 179–96.

[15] Hahn, *Bibliothek* #154; Kelly, *Creeds* 268–70.

[16] Hahn, *Bibliothek* #157. See also M. Tetz, "Ante omnia de sancta fide et de integritate veritatis: Glaubensfragen auf der Synode von Serdika (342)," *ZNTW* 76 (1985) 243–69, who has a new critical edition of the text, and a commentary; and I. Opelt, "I dissidenti del Concilio di Serdica," *Augustinianum* 25 (1985) 783–91.

Athanasius convoked in Alexandria marked the first time that he admitted that the phrase "three *hypostaseis*" might be understood of God in an orthodox way, although he still preferred "one *hypostasis*."[17] Marcellus and the clergy who remained faithful to him wrote to Athanasius ca. 371 and asked him to approve their doctrine. They had given up all of Marcellus' distinctive beliefs but held tenaciously to the doctrine of one divine *hypostasis*.[18] But the Synod of Alexandria had little immediate effect. Gregory of Nazianzus could still say, ca. 380, that the Westerners suspect Arianism whenever they hear "three *hypostaseis*."[19]

Hence the way of using the word *hypostasis* characterized the two opposing parties for much of the fourth century; one preferred to speak of one *hypostasis* in God, the other of two (or three, if the Holy Spirit is considered). I suggest calling the two conflicting theological systems "miahypostatic" and "dyohypostatic" theology, the theology of one *hypostasis* and of two *hypostaseis* respectively. These terms signal a profound difference in theology, one that touched not only the way God—Father, Son, and Holy Spirit—was understood, but also the way Christ's person and saving work were described.

DYOHYPOSTATIC THEOLOGY

As a coherent system, dyohypostatic theology can be described in a typical or ideal form. No one author mentions all of the following characteristics (although Eusebius of Caesarea comes close). But it is a fair description of a type of theology found in many authors.

There is one God, who is the *archē*—the beginning, the first principle, the ultimate source, and the cause of everything else that exists. He is eternal and underived, and utterly transcendent, even unknowable, best described by the *via negativa*: as *anarchos* (without source), *agen(n)ētos* (unoriginate or unbegotten), *akatalēptos* (incomprehensible). This God, the Father, and only He, is God in the truest and fullest sense of the word.

Besides the Father, there also exists another *hypostasis*, which Scripture calls Son, Word, Image, Wisdom, Power, and "the firstborn of all creation" (Col 1:15). The Son of God holds a rank somewhere beneath

[17] The *Tome to the Antiochenes* (PG 26, 796-809; Engl. tr. in NPNF 2/4, 483-86). See M. Tetz, "Über nikäische Orthodoxie: Der sog. Tomus ad Antiochenos des Athanasios von Alexandrien," *ZNTW* 66 (1975) 194-222; and L. Abramowski, "Trinitarische und christologische Hypostasenformeln," *ThPh* 54 (1979) 38-49, who also analyzes the *Tomus ad Antiochenos*.

[18] Eugenius of Ancyra, *Expositio fidei ad Athanasium*, critical ed. and analysis by M. Tetz, "Markellianer und Athanasios von Alexandrien: Die markellianische Expositio fidei ad Athanasium des Diakons Eugenios von Ankyra," *ZKG* 64 (1973) 75-121.

[19] *Oration* 21, 35; Engl. tr. in NPNF 2/8, 279.

God but above all creatures, or all other creatures. This tradition does not make any clear distinction between "begetting" and "creating." The decisive point is that the Father is the source of the Son's being; the Son depends on the Father for his being. Collectively, the tradition is wary of materialistic thinking and strives to avoid language that might suggest that the Father's essence is divided to produce the Son, or that the Son is an effluence of, or an emanation from, the Father.

The Son's relationship of dependence excludes predicating "eternity" of the Son. He may be said to have been begotten "before all ages," outside of time, since time too is one of the creatures that came to be through him; but if he were truly eternal, he would be a second first principle.

The Son is naturally and obviously subordinate to the Father. Scripture affirms this when it has the Son say, "The Father is greater than I" (Jn 14:28). And reason confirms it, since a first principle or source (*archē*) is superior to what derives from it. Hence the passages of the Old and New Testaments that imply the Son's subordination to the Father pose no problem for the dyohypostatic tradition.

The Son's principal function is that of a mediator; Scripture calls him the "mediator between God and men" (1 Tim 2:5). As mediator, he is the instrument through which God created the universe: Scripture distinguishes the Father, "from whom are all things," from the Son, "through whom are all things," and says of the Son, "all things were made through him" (1 Cor 8:6; Jn 1:3).

As mediator, the Son is also revealer and teacher. The dyohypostatic tradition often attributes the Old Testament theophanies to the Son: the Son walked in the garden in the cool of the evening, wrestled with Jacob, appeared in the burning bush, gave the law to Moses, and spoke through the prophets. In particular, the Son reveals God because he is "the image of the invisible God" (Col 1:15).[20]

The incarnate Son is Savior of the human race, principally by fully revealing God the Father, teaching the fulness of truth, and being a model of virtue. He cannot save the human race by divinizing it or uniting it to the divine nature, because he is not divine in the fullest sense of the word. At a moment in history that God determined, the Son took flesh from the Virgin Mary. But the Incarnation was not a radically new state of the Son's existence; the Son was temporarily incarnate when he wrestled with Jacob.[21] The incarnate Christ simply continues his work as revealer, teacher, and model. His human flesh has no new personality

---

[20] See further R. P. C. Hanson, "The Arian Doctrine of the Incarnation," in Gregg, *Arianism* 181–211.

[21] First Creed of Sirmium, anathema 16 (Hahn, *Bibliothek* #160).

or will; the Son in his human flesh continues in perfect harmony of will with the Father, just as he was before he assumed this flesh. His suffering and death on the cross are a model of patience and selflessness.

Put another way, salvation takes place in the order of will;[22] it is not a new state, but an offer of knowledge. The Son reveals the truth and is a model of a God-pleasing life; Christians are saved when they accept the truth and live it. Neither the Incarnation nor the cross and resurrection brought about, of themselves, any ontological change in the human condition. There is no assumption of the human race by the Godhead, no deification of human beings without their co-operation. But with the help of the truth that Christ revealed, and by following his example, the way that leads to salvation can be freely chosen.

The dyohypostatic theology has obvious strengths and weaknesses. It easily accounts for the distinction between the Christ of the Gospels and his divine Father. Further, it offers a good explanation for the many passages in the New Testament that imply the Son's subordination to the Father. Finally, it gives full play to human freedom in the process of salvation.

But this theology also has serious shortcomings. Its chief flaw is its inability to provide a satisfactory account of monotheism. Eusebius of Caesarea's suggestion that the Son is God but not the "only true God"[23] is only the most awkward of the explanations; the others do not differ essentially from it. The dyohypostatic theology cannot avoid positing a second, lower-ranking God. Then too, this theology offers a concept of salvation that is really no more than moralism.[24] The help that Jesus offers is ultimately no more than his teaching and his inspiration.

These authors think habitually, or prereflectively, in terms of the Greek notion of the great chain of being, a way of thinking or conceiving all that exists by situating each existent somewhere on a scale or in an order, with God Himself at the top and brute matter at the bottom.[25] They do not make any clear distinction between the uncreated and the created as the two primary or ultimate categories of being.

This habitual thinking in terms of the great chain of being explains

[22] Seen clearly by R. C. Gregg and D. E. Groh, *Early Arianism—A View of Salvation* (Philadelphia: Fortress, 1981). See also iidem, "The Centrality of Soteriology in Early Arianism," *ATR* 59 (1977) 260–75, and B. Studer, *Gott und unsere Erlösung im Glauben der alten Kirche* (Düsseldorf: Patmos, 1985).

[23] Opitz, Urkunde 3. The phrase "true God from true God" in the Creed of Nicaea refutes this view.

[24] E. P. Meijering, in his review of Gregg and Groh, *Early Arianism*, asks: "Can a doctrine which advocates the imitation of the perfect creature Christ be called a doctrine of *salvation*? Is this not moralism?" (emphasis his). The review is in *VC* 36 (1982) 67–68.

[25] See A. O. Lovejoy, *The Great Chain of Being* (Cambridge, Mass.: Harvard Univ., 1936).

the ease with which some of the Eusebians call the Son "God," while others call him "a creature." The significant point is not the distinction between these two terms, but the fact that the Son ranks below God but above all the rest of creation.

This dyohypostatic theology has obvious similarities to Middle Platonic cosmology, especially Numenius'.[26] This is clear also because there is little room for the Holy Spirit. The Holy Spirit is mentioned in the rule of faith, but hardly plays a role in reflection or speculation.

MIAHYPOSTATIC THEOLOGY

The miahypostatic tradition can also be described in a typical or ideal form. The miahypostatic theology takes strict Christian monotheism as its point of departure. There is one God. This one God is one real existent: one *hypostasis*, one *ousia*, and (in some authors) one *prosōpon*.

This one God utters a Word, or begets a Son, and sends forth His Holy Spirit. The miahypostatic tradition does not hesitate to take over these names from the rule of faith, and willingly confesses faith in the Father, the Son, and the Holy Spirit. It does, however, at least in its earlier stages, have difficulty explaining, in speculative language, the essence or nature of the Word and the Spirit. It hesitates to assign any plurality to the Godhead, and hence insists on the expression "one *hypostasis*." In general, in speaking of God, saying "one" is always safe, whereas saying "two" is always dangerous. Plurality is rather located in the Incarnate.

The Son, for the miahypostatic tradition, is God in the same way that the Father is: *homoousion tō patri*, although its representatives seldom appeal to the Creed of Nicaea until several decades after the Council.

The Incarnation is the decisive moment in the history of salvation and marks a new stage in the history of the Logos. At the Incarnation God Himself is united with a human nature and thereby with human nature itself. This tradition conceives of human nature as a collectivity, so that, when the Word assumed *ho anthrōpos*, he also assumed—and thereby elevated—*hē anthrōpotēs*.

The miahypostatic theology applied to the incarnate Christ, or even to Christ's flesh, all the biblical texts that suggested the Son's subordination to the Father. It is the Incarnate, as man, who says, "The Father is greater than I" (Jn 14:28), or who knows neither the day nor the hour (Mk 13:32). In principle, at least, this gave these authors an opportunity

[26] See J. Dillon, *The Middle Platonists: 80 B.C. to A.D. 220* (Ithaca: Cornell Univ., 1977) 361–79, and the articles of F. Ricken noted below.

to reflect on Christ's human soul or mind.[27]

Salvation, in this tradition, is essentially a divine act by which the human race is elevated and deified. Salvation takes place in the order of being: God acts, and thereby the human race is saved. Athanasius expressed this in his famous axiom, "God became man so that man might become divine."[28]

Marcellus of Ancyra[29] held a distinctive form of the miahypostatic theology, and several points distinguish his thought from the general outline just sketched. He propounded a radical monotheism. God is one *ousia*, one *hypostasis*, and one *prosōpon*. *Ousia* and *hypostasis* mean "being" or "existent." *Prosōpon* means "source of action," and especially of rational discourse. The term that Marcellus preferred for God was the third, *prosōpon*. God had to be one *prosōpon*, because Marcellus could not conceive of two "I"s in the Godhead; *hypostasis* means the reality behind the *prosōpon*.

The Word, as God's *dynamis* or power, is eternal; when God speaks, then His Word became an active power. The only title that is proper to the Preincarnate is "Word"; all other titles are titles of the incarnate Christ. The Word "goes forth" from the Father; "begetting" is better reserved for the Virgin's conceiving. The Holy Spirit proceeds from the Father and receives His mission through the Son.

God's activity appears to expand the *monas* or unity into a triad; but the *monas* is indivisible in *dynamis*, that is, indivisible into two or three distinct subjects; and the nature of the expansion is left unexplained, except that it is in *energeia monē*.

When Marcellus writes abstractly of Christ's humanity, he calls it *sarx*; but when he thinks of it functionally or soteriologically, he calls it *anthrōpos*.

When writing of the Savior's work (and "Savior" is the title he prefers for the Incarnate), he does not distinguish between Christ's human nature and human nature in general and thus grounds his doctrine of deification. Marcellus taught that when the Word assumed *ho anthrōpos*, it assumed not only an individual man but the whole human race, and the latter

[27] Marcellus of Ancyra began such reflection when he wrote that Jesus' words in the Garden of Olives indicated an *asymphōnia* between him and the Father. See below; and cf. G. C. Stead, "The Scriptures and the Soul of Christ in Athanasius," VC 36 (1982) 233–50, and R. Lorenz, "Die Christusseele im arianischen Streit: Nebst einigen Bemerkungen zur Quellenkritik des Arius und zur Glaubwürdigkeit des Athanasius," ZKG 94 (1983) 1–51.

[28] De inc. Verbi 54; cf. C. R. Strange, "Athanasius on Divinization," StPatr 16/2 (= TU 129; Berlin: Akademie, 1985) 342–46.

[29] What follows is the result of a study of the extant fragments of Marcellus' Contra Asterium. See also J. T. Lienhard, "Marcellus of Ancyra in Modern Research," TS 43 (1982) 486–503, for a survey of the literature on Marcellus.

precisely as sinful and deceived.

Marcellus also sees the need for a human soul or mind in Christ. Asterius had explained that Jn 10:30 ("I and the Father are one") signified their "perfect harmony of will in every word and deed." But Marcellus points out that Mt 26:39 ("not as I will, but as you will") demonstrates that their wills were not always in harmony; hence Christ had a distinct center of consciousness.[30]

With careful attention to 1 Cor 15:24–28, Marcellus teaches that Christ's partial kingdom will, at the end of time, be absorbed into God's whole kingdom.[31] Even when he wrote the *Contra Asterium*, however, he admitted a problem with this theory, namely, his inability to explain what would happen to Christ's flesh at the consummation of time.

Manuals often take Marcellus' doctrine of God as a Monad that temporarily expands into a Triad as the most typical element of his theology. But these terms are not frequent in the extant fragments of the *Contra Asterium*. Marcellus' speculation is rather dominated by a full and emphatic account of Christian monotheism but lacks a term, or a place, for the hypostatic existence of the (preincarnate) Word and the Spirit. He can call God a Triad but cannot say what is triadic in God. On the other hand, he distinguished clearly between the preincarnate Word and the incarnate Christ, and had the rudiments of a Christology that gives an adequate place to Christ's complete human nature.

At least potentially, the miahypostatic tradition recognizes that the first and most important distinction among existents is that between the uncreated and the created. The uncreated is divine and eternal, the created is finite and temporal. No series of steps, no great chain of being, can bridge the gap between God and creatures. The only possible bridge is a free act of God's, the act of creating. Further, while both the Word and creatures have their source in God, the way they proceed from the source is radically different. The Son is begotten, that is, he comes from God's essence. Creatures are made; they come from God's will.

THE TWO TRADITIONS COMPARED

When the two traditions are compared, their strengths and weaknesses, measured against the later, orthodox resolution, become clear.

---

[30] Frag. 73. Grillmeier (*Christ in Christian Tradition* 285–86) writes: "We can hardly be wrong in seeing the assertion of 'two wills' in Christ as a contrast to the Arian doctrine of the mutable will of the Logos which marks him out as a creature.... This is a new step of Marcellus in Christology.... This already seems to introduce a Word-man Christology." See also frag. 74, in which Marcellus also attributes disharmony of will to the flesh that the Word assumed.

[31] See J. T. Lienhard, "The Exegesis of 1 Cor 15, 24–28 from Marcellus of Ancyra to Theodoret of Cyrus," *VC* 37 (1983) 340–59.

428   THEOLOGICAL STUDIES

Speaking of one *hypostasis* makes the defense of Christian monotheism easy, but allows little room for an explanation of the Trinity that sees plurality in the Godhead itself and not simply in God's activity or in the *oikonomia*. The language of two or three *hypostaseis* allows for a clear explanation of biblical Trinitarianism, but makes it difficult to maintain consequential monotheism and, at least in the fourth century, falls almost by necessity into the Platonic, subordinationist pattern of the great chain of being.

In Christology the dyohypostatic tradition, which already sees the Son as naturally subordinate, the lesser *hypostasis* who, as God's instrument, reveals the transcendent God and is the mediator between God and the world, sees the Son as active, in this role, from the moment of creation on through all the revelations and theophanies of the Old Testament and continuing, in a natural progression, into the Incarnation. The mediator is naturally instrument, revealer, teacher, and model. There is no need to postulate a finite, human mind in Christ; the Son is always in *symphōnia*, harmony of will, with the Father. The miahypostatic tradition, in contrast, sees the Incarnation as a radically new stage in the existence of the God the Logos. Because the Logos is God, the Incarnation is a profound, new mystery.

There is little speculation on Christ's human soul in the early fourth century; but what there is begins on the side of the miahypostatic tradition, particularly in Eustathius of Antioch and Marcellus of Ancyra. It is striking that Marcellus of Ancyra accuses Eusebius of Caesarea of psilanthropism for saying that Christ is the "one mediator between God and men" (1 Tim 2:5) and Eusebius accuses Marcellus of psilanthropism for saying that Christ had a human soul or mind.[32]

But the doctrine on which the two traditions may best be tested is the doctrine of salvation. In a sense, salvation is the most basic of all religious concepts. Every religious system offers some kind of salvation. Each presupposes that there is a gap or a rift between the human and the divine, and offers to close or heal it. The doctrine of salvation finally answers the simple but honest question, "What's in this for me?"

It would be simplistic and unfair to say that the dyohypostatic tradition is cosmological and the miahypostatic soteriological. Both are reflections on the saving event in Christ. Neither is adequate in itself. The two types of theology may be reducible to two ways of conceiving salvation—or

---

[32] Marcellus, frags. 100–102; Eusebius, *De eccl. theol.* 1, 20, 43, and 45. On Eustathius see Grillmeier, *Christ in Christian Tradition* 296–301; further R. V. Sellers, *Eustathius of Antioch and His Place in the Early History of Doctrine* (Cambridge, Eng.: University Press, 1928); H. Chadwick, "The Fall of Eustathius of Antioch," *JTS* 49 (1948) 27–35; and R. P. C. Hanson, "The Fate of Eustathius of Antioch," *ZKG* 95 (1984) 171–79.

rather, to two different ways of interpreting what the New Testament says about Christ's saving work. Salvation has both a divine element and a human element; no Christian would deny that. It is God who offers salvation and man who in some sense co-operates with God, at least by receiving the gift of salvation. The miahypostatic theology concentrates on God's action. It interprets salvation as a gift from above, a change in the order of things effected by God's decree, or, in a classic term of Greek theology, as deification. God acts to unite humanity to Himself and thereby save it. The dyohypostatic theology concentrates on the human response. It reserves a place for man's free acceptance of God's offer of salvation and therefore for his free choice. God's offer is seen as revelation, teaching, and example.

As already stated, the dyohypostatic tradition sees salvation in the order of will: Christ is essentially a revealer and teacher. The advantage of such a view is that it better preserves human freedom; the disadvantage is that it can lapse into mere moralism. The miahypostatic tradition sees salvation in the order of being: God acts definitively in Christ to save fallen man. Such a view runs the risk of making salvation part of a process in which man is passive; but it preserves the unique moment of God's gracious and effective love of His sinful creatures.

The question of the sources of these two traditions is difficult, if not insoluble. To say that one tradition is Origenist is not particularly helpful, and might be misleading; Marcellus too can quote Origen in his own defense.[33] Friedrich Loofs tried to distinguish a theology that arose in Asia Minor or Antioch, which was biblical and historical, and found in Irenaeus of Lyons, for example, from a theology that is typical of Alexandria, and that was speculative and philosophical, and found, for example, in Justin Martyr and Origen.[34] But the alliance of Eusebius of Caesarea, the admirer of Origen and pupil of Pamphilus, with Arius, the pupil of Lucian of Antioch, makes these categories practically useless.

The majority of bishops in Asia Minor and Syria were sympathetic to the dyohypostatic tradition. Athanasius, Marcellus, and the Westerners represent the miahypostatic tradition. Westerners, especially Romans, are probably rightly said to have held on to the spirit of the monarchian theology of the late second and early third centuries and thereby virtually to have ignored Tertullian.

But in the last analysis the search for sources may be fruitless. Perhaps

---

[33] Frags. 39, 86. On Arius' relation to Origen, see R. Lorenz, *Arius Judaizans? Untersuchungen zur dogmengeschichtlichen Einordnung des Arius* (Göttingen: Vandenhoeck & Ruprecht, 1980).

[34] See, e.g., his *Leitfaden zum Studium der Dogmengeschichte*, ed. K. Aland (7th ed.; Tübingen: Niemeyer, 1968), and the summary in Lienhard, "Marcellus" 493–94.

these differing theological systems can best be categorized by their emphasis, in the doctrine of salvation, on divine initiative or human response. In a sense Arius, Nestorius, and Pelagius all in their own ways emphasize human response, while Athanasius, Cyril of Alexandria, and Augustine all stress the divine initiative. It is safer, perhaps, to say no more than this.

HISTORY OF THE TWO TRADITIONS

The history of the two traditions in the fourth century can only be sketched here in outline. The first period is that from the crisis Arius caused in Alexandria to the Council of Nicaea. In this period Arius' expulsion from Alexandria caused more than a few theologians in the dyohypostatic tradition to attempt to formulate their theological views. Most of these attempts were in the form of letters.

In 318 or 319 Eusebius of Caesarea wrote a letter to Euphration of Balaneae[35] in which he argued that the Father must exist before or precede the Son, and is superior to the Son because He causes the Son's existence; the Son is God, but not "true God" (Jn 17:3). In 320 or 321 Eusebius of Nicomedia wrote a letter to Paulinus of Tyre (the letter that Asterius later tried to defend)[36] in which he aggressively rejects the assertion that the Son is of or from the Father's essence (ek tēs ousias); he is rather from the Father's will, a perfect creature. There is "one Unbegotten," he can write, "and one made by Him." The letter, G. C. Stead remarks, "became something of an Arian classic."[37] Paulinus of Tyre[38] wrote a letter, perhaps addressed to Alexander of Alexandria, in which he called Christ "a second God," "a more human God," and "a creature."[39] In 325 Narcissus of Neronias, in a letter to Eusebius of Nicomedia and others, wrote of a first and second God, and of two or

[35] Opitz, Urkunde 3. On Eusebius's theology see below.
[36] Opitz, Urkunde 8. See A. Lichtenstein, *Eusebius von Nicomedien: Versuch einer Darstellung seiner Persönlichkeit und seines Lebens unter besonderer Berücksichtigung seiner Führerschaft im arianischen Streite* (Halle: Niemeyer, 1903). There are two recent studies of the letter: G. C. Stead, "'Eusebius' and the Council of Nicaea," *JTS* 24 (1973) 85–100, and C. Luibhéad, "The Arianism of Eusebius of Nicomedia," *ITQ* 43 (1976) 3–23.
[37] Stead, "Eusebius" 86.
[38] On Paulinus see G. Bardy, "Sur Paulin de Tyr," *RevScRel* 2 (1922) 35–45. Paulinus was a close friend of Eusebius of Caesarea; Eusebius dedicated the tenth book of his *Ecclesiastical History* to him and composed his *Onomasticon* at Paulinus' request. According to T. Kopecek (*A History of Neo-Arianism* 1 [Cambridge, Mass.: Philadelphia Patristic Foundation, 1979] 64), the later neo-Arian Aëtius studied Scripture under Paulinus at Antioch.
[39] Opitz, Urkunde 9.

three divine *ousiai*.[40] But the most significant partisan was probably Asterius the Sophist.[41] Before Nicaea, Asterius wrote a booklet (*syntagmation*) which became the theological manual of the Eusebian party and qualified Asterius to be the spokesman or publicist of dyohypostatic theology. In this pamphlet Asterius defined "ingenerate" precisely as "what was not made, but always is." He also speaks of a double power and a double wisdom: one natural to God and hence eternal, unoriginate, and unbegotten, and another, manifested in Christ, which is created. Asterius states more clearly than the others that Christ is the necessary, created instrument by which God created.

Arius too, far from being an original thinker, was simply one more adherent of the dyohypostatic tradition,[42] albeit one who, in his earlier statements in Alexandria, expressed himself awkwardly or provocatively, and who, further, had the bad luck of using the language of dyohypostatic theology in an atmosphere—Alexandria—where it was unfamiliar and hence easily misunderstood.

In this early period the miahypostatic tradition is sparsely represented; dating Athanasius' *Contra gentes et de incarnatione uerbi* before 318 has been abandoned by most scholars.[43]

The second period is that from Nicaea to the Dedication Council of Antioch. After Nicaea the language used by the representatives of the dyohypostatic tradition is more guarded; phrases like "two Gods" and "two *ousiai*" disappear. Asterius the Sophist wrote his letter[44] defending Eusebius of Nicomedia's own letter to Paulinus of Tyre during this time, probably in 327. The occasion of his writing may have been Eusebius' effort to have his deposition reversed and regain his see. Perhaps under the influence of Nicaea, Asterius took a creed (albeit a simple one) as his point of departure. From there he asserts that the triple name must refer to a triple reality. The Father and the Son are two natures, he writes, two *hypostaseis*, and two *prosōpa*. The two are one, he insists, in harmony

[40] See W. Ensslin, "Narkissos, Bischof von Neronias," *RE* 16 (1935) 1733-34. Fragments of the letter: Opitz, Urkunde 19.

[41] See G. Bardy, *Recherches sur saint Lucien d'Antioche et son école* (Paris: Beauchesne, 1936) 316-57 (which includes an edition of the fragments of the *syntagmation*); Grillmeier, *Christ in Christian Tradition* 206-14; and particularly M. F. Wiles with R. C. Gregg, "Asterius: A New Chapter in the History of Arianism," in Gregg, *Arianism* 111-51.

[42] R. D. Williams ("The Quest for the Historical Thalia," in Gregg, *Arianism* 1-35) speaks (p. 27) of Arius conscripted by the Lucianists, so that his own teaching soon became irrelevant.

[43] For the relevant literature, see Lienhard, "Marcellus" 487 n. 8, and F. Young, *From Nicaea to Chalcedon* (Philadelphia: Fortress, 1983) 68-70 and 300 n. 41, and add A. Pettersen, "A Reconsideration of the Date of the *Contra Gentes—De Incarnatione* of Athanasius of Alexandria," StPatr 18/3 (Oxford and New York: Pergamon, 1982) 1030-40.

[44] Fragments in Bardy, *Recherches*.

of wills. On the other hand, he virtually abandons Eusebius of Nicomedia's insistence that the Son is from the Father's will and accepts a more credal "begotten from Him."

It was Asterius' letter that provoked the first extended written work after Nicaea expressing the miahypostatic tradition, Marcellus of Ancyra's *Contra Asterium*. But Marcellus undertook a refutation not only of Asterius' letter, but of four other letters: those of Eusebius of Caesarea, Eusebius of Nicomedia, Paulinus of Tyre, and Narcissus of Neronias, all mentioned above. Marcellus probably had a dossier of letters put together by representatives of the dyohypostatic tradition, perhaps Arius himself.[45]

But the dyohypostatic tradition in the early fourth century is most clearly and fully represented by Eusebius of Caesarea. In the older literature Eusebius was treated as a historian and a compiler, but not as a theologian of any standing. Research in the past 50 years has changed that impression, and shown that Eusebius thought of himself as a theologian and that he has a theological system well worth studying.[46]

[45] Socrates (*Ecclesiastical History* 1, 6) records that Arius made a collection of letters favorable to himself; Marcellus probably had this collection. On theological alignments in the fourth century, see the interesting observations of C. Sansbury, "Athanasius, Marcellus, and Eusebius of Caesarea: Some Thoughts on Their Resemblances and Disagreements," in Gregg, *Arianism* 281–86.

[46] H. G. Opitz began the revision with his article "Euseb von Caesarea als Theologe: Ein Vortrag" (*ZNTW* 34 [1935] 1–19). H. Berkhof (*Die Theologie des Eusebius von Caesarea* [Amsterdam: Uitgevermaatschappij Holland, 1939]) studied Eusebius' *Praeparatio euangelica, Demonstratio euangelica*, and his two works against Marcellus (*Contra Marcellum* and *De ecclesiastica theologia*). His book is an excellent guide to the many theologically interesting passages in Eusebius, although Berkhof forced Eusebius' thought into the outline of later dogmatic theology and too easily assumed direct continuity between Origen and Eusebius. He concluded (p. 39) that "Origen is not a theologian in the proper sense of the word." G. Ruhbach, in a dissertation (*Apologetik und Geschichte: Untersuchungen zur Theologie Eusebs von Caesarea* [Diss. Heidelberg 1962]), unfortunately never published, showed that Eusebius revered Origen but considered himself not a spokesman for Origen but an independent theologian. A. Weber, in a small monograph on Eusebius' Christology (*ARXH: Ein Beitrag zur Christologie des Eusebius von Caesarea* [Munich: Neue Stadt, 1965]), studied Eusebius' interpretation of Prov 8. F. Ricken has investigated Eusebius' dependence on Middle Platonic thought in several articles: "Die Logoslehre des Eusebius von Caesarea und der Mittelplatonismus," *ThPh* 42 (1967) 341–58; "Nikaia als Krisis des altkirchlichen Platonismus," ibid. 44 (1969) 321–41; "Das Homousios von Nikaia als Krisis des altkirchlichen Platonismus," in *Zur Frühgeschichte der Christologie*, ed. B. Welte (Quaestiones disputatae 51; Freiburg: Herder, 1970) 74–99; and "Zur Rezeption der platonischen Ontologie bei Eusebios von Kaisareia, Areios und Athanasios," *ThPh* 53 (1978) 321–52. See also H. v. Campenhausen, "Das Bekenntnis Eusebs von Caesarea (Nicaea 325)," *ZNTW* 67 (1976) 123–39; C. Luibhéad, *Eusebius of Caesarea and the Arian Crisis* (Dublin: Irish Academic Press, 1978); J. R. Lyman, "Substance Language in Origen und Eusebius," in Gregg, *Arianism* 257–66; and Ritter, "Dogma und Lehre" 152–55.

Marcellus' *Contra Asterium* brought about a full reaction from Eusebius of Caesarea, first in his rather hasty and superficial *Contra Marcellum*, and then in his more carefully constructed and more theological *De ecclesiastica theologia.*
The third period is that from the Dedication Council to the death of Constantius. As suggested above, the year 341 marks the rise of two clearly distinguishable parties, with the majority of the Eastern bishops on one side and Athanasius, Marcellus, and most of the Westerners on the other side. Julius of Rome's vindication of Athanasius and Marcellus, recounted in his letter to the Easterners, provoked their reaction to him at the Dedication Council in 341. The Synod of Sardica (Philippopolis) (342 or 343) is the nadir of the relations between East and West. The Western statement calls the Easterners heretics, and the Eastern statement execrates Athanasius and Marcellus and calls Marcellus "omnium haereticorum execrabilior pestis."[47] Both sides probably regretted their excesses, and the Eastern *Ekthesis makrostichos* or Creed of the Long Lines (344) is deliberately conciliatory and even avoids the contested word *hypostasis* altogether.

But the dyohypostatic theology continued, apart from the formation of parties and the decrees of synods. In the two decades after the Dedication Council, this theology has two characteristics: it sees Marcellus of Ancyra, in a more and more stereotyped picture, as the opponent par excellence; and it becomes increasingly moderate and nuanced, so that one of its last forms is the homoeousian theology proposed around 358.

Eusebius of Caesarea died in 339, and Acacius succeeded him. Acacius wrote a work against Marcellus, probably soon after 341; in the extant fragments he is much concerned with the title "image" for the Son, and heavily dependent on the second creed of Antioch.[48] The sermons of Eusebius of Emesa (ca. 300–ca. 359),[49] which are preserved in a Latin

[47] Hilary of Poitiers, *Fragmenta historica* A, IV, 1, 1 (CSEL 65, 49).

[48] Epiphanius of Salamis preserves some fragments in *Panarion* 72, 6–10 (GCS Epiphanius 3, 260–64). See J.-M. Leroux, "Acace, évêque de Césarée de Palestine (341–365)," StPatr 8 (= TU 93; Berlin 1966) 82–85.

[49] See E. M. Buytaert, *L'Héritage littéraire d'Eusèbe d'Emèse: Etude critique et historique* (Louvain: Bureaux du Muséon, 1949); Eusèbe d'Emèse, *Discours conservés en latin: Textes en partie inédits,* ed. E. M. Buytaert (2 vols.; Louvain: Spicilegium Sacrum Lovaniense, 1953, 1957); P. Smulders, "Eusèbe d'Emèse comme source du *De trinitate* d'Hilaire de Poitiers," in *Hilaire et son temps* (Paris: Etudes Augustiniennes, 1969) 175–212; and I. Berten, "Cyrille de Jérusalem, Eusèbe d'Emèse et la théologie sémi-arienne," *Revue des sciences philosophiques et théologiques* 52 (1968) 38–75. Smulders provides a good summary of Eusebius' theology, and shows that Hilary of Poitiers knew and used Eusebius of Emesa's sermons (in Greek). He believes that Eusebius of Emesa is a direct link between Eusebius of Caesarea and the Homoeousians on the one hand, and a source of Hilary of Poitiers'

434   THEOLOGICAL STUDIES

translation, show a theology that is also a later form of the dyohypostatic theology. Eusebius insists with equal vigor both on the deity of the Son and on his subordination to the Father. Piet Smulders shows that Eusebius has the beginnings of a dyoprosopic Christology, which he is led to by his reflection on Jesus' agony in the garden and his suffering on the cross.[50] Eustathius of Antioch and Marcellus of Ancyra had already suggested that Jesus' human will had to be considered; in Eusebius of Emesa a representative of the dyohypostatic theology comes to the same insight. The one "heretic" whom Eusebius of Emesa attacks with any emotion is Marcellus of Ancyra.[51] Smulders writes of him that "the person of Eusebius leads us to the heart of the homoeousian group."[52] Cyril of Jerusalem is another clear representative of the dyohypostatic theology.[53] Like Eusebius of Emesa, Cyril too attacks only one living Christian in his Catecheses, namely Marcellus of Ancyra.[54]

In 358 the short-lived homoeousian party arose, which, if the analysis presented here is correct, is the last representative of the older dyohypostatic theology. The "Blasphemy of Sirmium" of 357 called attention to the words ousia, homoousios, and homoiousios by attempting to prohibit their use,[55] and, ironically, prepared the way for an ultimate solution.

During this same period the miahypostatic tradition is represented

---

Trinitarian theology on the other. Berten concludes that Cyril of Jerusalem depends on Eusebius of Emesa, who in turn depends on Eusebius of Caesarea.

[50] Smulders, "Eusèbe" 202, 211.

[51] Sermon 3, 24. Sermons 3 and 4 in Buytaert's edition have the titles De fide and Aduersus Sabellium respectively. The latter has Marcellus in mind.

[52] Smulders, "Eusèbe" 176.

[53] See E. J. Yarnold, "Cyrillus von Jerusalem," TRE 8 (1981) 261–66; and further J. Lebon, "La position de saint Cyrille de Jérusalem dans les luttes provoquées par l'arianisme," RHE 20 (1924) 181–210, 357–86; A. A. Stephenson, "St. Cyril of Jerusalem and the Alexandrian Heritage," TS 15 (1954) 273–93; idem, "St. Cyril of Jerusalem and the Alexandrian Christian Gnosis," StPatr 1 (= TU 63; Berlin 1957) 142–56; idem, "General Introduction," in Works of Saint Cyril of Jerusalem 1, tr. L. P. McCauley and A. A. Stephenson (FC 61; Washington: Catholic Univ. of America, 1969) 1–65; idem, "St. Cyril of Jerusalem's Trinitarian Theology," StPatr 11 (= TU 108; Berlin 1972) 234–41; H. A. Wolfson, "Philosophical Implications of the Theology of Cyril of Jerusalem," Dumbarton Oaks Papers 11 (1957) 1–19; W. R. Jenkinson, "The Image and Likeness of God in Man in the Eighteen Lectures on the Credo of Cyril of Jerusalem (c. 315–387)," EThLov 40 (1964) 48–71; I. Berten, "Cyrille de Jérusalem"; and R. C. Gregg, "Cyril of Jerusalem and the Arians," in Gregg, Arianism, 85–109. Much worry over St. Cyril's Nicene orthodoxy could have been avoided by recognizing that he belongs to the dyohypostatic tradition, which, when he wrote ca. 348, had theological shortcomings, just as the miahypostatic tradition did, but was not heretical.

[54] Catechesis 15, 27.

[55] Hahn, Bibliothek #161; Kelly, Creeds 285–88.

most fully by Athanasius.[56] Marcellus' last clearly authentic writing is a letter he addressed to Pope Julius of Rome in 341.[57] The writings that have recently been attributed—probably too hastily and too facilely—to Marcellus[58] perhaps belong rather more generally to the miahypostatic tradition of the fourth century. Once this category is established, there is no need to insist that only Marcellus could have written these works.

Besides unnuanced and increasingly stereotyped open opposition to Marcellus by Eusebius of Caesarea, Acacius of Caesarea, Eusebius of Emesa, Cyril of Jerusalem, and many of the Eastern councils and synods, another strain of opposition to Marcellus developed that was more subtle, more sophisticated, and—ultimately—theologically much more productive. This opposition is found in four writings that have several important characteristics in common. Each refers to Marcellus under the code name "Sabellius"; each uses the word *homoousios*, but only once or twice, and without making it a touchstone of orthodoxy; each is as explicitly opposed to Arius as it is to Marcellus; each accepts, at least in principle, the validity of the phrase "two *hypostaseis*" while rejecting the subordination that the dyohypostatic theology considered necessary to preserve monotheism; and each teaches the eternal generation of the Son. In other words, these writings draw elements from both the miahypostatic and

[56] On Athanasius' theology see, most recently, Ritter, "Dogma und Lehre" 178–85, and C. Kannengiesser, "The Athanasian Decade 1974–1984: A Bibliographical Report," *TS* 46 (1985) 524–41.

[57] Frag. 129. The interpretation of this letter is crucial to the understanding of Marcellus and the development of the miahypostatic tradition. Most authors have assumed that the *Contra Asterium* contains Marcellus' definitive theology, and that his letter to Julius conceals his real convictions. But it seems more probable that, just as the Eusebians corrected their vocabulary after Nicaea, Marcellus too moderated his views and made his thought more consistent between the composition of the *Contra Asterium* and his letter to Julius ten or fifteen years later. Marcellus had the chance to read Eusebius' extended criticism of his work and to talk with Athanasius in Rome for several months in 340 or 341. In his letter Marcellus gave up insisting that the Preincarnate may only be called Word and saying that Christ's reign will end, precisely in order to maintain the theological value of the title "Logos," the eternal existence of the Son-Word, and the one hypostasis of God. Marcellus also stands behind Eugenius of Ancyra's *Expositio fidei ad Athanasium* (ca. 371; see above). His followers are last heard from ca. 377 in their letter to Egyptian bishops, preserved by Epiphanius of Salamis (*Panarion* 72, 11–12).

[58] The principal writings attributed to Marcellus in recent decades, with their numbers from M. Geerard, *Clavis Patrum Graecorum*, are: Ps-Anthimus of Nicomedia, *De sancta ecclesia* (CPG 2802); *Homilia in Canticum canticorum* (CPG 2239); *Homilia de semente* (CPG 2245); *Sermo maior de fide* (CPG 2803); *Contra Theopaschitas* (CPG 2805); *Expositio fidei* (CPG 2804); *De incarnatione et contra Arianos* (CPG 2806); and *Epistula ad Euagrium monachum* (CPG 3222). For the literature on these works, see the *CPG* and Lienhard, "Marcellus"; and add R. P. C. Hanson, "The Date and Authorship of Pseudo-Anthimus De sancta ecclesia," *Proceedings of the Royal Irish Academy* 83 (1983) 351C-354C.

the dyohypostatic traditions and point the way toward the Cappadocian resolution. The writings are not hostile to Marcellus personally, but to a caricature of his teaching; implicit in their thought is an opening through which Marcellus might join them. Theologically, it is the concept of the eternal generation of the Son that allows these authors to escape from the subordinationism of the dyohypostatic theology and its reflex thinking in the pattern of the great chain of being, and to teach the essential equality of Father and Son and thus the Son's saving work as deification.

The works are Ps.-Athanasius, *Fourth Oration against the Arians*;[59] Ps.-Athanasius, *Contra Sabellianos*;[60] Basil of Caesarea, *Contra Sabellianos et Arium et Anomoeos*;[61] and (Ps.?) Gregory of Nyssa, *Aduersus Arium et Sabellium*.[62] They are difficult to date, but undoubtedly fall between 340 and 380.

If this analysis is correct, then a famous thesis, proposed by Theodor Zahn in 1867, is shown to be incorrect. Zahn believed that the Council of Nicaea had, with the word *homoousion*, professed the numerical identity or unity of the divine essence, but that the Cappadocian Fathers had taken the word to mean generic identity, and thus no different in meaning from *homoios kat' ousian*.[63] Practically, Zahn believed, the

[59] Critical ed. by A. Stegmann, *Die pseudoathanasianische "IVte Rede gegen die Arianer" als "kata Areianôn logos": Ein Apollinarisgut* (Rottenburg a. N.: W. Bader, 1917). In chap. 13 the author addresses his opponent in the singular, and warns him that his teaching leads to Sabellius'. This shows, as clearly as any passage, that the "Sabellius" of the fourth century is not the third-century heretic; he can only be Marcellus.

[60] Text in PG 28, 96–121. See R. Hübner, "Die Hauptquelle des Epiphanius (Panarion, haer. 65) über Paulus von Samosata: Ps-Athanasius, Contra Sabellianos," *ZKG* 90 (1979) 201–20; idem, "Epiphanius, Ancoratus und Ps-Athanasius, Contra Sabellianos," *ZKG* 92 (1981) 325–33; and J. T. Lienhard, "Ps-Athanasius, Contra Sabellianos, and Basil of Caesarea, Contra Sabellianos et Arium et Anomoeos: Analysis and Comparison," *VC* 40 (1986) 365–89.

[61] Text in PG 31, 600–17. See Lienhard, "Ps-Athanasius."

[62] Ed. F. Müller, *Gregorii Nysseni opera* 3, 1 (Leiden: Brill, 1958) 71–85. See also K. Holl, "Über die Gregor von Nyssa zugeschriebene Schrift 'Adversus Arium et Sabellium,'" *ZKG* 25 (1904) 380–98, reprinted in his *Gesammelte Aufsätze zur Kirchengeschichte* 2 (Tübingen: Mohr, 1928) 298–309; J.Daniélou, "L'*Adversus Arium et Sabellium* de Grégoire de Nysse et l'origénisme cappadocien," *RechScRel* 54 (1966) 61–66; M. van Parys, "Exégèse et théologie trinitaire: Prov 8:22 chez les Pères cappadociens," *Irénikon* 43 (1970) 362–79; R. Hübner, "Gregor von Nyssa und Markell von Ankyra," in *Ecriture et culture philosophique dans la pensée de Grégoire de Nysse*, ed. M. Harl (Leiden: Brill, 1971) 199–229, esp. 211 n. 1; and idem, *Die Einheit des Leibes Christi bei Gregor von Nyssa: Untersuchungen zum Ursprung der "physischen" Erlösungslehre* (Leiden: Brill, 1974) esp. 31 n. 19. Holl ascribed the work to Didymus the Blind of Alexandria; Müller, its modern editor, leaned toward authenticity, and thought it might be one of Gregory's earliest works; Daniélou was convinced of its authenticity; van Parys and Hübner consider it unauthentic.

[63] Th. Zahn, *Marcellus von Ancyra: Ein Beitrag zur Geschichte der Theologie* (Gotha: Fr. A. Perthes, 1867) 87. See A. M. Ritter, "Arianismus," *TRE* 3 (1978) 706, who tries to

Cappadocians were heirs, not of Nicaea and of Athanasius, but of the Homoeousian party of Basil of Ancyra and George of Laodicea. But the Homoeousians represented rather the end of the dyohypostatic tradition, and the Cappadocians inherited the corrected theology of these "anti-Sabellian" writings.

After 361 the categories "miahypostatic theology" and "dyohypostatic theology" lose their relevance. Traces of the parties do remain: some Ancyran clergy remained faithful to Marcellus, and the schism in Antioch between Paulinus and Meletius corresponds to these categories.[64] But the gradual rapprochement of the two traditions was advanced by several events. The rise of the Neo-Arians is the immediate cause of the rise of the Homoeousian party:[65] the Blasphemy of Sirmium attempted to prohibit the use of the words *homoousios, homoiousios,* and *ousia,* and thereby drew attention to them. Athanasius, in his *Tome to the Antiochenes* of 362, admitted for the first time that besides one *ousia* and one *hypostasis,* there was also a sense in which one could rightly say "three *hypostaseis*" of the Godhead. And the rise of the Neo-Arians makes Eunomius of Cyzicus the chief opponent of Homoeousians and Cappadocians alike.

Nevertheless, the categories "miahypostatic" and "dyohypostatic" are useful for analyzing theology in the earlier part of the fourth century. They show that the "Arian" controversy was in reality a collision between two theological systems, neither of which was quite adequate; but the very collision prepared the way for a resolution.

---

continue Zahn's thesis that the Fathers of Nicaea intended *homoousion* to mean numerical identity, but admits that he is opposed by Ricken, Stead, Simonetti, and Grillmeier. But cf. Ritter's "Dogma und Lehre" 200 and 202, where he has given up his defense of Zahn's hypothesis.

[64] See J. N. D. Kelly, *Jerome: His Life, Writings and Controversies* (London: Duckworth, 1975) 38 and passim, and F. Cavallera, *Le schisme d'Antioche (IVe-Ve siècle)* (Paris: Picard, 1905).

[65] See Kopecek, *Neo-Arianism,* for the history of the movement.

'EUSEBIUS' AND THE COUNCIL OF NICAEA

IN an effort to dissipate some of the obscurity which surrounds the Council of Nicaea, I will pose two questions in this paper. First, what contrast can be seen between the theology of Eusebius of Caesarea and that of his namesake of Nicomedia? I shall attend particularly to the latter's *Letter to Paulinus*,[1] and to the phrase ἐκ τῆς οὐσίας which it discusses; this is partly because the first draft of this paper was written at fairly short notice for a patristic conference, and made use of material already collected; but the letter is a revealing document, and the disputed phrase a serviceable test-piece. Secondly, I shall try to elucidate the part played in the Council by these two theologians.

Although the terms οὐσία and ὁμοούσιος came in for discussion at an early stage in the Arian controversy, they were not the original focus of conflict. It seems rather that Arius reacted most sharply against the teaching of his bishop Alexander that the Son is coeternal with the Father; Arius wished to assert the priority of the Father, though this was for him not strictly a priority in time, since he was willing to set the origin of the Son 'outside time' and 'before the ages';[2] he was convinced, however, that only the Father was strictly 'without origin'; hence 'there was—though there was not a time—'[3] when the Father was not yet Father and the Son 'was not'. The terms οὐσία and ὁμοούσιος were drawn into the dispute in view of two consequent points: the Arian claim that the Father is necessarily superior to the Son in status, and the view that the Son derives from the Father by a pure act of will, which would not infringe the divine immutability; he is not therefore 'of his substance', nor 'consubstantial with him'. But the issue of the Father's priority seems to be put first by Arius in his letter to Eusebius of Nicomedia (Opitz, Urkunde 1) and in the creed which he submitted to Alexander (ib. 6: οἴδαμεν ἕνα θεόν, μόνον ἀγέννητον, μόνον ἀίδιον, μόνον ἄναρχον); and equally in Alexander's Encyclical (ib. 4b, § 7) and in the dogmatic letter which he circulated later (ib. 14; see § 10, which begins his summary of Arian doctrine; § 15, which begins his reply; and §§ 22–7).

Arius considered that the official teaching involved the absurdity of postulating two independent first principles; and also that it suggested

---

[1] Text in H. G. Opitz, *Urkunden zur Geschichte des Arianischen Streites* (Athanasius' *Werke*, Bd. iii, Teil 1), Urk. 8.

[2] Urk. 1, § 4; 6, § 3; for the phrase πρὸ αἰώνων see Ps. liv. 20 LXX.

[3] H. M. Gwatkin, *Studies of Arianism*², p. 24.

[Journal of Theological Studies, N.S., Vol. XXIV, Pt. 1, April 1973]

a physical process of generation which would involve the Father in change and diminution. He himself seems not to have been entirely consistent in the way he formulated his views; or, possibly, he made some concessions in the hope of reaching agreement. Thus in his letter to Eusebius of Nicomedia he seems to have criticized the doctrine that the Son is 'from God himself' (ἐξ αὐτοῦ τοῦ θεοῦ, Urk. 1, §2); but in his more conciliatory letter to Alexander (ib. 6) he admits, in slightly different terms, that the Son 'received his being from the Father' (τὸ εἶναι παρὰ τοῦ πατρὸς εἰληφότα)[1] and 'was constituted by the Father' (ὑπὸ τοῦ πατρὸς ὑπέστη); and in the *Thalia* he says directly that he originated 'from God . . . from the Father' (ἐκ θεοῦ ὑπέστη . . . τὸν ἐκ πατρὸς ὄντα: Athanasius, *synn*. 15, Bardy, *Lucien*, p. 257). He did not of course reject the traditional titles 'Father' and 'Son', nor the metaphor of procreation which they imply, for the *Thalia* speaks of the Father's 'begetting' (γεννᾶν, τεκνοποιεῖν, ib. pp. 256–7); but he wished to define their sense. The only acceptable safeguard, he considered, was the proviso that the Son originated from the Father at a moment (though not in time) and by an act of will which had no association with division or change.

It was in some such circumstances that the phrase 'from the Father's substance' (ἐκ τῆς οὐσίας τοῦ πατρός) attracted the criticism of the Arian party. With slight variations, it occurs five times in the letter of Eusebius of Nicomedia to Paulinus, a document which became something of an Arian classic. It was largely reproduced in Latin by the Arian Candidus, and the full Greek text is given by Theodoret. Further, there seems a reasonable probability that it was this letter which was strongly criticized from the Nicene side, and defended by Asterius, who himself was attacked by Marcellus;[2] this in turn induced Eusebius of Caesarea to write against Marcellus, some years after the letter itself was written. Indeed, it is not impossible that the letter in question was read at Nicaea, and provided a reason for including the controversial phrase ἐκ τῆς οὐσίας in the Creed itself.

From a close examination of the letter, it appears that the objections posed by Eusebius of Nicomedia have a basis in tradition. He begins, much like Arius, by protesting against any doctrine of 'two ingenerates, or of one divided into two or suffering any bodily change' (οὔτε γὰρ δύο ἀγέννητα ἀκηκόαμεν οὔτε ἓν εἰς δύο διῃρημένον οὐδὲ σωματικόν τι πεπονθὸς μεμαθήκαμεν); rather, there is One who is ingenerate, and One who is truly generated by him, and not from his *ousia*, in no way partaking of

---

[1] Contrast Origen, *in Jo.*, fr. 9, where παρὰ πατρός (John i. 14) is held to support the Son's unique derivation ἐκ τῆς οὐσίας τοῦ πατρός, whereas creatures come into being ἐκ θεοῦ.

[2] Eusebius, *c. Marcell.* i. 4 (Klostermann, pp. 19–20).

the ingenerate nature or being of his *ousia* (ἀλλ' ἕν μὲν τὸ ἀγέννητον, ἕν δὲ τὸ ὑπ' αὐτοῦ ἀληθῶς καὶ οὐκ ἐκ τῆς οὐσίας αὐτοῦ γεγονός, καθόλου τῆς φύσεως τῆς ἀγεννήτου μὴ μετέχον ἢ ὂν ἐκ τῆς οὐσίας αὐτοῦ). The two clauses containing *ousia* seem to make two slightly different points; the first is clearly concerned with the origin of the second person, the second may be intended rather to reinforce the statement that he does not share the nature of the ingenerate first principle. A little later, Eusebius quotes Proverbs viii. 22-3, 25: 'The Lord created me the beginning of his ways . . . before the ages he founded me . . . before all the hills he begets me.' He argues that the terms 'created' and 'founded' show that the second person did not proceed 'out of him, that is, from him, as a part of him, or from an outflow of his *ousia*' (εἰ δὲ ἐξ αὐτοῦ, τουτέστιν ἀπ' αὐτοῦ ἦν ὡς ἂν μέρος αὐτοῦ ἢ ἐξ ἀπορροίας τῆς οὐσίας, οὐκ ἂν ἔτι κτιστὸν οὐδὲ θεμελιωτὸν εἶναι ἐλέγετο); while the term 'begets' cannot imply any 'origin from the paternal *ousia* or sameness of nature derived from him' since it is applied to beings who are wholly unlike him in nature, e.g. to men. (The excluded possibility is ὡς ἂν ἐκ τῆς οὐσίας τῆς πατρικῆς αὐτὸν γεγονότα καὶ ἔχειν ἐκ τούτου τὴν ταυτότητα τῆς φύσεως.) A little later he declares, 'For nothing is from his *ousia*, but all things coming into being by his will, each one exists just as it came into being.'

It is not easy to determine the sense which Eusebius gives to *ousia*, since, in all the five cases we have noticed, it is used to express a view which he condemns. Further, his two main concerns, for God's uniqueness and for his immutability, seem to call for slightly different exegesis of the phrase ἐκ τῆς οὐσίας. God's uniqueness would be infringed (*per impossibile*) by the mere existence of an exact double, another first principle, who would be ἐκ τῆς οὐσίας in a purely formal sense, as *sharing* his unique position of primacy; his immutability would suffer if such a being *issued from* his being by some quasi-physical process of generation implying change or loss (σωματικόν τι πεπονθός, ἀπόρροια). The only time Eusebius himself adopts *ousia*, it seems to have the sense of 'rank' or 'metaphysical status'; he speaks of the Lord as 'created and founded and generated in respect of his *ousia* and his immutable and ineffable nature and likeness to his maker' (κτιστὸν . . . καὶ θεμελιωτὸν καὶ γεννητὸν τῇ οὐσίᾳ καὶ τῇ ἀναλλοιώτῳ καὶ ἀρρήτῳ φύσει etc., § 4). Eusebius is clearly expressing a fairly radical form of Arian doctrine, and makes some points which we have no direct evidence for attributing to Arius himself; and it may be significant that he nowhere refers directly to 'the Father' or 'the Son'; but even he stops well short of the later Anomoean position; the second person, though 'wholly distinct in nature and power', has come into being 'for perfect likeness to the disposition and power of his maker' (πρὸς τελείαν ὁμοιότητα διαθέσεώς τε καὶ δυνάμεως τοῦ πεποιηκότος, § 3); and if it seems disconcerting that the theme of 'perfect likeness' is treated only prospectively, as if it were a task to be fulfilled by the Logos, we still cannot say that Eusebius ranks him with the created order; he is in no way comparable with men, who are 'in all respects unlike him in nature'.

To trace the history of the phrase ἐκ τῆς οὐσίας it is necessary to go back about a hundred years. Tertullian was possibly the first Christian writer to adopt it, though Irenaeus uses the concept of emissions or emanations from a divine spiritual stuff in his comments on Valentinian theology. Tertullian however boldly appropriates the Valentinian term 'projection' (προβολή: Prax. 8) and declares, 'I derive the Son from no other source than from the Father's substance' (filium non aliunde deduco, sed de substantia patris, ib. 4). Tertullian pictures God as a mind which contains within itself the Word as its 'plan' or 'thought', yet one which is sufficiently distinct to be addressed as a 'partner in dialogue' (ib. 5). At the moment of creation, however, this thought is uttered, and becomes sermo, spoken word, in place of ratio; and now for the first time can be regarded as 'Son' in the full sense. So Tertullian applies the text 'This day have I begotten thee', and comments: haec est nativitas perfecta sermonis, ib. 7, an expression which brings together the two concepts of spoken word and begotten son; and then adds that he is not (as sermo might suggest) a mere utterance, or a mere physical effect, but ranks as a substance himself, proceeding from the substance of the Father: nec carere substantia quod de tanta substantia processit et tantas substantias fecit.

Novatian follows Tertullian fairly closely, making a more guarded use of the controversial term 'projection', and teaching that the Word-Son was born from the Father 'when he willed' and in substantial form (ex quo, quando ipse voluit, sermo filius natus est; qui non in . . . tono coactae de visceribus vocis accipitur, sed in substantia prolatae a deo virtutis agnoscitur, Trin. 31); he calls him 'a divine substance coming forth from the Father', 'God from God'.

Origen differs from these Latin fathers in holding that the Son is eternally generated, and in showing more concern about possible materializing interpretations of the term 'generation'; this leads him to make constant use of the alternative metaphor of an act of will proceeding from the mind, even though this metaphor calls for the further corrective that God's Word and Wisdom is to be understood as a substantial second being, not a mere utterance or act of will. He also shows a marked interest in the great metaphors of Wisdom vii, especially 'breath', 'effulgence', 'image' (= ἀτμίς, ἀπαύγασμα, εἰκών, vv. 25-6), which can suggest an intangible and mysterious process of generation and avoid the distasteful suggestion of a physical 'effluent' (ἀπόρροια, ib.).

Both Tertullian and Origen seem to switch rather abruptly between the metaphors of proclamation and procreation; and it may be worth remarking that in the light of Stoic theory the contrast between them would be rather less extreme than it seems today. Both writers were at least familiar with the view that the emission of human seed is of itself sufficient to release a fully individualized offspring in germinal form, which only needs shelter and nourishment within the womb. Procreation would then be in principle asexual; it is (like speech) an activity of the 'spirit' in man; and the seed itself embodies a 'logos' and was thought to proceed direct from the brain by way of the spinal cord. Both Tertullian and Origen of course make clear that these human processes offer only the remotest analogy for divine realities; my point is simply that in their thinking the two alternative bases for analogy were less widely separated than they are for us.

I have called attention to the physical associations of the term 'effluence', and indeed 'substance' itself, in order to illustrate Origen's hesitation over accepting the phrase 'from God's substance'. In his Commentary on St. John (xx. 157–8) he suggests that it could imply that the Father would lose some of his substance in procreation: 'Others explained "I came forth from God" as "I was begotten of God", and these would consequently say that the Son was begotten from the Father's substance, as if God were diminished and lacking in the substance which he had before, when begetting the Son, as . . . in the case of those who are pregnant.' (This is clearly one of the points that Eusebius takes up.) In his De Principiis also Origen condemns all materializing notions of the Son's generation, preferring to speak of 'will from mind', though in fact it is a substantive reality, *virtus altera in sua proprietate subsistens*, not a mere act of will; so far as I can discover, he does not use the phrase 'from the substance' in this work. But there are at least three passages elsewhere which support the phrase. In fragment 9 of the Commentary on St. John it is used to emphasize the contrast between the Son, who comes 'out from the Father', and creatures, who have their being 'from God': Τὸ Ὡς μονογενοῦς παρὰ πατρὸς νοεῖν ὑποβάλλει ἐκ τῆς οὐσίας τοῦ πατρὸς εἶναι τὸν υἱόν. οὐδὲν γὰρ τῶν κτισμάτων παρὰ πατρός, ἀλλ᾽ - ἐκ θεοῦ διὰ τοῦ λόγου ἔχει τὸ εἶναι. In his Commentary on Romans (iv. 10: P. G. 14. 998A) he argues that Christ's death is a proof of divine goodness: *Nisi enim esset hic ex illa veniens substantia*—'For unless he had come from that substance, and had been the Son of that Father [who is good], he could not have shown such great goodness towards us.' These two passages are noteworthy as

115

exhibiting an apparently spontaneous and unforced use of the phrase; in the Commentary on Hebrews, as preserved by Pamphilus, a slightly more apologetic note appears when Origen quotes Wisdom vii. 25 and explains that the Scripture uses corporeal metaphors to express spiritual truths; he concludes: *sic et sapientia ex eo procedens, ex ipsa Dei substantia generatur.*

Not unnaturally, the followers of Origen are not agreed as to the value of the phrase 'from God's substance'. Athanasius was able to quote in its favour a passage from Theognostus where the writer clearly alludes to Wisdom vii. 25–6 so as to show that the Son is not alien to the Father's substance, but emanates from it without causing any division or alteration: οὐκ ἔξωθέν τίς ἐστιν ἐφευρεθεῖσα ἡ τοῦ υἱοῦ οὐσία οὐδὲ ἐκ μὴ ὄντων ἐπεισήχθη, ἀλλὰ ἐκ τῆς τοῦ πατρὸς οὐσίας ἔφυ ὡς τοῦ φωτὸς τὸ ἀπαύγασμα, ὡς ὕδατος ἀτμίς ... καὶ οὔτε ... αὐτός ἐστιν ὁ πατὴρ οὔτε ἀλλότριος, ἀλλὰ ἀπόρροια τῆς τοῦ πατρὸς οὐσίας, οὐ μερισμὸν ὑπομεινάσης τῆς τοῦ πατρὸς οὐσίας. ὡς γὰρ μένων ὁ ἥλιος ὁ αὐτὸς οὐ μειοῦται ταῖς ἐκχεομέναις ὑπ' αὐτοῦ αὐγαῖς, οὕτως οὐδὲ ἡ οὐσία τοῦ πατρὸς ἀλλοίωσιν ὑπέμεινεν εἰκόνα ἑαυτῆς ἔχουσα τὸν υἱόν (*decr.* 25). It would perhaps be unwise to infer too much about Theognostus' general standpoint from this single passage; indeed Athanasius' reference to his 'previous discussion by way of an exercise' suggests that the Arians also could invoke his authority,[1] as they certainly did that of Dionysius. On the other hand Pamphilus, who quotes the passage from Origen in support of the *homoousion*, seems to have no hesitation about the phrase 'from God's substance'; his comment is: *Satis manifeste, ut opinor, et valde evidenter ostensum est, quod Filium Dei de ipsa Dei substantia natum dixerit, id est* ὁμοούσιον, etc.

Eusebius of Caesarea gives us much more abundant material for study, having left us at least one major work on dogmatic theology, the *Demonstratio Evangelica*, which was completed before the Council of Nicaea, and largely written before the Arian controversy attracted attention. His teaching on the Son's origin is complex and not entirely consistent. He does not, like Origen, uphold his eternal generation, but regards him as having originated by an act of the Father's will, so that the Father is in existence before the Son (ὁ δὲ πατὴρ προϋπάρχει τοῦ υἱοῦ καὶ τῆς γενέσεως προϋφέστηκεν, *D.E.* iv. 3. 5); on the other hand he places the Son's generation 'before the ages', and admits—quite shortly after the passage just quoted—that he was *not* 'at some times nonexistent, and originating later, but existing and pre-existing before eternal times' (οὐ χρόνοις μέν τισιν οὐκ ὄντα, ὕστερον δέ ποτε γεγονότα,

---

[1] Cf. Photius, cod. 106; for 'exercise' (γυμνασία) cf. the rather similar defence of Marcellus quoted by Athanasius in *Apol. c. Ar.* 47.

ἀλλὰ πρὸ χρόνων αἰωνίων ὄντα καὶ προόντα, ib. 13). He constantly emphasizes that the *manner* of the Son's generation surpasses our comprehension, and is decidedly circumspect in his use of the traditional images; in one passage he points out that a ray of light is no true parallel, being coexistent with its source and proceeding from it involuntarily (ib. 5); rather strangely, he takes refuge in the alternative metaphor of a fragrant odour (ib. 9).

In the course of these discussions on the Son's origin we find a list of objections to materializing theories, which occurs several times in almost standardized from:

iv. 3. 11: οὔτι πω κατὰ στέρησιν ἢ μείωσιν ἢ τομὴν ἢ διαίρεσιν ('not by deprivation or diminution or severance or division').

ib. 13: οὐ κατὰ διάστασιν ἢ τομὴν ἢ διαίρεσιν ἐκ τῆς τοῦ πατρὸς οὐσίας προβεβλημένον.

iv. 15. 52: οὐ κατὰ προβολὴν ἢ κατὰ διαίρεσιν ἢ τομὴν ἢ μείωσιν ...

v. 1. 8: μήτε κατὰ προβολὴν μήτε κατὰ διάστασιν ἢ διαίρεσιν ἢ μείωσιν ἢ τομήν ...

ib. 9: μηδὲ ... οὐσίαν ἐξ οὐσίας κατὰ πάθος ἢ διαίρεσιν μεριστὴν καὶ χωριστὴν ἐκ τοῦ πατρὸς προεληλυθέναι τὸν υἱόν.[1]

It will be seen that the phrase ἐκ τῆς οὐσίας, or its near equivalent, occurs twice over within this list of condemned phrases. But a little later, Eusebius embodies it in a cautiously worded positive statement. Beginning from the familiar text 'Who shall explain his generation?' he continues: 'But if anyone ventures to go further and compare what is totally inconceivable with visible and corporeal examples, perhaps he might say that the Son came forth from the unoriginate nature and ineffable substance of the Father (ἐκ τῆς τοῦ πατρὸς ἀγενήτου φύσεως καὶ τῆς ἀνεκφράστου οὐσίας) like some fragrance and ray of light ...', v. 1. 18; but he almost immediately points out the limitations of all such metaphors, and once again associates the phrase ἐξ οὐσίας with the notion of change and division: οὐδὲ γὰρ ἐξ οὐσίας τῆς ἀγενήτου κατά τι πάθος ἢ διαίρεσιν οὐσιωμένος, οὐδέ γε ἀνάρχως συνυφέστηκεν τῷ πατρί etc., ib. 20. It must be said that Eusebius looks on the phrase 'from the substance' with marked disfavour, even though he does not reject it consistently, like his namesake of Nicomedia; so that his reluctant acceptance of it at Nicaea has some support in what he had previously written.

The evidence so far produced might still suggest a certain difference in manner between the two Eusebii. In the Caesarean, who of course

---

[1] These terms are taken up in Eusebius' Letter to his Diocese (Opitz, Urk. 22), in § 12: οὔτε γὰρ κατὰ διαίρεσιν τῆς οὐσίας οὔτε κατὰ ἀποτομήν, ἀλλ' οὐδὲ κατά τι πάθος ἢ τροπὴν ἢ ἀλλοίωσιν τῆς τοῦ πατρὸς οὐσίας τε καὶ δυνάμεως. In § 7 he attributes rather similar disclaimers to Constantine.

provides far more material for study, we can trace occasional signs of an accommodating temper, a willingness to see some merit in theological phrases of which he does not wholly approve. But there is a qualification to be made here. Eusebius also thought that others should be accommodating; and, in particular, he thought that Alexander should be more accommodating towards the Arians; this is shown by his letter to Alexander, Urk. 7. We can, I think, go further (on the strength of his letter to Euphration, Urk. 3) and say that at the beginning of the controversy Eusebius was fairly strongly inclined to take the Arian side; and this inclination may well have been reinforced when Arius appeared to plead his cause in person, and again when Alexander rebuffed Eusebius' attempts to make peace. In this case, can we still maintain that there was a noticeable difference of standpoint between the two Eusebii, and that Eusebius of Caesarea took the more moderate line? I shall suggest that this thesis should be abandoned.

II

Eusebius in his *Vita Constantini* gives us some useful information about the circumstances and setting of the Nicene Council, but makes no serious attempt to describe its dogmatic debates. On this subject, our information is scanty, and there are only three contemporary witnesses. The first is Eusebius himself, whose Letter to his Diocese gives a valuable, if tendentious, account of the composition of the Creed; it is well known and, for the moment, I shall not consider it further. The second is Athanasius, whose references to the debates seem to me disconcertingly vague and schematic. The third is Eustathius, Bishop of Antioch, from whom we have a brief description of the Council preserved in Theodoret's *Ecclesiastical History* i. 8, which I think deserves some further discussion. Eusebius' account has the great advantage of having been written immediately after the event; Athanasius' first surviving references to it occur in his *De Decretis*, written some twenty-five years later. Eustathius' comments are probably intermediate in date; they cannot be strictly contemporary, since he refers to a subsequent revival of Arian fortunes (§ 4); but it is commonly held that he did not survive the Council by more than ten or fifteen years; so a date *c.* 330 would seem to be allowable, but it might be somewhat earlier: Quasten (iii. 304) suggests *c.* 329; Sellers (p. 27), 325–30; Spanneut (in *D.H.G.E.*), 327–8.

Some of the most tantalizing problems arise out of a phrase at the end of § 1 : ὡς δὲ ἐζητεῖτο τῆς πίστεως ὁ τρόπος, ἐναργὴς μὲν ἔλεγχος τὸ γράμμα τῆς Εὐσεβίου προὐβάλλετο βλασφημίας. We may distinguish three problems :

(1) *Εὐσεβίου*: which Eusebius is indicated?

(2) τὸ γράμμα: does this mean a creed specially prepared for the Council?

(3) προὐβάλλετο: does this mean that it was produced by the Arians on their own initiative?

Let me give a brief history of scholarly judgement on these three points. We can begin with Theodoret himself. It is not easy to discover his opinion on the first point; but I am inclined to think that, whether rightly or wrongly, he supposed that Eustathius was referring to Eusebius of Nicomedia, who is commonly intended when the name Eusebius is used without qualification. But on the other two points Theodoret's opinion is clear enough; he thinks the document is a credal statement produced by a group of prominent Arians and presented by them to the Council; this is evident from a passage in Chapter 7, § 15, where he writes, ὑπαγορεύσαντες δὲ καὶ πίστεως διδασκαλίαν ἐπέδοσαν τῷ κοινῷ· ἣν ἀναγνωσθεῖσαν εὐθέως διέρρηξαν ἅπαντες. The word διέρρηξαν is clearly a reminiscence of Eustathius' phrase διαρραγέντος ἐπ' ὄψει πάντων; so this passage gives Theodoret's version of the same incident. If he is right, we can translate Eustathius (with many moderns): 'When the pattern of the faith was under discussion, Eusebius' document was presented, which contained undisguised evidence of his blasphemy.'

The Renaissance translators seem not to have taken this point; Baronius, Christophorson, and Sirmond all render τὸ γράμμα by *litterae*, which need not suggest a credal statement; but Joachim Camerarius substitutes *libellus*, and this rendering is taken up by Valesius. Valesius has the great merit of seeing the significance of the last-quoted passage from Theodoret i. 7; he thinks of a credal document, deliberately propounded to the Council; but he adds the rather surprising judgement that it is Eusebius of Caesarea who is meant, basing his opinion on the fact that Socrates speaks of a dispute between this Eusebius and Eustathius, *H.E.* i. 23. However, Socrates is evidently thinking of a dispute arising well *after* the Council, when some of the disputants were having second thoughts about the term *homoousios*.

Subsequent historians have generally rejected Valesius' opinion that Eusebius of Caesarea was intended; though some distinguished scholars have taken this view; so, apparently, Léon Parmentier, if we may trust his Index to Theodoret; Eduard Schwartz; and, more tentatively, Professor A. H. M. Jones and Dr. Henry Chadwick.[1] It has been widely assumed that τὸ γράμμα refers to a credal statement; but there

[1] E. Schwartz, P.–W.–K. vi. 1413–14; A. H. M. Jones, *Constantine and the Conversion of Europe*, pp. 158 f.; H. Chadwick, *H.T.R.* liii (July, 1960), p. 171 n. 2.

has been no consensus on the question whether the Arians themselves produced it, or whether it was cited by their opponents. On the whole, the former view has been favoured by recent writers.[1]

As a first step in our present investigation, I submit that Theodoret's account of this stage of the Council's proceedings has no independent value, but is entirely based on his reading of Eustathius. This has been correctly seen by Dr. R. V. Sellers (*Eustathius*, p. 28 n. 1). We can, I think, understand how Theodoret came to infer that the document was a credal formula drawn up by a committee. Eustathius writes that 'the Eusebian gang' was discredited by the rejection of the document: τὸ ἐργαστήριον τῶν ἀμφὶ τὸν Εὐσέβιον σαφῶς ἑάλω, τοῦ παρανόμου γράμματος διαρραγέντος ὑπ' ὄψει πάντων ὁμοῦ. This meaning of ἐργαστήριον is quite well attested; see, e.g., Athanasius, *de sent. Dion.* 13. Theodoret, however, seems to have taken it to mean a 'working-party', and so assumed that the rejected document was their ἔργον, i.e. the joint production of the group of Arian theologians, whose names he could supply from other sources. But of course the fact that the Arian group was discredited by the rejection of the document would not prove that they were its joint authors; they need only have supported it; and in any case Theodoret's assumption conflicts with Eustathius' wording, which implies a single author: the reading of the document 'inflicted irremediable shame upon the writer', τῷ γράψαντι.

Secondly, I should like to comment on the curiously involved syntax of the phrase I have already quoted from Eustathius: ἐναργὴς μὲν ἔλεγχος τὸ γράμμα τῆς Εὐσεβίου προὐβάλλετο βλασφημίας. The difficulty here is that both ἔλεγχος and τὸ γράμμα seem to need some explanatory phrase; so it looks as if the phrase τῆς Εὐσεβίου βλασφημίας is meant to do double duty and qualify them both. (The Latin version of Valesius reproduces the difficulty: *tanquam manifestum argumentum liber Eusebianae blasphemiae proferebatur*; the English versions of A. E. Burn and J. N. D. Kelly conceal it: 'The formulary of Eusebius was brought forward, which contained undisguised evidence of his blasphemy.') This complicated construction is perhaps not too surprising when found in such a sophisticated stylist as Eustathius. But a simple solution is possible if we suppose that τὸ γράμμα has been previously mentioned, and therefore needs no further explanation. And this suggestion seems to me to be probable on other grounds. Anyone reading Dr. Spanneut's collection of the fragments of Eustathius must be struck by the remarkable difference in style and subject-matter between the highly polemical narrative we have been considering, which appears as fr. 32, and the

[1] e.g. J. N. D. Kelly, *Creeds*, pp. 212–13; I. Ortiz de Urbina, *Nicée et Constantinople*, p. 61; M. Spanneut, *D.H.G.E.*, s.v. Eustathius, vol. 16, col. 15.

preceding fragments 18–31, all drawn from the *Eranistes*, and all of an exegetical and theological character, with only passing references to opponents (fr. 23, καθάπερ οἱ συκοφάνται δοξάζουσιν: fr. 27, περιττῶς τοῖς ἀποστολικοῖς ἐπισκήπτουσιν ὅροις οἱ ἐναγεῖς). And why introduce a reference to the Council of Nicaea into an exegetical treatise? Obviously the text in question was a highly controversial one; but the simplest answer must be, because this text was quoted in the Arian document discredited at Nicaea. I would suppose that Eustathius began by referring to the text, and its Arian exegesis; went on to claim that this had already been rejected at the Council—fr. 32, which may well have come fairly near the beginning of his tract, though obviously not at the very beginning; and went on to give his own exegesis. Fr. 32 therefore originally preceded the other fragments, 18–31. This squares fairly well with the summary of the tract given by Theodoret, who says that Eustathius 'wrote about these things, recounting what happened and refuting their blasphemy and expounding the text from Proverbs', τά τε γεγενημένα διδάσκων καὶ τὴν βλασφημίαν ἐλέγχων καὶ τὴν παροιμιακὴν ἑρμηνεύων ῥῆσιν. We may also fairly infer that most of the tractate was exegetical, and that Eustathius gave no further account of the Nicene proceedings; for the fifth-century historians were greedy for details of this momentous and poorly attested event, and Theodoret would not have neglected to quote further evidence, if available, from a tract which he had studied in detail.

I pass to consider the significance of the word προὐβάλλετο. Προβάλλε-σθαι occurs twice in the extract from Eustathius; its second instance is a reference to some people τοὔνομα προβαλλόμενοι τῆς εἰρήνης; this use of the middle voice with the sense of 'pretending' or 'alleging' is common in the contemporary writers Eusebius and Athanasius. What of its first occurrence, in the imperfect indicative passive? Need it mean anything more than 'was produced'? Or can any further inference be drawn?

It is easy to see that if its second appearance carries the sense of 'insincerely alleging', its first could be taken to mean 'was speciously presented', 'was trumped up'; and if so, then Eustathius means that the Arians produced it. This indeed is how Theodoret probably understood the term; he himself uses it in the sense of 'introducing', e.g. in iv. 15 of the Arians introducing an anti-bishop, ἕτερον ἀντ' ἐκείνου προὐβάλοντο πρόεδρον. But this is extremely slender evidence for the assertion, quite commonly made by modern scholars, that the Arians took the initiative at the beginning of the Council. Is there any other evidence for this supposed Arian initiative? I am not aware of any; and there are some considerations which I think suggest that they were on the defensive from the first. For one thing, they must have realized that they were in a minority; and this probability is strengthened if we agree that a decision against them had been given by fifty-six bishops at Antioch some six months before. Again, if we are justified in taking Eusebius' reference to the 'Bishop who led the right wing' (*V.C.* iii. 11) as suggesting that the house had already divided for and against the Arian party at the start of the proceedings, the disparity in numbers would be even more evident. In such circumstances, their best hope would be to play upon Constantine's known desire for peace[1] and try to avoid provocative statements, leaving their opponents to incur the odium of starting the theological dispute. And this is consistent with the admittedly vague account given by Eusebius: Constantine appealed for peace, but almost immediately complaints began (*V.C.* iii. 13). He must mean that the anti-Arian party took the offensive; indeed Athanasius (*decr.* 3) records that the Arians were asked (politely) to explain themselves. Eusebius of Caesarea genuinely admired Constantine, and sympathized with his desire for peace; his namesake of Nicomedia was known as an able tactician; Eustathius was evidently no tactician at all.

There is, moreover, an alternative rendering, which I do not wish to advocate, but will mention as a possibility, since I am not aware that it has been suggested before. Προὐβάλλετο could mean 'was denounced' or 'rejected'. The *middle* verb, meaning 'to hold out one's arms', 'to take one's guard', is found in Demosthenes, *Philippics* i. 40, and reappears in Gregory of Nyssa, *c. Eun.* ii. 10; hence no doubt develops the sense 'to repulse' or 'reject' a person or thing. This use of προβάλλεσθαι is not very common, but it occurs in Xenophon (in the passive), Dionysius of Halicarnassus, Philo (at least three relevant instances), Josephus, Plutarch, and Clement of Alexandria; usually in the middle voice; especially in the perfect middle (Dionysius, Philo); and commonly in parallel with μισεῖν, to hate or reject (Philo, Plutarch, Clement). Josephus uses it in an extremely well-known account of the Essenes, which was quoted by Porphyry and Eusebius. It seems clear that an accomplished orator like Eustathius would have read most of these authors;[2] and it would be characteristic of him to use yet one more word bearing a pejorative sense.

Having written the above, I was inclined to abandon my suggestion, since I could not find evidence for this use of προβάλλειν among writers contemporary with Nicaea. But such evidence is in fact available in a very familiar text; no other than the treatise *De Incarnatione* of St.

---

[1] Cf. his letter to Alexander and Arius, Opitz, Urk. 17.
[2] His *other* use of προβάλλεσθαι proves to be an echo of Demosthenes, *Philipp.* iii. 8, presumably a well-known school text.

Athanasius himself. At the beginning of *c.* 24 he writes—according to the great majority of MSS.—τὰ δὲ καὶ παρ' ἑτέρων ἂν λεχθέντα, ταῦτα προβαλεῖν ἡμᾶς ἀναγκαῖον ταῖς ἀπολογίαις. The older printed texts, including those of Robertson and Cross, read προλαβεῖν, which gives the easy and natural sense 'to anticipate'; but the MS. evidence for this reading is not strong; it occurs in the Short Recension MSS. dCD, together with a small group of unreliable Long Recension MSS. (OON, with the corrector of B). And προλαβεῖν is clearly the *lectio facilior*; it could easily arise from a misreading or a mistaken emendation of the less familiar προβαλεῖν. St. Athanasius, then, must have written προβαλεῖν; Ryan (p. 110) notes this as the original Long Recension reading, and Thomson prints it in his text. But what can it have meant? There is (I think) no evidence at all that προβαλεῖν can mean 'to anticipate', a rendering which Thomson oddly retains; it is more likely to mean 'reject' or 'censure'; and Plutarch (*Adv. Col.* 22) enables us to confirm the much less common use of the active verb in a closely related sense, 'to hold something against someone', *alicui aliquid obicere*. Eusebius also uses the word (in the perfect middle) in *Laus Const.* 7 init., apparently with the sense of 'setting on' one combatant against another.

I would welcome further evidence upon this interesting word. Meanwhile, I still think it possible that Eustathius meant that an Arian writing was 'denounced' (or conceivably intended this meaning as part of a *double entendre*—to expound it was to expose it!). Even if he only meant that it was 'produced', it is surely more likely that he meant that it was produced *as* a proof of Eusebius' blasphemy, rather than the involved 'produced for approval but served as a proof . . .' I conclude that there is no sufficient evidence for the commonly held theory that the Arians took the initiative at the beginning of the Council. It rests on the unsupported testimony of Theodoret; and this testimony is worthless if (as we think) it is based on a faulty deduction from the words of Eustathius.

Next: if this be admitted, there is no particular reason to suppose that τὸ γράμμα refers to an Arian *Creed*; and there is one consideration which slightly inclines me to suppose that it does not. Eustathius observes that the document was 'read in the presence of all' (ἐπὶ πάντων ἀναγνωσθέν) and 'inflicted irremediable shame upon the writer' (αἰσχύνην δ' ἀνήκεστον τῷ γράψαντι παρεῖχεν). Eustathius' phrase suggests that the crime of Eusebius consisted in *writing* what he did; but if Eusebius had not only written a heretical statement but himself proclaimed it in the presence of the Council, it would surely be the proclamation and avowal of heresy which would cause the greater offence to Eustathius and his friends, and one would expect him to make this clear. If a modern bishop proclaimed in his cathedral, 'God is dead and buried, and a good thing too', one might naturally say that it is monstrous to *proclaim* such doctrines; even if he were in fact quoting a passage from his own book, it would be a curiously broken-winded comment if one said: 'When this passage was read in the presence of all, it brought final discredit upon the writer.' But Eustathius was not a man to waste his opportunities; so I prefer to think that τὸ γράμμα refers to some previous work of Eusebius which was denounced by his opponents.

I pass on to what is perhaps the most interesting and controversial point: which Eusebius was involved in this incident?

The traditional view, that it was Eusebius of Nicomedia, requires the assumption that the theological position of the two bishops was strongly contrasted. The unidentified Eusebius produced a statement which was condemned outright and which must therefore have been markedly Arian; but Eusebius of Caesarea, if we trust his own account, produced a creed which Constantine approved, with the single proviso that *homoousios* be added, and which formed the basis of the official Creed of the Council; so it used to be thought. The difficulty is that we have found much less disparity in the views of these two theologians than the traditional view requires.

But the opposing view, that it was Eusebius of Caesarea, also presents much difficulty. We have to believe that Eustathius, perhaps smarting under undeserved injuries, gives a picture of Eusebius which is quite out of line with our other evidence. For we know that Eusebius retained the Emperor's favour, and did not wholly forfeit the regard even of Athanasius, who was prepared to quote his creed as evidence of his substantial orthodoxy. And the difficulty is worse if we suppose that Eustathius and Eusebius are reporting *the same incident*, one with the comment that the impious document was torn to shreds in the sight of all, the other remarking that it offered no room for contradiction.

However, this is largely a matter of subjective impression, on which scholars will have already formed their opinions. I must turn to some other considerations which are perhaps a little less well worn.

1. I believe myself that the Synodal Letter of Antioch is authentic; but I also believe that its discovery produced an over-strong reaction against the traditional assessment of Eusebius of Caesarea. Tradition saw him as the virtual framer of the Creed; the evidence that he was provisionally excommunicated at Antioch certainly came as a shock. Obviously the *intention* was to discredit him; but the intentions of the Council of Antioch were not entirely fulfilled. They had already suffered a reverse in the transfer of the Council from Ancyra, under the wing of their friend Marcellus, to Nicaea, in the heart of pro-Arian Bithynia; and Constantine's resolve to work for harmony and

comprehensiveness must have been another disappointment. It seems to me that Constantine thought Ossius and Eustathius had acted too impetuously, and determined to revert to a policy more like that envisaged in his letter to Alexander and Arius; he now realized that Arius himself must be jettisoned, but was determined not to make more victims than he could help. In that case, both Eusebii had reasonable grounds for confidence, provided they kept their heads and took a moderate line. For that matter, whatever we think of the presidency of the Council, it seems likely that one or other of the Eusebii delivered the opening address. Eusebius of Caesarea identifies the speaker simply as ὁ τοῦ δεξίου τάγματος πρωτεύων; but this is a complimentary phrase, and suggests that it was either himself or one of his friends; and Eusebius of Nicomedia would have a good claim to welcome the Emperor, as the local metropolitan.[1]

2. Starting from traditional assumptions, Eustathius' account would seem to suggest that he thinks of three parties at the Council, not two, as Athanasius so often implies. First there are the Eusebians, οἱ ἀμφὶ τὸν Εὐσέβιον, who can presumably be identified with 'the raving Arians', οἱ Ἀρειομανῖται. Secondly there is the 'peace party', οἱ ἐκ συσκευῆς. Thirdly there is the group whom they put to silence, oddly described as 'the people who spoke best' (or perhaps, 'spoke the best sense'), τοὺς ἄριστα λέγειν εἰωθότας, obviously Eustathius himself and his sympathizers.

The traditional view connects 'the raving Arians' with Eusebius of Nicomedia, and contrasts him with his peace-loving namesake. I have already argued against this view. But if Eustathius begins by referring to Eusebius of Caesarea, then who are the peace party, who got their way when the Eusebians had failed? One would have to imagine a party which commanded broader support, and so, whose views were nearer to Eustathius' own, but nevertheless not acceptable to him. What is this group of theologians whose views were markedly more 'Nicene' than those of Eusebius of Caesarea, yet also distinct from those of (say) Alexander, whom Eustathius would have been bound to defend?

If, on the other hand, the initial reference is not to an Arian initiative or creed, but to some previous writing by a member of the Arian party, it becomes much easier to identify the 'peace party'; they will be the bishops who fell in with Constantine's policy of comprehensiveness, and may well have included Eusebius of Caesarea among their numbers; and we still get an adequate explanation of the subsequent feud between him and Eustathius. To put it another way, the 'Eusebians' are those who supported the discredited document; the 'intriguers' can also be Arians, but ones who have adopted a policy of dissimulation.

[1] So Lietzmann, iii (E.T., *From Constantine to Julian*), p. 117; E. Schwartz, *Kaiser Constantin*, p. 135; P.-W.-K. vi. 1413.

3. We learn from St. Ambrose (*de fide* iii. 15 (125) = Opitz, Urk. 21) that a letter of Eusebius of Nicomedia was read at the Council; but there is no suggestion that Eusebius himself read it. Ambrose writes: *Sicut auctor ipsorum Eusebius Nicomediensis epistola sua prodidit, scribens* —here follows a brief quotation, not otherwise identifiable: *si verum dei filium et increatum dicimus,* ὁμοούσιον *cum patre incipimus confiteri.* He continues: *Haec cum lecta esset in concilio Nicaeno,* etc. The report is perfectly consonant with my submission that Eustathius is referring, not to the production of an Arian creed, but to the indictment of Eusebius of Nicomedia by the anti-Arian party on the basis of his previous writings.

4. Although it cannot be the document mentioned by St. Ambrose, I have a good deal of sympathy with the view that the writing mentioned by Eustathius is no other than the letter to Paulinus. This does at least fulfil one of the necessary conditions, in that much of its argument is based on exegesis of Proverbs viii. 22–3, 25. Eustathius' extended references to the Incarnation, the human life of Christ, and the Passion may not at first sight seem to fit this context; but they can, I think, be understood as a reply to the phrase which I have already quoted, that the second person is 'created, established, and begotten in respect of his substance and his unchangeable and ineffable nature'. We can see from the fragments that Eustathius attached great importance to the distinction between the Logos and the man Jesus; so presumably his contention was that Christ was created and established and had a beginning only in respect of his human nature, and so was directed precisely at this phrase from Eusebius. But I must not pursue this topic.

We are left, then, with an impression of the Nicene Council which is a good deal less colourful than that commonly accepted, but possibly more reliable. There is no marked contrast in the standpoint or the tactics adopted by the two bishops bearing the name Eusebius. If anything, it was Eusebius of Caesarea who had put himself in the more dangerous position by his outspoken defence of Arius, to which his namesake alludes (Urk. 8 init.); but it was his colleague who, in view of his position, presented the more tempting target for the anti-Arian party. He was therefore sharply attacked; but the two bishops and their associates avoided provocative statements and made the most of Constantine's desire for peace and comprehension. For the moment they were unable to stand by Arius, and their hopes of a purely non-committal statement of doctrine were not fulfilled; but they were able to defend themselves against their outright opponents, and obtained a creed which, with manifest reluctance, they were nevertheless able to sign.   G. C. STEAD

Journal of Ecclesiastical History, Vol. XXIV, No. 2, April 1973

Insight or Incoherence? The Greek Fathers on God and Evil[1]

by FRANCES M. YOUNG
Lecturer in Theology, University of Birmingham

This paper attempts to explore a number of inter-related ideas—inter-related in so far as they are all concerned in one way or another with evil, and God's relationship with it.

The belief most characteristic of Christianity is the assurance that redemption from evil has been achieved for mankind in the life, death and resurrection of Jesus Christ. Our first enquiry is concerned with a basic contradiction in the accounts of this belief given in Greek Patristic literature. Secondly, attention will be drawn to the tension between this characteristically Christian affirmation and the efforts of Christian thinkers of the period to produce a rationally-based theodicy—that is, their treatment of the problem of evil as traditionally understood. The conclusion raises the question whether our findings require us to charge the Greek Fathers with incoherence in their theology.

The work of Christ took place in the context of a cosmic drama. Since Aulen's study,[2] it is no longer possible to escape from the fact that the early Church presupposed some form of dualism in its presentation of Atonement. From the New Testament to the Cappadocians, the Christian felt himself to be involved in the warfare between God and the devil, good and evil, light and darkness, life and death, righteousness and sin. This conflict was typified in the Christian campaign against idolatry and superstition, magic and astrology. The martyr felt himself at war with the opposing forces of evil when he died for his faith. With the powers of evil, God had to do battle or business, and the supreme moment of victory was the Cross of Christ. Christ achieved the victory; his followers were merely bringing the rout to its final conclusion. So the Fathers understood 'the idea of Atonement as a divine conflict and victory; Christ—Christus Victor—fights against and triumphs over the evil powers of the world, the "tyrants" under which mankind is in bondage and suffering'.[3] 'Christus Victor' conquered death by his resurrection, spiritual blindness by the light of

---

[1] This paper was originally composed for the Oxford Society of Historical Theology. I am grateful to the society for their discussion.

[2] G. Aulen, *Christus Victor*, E.T., London 1931. See my discussion of Aulen's view of Atonement in the Greek Fathers, in 'The Use of Sacrificial Ideas in Greek Christian Writers from the New Testament to John Chrysostom', Cambridge University Ph.D. thesis, (1967).

[3] Aulen, op. cit., 20–1.

113

his teaching and ignorance by his revelation, and all the various aspects of this victory can be described mythologically by reference to the defeat of the devil and his angels.

To illustrate the pervasiveness of this concept of God's atoning work, I draw your attention to the soteriology of Origen. Origen's ideas on salvation are expressed in a vast range of imagery,[1] for he was untiring as an exegete and as a collector of scriptural passages which applied to any given problem. There is a confusing array of ideas, but nevertheless a basic pattern can, I believe, be discerned. This is a pattern of conflict between good and evil, in which Christ achieves the victory. I would argue that Origen *basically* thought of the Atonement in terms of the dualist outlook described—that is, his use of this theory was not an occasional descent to the level of the 'simpliciores', an element foreign to his philosophical outlook, as some scholars have imagined, but rather it is absolutely central to his understanding of salvation.

Most expositors of Origen's thought have regarded as his characteristic view of Christ's saving function, his understanding of Christ as revealer, educator and enlightenment, that is, as Logos of God. That this should be Origen's main account of Christ's work in the *De Principiis* is not surprising,[2] since this is a work dominated by philosophical issues and ideas. It is also prominent in the *Commentary on John*,[3] as the brightness of God's glory. Christ enlightens the whole creation and, as the Word, he interprets and presents to the rational creation the secrets of wisdom and the mysteries of knowledge. This approach is scattered throughout Origen's work and needs no detailed exemplification.

As far as our argument is concerned, however, the important point is that even this description of Christ's work fits into the dualist pattern. Not only is it expressed in the simple opposition of light and darkness, knowledge and ignorance, but it is seen in the context of the war between good and evil, God and the devil. Thus Origen can maintain that Christ as Word conquers the opposing powers by reason, 'by making war on his enemies by reason and righteousness, so that what is irrational and wicked is destroyed'.[4] Right doctrine is a means of conquering sin.[5] The light shines not only in the darkness of men's souls, but has also penetrated to where the rulers of this darkness carry on their struggle with the race of men; and, shining in the darkness, the light is pursued by darkness, but not overtaken.[6]

---

[1] See, e.g., his collection of titles expressing the nature and work of Christ in *Comm. Jn.*, i. 22 ff.; Light of the world, Resurrection, the Way, the Truth, the Life, the Door and the Shepherd, Christ and King, Teacher and Master, Son, True Vine and Bread, First and Last, Living and Dead, Sword, Servant, Lamb of God, Paraclete, Propitiation, Power, Wisdom, Sanctification, Redemption, Righteousness, Demiurge, Agent of the Good God, High-Priest, Rod, Stone, Flower, Logos.

[2] *De Princ.*, i. 2, 6, 7, 8; iii. 5, 8.

[3] E.g., *Comm. Jn.*, i. 23, 24, 27, 42.

[4] Ibid., ii. 4.

[5] *Comm. Rom.*, vi. 3.

[6] *Comm. Jn.*, ii. 21.

114

This dualist basis to Origen's thought could be illustrated whichever characteristic image we might adopt as example,[1] but I shall not delay further at this point. I simply draw attention to its presence even in one of the most sophisticated of Christian thinkers. The idea is so widespread elsewhere that it is hardly necessary to document it. From the exorcisms of the New Testament to the spiritual struggles of the monk Antony against temptation, the same view prevails, and it is difficult to understand why it has for so long been played down by scholars. The explanation is no doubt to be found in the influence of theologians who, in the interests of their own views of Atonement, portrayed ransom-theories as uncharacteristic aberrations.[2]

In the context of this basic dualism, it was not unnatural that redemption was seen in terms of God ransoming man from the power of the devil. Paul had spoken of men being 'slaves to sin', of being 'sold to sin'; furthermore he had described man as being bought with a price, the blood of Christ.[3] Λύτρον, λύτρωσις were current in the language of the Church, and provided a natural means of expounding the nature of Christ's work of worsting the evil powers.

But the Church also used cultic language of Christ's death, describing it as a sacrifice. According to Aulen, sacrifice is naturally regarded as offered *to* God, whereas ransom indicates the price paid *by* God to the devil.[4] But how could the death of Christ be both a sacrifice to God and a ransom to the devil? If the conquest of the devil was the basic requirement for dealing with evil, why should sacrifice to God be necessary? How could a ransom offered *by* God, be also a sacrifice *to* God?

There can be little doubt that for many Church members this contradiction was never spelled out, but was endemic in their outlook. The most frequent understanding of the idea of sacrifice in Greek pagan literature is placatory, the offering of gifts or bribes to get the favour of the gods. Such an idea had been much criticised by philosophers,[5] and in the Old Testament, while traces remain, it had been considerably refined[6]; for the sacrificial system was part of God's law, given by God for dealing with sin and keeping the covenant-relation intact. But philosophical considerations did not much affect popular piety, and the Old Testament was interpreted in accordance with pagan presuppositions. So Christ's death on the cross was certainly understood by the majority of Gentile Christians as a sacrifice placating God's wrath.

This is reflected in the writings even of those who had had an educa-

[1] For further development, see my dissertation, cited above, 232 ff.
[2] E.g., H. Rashdall, *The Idea of Atonement in Christian Theology*, London 1919; J. Rivière, *The Doctrine of the Atonement*, E.T., London 1909.
[3] *Rom.*, vi. 17, 18; vii. 14; *I Cor.*, vi. 20; vii. 23.
[4] Aulen, op. cit. See his chapter on 'The Double Aspect of the Drama of the Atonement'.
[5] The points made in this paragraph are developed more fully in my dissertation, cited above.
[6] *Gen.*, viii. 21; *I Sam.*, xxvi. 19; *II Sam.* xxiv. 25. For discussion, see G. B. Gray, *Sacrifice in the Old Testament*, Oxford 1925.

115

tion in Origenist theology, and who would therefore feel embarrassed by the idea of God's anger. Eusebius in his *Demonstratio Evangelica*[1] discusses the meaning of sacrifice, providing a rationale to cover Old Testament types and their antitype, the sacrifice of Christ. The blood of the animal is offered to propitiate God; it is the life offered in place of the sinner's life, as an ἀντίψυχον, a ransom and substitute. Christ became the victim who was the substitute offered to God for the life of sinful man; as High-priest, he offered the perfect sacrifice pleasing to the Father, his own body.

John Chrysostom in his *Homilies on Hebrews* consistently explains Christ's work as propitiating the Father, reconciling us to an angry and hostile God. 'The Father was wroth against us, and displeased with us as being estranged from him; he (the Son) accordingly became mediator between us and him, and won him over'.[2] 'He went up with a sacrifice which had power to propitiate the Father'.[3]

These statements are clear and incontestable. Christ offered a propitiatory sacrifice to God. Yet, alongside this interpretation, we find references to the more widespread view that Christ was God's agent conquering the powers of evil. Chrysostom explains that 'he dissolved death, banished us from the tyranny of the devil, freed us from slavery . . .'[4] After dealing with the Destroyer, 'God led us out of Egypt, out of darkness, out of idolatry . . .'.[5]

Eusebius thinks of the ransom as a price paid by God to the devil,[6] as well as being the substitutionary sacrifice offered to God. In fact, Eusebius's discussion proves that the contradiction was marked by linguistic confusion; Aulen's distinction between ransom and sacrifice does not apply. The terms were interchangeable, and applicable within either picture of Christ's atoning work.

Yet some did feel a certain embarrassment. Chrysostom consistently stresses the φιλανθρωπία of God which motivated the offering of his Son.[7] On one occasion, having stated that Christ propitiated the Father, he corrects himself, and says rather lamely that it was not God but the angels who were hostile.[8] The uncomfortable tension between a sacrificial understanding of Christ's death, and the prevailing picture of God acting in Christ to overcome evil because of his love towards men, is apparent, though not resolved.

However, some feelers towards resolution had been advanced. Origen provides an instructive example, instructive because his successors failed to grasp what he was getting at. Because of his wide-ranging exegetical work, the sacrificial interpretation of Christ's death had become more

[1] *Dem. Evang.*, i. 10.
[2] *Hom. Heb.*, xvi. 1.
[3] *Hom. Heb.*, xvii. 1.
[4] *Hom. Heb.*, v. 2.
[5] *Hom. Heb.*, xxvii. 1.
[6] *Dem. Evang.*, x. 8.
[7] E.g., *Hom. Heb.*, iv. 3; v. 2; xxv. 1; etc.
[8] *Hom. Heb.*, xvii. 1.

116

prominent in his writings than in previous literature. The rituals described in Leviticus were given a Christological interpretation in his Homilies. Here it is not perhaps surprising to find frequent reference to the sacrificial death of Christ, but the image is also found in many other contexts. Yet, as we have seen, Origen's predominant theory of Atonement was the idea of divine victory over evil. How then did he understand Christ's sacrifice? Origen's rationalisation of God's anger and emotion is well-known, and we should, therefore, be surprised if he accepted the notion of propitiation. 'When we speak of God's wrath, we do not hold that it is an emotional reaction on his part, but something which he uses in order to correct by stern methods those who have committed many terrible sins'.[1] His anger then is a means of discipline. It is reformative rather than retributive.[2] So the concept of propitiation is ridiculous, and Origen recognises this. There is no mercy in letting off a sinner unless punishment has had its effect.[3] Mercy cannot be bought or wrath propitiated.

Yet Origen does use the language of propitiation. Was he aware of this contradiction? I believe he was, and that his use of propitiation-language was subtly different from popular usage, directing attention to the removal of sin, the transformation of mankind which is required for reconciliation with God.[4] In the Commentary on John, for example, he asks how Christ could have been Paraclete and Atonement and Propitiation, if the power of God which makes an end to our weaknesses, did not flow over the soul of believers, administered by Jesus, who is himself the power of God.[5] Furthermore, I think it can be shown that his understanding of Christ's sacrifice was not inconsistent with his general view of Atonement. Often he speaks of it as a mystery, and at times confesses himself baffled; but when he seeks an explanation, he shows himself very unhappy with the idea that his sacrifice was offered to God, and solves his problem by suggesting that God allows Christ and the martyrs to suffer in order to *overthrow the evil powers*, instancing as a comparable case the Gentiles who were said to have offered themselves as victims for the public good.[6] He uses this analogy several times, referring to stories of men who sacrificed themselves to check epidemics of plagues and famines,[7] and regards this as the only possible way of solving the problem of how Christ's sacrifice dealt with evil.

Now in using this analogy, Origen is turning to a different understand-

---

[1] C. Cels., iv. 72 (trans. H. Chadwick).
[2] N.B. the images used to express this: a father disciplining his child (*Hom. Jer.*, xviii. 6; Comm. Rom., vii. 18); a doctor inflicting pain in order to heal, a schoolmaster chastising in order to improve (C. Cels., iv. 56).
[3] Comm. Rom., ii. 1; iii. 1.
[4] N.B. 'sin' or 'men' appear as the *object* of the verb not God; for further detail, see the dissertation, cited above.
[5] Comm. Jn., i. 38.
[6] Comm. Jn., vi. 35-6.
[7] C. Cels., i. 31; Comm. Rom. iv. 11. N.B. the same analogy is used of the deaths of martyrs in *I Clement*, 55. Philo uses it to explain Abraham's sacrifice of Isaac in *De Abrahamo*, 33.

117

ing of sacrifice. In primitive Greek religion, sacrifices of aversion were offered to ward off the gods of the underworld, the evil spirits, plagues and disasters.[1] These superstitious rites were still very much alive, and for the Neoplatonist, Iamblichus, this was the most important aspect of sacrificial worship, the aversion of evil so that the purified soul might be united with the divine.[2] When Origen reflects on the character of Christ's sacrificial work, he sees it in terms of God offering a sacrifice to avert and conquer evil, so it *is* consistent with his concept of Atonement and his rationalisation of God's anger.

Yet this view is hardly argued in a clear and compelling fashion. Hints and gropings are all we find. So Origen's successors failed to discern it, and lived with the uncomfortable tension outlined earlier. There was a fundamental contradiction between the understanding of Christ's death as a propitiatory sacrifice, and the prevailing view of God's atoning work as the conquest of evil.

In discussion, the ideas in the following section have elicited the comment 'What an indictment of the Fathers as systematic thinkers!'.[3] The comment is fair to the extent that my conclusions expose inconsistencies and ill-perceived ambiguities; it is not fair in so far as many of the same short-comings can be detected in the thinking of pagan contemporaries with whom the Fathers shared a considerable cultural sophistication. No philosopher is entirely isolated from contemporary habits of thought, though nowadays we are more aware of cultural conditioning, and, one hopes, less inclined to make claims to absolute truth. The following case-history diagnoses some causes of blindness, as well as reporting its occurrence in the Fathers' treatment of a perennial and intractable problem.

The problem with which I am concerned here has been described as 'a paradox, a problem in the problem of evil'.[4] The difficulty is that on the one hand evil in the world presents a problem for theistic belief, and yet on the other hand, it is a necessary condition of any religion of redemption. Both theodicy and atonement are concerned with evil, but the approach is very different. One proclaims the conquest of evil, the other seeks to explain its existence; one asserts the power of God over evil, the other regards evil as a threat either to God's goodness or his sovereignty.

In the writings of the Greek Fathers, there is little awareness of this contradiction, even though it is present in a particularly acute form. As we have seen, the early Church presupposed a form of dualism in its presentation of Atonement. Yet, in the face of Gnostics and Manichaeans, who presupposed an ultimate dualism, the Church engaged in the enterprise of

[1] J. E. Harrison, *Prolegomena to the study of Greek Religion*, 3rd ed., Cambridge 1922; G. Murray, *Five Stages of Greek Religion*, Oxford 1925; H. J. Rose, *Ancient Greek Religion*, London 1948; R. K. Yerkes, *Sacrifice in Greek and Roman Religion and in early Judaism*, London 1953.
[2] *De Mysteriis*, v. 6 ff.; dissertation, cited above, 32 ff.
[3] G. C. Stead, at the Sixth International Conference on Patristic Studies, Oxford 1971.
[4] Patterson Brown, 'God and the Good', *Religious Studies* ii, 1967, 269–76.

118

theodicy, of vindicating God's goodness as Creator.[1] When considering the nature and origin of evil, the Church could not stomach a philosophical dualism, even though their faith was dualistic in its presuppositions. Yet they appear largely oblivious to this inconsistency.

So, in the Greek patristic literature, we find another unresolved and ill-perceived tension in their understanding of God and his relationship with evil. Can we trace any reasons for their blindness? I think we can.

In the first place, discussion of evil arose in two different theological contexts; so the lack of consistency was not immediately apparent. Theodicy sprang out of controversy; the debate with rival philosophers, critics and heretics produced a stock of philosophical arguments defending monotheism, the providence of God, the goodness of the creation, and so on. Thus a philosophical theodicy was built up. On the other hand, in presenting the message of salvation, and exhorting congregations to the Christian life, the struggle against evil was depicted in highly graphic terms. Salvation tended to be understood as an escape from, or victory over the evils of the world.

Even in the work of the Cappadocians we find a marked separation between tackling questions of theodicy and preaching redemption. For esample: Basil's *Hexaemeron* is a work of philosophical theodicy, asserting the goodness of God in creation and providence. The legacy of Aristotle and the Stoics is evident in the use of final causes as examples of providence in the natural world.[2] Facts apparently fatal to this theory are given rational explanations, mostly along the lines of Origen's theodicy: God, like a schoolmaster, uses corporal punishment for our good.[3] So the whole creation becomes a vast teaching-machine, with lessons at every turn: even poisonous plants[4] and ravenous beasts[5] have such a providential purpose. Here, then, is a remarkable adaptation of contemporary science to theistic argument, but in the whole collection of homilies, there is not a single reference to faith in redemption from evil, since the existence of evil in creation is simply not admitted. Indeed, there is only one specifically Christian, as distinct from theistic, point, and that is a dubious piece of exegesis relevant to current Trinitarian debate.[6] The doctrine of redemption finds no place in discussion of the doctrine of creation.

On the other hand, Gregory Nazianzen's *Orations*, particularly his Easter sermons,[7] illustrate forcibly the dualist presuppositions of much Christian preaching. They are rhetorical pieces which perhaps overdo the antitheses; but, nevertheless, the reality and power of evil is assumed

---

[1] Cf. W. G. Floyd, *Clement of Alexandria's treatment of the problem of evil*, Oxford 1971.

[2] Y. Courtonne, *Saint Basile et l'Hellénisme*, Paris 1934; S. Giet, *Basile de Césarée, Homélies sur l'Hexaemeron*, Introduction (Sources Chrétiennes), Paris 1949.

[3] *Hexaemeron*, i. 5, 6; ix. 5.

[4] Ibid., v. 4.

[5] Ibid., ix. 5.

[6] Ibid., ix. 6.

[7] *Orat.*, i and xlv.

119

without question in the proclamation of the Gospel of redemption, and the call to partake in Christ's successful campaign against evil.

Thus, context often determined the approach. In a good many cases, however, this explanation breaks down. For example, in the pastoral situation, tragedies were confronted which called providence in question; explanations were drawn from the traditional arguments of theodicy, consolation and encouragement from scripture and the example of God's redemptive love in Christ. Inconsistency between the different approaches was disregarded. An analogy provides a possible explanation: Origenist exegesis of scripture approved a multiplication of meanings, however incompatible; likewise, in the vindication of God's providential love, any mitigating argument or insight was worth adding to the pastor's stock, regardless of inconsistency between the different suggestions.

Sermons provide examples of the intermingling of popular theodicy and scriptural consolation. One of Basil's extant homilies was delivered during a period of drought and famine.[1] The occasion of Gregory Nazianzen's *Sixteenth Oration* was a hailstorm which totally destroyed the crops of his parishioners. Such disasters have always called providence in question; but for Basil and Gregory it was unthinkable to deny either divine causation or divine goodness. Arguments of theodicy were used to prove that these terrible events were providential in drawing the attention of the congregation to its failure to live in a way worthy of Christ. Elsewhere in Gregory's *Orations*, we find similar claims of popular theodicy: sickness is a means of cleansing, recovery a proof of God's grace.[2] God's chastening in history is seen in wars, plagues, etc.[3] However, suggestions of another kind also appear, suggestions which are only marginally consistent with this theodicy. In the face of evil, people should not be crushed and vanquished, but should apply the blood of the new covenant in order to rise again;[4] the suffering of the innocent, nobly born, though a scandal to unbelievers, is nevertheless a testimony to God's love and a sharing in Christ's sufferings;[5] the suffering of Christ and of the martyrs was exemplary and an instrument of our salvation.[6] In his sufferings, the Son of God experienced our condition.[7] Furthermore, a vivid sense of the reality of the powers of evil with which Christians have to contend, sometimes embodied in characters like Julian the Apostate,[8] sometimes directly inspiring idolatry and wickness,[9] contrasts with the confident assertion of God's goodness and sovereignty, witnessed in creation and providence.[10] Often

[1] *Homilia dicta tempore famis et siccitatis*, in P.G., xxxi. 304 ff.
[2] *Orat.*, xviii. 28; viii. 15, 17, 18.
[3] *Orat.*, xxxviii. 13.
[4] *Orat.*, xvi. 12.
[5] *Orat.*, viii. 15.
[6] E.g., *Orat.*, xv; xxiv. 19; xxxiii. 9.
[7] *Theol. Orat.*, iv. 5–6.
[8] *Orat.*, iv. 65–71.
[9] *Theol. Orat.*, ii. 15.
[10] *Theol. Orat.*, ii passim.

120

these viewpoints appear on different occasions, but sometimes both are expressed in a single sermon.

Here, then, we find an oscillation between theodicy and atonement doctrine, varying suggestions employed side by side, and consistency between them neither sought nor demanded. We see here the response of groping believers, not a coherent answer to a philosophical problem.

In the case of systematic attempts to account for evil and the need for redemption, the factors so far discussed are obviously irrelevant. Here the paradox was concealed by the very nature of the arguments used.

In the first place, a sharp distinction between physical and moral evil allowed quite different solutions to each problem. Basil's homily, *Quod Deus non est auctor malorum*,[1] seeks to absolve God of responsibility for evil, largely by establishing this distinction. Things that we call evil, like sickness, poverty, death, plagues, droughts, famine, earthquakes, floods, etc. are not so; they have their purpose as a means of testing and discipline. The only thing that is really evil is sin, which arose out of our own choice. Thus physical evils were dissolved away by arguments of theodicy; moral evil alone was regarded as serious. Dealing with the latter problem was the object of God's work of redemption.

In this way, theodicy and atonement were virtually consigned to separate compartments, and their paradoxical relationship went unobserved. Only in explaining the genesis of moral evil did they overlap, and here a consistent account appeared to be available in attributing its origin not to God but to the free choice of morally free creatures. However, this apparently consistent account was itself unsatisfactory, for it was based on a certain ambivalence of meaning in the commonly accepted definition of evil. This was, in fact, the most serious factor in concealing the paradox with which we are concerned.

Evil was defined as non-Being. The definition arose out of the following argument: All Being is good. Evil is the opposite of good. Therefore it is not in Being. It has no hypostasis of its own; it is simply absence of good.

This definition was Platonic. So well-known is its use in Augustine, and previously in Christian Platonist writings from Clement of Alexandria onwards, that I need not document it. It was adopted as an argument against dualism, and it served as a method of theodicy: if evil is not in Being, it is neither a power equivalent to good, nor was it created by God.

The argument then really belongs to theodicy, and there it most often appears. But it was rapidly adapted to serve as an explanation of the origin of evil and the need for salvation. Thus moral evil as well as physical evil was defined as absence of good; its origin was attributed to the fact that beings created with freewill turned away from the good, and preferred created things to the Creator. So, for example, Gregory of Nyssa explains the fall of Satan and his angels, and sets the scene for his dramatic account of redemption. The same argument served as explanation of the fall of man.[2]

---

[1] P.G., xxxi. 329 ff.   [2] See especially the *Catechetical Oration*.

121

Gregory, then, assumed, like many other apologists,[1] that this definition of evil provided a satisfactory background to the story of redemption, even though it originated in the context of theodicy. Its weaknesses for this task are well-known: (a) if evil is merely deprivation of good, why should morally free agents choose it in preference to good? (b) if evil is the absence of good, whence comes malicious evil, deliberate rebellion such as is envisaged as the background to a redemption-doctrine? In fairness to Gregory and his predecessors, we should note the closely parallel accounts of evil found in Porphyry's *Letter to Marcella*[2] and Sallustius's treatise *On the gods and the universe*.[3] It was not the fault of Christian thinkers *alone* that these weaknesses went undetected.

More serious than these weaknesses, however, is the fact that the consistency is merely superficial. The argument cannot retain its force in both contexts at once, since the notion of non-Being is different in each.

The prevailing intellectual climate encouraged a certain confusion over the status of non-Being. The problem arose from the identification of value-judgements and existential statements. Plotinus expresses the difficulty: 'Evil cannot be in Being or in that beyond Being: for they are good. It remains then that, granted there is evil, it must be in a class of non-Beings, existing as a sort of form of non-existence. "Non-Being" here, of course, does not mean "that which is absolutely non-existent" but only "that which is other than Being"'. Just as there is Absolute Good, he argued, so there must be Absolute Evil.[4] So Plotinus. His position is comparatively clear, if paradoxical.[5]

It was, of course, no more paradoxical for Christian apologists to define evil as non-Being and yet be extremely conscious of its presence and power in the world. But if Plotinus was comparatively clear, the arguments of Athanasius and Gregory suggest that clarity was easily lost. They are far less aware of the ambiguity involved in the notion of non-Being, a situation aggravated by the parallel ambiguity of the word 'death' in scripture, where the literal and moral senses run together. In Athanasius's formulation, death is a return to the nothingness out of which men were created; death, evil and non-Being are the opposites of life, good and Being. According to this definition, failure to choose the good should mean decay, dissolution, oblivion; but, in fact, the fall meant rebellion, positive wickedness and enslavement to the powers of evil. Death is not simply a return to nothing, but a power hostile to the purposes of God, which must be conquered. Evil has no οὐσία but its power cannot be denied. It is far from merely negative. Only the triumph of the incarnation could redeem mankind from the powers of death and sin. Such is the position outlined in Athanasius's *De Incarnatione*, followed in Gregory

---

[1] E.g., Athanasius, *De Incarnatione*; Basil, *Quod Deus non est . . .*, cited above,121 n. 1.
[2] Ed. A. Nauck, 1886 (Teubner ed.).
[3] Ed. A. D. Nock, Cambridge 1926.
[4] *Enneads*, i.8.3 (trans. A. H. Armstrong).
[5] For Plotinus, matter, too, had this paradoxical status. For discussion, see J. M. Rist, 'Plotinus on Matter and Evil in Phronesis', vi (1961), 154 ff.

122

of Nyssa's *Catechetical Oration*, and implied throughout the writings of the Cappadocian Fathers.

'Non-Being' then does not necessarily mean non-existent. Once introduce a need for redemption, and the existence of evil in some sense is implied. In terms of contemporary philosophy, this position might be acceptable; but once allow that evil exists in some sense in the universe, and you attribute some responsibility to the Creator. If non-Being does not mean non-existence, then the argument is emptied of its original force as a means of theodicy. This definition of evil cannot do both jobs at once without a fatal loss of effectiveness.

So the Greek Fathers failed to observe that theodicy and atonement-doctrine are uncomfortable bed-fellows, largely because the conventional definition of evil appeared to be viable in both contexts; but the appearance was deceptive.

We have explored two areas of contradiction, tension or ambiguity in the Fathers' treatment of God's relationship with evil. These two areas are not unrelated. The inconsistencies between theories of atonement and theodicy were further confused by the unresolved contradiction between different theories of atonement sketched earlier. The predominant argument of theodicy, as we have seen, derived from Origen, and attributed sickness, droughts, earthquakes and other external evils, to God's purpose of disciplining mankind. Origen may have been unhappy with ideas of propitiation, but his theory lent itself in popular preaching, no doubt under the influence of the prophetic writings of the Old Testament, to demands for repentance and reform as a means of propitiating an angry God who punished the people by sending drought or hailstorm to destroy their crops.[1] The offering of such spiritual sacrifices fitted into the pattern of ideas which fostered the propitiatory theory of Christ's sacrifice, but was not consistent with the dualism that dominated thinking about redemption.

Monism or dualism? Ultimately both the problems we have considered resolve themselves into this question, and the tensions arose because the Fathers had reasons for wanting to maintain both at once. They conceived of God as source of all; they also conceived of God as all goodness, opposed to and triumphant over evil.

The nub of the problem, then, was how far responsibility for evil could be attributed to God. There were inbuilt pressures against allowing God any responsibility at all for evil: he was identified with the One and the Good of the philosophers; and the Christian Gospel rested on a confident assertion of his saving goodness overcoming evil. Origen and Gregory of Nyssa represent the most consistent acceptance of such views, but this line of reasoning led them into the second trap we have explored: on the one hand, to maintain that evil was really non-existent, but on the other hand, to produce the most vivid, and to modern minds, the most repugnant ac-

---

[1] Cf. especially Gregory Nazianzen, *Orat.*, xvi, discussed above.

123

counts of God's trafficking with the devil. Gregory's fish-hook is notorious,[1] but was undoubtedly motivated by a deep awareness of God's goodness and love towards mankind.

The vast majority, however, were less consistent in their understanding of God's nature. Traditional patterns of thought were adopted without a real appreciation of the contradictions involved. God is love; God is angry. God is ultimately responsible for everything; the devil is responsible for evil.[2] God sent his Son to overcome evil; God was placated by his Son's sacrifice. Insight or incoherence? Surely we can only charge them all with the latter.

And yet, does not this very incoherence imply at least a sensitivity to the ambiguous and elusive character of God and his relationship with evil? An entirely convincing solution continues to elude us.[3] Perhaps the nearest thing we can get to a characteristically Christian theodicy, as distinct from a general theistic one, is to say that on the Cross, God in Christ entered into the suffering and evil of *his* world, so demonstrating that he *does* take responsibility for it, and at the same time dealing with it. But this is perhaps poetic understanding or the insight of faith, rather than a theological conclusion based on logical argument. It was in any case, not open to the Greek Fathers because of certain philosophical presuppositions that barred the way. They not only denied the reality of evil and suffering but also denied the possibility of God changing or suffering. Their affirmation of the incarnation was in spite of their theology rather than consonant with it.

Nevertheless, one of the Greek Fathers does reconcile the various elements up to a point, and in spite of the difficulties imposed by contemporary presuppositions, seems to feel his way towards a more subtle appraisal of the situation. This is Athanasius.

Athanasius's *De Incarnatione* is a major attempt to present the Christian Gospel of redemption in a systematic way. It takes up the traditional language of Christian preaching, the traditional accounts of the fall and redemption. It is, to our minds, refreshingly free of the demonology of most early Christian writing, and concentrates on the fall of Man, rather than the prior fall of the devil. However, it would be foolish to imagine that the devil is entirely absent,[4] and in any case the principal motif of his soteriology is the idea of victory over death,[5] sin and ignorance, a major proof of this being seen in the destruction of idolatry which Christianity was effecting. The Cross is a trophy,[6] the Gospel, a cry of victory: 'The devil's tyranny has come to an end'.[7]

[1] *Cat. Orat.*, 24.
[2] E.g., Gregory Nazianzen, *Orat.*, xliii. 41, where evil in the Church is attributed to the devil. Other examples would not be far to seek.
[3] E. H. Madden and P. H. Hare, *Evil and the concept of God*, Springfield, Illinois 1968, is a searching critique of most modern attempts at theodicy.
[4] *De Inc.*, v. 1–2; vi. 5, 6; x. 4; xii. 6; xx. 6; etc. See especially, *De Inc.*, xxv (Long Recension), and *Vita Antonii*, passim.
[5] Note the virtual personification of death in *De Inc.*, e.g. *De Inc.*, iv. 2; v. 2; etc.
[6] *De Inc.*, xix. 3; xxiv. 4; xxvi. 1; xxx. 1.   [7] *C. Arianos*, ii. 73.

124

But Athanasius recognised that the picture of a straightforward conflict between good and evil, did not do justice to the complexity of the problem. Following the traditional monism, he used the non-Being argument, failing, like the others, to observe its weaknesses. The significant thing, however, is that he *did* allow a measure of responsibility to God for the mess from which mankind needed salvation. He suggested that man's disobedience had produced an intolerable tension between God's integrity and his goodness.[1] It put God into a dilemma. It was unthinkable that he should go back on his word, and Man, having transgressed, should not die; God could not falsify himself. But it was not worthy of his goodness that his creation should perish, especially in the case of creatures who had been endowed with the nature of the Logos himself. It would have been better never to have created them. Repentance could have solved the problem, if it had not been for that decree, and the corruption of nature which therefore ensued when Man committed sin. The debt to death had to be paid. Somehow God's integrity had to be salvaged while the demands of his love were met. The sacrifice of Christ was the solution to this dilemma; it was a sort of 'self-propitiation', offered by God to God, to make atonement for the existence of evil in his universe.[2]

This account does seem to do justice to the conflicting traditions about God's relationship with evil which we have been examining. No doubt such a solution was latent in earlier Christian thought, but I do not think it was explicitly expressed and it was probably hardly grasped.[3] In the writings of the two Cappadocian Gregories, we find no explicit use of these ideas. Gregory of Nyssa, as we have seen, follows Origen in seeing Atonement in radically dualistic terms. Gregory Nazianzen *may* have been feeling towards something like the Athanasian solution. He explicitly enquires in one passage[4] whether the ransom was given to the devil, and dismisses the idea as ὕβρις. The offering was therefore made to God; but why? His reply is 'because of the economy'; God did not need such a sacrifice, but it was his method of purifying human nature.

---

[1] *De Inc.*, viii. ff.

[2] This is not quite Athanasius's terminology, but see *C. Arianos*, ii. 7 ff. The argument of this passage as a whole stresses the idea that the sacrifice of Christ was offered by God to God to reconcile himself, and includes the unusual phrase: ἱλασκόμενος τὰ πρὸς τὸν Θεόν. This phrase is particularly significant because Athanasius rarely uses propitiation-language (except in scriptural quotations), and here he has deliberately avoided saying Christ propitiated God. He, of all people, could not allow a distinction between God and the Logos.

[3] Here I differ from Aulen, in his chapter on 'The double aspect of the drama of atonement', where he outlines a similar theory of divine self-reconciliation, maintaining that, while the Fathers had a dualistic outlook, it was modified by the view that the devil was ultimately God's creature and under God's authority (à la Job, presumably). Thus he describes the death of Christ both as a ransom offered by God to the devil, and as a sacrifice offered by God to himself. Undoubtedly there is some measure of truth in this, particularly, as we have seen, in the case of Athanasius. But it is far from explicit in other patristic writings.

[4] *Orat.*, xlv. 22.

125

'Because of the economy'. Ultimately that is an honest admission that the whole matter is a mystery. The gropings of the Greek Fathers seem to be incoherent, but perhaps their refusal to adopt oversimplifying ideas, their refusal to ignore or forget conflicting elements of the tradition, does reflect some insight, perhaps unconscious, into the complexity of the problems.

TRADITION, EXEGESIS, AND THE CHRISTOLOGICAL CONTROVERSIES

ROBERT L. WILKEN, *Assistant Professor of Church History, Lutheran Theological Seminary at Gettysburg*

In 430, Cyril, bishop of Alexandria, wrote in his treatise *Adversus Nestorium* that we must put away idle questioning and "receive with faith the simple and undefiled tradition."[1] Which tradition did he have in mind? About the same time, Nestorius, bishop of Constantinople, defended a priest who denied the appellation *theotokos* to the Virgin Mary.[2] Nestorius claimed the term was not in accord with the tradition. Which tradition did he have in mind?

Both Cyril and Nestorius made quite clear that they were referring to the ancient tradition which the apostles received from Jesus and later handed on to the bishops of the Church. As bishops of two of the most important sees in Christendom—Alexandria even claimed to be founded by Mark—each believed that he had received from his predecessors this tradition handed over by the apostles. And though they might have been reluctant to admit it in 430, they thought this tradition was the common possession of all orthodox bishops in the Empire.

On examination, however, it is doubtful whether the tradition would have appeared as unified as they would have us believe. In fact, Cyril's own explication of the "undefiled" tradition betrays a suspiciously Alexandrian caste; and Nestorius' reasons for denying Mary the *theotokos* sound surprisingly like other writers in the orbit of Antioch. The twelve anathemas sent to Nestorius by Cyril are a good case in point. They were offered as a statement of the faith of the total Church, as a common and universally acceptable tradition, but they were nothing of the sort and bore all the marks of a peculiarly Alexandrian Christology.[3] In fact, as Liébaert has shown, much of Cyril's "undefiled" tradition is simply Athanasius lifted bodily—without notes—from his *Orationes Contra Arianos.*[4] Was Cyril, then, really referring to the ancient tradition supposedly shared by all? Or did he, without realizing or admitting it, really mean the particular redaction of the faith transmitted in the Church of Alexandria?

If we put the same question to Nestorius we discover immediately that he was wrong about the *theotokos* . The term had been in use for several centuries and could be documented in the writings of important fathers.[5] Cyril knew this and could produce telling evidence. Does this, however, mean that Cyril was right and Nestorius a dangerous innovator? Unfortunately the matter cannot be so easily decided, for, though wrong about the *theotokos,* Nestorius certainly had much more in mind than a few Greek letters. It hardly vindicates Cyril, as many have supposed, simply to cite passages containing *theotokos* in earlier orthodox writers.[6] Cyril had indeed outflanked him on the term, but this did not wholly undercut Nestorius' position or the argument behind his rejection of *theotokos*.

Now it was hardly a new phenomenon in Christian history to appeal to tradition. For several centuries theologians had appealed to tradition in defense of the faith against heretics. Ireneaus had done it; Hippolytus had done it; and Tertullian gave the argument classic form in his *De Praescriptione haereticorum*. But things were different in the second century, for heretics were seldom, if ever, bishops of important sees, and most bishops could offer proof—at least to their own satisfaction—that they possessed authentic apostolic tradition. But how things had changed by the fifth century! Here we behold bishops of the two most important and influential sees of the East engaged in a vicious and relentless battle, each marching forth armed with the conviction that he alone possessed the truth and appealing to what was considered one and the same tradition. What had happened to enflame such passion, bitterness, and profound misunderstanding? On the surface two patriarchs disagreed over a theological point. But this had happened before. Some have argued that the conflict be read primarily in political terms: the pope of Alexandria was seeking to crush the see of Constantinople, a young upstart challenging Alexandria's primacy in the East.[7] But this also was not new, for Theophilus, Cyril's predecessor, had sailed from Alexandria only a few years earlier to humiliate and destroy Chrysostom in Constantinople. The consequence of this encounter hardly equalled the disaster which sprang from the meeting of Cyril and Nestorius a generation later.

The following does not intend to suggest a new key to explain and interpret the Christological controversies of the fifth and sixth centuries. Nor does it seek to isolate theological factors at the expense of political and ecclesiastical factors.[8] Hopefully we have learned that any series of historical events can only be interpreted within a total web and complex of factors. While recognizing the multitude of factors which must be considered in any thorough and complete description of the events, I should like here to point to several aspects of the controversy which have generally been overlooked. How does the conflict look when viewed from the perspective of the exegetical tradition preceding Cyril and Nestorius?

When the question is phrased in this way we observe immediately that, beneath the surface of theological rhetoric and high-flown ecclesiastical maneuvering, there moved deep and disturbing currents soon to surface with massive destructive power. This article will try to locate these currents as they emerged in the exegesis of Cyril and Nestorius. At the same time it touches on the more general problem of tradition in the ancient Church. For the classical argument from tradition, so finely etched into the mind of the Fathers, claimed to preserve the correct interpretation of the Scriptures. But it is precisely at this point that its limitations become most apparent. Perhaps the bishops of the fifth century were oblivious to what was happening, but it is plain: the argument is breaking into a thousand pieces. Once it had risen to its task, but now it is crushed by a burden it was never meant to bear. Though this article is primarily concerned with the Christological controversies, it tries, by suggesting what the controversy might mean for the argument from tradition, to place the upheaval of the fifth century into a wider Church historical and theological perspective.

What factors contributed to the explosion of the fifth century? What set Cyril and Nestorius on a fixed collision course destined to crash and explode like two express trains smashing each other at 100 m.p.h.? Without seeking a scapegoat or attempting to excuse Cyril or Nestorius, it must be granted that the trouble began with Arius and the varying responses to his teaching.

To be sure, his doctrine had been condemned at Nicaea long before the time of Cyril and Nestorius, but this was only a prelude to the violent battle stretching across the fourth century. The dismal procession of orthodox, semi-Arian, and Arian councils stretching from Nicaea to Constantinople is a striking reminder that Arianism was still very much alive. Historically, in fact, the dispute had supposedly been settled in the latter part of the century under the reign of Theodosius I at the Council of Constantinople. But was it? Could the churches now turn to other matters? One would expect this to be so, but our sources reveal a quite different picture. Surprisingly the years between 380 and 430 bear witness to condemned but nevertheless very lively Arian sects, with educated and resourceful leaders.

Just how important Arianism actually was during this period is revealed by the legislation against heretics from 380-430. In the *Codex Theodosianus* there is a constant stream of laws condemning the Arians or one of the sister heretical groups, the Eunomians or Macedonians. Only the Donatists can claim the dubious distinction of having as many laws proclaimed against them as the Arians. At this time Donatism was at the height of its power and influence and the churches in North Africa were continually faced by its threat. Extensive legislation against it could be expected. Arianism, however, was supposedly finished business, but specific references to Arian sects in the *Code* occur more than twenty times during this period.[9] Furthermore, the laws do not simply repeat ritual formulas of condemnation—as, for example, the condemnation of pre-Nicene heresies—but they prohibit proselytizing and gathering of assemblies. Apparently the Arians did not comprise a few scattered individuals or communities, but were or-

ganized groups capable of commanding the attention of the theologians
and disturbing the life of the churches.

Laws, however, can be deceptive and frequently do not offer the
kind of information needed for accurate historical judgments. But
if the inferences drawn from legislation only provide suggestions, the
ecclesiastical histories of the period support the suggestions with a
fuller and more satisfying account.

Socrates and Sozomen, who record the events of the fourth century and early fifth century, devote what seems an inordinate amount
of space to a dying sect. At one place Socrates describes a tumult in
Constantinople in 388 in which Arians burned the house of Nectarius,
patriarch of the city. Elsewhere he tells of nocturnal assemblies of
Arians even though Chrysostom had forbidden them to congregate. In
these gatherings the Arians, whom he tells us were "very numerous,"
sang responsive verses adapted to their teaching. He also describes
measures taken by Nestorius soon after his consecration in Constantinople to meet the menace of Arianism in that city.[10]

Finally, the literary remains of this period confirm the impression given by the laws and histories. Though we do find treatises on
specifically Christological rather than Trinitarian topics, the bishops
continued to deal with questions raised by the Arians and at this point
they concentrated much of their polemic. The abortive attempt of
Apollinaris to raise and answer the Christological questions implied by
the dogma of Nicaea was shortlived.[11] In certain parts of the Empire
he initially gained considerable support, but the swift condemnation
of his teaching nipped in the bud the growth of this new heresy. For
this reason the majority of the writings between 380-430 are concerned with Arius and the doctrine of the Trinity. In his sermons
John Chrysostom, even while in Antioch, preached frequently on Arian
perversions and regularly expounded his text in terms of Arian objections.[12] Didymus the Blind, writing in Alexandria, composed at
least two works on the Trinity.[13] Theodore of Mopsuestia wrote a
treatise against Eunomius and expressly mentions this polemical concern as part of the task he saw in expounding the Gospel of John.[14]
And Cyril of Alexandria is almost exclusively concerned with the
Trinity in his earlier writings. He wrote two massive dogmatic works
on the subject, a *Commentary on John* which deals extensively with
the Arians, and he frequently took up related questions when the occasion arose in his Old Testament commentaries.[15]

Thus at the beginning of the fifth century, Arianism in one form
or another is still much on the scene. This led to a certain ossification
of theological reflection and formulation, for the questions had really
been answered years before; and it promoted a restricted vision,
limited by the blinders of old questions, arguments, and answers. Even
if something new had been sensed before Nestorius, it is doubtful the

bishops would have recognized it much less known what to do with it.[16] As Grillmeier points out, there was no "method" present in the early fifth century which could adequately deal with the issues raised by Nestorius: "At the time of the Ephesinum, the Church possessed no finished theological method that might have produced a scientific evaluation of the teaching of Nestorius."[17]

In terms of the controversy between Cyril and Nestorius this situation meant that the immediate background and presupposition of the controversy was not so much a question of Christology, but of the Trinity. Once hostilities began the uniquely Christological question came quickly to the fore; but much of the initial misunderstanding stems from the inability of both parties to even faintly understand their differing approaches to Arius. They both agreed on the orthodox dogma proclaimed at Nicaea and Constantinople; what they did not know, however, was that each had received a different tradition of how to get to it. In their opposition to Arius they were indeed united; but they opposed him with different arguments. And here was the rub.

Among the controversial points between the Athanasian and Arian parties, one centered on the proper interpretation of certain passages of the Gospels. The Arians were quick to point to any passage which explicitly stated or implied that Jesus did not bear the characteristics of God. For example, they singled out Luke 2:52, "Jesus increased in wisdom and in stature" and claimed this showed he was not equal with the father, because the text says he grew. God, it was assumed, could not "grow" in wisdom or change in any way. Other examples were the Baptism of Jesus, which showed he had to receive the Spirit; the statement that the "Son of man did not know the day or the hour," (Mk. 13:32; Mt. 24:36); Jesus' words: "My soul is troubled unto death" (Mt. 26:38; John 12:27; Mk. 14:34); and others.

Supported by such passages from the Scriptures the Arians had little difficulty in presenting the Nicene theologians with a powerful argument. Eudoxosius of Constantinople wrote: "Let them (the Nicenes) answer how one who is passible and mortal can be *homoousios* with the God who is above these things and who is beyond suffering and death."[18] What makes this argument difficult to refute is that its assumptions are shared by both sides of the debate. Both the Nicenes and Arians agreed that God is beyond suffering and death and that such predicates as "change" or "alteration" or "ignorance" could not be predicated of the deity. At the same time both sides agreed that the accounts of Jesus in the gospels were reliable and had to be taken into consideration in answering the problem. Hence, while disagreeing on the inferences drawn by the Arians, the Nicenes were coaxed into a debate in which all shared much the same ground rules. Any answer had to be given within these pre-established limits.

Recently Francis Sullivan in his monograph on Theodore of Mopsuestia outlined in syllogistic form the specific pillars in this Arian argument. His analysis not only provides a useful framework in which to interpret the Arian approach, but it also shows clearly the initial divergence between Alexandrian and Antiochene responses to the Arians. The syllogism runs as follows:

> The Word is the subject of the human operations and sufferings of Christ.
>
> Whatever is predicated of the Word must be predicated of him according to his own nature (*kata physin*).
>
> *ergo*, the nature of the Word is limited and affected by human operations and sufferings of Christ, and is subordinate to the Father.[19]

On the part of the Nicene theologians this situation required an adequate defense and an effective reply to the Arian argument, and at the same time it demanded a comprehensive pattern for interpreting the "problem passages" in accord with Nicene theology.[20] At this point the tradition diverged and this divergence set the stage for the later conflict. What was, however, to cause such difficulty for Nestorius and Cyril was not simply the divergent replies, but the inability to distinguish the defense from the doctrine it sought to defend. By the end of the fourth century the Nicene dogma had become Catholic tradition, but its defense rested on the peculiarities of local traditions. By the fifth century this two-fold defense had molded and shaped two theological traditions. The confusion between contrasting theological traditions and the universally acceptable tradition of Nicaea eventually helped undercut any serious appeal to tradition.

Athanasius, who sets the pattern for the later Alexandrian position, countered the Arians by exposing the weakness of the second (minor) premise. It is false, argued Athanasius, to claim that any action predicated of the Logos must be predicated of him according to his own nature (*kata physin*). For the gospel teaches us that the divine and eternal Logos took on human flesh and became a man. When he became man he assumed the characteristics of man such as weakness, hunger, suffering, etc. Therefore we can rightly say that it is the Logos who hungers, suffers, etc.; but we do not say he does so according to his own nature. Rather he suffers according to the flesh, according to his humanity (*kata sarka*). Such predicates differ from "eternity" and "unbegotten" for these belong to the Logos *qua* Logos, i.e., as he is according to his own nature. Thus two types of predication are possible, and it is of fundamental importance to distinguish between them. In Book III of his *Contra Arianos* he writes:

> This then is the scope (*skopos*) and character of the Holy Scripture, as we have often said; in the gospel there is a double (*diplēn*) account of the Savior; that he was always God and is Son, being the Logos and radiance and wisdom of the father; and that afterwards, he took flesh from the

Virgin Mary, the *theotokos,* and became man. And this (*skopos*) is to
be found signified throughout all the inspired Scriptures.[21]

By establishing the necessity of two types of predication of the Logos,
Athanasius sought to safeguard the divinity of the Son and at the
same time recognize the reality of the Incarnation and life of Jesus.
His interest is completely Trinitarian, but the lines along which he
shaped his answer were to provide the center of the later Alexandrian
passion for the unity of Christ.

When applied to particular texts of the gospels Athanasius' exegetical principle provides a ready key to all the difficulties raised by
the Arians. At times the Logos does things "divinely," such as heal
the sick, raise the dead, know the thoughts of men; at other times he
does things "humanly," such as hunger, thirst, suffer, etc. Of Lk.
2:52 Athanasius asks: If Jesus Christ is truly the Son of God how
can he advance? It is obviously not the Word, qua Word (*ei logos
estin*) who advanced, he answers; what is meant is that the Logos advances "humanly" (*anthropinōs*) since advance is proper to man.
"Wherefore he (the evangelist) did not say 'the Logos advanced' but
"Jesus" by which name the Lord was called when he became man, so
that there is an advance of the human nature."[22] Thus Athanasius'
strategy is to hold fast to the conviction that in both human and divine matters the subject remains constant. Be it divine or human actions which the Evangelists describe, the subject is always the divine
Son. But depending on the kind of action described, they must be assigned to the Son either as he is in himself, or as he is according to
his humanity.

But this was only one side of the reply to Arius. On the other
side men such as Eustathius of Antioch hammered out a wholly different defense and a correspondingly different pattern for interpreting the passages from the gospels.[23] They also granted the initial assumption concerning the nature of the deity as well as the conviction
that certain predications were improper for the deity. But in contrast to Athanasius they denied the major premise of the syllogism
and granted the minor premise. This meant they said that only one
type of predication was possible, namely predication according to the
nature of the Logos (*kata physin*). But this suggested that the Logos
hungers, thirsts, suffers according to his own nature (*kata physin*)
and is therefore limited. If caught in this dizzy circle they would
eventually have to grant the Arian claim that the Logos is subordinate
to the Father. Therefore they answered that the Word is not the subject of the human operations and sufferings of Christ. Rather, passages which speak of suffering must not be attributed to the Logos,
either by nature or according to the flesh, but they must be ascribed
to the man Jesus. It is he who advances in wisdom, who does not
know the day or the hour, who hungers, thirsts, and suffers. Here,

as in Athanasius, the argument is primarily concerned with a Trinitarian question; and it is in terms of this particular historical problem that it must be considered. It provided a way out of the dilemma posed by the Arians and set the pattern for the later Antiochene exegesis of the Gospels.

In briefest terms, then, this is the great fork in the road which divides the two orthodox replies to Arius and his followers. Both provided a defense of Nicene theology, a refutation of the Arian arguments, and a schema for expounding the gospels. The one seldom had difficulty recognizing that the Jesus of the gospels was God, but it tended to diminish the importance—if not the reality—of the human portrait of him presented in the gospels. The other seldom had trouble taking seriously this portrait, but it always found it difficult, as Theodore's exegesis of John amply demonstrates,[24] to say how this Jesus could be one with God. The one, initiated and worked out by Athanasius, was to find expression in his successor in the see of Alexandria, Cyril; the other, shaped by men like Eustathius, was to dominate the tradition centered about Antioch and to find expression in the fifth century in Nestorius, Theodore of Mopsuestia, and Theodoret of Cyrus. And it was the divergence of these two traditions which led to the mighty upheaval when the Alexandrian, Cyril, began reading what the Antiochene, Nestorius, had to say about Jesus.

Shortly after Nestorius was consecrated patriarch of Constantinople, he preached a series of sermons. Of these only fragments remain with one important exception: a sermon preached on Hebrew 3 and the priestly work of Christ.[25] Not only is it the only complete sermon preserved in Greek, but since it was forwarded to Cyril shortly after it had been preached (with a number of other writings), it provides an important document to observe Cyril's initial reaction to Nestorius. In fact, Cyril discussed in some detail and with quotations this particular sermon in Book III of the treatise *Adversus Nestorium*. Furthermore, the sermon is significant, for it deals precisely with the issue which had caused so much difficulty with the Arians, namely, how to interpret the biblical statements ascribing to Jesus human characteristics and emotions. For these reasons it sheds light on the beginnings of the Nestorian controversy before the strife began, shows the importance of the exegetical tradition to the controversy, and points to the way trinitarian questions are transformed to major problems of Christology.[26]

The text of the sermon is Heb. 3:1ff.

"Therefore, holy brethren, who share in a heavenly call, consider Jesus, the apostle and high priest of our confession. He was faithful to him who appointed him, just as Moses also was faithful in God's house." (RSV)

At the outset, says Nestorius, we must remember that, when expounding the doctrines of the faith and the Holy Scriptures, we are dealing with weighty and serious matters. For the faith is holy and precious and frequently beyond our grasp and comprehension. The heretics (i.e. the Arians), failing to recognize the profundity of the divine, throw all caution to the wind when they proceed to interpret heavenly matters. This passage is a good example, for they twist and turn it to match their purposes, "imagining themselves to have something of greater value in theology."[27] They dare to say that the text means the "son is created" (*tou ektisthai ton uion*) because St. Paul (i.e. the writer to the Hebrews) says that God made him (*poiesanti auton*).

Nestorius, with other opponents of the Arians, is placed on the defensive because of the words of Hebrews which seem to suggest that the Son is "made" (*poieō*) by the father. If this is the case the Son cannot be equal to the father nor can he have existed from all eternity. This passage, like the others discussed above, was at issue between the Arians and orthodox long before the fifth century, for it offered the Arians the same kind of support as certain texts from the gospels. Hence the question Nestorius places at the head of his sermon focuses on a theological as well as an exegetical problem which had been at the center of discussion for many years. At the height of the conflict with the Arians Athanasius produced a lengthy discussion of Heb. 3 along the lines of the developing Alexandrian pattern.[28]

Unfortunately it is difficult to trace the Antiochene exegesis of this passage in the fourth century, because the few remaining fragments do not touch on it. The most extensive and important evidence does not appear in our sources until Nestorius and Theodoret of Cyrus. Their exegesis, however, conforms so closely to the Antiochene pattern outlined above that we can safely conjecture that earlier writers had shaped the scheme which they follow. It is particularly disappointing that the fragments of Theodore of Mopsuestia's *Commentary on Hebrews* do not deal with this passage; but, in spite of this gap, it is clear from other sections of the commentary that he would have expounded it as did Theodoret.[29] In his reply to the *Twelve Chapters* of Cyril Theodoret immediately raises the Arian issue. We note, says Theodoret, that the writer to the Hebrews uses the term "made" when referring to Christ. The Arians, recognizing the support this gives to their argument, quickly jump to the conclusion that Hebrews says the Word was made and is therefore a creature like men. For if the Word is "made" then he must be subordinate to the Father. Therefore, we cannot apply this passage to the Word and remain orthodox. Furthermore, it is surely incorrect to say that the Word assumed the rank of the priesthood of Melchizedek, for this leads us to the same heretical conclusions of the Arians. Rather we say that the "one from the seed of David" was our priest and became a victim by offering himself to God for us.[30]

From these remarks it is clear how rigidly Theodoret conforms
to the Antiochene type of defense against Arianism and the exegetical principles associated with it; furthermore it is striking how deeply
he is concerned in 431 to guard his flank against Arians though he
is in fact engaged in new conflict with Cyril. These remarks were
written after the lines of the Christological debate had been sharply
drawn. Thus, while answering Cyril's Christological extremism, Theodoret puzzles how Cyril could "confute the blasphemy of the heretic"
(Arius) when he says that such passages as "The Son of Man does
not know the day or the hour" can be assigned to the Divine Word.[31]

Let us now turn to Nestorius who, as it will be seen, stands precisely in this same tradition. When the Arians read the words "made
him" in Hebrews they wrongly attribute these words to the Divine
Logos and conclude from them that the Son is subordinate to the
Father. Similarly, "when they hear the word 'apostle' they think that
God the Word is the Apostle; when they read 'office or priest' they
imagine that the Godhead is priest."[32] Such exegesis is customary
among heretics, for it is their custom to say that human characteristics
such as being a priest, or being "made" show that the divine Logos
is not one with the Father. In the exposition of this passage then,
orthodox exegetes must show the error of the Arian interpretation
and the conclusion they draw from it, namely, that the Son is not
truly God.

What then is the correct interpretation and how do we meet their
objections? We must ask the Arians: "If divinity is a high priest,
who is honored by the service of the high priest? If God is the one
who makes the offering, there is no one to whom the offering is made."
What could be greater than God to receive such an offering. Only a
priest who is himself in need of perfection could bring an offering
to God; someone who is perfect would hardly need to make offering.
Every high priest "is bound to offer sacrifice for his own sins as well
as those of the people" (Heb.). But God does not lack perfection.
"Whence therefore is the Word of God thought to be called priest
by them, he who did not need sacrifices for his own improvement as
other priests?"[33]

To support this exegesis against his Arian critics Nestorius turns
to the context of the passage. Immediately prior to the text, St. Paul
says that Christ is "made like his brethren in every respect." This
surely means that the text refers to Jesus, for Paul says it is "not
with angels that he is concerned but with the descendants of Abraham." "Is the Godhead the seed of Abraham?" asks Nestorius. Furthermore "the lifegiving God does not suffer," as Arians read the
texts, "but it is the seed of Abraham" who suffers.[34] This interpretation is confirmed by the Gospels, for here we observe a similar dis-

tinction. Some texts refer to the Logos as for example, "Before Abraham was I am." But this is not parallel to the passage in Hebrews. In this connection Luke is more appropriate where we read: "Jesus increased in wisdom and stature." Therefore, concludes Nestorius: "Humanity was anointed, heretic, not the divinity. This one (i.e. Jesus) is he who was made a faithful priest to God for he became a priest and did not exist as such from eternity."[35]

While there is much in this argument of importance for Nestorius' views on Christological questions, it is noteworthy that he is engaged primarily in a discussion of the Trinity. That is to say, he is determined to defend the Nicene Dogma against Arian perversions and show that the Son is truly the second person of the Holy Trinity, equal to the Father and begotten before all ages. Furthermore he supports his argument with the exegesis of a "problem" text that conforms precisely to the pattern set down by a writer such as Eustathius of Antioch. The Arian claim that such statements of the Scripture apply to the Logos cannot stand; for they refer to the man Jesus, the "one called the seed of Abraham, the one who in all things is similar to his brother, who became a high priest in time, who was perfected through sufferings."[36]

Once Nestorius is satisfied he has answered the Arian objections he takes up the question of the priestly work of Christ and its relation to the teachers and prophets of the Old Testament. Here he moves from the polemical situation to a more relaxed exposition of what kind of priest was called for.

> "A high priest, then, was needed to mediate the blessing, on the one hand from the race of Abraham by nature (*tei phusei*) and on the other hand, in honor above the prophets. He must be meek and blameless, capable of suffering as a descendant of Abraham, but who knew in times of danger to call out to God, 'not my will but yours.' Christ was born for this, not clothed with the nature of angels, for God did not promise a blessing to men from the race of angels, but from the seed of Abraham of the same (seed) as those who received the Gospel."[37]

The uniqueness of Christ does not lie in some innate quality or capability, for he is like other men in every respect. Rather his uniqueness lies in what he did: he lived a perfect life and offered to God a perfect sacrifice. In this he is greater than all the prophets and priests of the Old Testament.

This sermon can, I believe, be taken as an accurate reflection of the theological and ecclesiastical situation on the eve of the Christological controversies. While Nestorius does treat Christological matters in the latter part of the sermon, he is first and foremost interested in refuting the Arians rather than in developing a proper understanding of the person of Christ. It is the relation of the Son to the Father, not the relation of the Son to mankind which provides the basis for his exposition. And though he borders on questions soon to be raised, he does so from the perspective of the controversies of the fourth century. With respect to the Trinitarian controversy he stands in the tradition of Antioch and its particular reply to Arianism, both exegetically and theologically. When Nestorius speaks of preserving the tradition of the fathers, it is this tradition which he has in mind. Unfortunately Nestorius could not, as Cyril also could not, see that this tradition was shaped and colored by particular historical and theological factors in the fourth century. And though he may have thought he gave expression to apostolic teaching, he is in fact reflecting the central strand of a particular rather than universal tradition.

It was this tradition which laid the groundwork for his rejection of the appellation *theotokos*.[38] Whether others before him had also rejected it is a moot question, but the basis on which he was able to reject it is clearly evident. When placed against the backdrop of the trinitarian discussion, instead of the Christological, the *theotokos* takes on a somewhat different character. For here it seems to suggest that the Logos bears all the characteristics of humanity and is limited by human affections. And, following the Antiochene argument, if it is only possible to predicate of the Logos *kata physin*, the term means that according to his very nature the Logos is born of a woman, and therefore grows and increases, is ignorant, hungers and thirsts, suffers and dies. But from this the Arians conclude that he is really not God, for God cannot be born of a woman, grow, be hungry, suffer and die. The conclusion seems inevitable; the Logos is not really God, but subordinate to the Father. As we have seen, it was to avoid this implication that the Antiochenes framed their exegesis and reply to the Arians. For this reason the *theotokos* can and must be placed in the same category with all the other statements in the Scriptures which caused such difficulty; that is to say, it raised the same problem as did the passage from Hebrews 3. The rejection of the term is totally consistent with the Antiochene exegetical and theological tradition. In view of the many passages in Scripture which seemingly gave support to the Arians, why, they asked, should we add another non-scriptural term to the debate. It only adds fuel to their fires and makes the orthodox defense doubly difficult. Whether ecclesiastical considerations made the use of the term unwise is another question; and Nestorius can perhaps be rightly criticized at this point.[39] But, he certainly saw the implications of the term and had good and substantial grounds for discouraging its use.

This sermon and others were quickly forwarded to Cyril in Alexandria. His response was swift and decisive, and it was destined to initiate a most bitter exchange between him and Nestorius. As a result of it the Church was never again to see or know the peace and unity—even with its divisions, competing parties, and controversies —it had known since the Council of Constantinople. Cyril's initial reaction to Nestorius came in a letter to the monks of Egypt, and it is to this letter that we must now turn. Cyril's Christology and his attack on Nestorius have been the object of many studies, and it is not our intention to contribute to this discussion here. The following remarks are only intended to pinpoint the immediate response of Cyril and place it in the historical perspective of the two traditions being discussed here.[40]

Cyril begins by explaining the reason for his letter. He had heard that some questioned whether the Virgin Mary should be called *theotokos* and, since this caused no little disturbance, he proposes to say a few things apropos of the question. He expresses the hope that his remarks will not lead to more arguments but that they will assist the monks in opposing error, avoiding difficulties, and helping others to learn the truth. Either Cyril was unbelievably naive about theological controversy—and this is incredible after the events of the fourth century—or he had no idea of the magnitude of the problem on which he ventured to suggest an answer. Perhaps this is simply another indication of the deep and unbridgeable chasm which separated the two respective traditions. Cyril goes forth to battle with weapons poised and the banner of truth as standard; but he fails to grasp even at the most primitive level either the reasons upon which Nestorius denied the *theotokos* or the consequences of his deeds for the Church.

But monks are loyal and faithful, and Cyril is certain they are persuaded of the "faith once handed down to the churches from the Holy Apostles."[41] Because they possess this true and faithful tradition they can oppose the heretics and convince the gainsayers. About others Cyril can only express amazement, for it is beyond comprehension how anyone can be in doubt about the *theotokos*. "The blessed disciples handed over this faith to us even though they did not mention the term itself. And thus we were taught to think by the holy fathers."[42] Blessed Athanasius, who ruled the Church in Alexandria for 46 years opposed the Arians and wrote books against them. In Book III of his *Contra Arianos* Athanasius expressly calls the Virgin Mary *Theotokos*.[43] And though he was not yet bishop he defended this faith against error in the great and holy Synod of Nicaea.

Realizing that the term does not occur in Scripture, Cyril proceeds to explain why it is nevertheless appropriate. Some at the Council thought it best to employ terms which do occur in Holy Scripture and therefore did not mention *theotokos*. Cyril does not seem to be troubled by the number of other terms in the same category, notably *homoousios*. If, however, we consider the mystery of Christ as the fathers, guided by the Spirit have expressed it, the answer is plain. For if God is born of the Virgin Mary surely she is *theotokos*.[44]

Let us now look more closely, says Cyril, at the symbol of Nicaea: (The text of the creed follows.) The inventors of heresy do not confess the creed with us, but say that "the son is a latecomer (*prosphaton*) and created by the God and Father just as other creatures. . . These wretches do not even blush to ascribe to him a beginning in time."[45] In fact they make of him a sort of intermediate creature between God and other creatures and then outrightly disobey the Scriptures by worshipping what is not God.

Cyril's reply is highly characteristic. He appeals to Athanasius and the tradition of the Alexandrian Church as though it were the ancient tradition handed to the Church by the apostles. While he is aware of the impossibility of finding Scriptural support for the term, and recognizes the difficulty of appealing to Nicaea, this does not deter him. What he fails to recognize, however, is that not everyone saw things the way Alexandrians did and that his own expression betrays a multitude of distinctively Alexandrian terms and concepts. This is especially evident in the latter part of the letter where he outlines his view of the Incarnation.

Secondly, though he lapses into a discussion of a Trinitarian question and reiterates the reply to Arius given by Anthanasius, he does not give any indication that this question might be related to Nestorius' criticism of the *theotokos*. Cyril is totally oblivious to the concern which prompted Nestorius' remarks and demonstrates no understanding whatsoever of the reasons behind them. As far as Cyril could see, what Nestorius had to say about Arianism and the *theotokos* was wholly beside the point. The answer to Arius had been worked out in detail and with great precision; in fact Athanasius had done such a good job that Cyril did not think it worth the time to formulate his own objections. From the time of Athanasius to Cyril the Alexandrian reply had undergone few, if any, alterations. The seriousness of the clash and the extent of the misunderstanding created by their respective exegetical traditions is perhaps best reflected in the widely divergent views of Christ's priestly work. We have already seen the shape of Nestorius' view of the priesthood as well as the reasons underlying it. Let us now turn briefly to the answer hurled across the Mediterranean by Cyril in his twelve anathemas.[46]

In the anathemas or chapters Cyril sought to isolate what he considered the most important points where Nestorius diverged from the tradition. Written in "anathema" style they first stated the true teaching as Cyril saw it, continued with an "if not" clause concerning this teaching, and concluded with the familiar "let him be anathema." The anathemas touch on a variety of issues such as the *theotokos,* the union of the Word and human flesh, the worship due the "god-man," the nature of Christ's flesh, et al. Of these the only anathema dealing specifically with an exegetical issue is Anathema 10 on the priesthood of Christ as expressed in Hebrews.[47] Anathema 4 lays down the Alexandrian exegetical principle concerning the proper interpretation of "problem" texts from the Gospels, and though it is couched in more technical language than the rule enunciated by Athanasius in his *Contra Arianos*, the meaning and intention are the same.

> "If anyone assigns to two persons or hypostases the words of the evangelic or apostolic writings, which are spoken either of Christ by the saints or of himself by Himself, and applies some to a man considered apart from the Word who is from God, and others, as God-befitting, solely to the Word from God the Father, be he anathema."[48]

As we have seen, this principle was forged by Athanasius in the heat of the Arian controversy and it became normative for the Alexandrian Church. Cyril, however, states the Alexandrian position here in primarily Christological rather than Trinitarian terms. He is no longer concerned, as was Athanasius, to provide an interpretation of the texts of the New Testament which could defend the faith against Arius; rather he turns this initial insight into Christological form by setting it against the Antiochene pattern of exegesis.

The tenth anathema discusses the same question in more particular terms. Cyril could have used a number of other examples, but the priestly work of Christ was the most natural, for he had observed Nestorius' exposition of it in the sermon. But before considering Cyril's interpretation of the text from Hebrews, let us look briefly at the manner Athanasius approached the question. As we have already noted, Heb. 3 apparently played an important role in the controversies with Arius, and Athanasius devoted a long section of the *Orations* to its exposition. When we look at the problem faced by Athanasius we quickly discover that it is precisely the same problem Nestorius posed in his sermon. Athanasius was pressed to answer how it could be that the Son was equal to the Father when the Apostle in Hebrews says that he was "made." If any passage gave support to the Arian cause this seemed to do so. For if the Son is "made" that means he is a "work," a "creature" and therefore not equal to God. Athanasius, in a lengthy and repetitive discussion, sets forth two lines of rebuttal. The first argues that, though the term "made (*poieō*) is indeed used, it does not mean made, but rather "begat," i.e., the word traditionally used of the generation of the Son. "Wherefore also when the essence (*ousia*) is a work or creature, then, the words 'he made,' and 'he became,' and 'he created' are properly spoken of it and designate the work. But when the essence is an Offspring and Son, then 'he made,' and 'he became,' and 'he created' no longer properly belong to it, nor designate a work; but in place of 'he made' we use without distinction 'he begat.' "[49]

This would perhaps be sufficient as a guiding principle for passages using such terms, but Athanasius proceeds to another explanation. Here he outlines the familiar pattern of the "two nature" exegesis displayed elsewhere in these *Orations*. Many passages in the

Scriptures are properly assigned to the Son according to his divine nature; but we also read passages which cannot be interpreted in this fashion and must be assigned to the Word "when he has become man, i.e., to his humanity."[50] Heb. 3 belongs to the latter category, for it signifies "his descent to mankind . . . and that in the process of time, when God willed, he became a high-priest."[51] Hence the expressions "he became" and "he was made," "must not be understood as if the Word considered as the Word were made, but that the Word, being Demiurge, afterwards was made High Priest, by putting on a body which was originate and made, which he is able to offer for us; wherefore he is said to be made."[52] In briefest terms this is Athanasius' exegesis of the passage from Hebrews in reply to the Arians. Instead of supporting the notion that the son is subordinate to the Father, as the Arians claimed they do, these passages point, says Athanasius, to the nature of the Son after he has become man, i.e., as he is *kata sarka,* according to his human nature. In conclusion Athanasius summarizes his view:

"For so long as we confess that He became man it makes no difference, as was said before, whether 'he became,' or 'he has been made,' or 'created,' or 'formed,' or 'servant,' or 'son of an handmaid,' or 'son of man,' or 'was constituted,' or 'departed (life),' or 'bridegroom,' or 'brother's son,' or 'brother.' All these terms are proper to man's constitution; and as such they do not designate the essence of the Word, but that he has become man."[53]

When this exegesis is compared with that of Nestorius it becomes clear that they were both wrestling with the same problem—a problem concerning the Trinity. Each believes the Arians perverted and misunderstood the Scriptures by subordinating the Son to the Father; and each proceeds in his own fashion to refute the arguments of the Arians. What is striking about the parallel between Nestorius and Athanasius is that they lived almost 100 years apart. Though the dating of the *Orations* is somewhat disputed, at the inside at least 75-80 years (perhaps even 90) intervened between them and Nestorius' sermon on Hebrews. And in each case Athanasius and Nestorius are disturbed about the same question.

When we return to Cyril we note again that similar questions exercised him during the early part of his episcopate and provided the occasion for many of his dogmatic and exegetical writings. In the reply to Nestorius, however, we see the initial shift of emphasis which was eventually to frame the peculiarly Christological questions of the two centuries after Cyril. But, even though he does shift the question to new ground, his approach is fundamentally set by Athanasius and the direction his theology took in response to Arius. In the attack Cyril did not contribute in a substantive fashion to the theological tradition of Alexandria—at least not at this point—but he had ceased worrying about the Arians. And this in itself is no insignificant step forward. Cyril was certain the divinity of the Son had been established beyond further refutation, and it was time now to turn to the implications of this conviction.

The anathema reads as follows:

"The divine Scripture asserts that Christ was made 'the High Priest and Apostle of our confession'; moreover he offered himself for us 'as an odour of sweet savor' to God even the Father. If anyone therefore says that it was not the Word himself who is from God who was made High Priest and our Apostle when He was made flesh and man like us, but as it were another one born of a woman, considered separately from Him: or if anyone says that He offered the sacrifice for himself also and not rather solely for our sakes—for he 'who knew no sin' would have no need of a sacrifice—let him be anathema."[54]

Cyril begins with a straightforward statement of the content of the passage from Hebrews. Then, secure in the conviction that human predications no longer call into question the divinity of the Word, he says that it was the Word who was made High Priest and Apostle. This did not happen before he became man, i.e., in his pre-existence, but he became high priest "when he became flesh." Furthermore, if it was the Word who was high-priest it is obvious that he did not have to make offering for himself, even though he was a man. At two points he goes beyond Athanasius.[55] First of all, instead of arguing that Hebrews does not mean the Son is not equal to the Father, he assumes the Son *is equal* to the Father and seeks to show what it means that the Word was made man and became a priest. Athanasius could never move the discussion to this point—even if he wished to—for he was too pressed by his opponents to defend the prior point. Secondly, Cyril opens the question concerning the nature of Christ's priesthood. As high priest Christ is perfect and without sin and for this reason the sacrifice he offers is not offered for himself but for other men.

In the accompanying letter Cyril explains himself more fully. If Christ is truly God, then the sacrifice must be appropriate to him. It must be perfect and without blemish and offered for others because he himself is spotless and without sin.

"For what offering or sacrifice did he need for himself, who as God was superior to all sin?"[56]

Cyril's understanding of priesthood is not pulled out of the air to criticize Nestorius; already many of these concepts had been developed and explained at length in his commentaries. In the course of the controversy Cyril took occasion to explain further the intention of the anathema, but it was in the treatise *Adversus Nestorius* (Book III) where he most fully articulated together the exegetical and theological dimensions of Christ's priestly work.[57] While important for Cyril's own Christology, a discussion of this cannot detain us here.

Before concluding, one final piece of evidence should be added

to the discussion. We have now seen that Nestorius was concerned
in his sermon to refute Arian subordinationism. From his approach
to the text and the problem he discussed, it became clear that he was
troubled by the same questions which troubled Athanasius in the
fourth century. When Cyril read Nestorius he saw red, for in his
view, Nestorius had radically broken with the tradition he had received. Furthermore, Cyril, though working within the Trinitarian
framework set down by Athanasius, saw Nestorius in Christological
terms and gauged his comments accordingly. But how did Cyril's
theology look to the Antiochene theologians who stood in the same
tradition as Nestorius?

The best example here is Theodoret of Cyrus, because he sought
to refute Cyril's anathemas. Theodoret's own Christology is an important representative of the Antiochene school without many of the
exaggerations and infelicities of Nestorius or Theodore. What interests us here, however, is not his own Christology but the way he
looked at Cyril's anathemas. In his remarks on the fourth anathema,
which dealt with the proper exegesis of the texts from the Scriptures,
Theodoret notes that Cyril is proud of his ability to contest Arius
and Eunomius and other heresiarchs. But, says Theodoret, "let the
exact professor say how he answers the blasphemy of the heretics
when he says that the things spoken humbly and appropriately of the
form of a servant apply to the divine Word."[58] For in these cases the
Arians try to show that the Son is inferior, a creature, something made,
and a servant.

Even though the controversy has by the time of this writing become explicitly Christological, Theodoret is still troubled by the Arians.
And he misunderstands Cyril and the Alexandrian reply to Arius just
as totally as Cyril misunderstood Nestorius and the Antiochenes.
Neither had any inkling of the profound and unbridgeable chasm their
predecessors had created when they refuted Arius. Consequently
Theodoret proceeds to defend the divinity of the Son against Arius,
though his supposed task is to refute Cyril. He simply cannot break
loose from the old question, for Cyril's own view of the matter seems
to open the floodgates to the perversions which the Church had fought
for so long. "To whom," says Theodoret, "shall we apply the hunger
and thirst, the weariness and sleep? To whom the ignorance and
fear? . . . If these belong to God the Word, how was wisdom ignorant?"[59] Finally, at the end of his discussion he links both his own
interpretation of the passages and the heresy of Arius. Unless, says
Theodoret, these parts of the Gospels are applied to the form of a
servant, we cannot hope to withstand the onslaughts of the Arians. "We
shall therefore apply what is divinely spoken and done to God the
Word; on the other hand we shall apply what is said and done humbly

to the form of a servant, in order that we are not infected by the blasphemy of Arius and Eunomius."[60]

In summary, let us now bring together the results of the foregoing analysis. The task before us was to show that on the eve of the Christological controversies the Trinitarian questions of the former century were still very much alive. The presence of Trinitarian questions was not incidental to the beginning of the Christological controversy, for they contributed to the direction the debate finally took as well as the profound misunderstanding between the competing figures. In part, the presence of Trinitarian questions springs from the very real presence of Arians in the empire during the years immediately prior to 430. Contrary to what one might expect as a result of the condemnation of Arianism at Constantinople, Arianism continued to exist and to foster troublesome sects with resourceful and capable leadership. It was against Arian teaching as well as Arian groups that laws were instituted and theological treatises written. And, though Apollinarism did indeed portend the questions of the future, it was Arianism which shaped the theological literature of the period.

To this theological and ecclesiastical situation, however, must be added the confusing fact of the divergent replies given to Arianism. The immediate occasion for the two types was a series of passages from the New Testament which seemed to suggest the Son of God was subordinate to the Father. In defense Alexandrian theologians argued that such passages were properly applied to the Son of God, but *kata sarka,* according to his human nature; Antiochene theologians, however, did not see how such passages could be applied to the Son of God without capitulating to Arian subordinationist claims. Taking another course, these theologians referred such passages to the man Jesus, the seed of Abraham, or the form of a servant. Cyril as an Alexandrian theologian stands in the former exegetical and theological tradition; Nestorius stands in the latter.

Trouble began when Cyril read what Nestorius had been preaching about one of these problem passages and about the *theotokos.* What Cyril did not realize, however, was that to Antiochene theologians the term *"theotokos"* raised the same problem as did these passages, for it suggested to the Arians that Christ was subordinate to the Father. In short, *theotokos* was for the Antiochenes a Trinitarian, not a Christological term. It seemed to give support to the opponents of the Divinity of the Son. Totally oblivious to the reasons why Nestorius rejected the *theotokos,* Cyril bombards him with a battery of Alexandrian arguments and expressions which only seem to betray his own parochial orientation. In the process Cyril does not stray from the basic Trinitarian pattern set down by Athanasius, but he does begin to shift its emphasis from a "Trinitarian" to "Christological" question. While

this shift is of great magnitude for the eventual development of the
doctrine of Christ, in the immediate situation it only contributed to
misunderstanding. Theodoret, who replied to Cyril's attack on Nestorius, is not only dissatisfied with some of Cyril's statements about
Christ, but he is utterly bewildered how Cyril can say what he does
and still hold out against the Arians. Thus, even after Cyril has begun to shift the center of the question, Theodoret is still disturbed
by the prior question—now over 100 years old.

As this is happening we behold crumbling before us the classical
argument from tradition, so dear to the Fathers. It is not, I believe,
romantic to claim that there was a time in which, even amid diversity,
the bishops could in truth appeal to a common tradition. But by the
fourth century Athanasius could hardly point to a unified and consistent tradition.[61] In fact much of his difficulty arose precisely because he was an innovator who claimed that his innovations were
absolutely necessary if the Church's faith was to be rescued from a
theology which would surely destroy it. Similarly Augustine, writing against the Donatists, had to grant that the Donatists had Cyprian
on their side. Nevertheless he argued that, by innovating and changing, he was more faithful to the Church's tradition than they. Each
appealed to the tradition within the tradition, that is to a deeper meaning which gave unity, purpose and cohesion to its diversity. Athanasius spoke of the "scope" and "meaning" of the Scriptures and the
tradition; Augustine appealed to the Catholic spirit, the bond of peace
and love.

But in the case of Cyril and Nestorius, neither seemed able to
offer the Church a "scope" or "meaning" or interpretation capable
of demonstrating the unity and cohesion of the tradition. For, tragic
though it be, there were in fact two "scopes" and two "meanings,"
each having the support of at least a century of exegetical and theological tradition. Neither man could see this; and, as a consequence,
neither was capable of formulating a solution which met the demands
of both traditions. In their madness each appealed to his own tradition and cast it in the face of the other, savagely hoping that, stripped
of the garments of logic and good sense, force would prevail. Whether
the collision which took place in 431 was resolved in 451 is, of course,
a hotly debated issue—even today. One thing is plain—the classical
argument from tradition had been forever destroyed, hopelessly crushed
by the weight of a load it was never meant to bear. But what is even
more tragic: it did not die. In fact, it blossomed anew and was transformed into what Harnack once called paleography, and Werner Elert
wryly labeled *Dogmengeschichte*—the gathering of citations from the
Fathers in support of one's own opinion.[62]

1. *Adversus Nestorii blasphemias*, iii.1; *Acta Conciliorum Oecumenicorum*, ed. by Eduard Schwartz (Berlin: Walter de Gruyter, 1914ff.), I,1,6, p.53; hereafter abbreviated A.C.O. Here as elsewhere the translation is my own, unless otherwise noted. For similar statements of Cyril cf. Ep. 1 (PG 77, 13b-c; A.C.O., I,1,1,10-11); Ep. 39 (PG 77, 176d; A.C.O., I,1,4,17).

2. A.C.O. I,5,1, p. 26; Friedrich Loofs, *Nestoriana* (Halle: Max Niemeyer, 1905), pp. 250ff. In a letter to Cyril Nestorius frequently appealed to the "traditions of the Fathers," and at one place to the "traditions of the Gospels" in support of his rejection of the *theotokos* (Ep. 5 inter epistolas Cyrilli, PG 77, 49-57, esp. col. 56a-b; Loofs 174ff.).

3. A.C.O. I,1,1,33-42. It is generally agreed today that the anathemas were not accepted by the Council of Ephesus in 431. For literature discussing this problem see Johannes Quasten, *Patrology* (Westminister, Maryland: The Newman Press, 1960), III, 134.

4. Jacques Liébaert, *La Doctrine Christologique de Saint Cyrille d'Alexandrie avant la Querelle Nestorienne* (Lille, 1951). In his recent article, "Das Scandalum oecumenicum des Nestorius in kirchlich-dogmatischer und theologiegeschichtlicher Sicht," *Scholastik*, XXXVI (1961), 327, Grillmeier points to Cyril's claim (Ep. 2, A.C.O., I,1,1,24) that Nestorius' teaching created an "ecumenical scandal." But this, it seems, can only be conceded if one chooses to side with Alexandria.

5. At least since Origen; see G.W.H. Lampe, *A Patristic Greek Lexicon* (Oxford: Clarendon Press, 1964), pp. 639-671; cf. also P.-Th. Camelot, *Éphèse et Chalcédoine* (Paris: Editions de l'Orante, 1961), pp. 13-14.

6. "C'est donc à la piété et à la foi traditionnelles que s'opposait Nestorius," writes Camelot, p. 14.

7. For the classical political interpretation see Eduard Schwartz, *Cyril und der Mönch Viktor* ("Akademie der Wissenschaften in Wien," Philosophisch-historische Klasse, Sitzungsberichte, Band 208, Abhandlung 4: Vienna, 1928).

8. Once again see Camelot: "Une chose du moins paraît certaine. Quels qu'aient pu être les défauts de son caractère, saint Cyrille n'a été mù que par le souci de la vérité et le zèle de la foi," p. 35.

9. Th. Mommsen and Paul Meyer (eds.), *Theodosiani Libri XVI cum Constitutionibus Sirmondianis* (Berlin, 1905), xvi.5, pp. 855-880; cf. in particular 5, 11 (383 A.D.); 5,17 (388); 5,23 (394); 5,34 (398); 5,49 (410); 5,59 (423); 5,64 (428), et al.

10. Socrates, *Historia Ecclesiastica*, v, 13. 20; vi, 8; vii, 29; Sozomen, *H.E.* viii 8. Socrates also tells of two Arian leaders, learned in Greek literature and the Scriptures and eloquent in speech. He expresses surprise they continue to confess Arian doctrine (vii, 6).

11. Hans Lietzmann, *Apollinaris von Laodicea und seine Schule* ("Texte und Untersuchungen von Hans Lietzmann, Vol. I; Tübingen: J.C.B. Mohr, 1904), pp. 26ff; see also *Reallexikon für Antike und Christentum*, I, 520.

12. PG, 59; see also his *Homilies on the Incomprehensible Nature of God* (PG 48, 701-812).

13. PG, 29, 671-774; PG, 39, 269-992.

14. Of the treatise against Eunomius only fragments remain. J. M· Voste (ed.), *Theodori Mopsuesteni Commentarius in evangelium Johannis Apostoli*; Text: CSCO, 115; Translation into Latin, CSCO 116 (Louvain, 1940). See also his Commentary on Psalm 2 (R. Devreesse, *Studi e Testi*, Vol. 93; "Pubblicazioni della Biblioteca Vaticana," Rome, 1939), pp. 11-12.

15. *Thesaurus de sancta et consubstantiali Trinitate* (PG 75, 9-656); *De sancta et consubstantiali Trinitate* (PG 75, 657-1124); *Commentary on John* (PG 73 & 74, 9-756); better edition of this commentary by P. E. Pusey, *Sancti patris nostri Cyrilli archiepiscopi Alexandrini in d. Joannis evangelium* (Oxford: Clarendon Press, 1872; 3 Vols.).

16. Interestingly, Nestorius was initially attacked as a heretic on Trinitarian grounds (Socrates, *H.E.* vii, 32); cf. also the *Obtestatio publice proposita* of Eusebius of Dorylaeum (A.C.O., I, 1,1, 101-2). Marius Mercator, Nestorius' western critic also made the same charge in his *Comparatio dogmatum Pauli Samosateni et Nestorii* (PL, 48, 753ff., A.C.O., I,5, 5-70ff.)·

17. Aloys Grillmeier, *Scholastik*, XXXVI (1961), 329.

18. August Hahn. *Bibliothek der Symbole und Glaubensregeln der alten Kirche*. 3rd Ed. by Ludwig Hahn (Hildesheim: Georg Olms Verlagsbuchhandlung, 1962; photographic reprint of 1897 ed.), p. 262. Cf. also Cyril of Alexandria's paraphrase of the Arian reaction to the account of Jesus' Baptism in the Gospels: They jump up, he says, with a "big laugh" and say: "What argument will you bring against what is written! The evangelist says the Spirit descends on the Son; he is annointed by the Father; he received that which he does not have." (PG 73, 196b-c; Pusey, I, 175).

19. Francis Sullivan, *The Christology of Theodore of Mopsuestia* (Rome: Gregorian University, 1956), pp. 158ff.

20. For a brief account of how these questions influenced the exegesis of the Gospel of John, cf. Maurice Wiles, *The Spiritual Gospel; The Interpretation of the Fourth Gospel in the Early Church* (Cambridge: The University Press, 1960), pp. 112-147.

21. PG, 26, 385a.

22. *Ibid.*, 436a.

23. See the statement of Eustathius: "Si enim in Christo, inquit, plenitudo divinitatis inhabit, primum quidem aliud est quod inhabit, aliud autem quod inhabitatur. Si autem natura differunt ab alterutris, neque mortis passionem neque cibi appetitum neque poculorum desiderium, non somnum, non tristitiam, non fatigationem, non lacrimarum fluxus, non aliam quamlibet mutationem plenitudini divinitatis coexistere fas est, cum sit inconvertibilis per naturam. Homini haec adplicanda seorsim sunt, qui ex anima constat et corpore." (Fragment 47); see also fragments 18, 27, 28, 41, 47, 48 in M. Spannuet, *Recherches sur les écrits d' Eustathe d'Antioche avec une édition nouvelle des fragments dogmatiques et éxégetiques* (Lille, 1948).

24. Cf., for example, the use of pronouns in the following passage: "Deus Verbum, qui *me* assumpsit *sibique* conjunxit, dat *mihi* cum fiducia victoriam iudicii. *Me* enim semel pro semper fecit *suum*, quando assumpsit *me;* atque evidens est *eum me* (!) non derelinquere ne temere agam." (Voste, CSCO, 116, p. 174). For other examples see T. Camelot. " De Nestorius à Eutyches." in A. Grillmeier and H. Bacht, *Das Konzil von Chalkedon* (Wuerzburg: Echter Verlag, 1951), I, 217ff.

25. Loofs, pp. 230-242. Text also in W.T. M. Becher, *Joannis Chrysostomi Homiliae* (Leipzig, 1839); reprinted in PG 64, cols. 479-492. Concerning the homily Loofs says (p. 107): "Der Text der Predigt bei Becher zeigt nicht die geringsten dogmatischen Korrekturen, erweist sich, an den Fragmenten gemessen, überall als intakt. Es liegt also in dieser Predigt der einzig in der Originalsprache vollständig erhaltene Sermon des Nestorius vor." See also Sebastian Haidacher. "Rede des Nestorius über Hebr. 3.1, überliefert unter dem Namen des heiligen Chrysostomus." *Zeitschrift für katholische Theologie*, XXIX (1905), 192-95.

26. It is not my intention to enter into a discussion of Nestorius' Christology, but to show how the exegesis of the sermon conforms to the pattern of Antiochene anti-Arian exegesis. For Nestorius' Christology, especially its dogmatic and philosophical aspects see Grillmeier, "Die theologische und sprachliche Vorbereitung der christologischen Formel von Chalkedon," *Chalkedon*, I, 144ff, and *Scholastik*, XXXVI, 321-56; Luigi Scipioni, *Ricerche sulla Christologia del 'Libro di Eraclido' di Nestorio* ("Paradosis: Studi di letteratura e teologia antica," Vol. XI: Freiburg, 1956); T. Camelot, "De Nestorius à Eutyches," *Chalkedon*, I, 213-229. The recent article by Carl Braaten, "Modern Interpretations of Nestorius," *Church History*, XXXII (1963), 251-67, is a helpful survey of the older literature; its usefulness is, however, limited, since it does not discuss these more recent works.

27. Loofs, p. 231.

28. *Oratio II Contra Arianos*, 1-10 (PG, 26, 145-168).

29. See the fragments in Karl Staab, *Pauluskommentare aus der griechischen Kirche* ("Neutestamentliche Abhandlungen," XV Band: Münster: Aschendorff Verlagsbuchhandlung. 1933), pp. 204-5: unfortunately we do not possess fragments of Diodore of Tarsus on Hebrews.

30. A.C.O., I,1,6,137. It is interesting that Theodoret in his more mature and less polemically oriented work, *Commentary on the Epistle to the Hebrews.* is more restrained in his comments. Here, in the exposition of Heb. 3:1, he assigns the passage to "*christos*," which title he calls the *mēnuma tōn duo physeōn* (PG, 82, 697b). Similarly John Chrysostom's exegesis of this section of Hebrews does not conform so rigidly to the Antiochene pattern: see his *Commentary on Hebrews* (PG, 63, pp. 45ff.).

31. A.C.O. I,1,6,137 (14-19).

32. Loofs, p. 232 (8-11).

33. *Ibid.*, pp. 232 (14)-233(4).

34. *Ibid.*, p. 234 (14-16).

35. *Ibid.*, p. 235 (5-6).

36. *Ibid.*, 236 (7ff).

37. *Ibid.*, p. 238 (8-31).

38. Cf. Nestorius. Ep. V inter epistolas Cyrilli (PG 77, 49-51: Loofs. 174-5). Nestorius argues that the term *theotokos* is not only unbiblical, but it suggests the Logos is passible (*pathēton*). This is, of course, said in light of the Arians and the support the term would give to their contentions. At the end of the epistle he explicitly mentions the Arians and links Apollinarism with Arianism. Both heresies, said Nestorius, made the Logos subject, according to his own nature, to human affections; and this, according to Arian logic, showed he was not God. This linking of Arianism and Apollinarism is characteristic of Nestorius and significant for understanding the Antiochene position vis-a-vis Alexandria. Cf. the numerous places where Nestorius lumps them together: Loofs. 166, 19: 170.30: 179.4; 181.18; 182.8; 184.15: 185,12; 194,10; 208,16; 267, 15; 273,7.

39. Socrates' description of Nestorius' phlegmatic and incautious character has become classic: see *H.E.* vii, 32.

40. Ep. I (PG, 77, 9-40; A.C.O., I,1,1, 10-23). The literature on Cyril's Christology is extensive. See the bibliography in Quasten, *Patrology*, III, 140-141. The most extensive recent work is Liébaert, *La doctrine Christologique*. . . ; but see also Grillmeier, *Chalkedon*, I, 160-93; G. Jouassard, "Une intuition fondamentale de saint Cyrille d'Alexandrie en christologie dans les premières années de son épiscopat," *Revue des Études Byzantines*, XI (1953), 175-186: and the discussion in the recent edition of two works of Cyril by G. M. de Durand, *Cyrille d'Alexandrie. Deux Dialogues Christologiques* ("Sources Chrétiennes," No. 97: Paris: Les Editions du Cerf, 1964), pp. 81-150.

41. Ep. 1 (PG, 77, 13b; A.C.O., I,1,1, 10).

42. *Ibid.*

43. *Ibid.*, 13c; A.C.O., I,1,1,11). The citation comes from *Oratio III Contra Arianos*, 29 (PG 26,385a).

44. *Ibid.*, 13d; A.C.O., I,1,1,11).

45. *Ibid.*, 16d; A.C.O., I,1,1,13).

46. A.C.O., I,1,1,40-42.

47. *Ibid.*

48. A.C.O., I,1,1,41; T. Herbert Bindley, *The Oecumenical Documents of the Faith*. 4th Ed. (London: Methuen & Co., 1950), p. 218.

49. PG, 26, 152c-153a.

50. *Ibid.*, 153c.

51. *Ibid.*, 161b.

52. *Ibid.*, 161d-164a.

53. *Ibid.*, 169a-b.

54. A.C.O. I,1,1,41; Bindley, p. 219.

55. Cyril had already discussed Hebrews 3 in his *Thesaurus* (PG 75, 361-3); here he was interested solely in the Trinitarian question and assigns the passage, following Athanasius, to the Incarnate Logos: "The Apostle is not explaining the nature of the Word, but the economy with flesh" (361b).

56. Ep. 17 (PG, 77, 117a; A.C.O., I,1,1 38).

57. A.C.O., I,1,7,65ff.; It is, I believe, important to note that Cyril's conception of the priestly work of Christ is not a hasty formulation shaped soley in response to Nestorius' sermon. Many of the concepts expressed in this work —blameless priest, spotless lamb, second Adam—were worked out in some detail in Cyril's commentaries before the controversy began. For the

second Adam cf. his *Commentary on John* i.9 (PG, 73, 157ff.; Pusey, I, 138ff.); ii.1 (PG, 73, 196bc; Pusey, I, 175); concerning priesthood, note the following discussions of terms and phrases which appear in the anathema: "sacrifice of God's Son," *In Joannem* xi.12 (PG, 74, 585b: Pusey, III. 20-21); "blameless sacrifice," *Ibid.*, xi.10 (PG, 74, 545d: Pusey, 724); "offering for mankind, but not for himself," *Ibid.* x.8 (PG, 74, 508c-d; Pusey, II, 689); *Ibid.* ix (PG, 74, col. 153a; Pusey, II, 378).

58. A.C.O. I,1,6,121. The felicitous phrase "exact professor" comes from the *NPNF* translator; the Greek itself is more prosaic though not without a touch of sarcasm: *ho tōn theiōn dogmatōn didaskalos akribēs*.

59. *Ibid.*

60. *Ibid.*, 122.

61. He had to write a book, *De Sententia Dionysii*, to show that his use of *homoousios*—a term Dionysius rejected in the third century—was faithful to authentic Christian tradition as well as responsive to the present problem (PG, 25, 479-522).

62. Werner Elert, *Der Ausgang der altkirchlichen Christologie* (Berlin: Lutherisches Verlagshaus, 1957), p.24; On the general practice of citing the fathers as authorities, see Robert M. Grant, "The Appeal to the Early Fathers," *Journal of Theological Studies*, N.S., IX (1960), 13-24; in particular see Hubert du Manoir de Juaye, "L'argumentation patristique dans la controverse nestorienne," *Dogme et Spiritualité chez Saint Cyrille d'Alexandrie* ("Études de Théologie et d' Histoire de la Spiritualité," ed. by Étienne Gilson and André Combes, No. 11: Paris: Librairie Philosophique J. Vrin, 1944), 454-490; Manoir correctly observes that the practice of citing extensive lists (*florilegia*) of quotations first begins with Cyril; at the same time he shows that the use of florilegia is of a piece with the earlier argument from tradition. Though I have not entered into a discussion of the intricacies of the new form of appealing to tradition, the intention of my remarks should be plain: the new development of undergirding one's theology by lists of citations of earlier fathers presupposes a view of tradition which has become unworkable by the ecclesiastical and theological situation of the late fourth and early fifth centuries. For further literature, see Marcel Richard, "Les florilèges diphysites du Ve et du VI siècle," *Chalkedon*, I, 721-748.

Journal of Ecclesiastical History, Vol. XXII, No. 2, April 1971

A Reconsideration of Alexandrian Christology

by FRANCES M. YOUNG

Lecturer in Theology, University of Birmingham

In modern Christological thinking, the tendency is to start with an affirmation of the real humanity of Christ. We recognise with ever-increasing realism that the man, Jesus, lived a life open to historical investigation, a life which was circumscribed within the limitations of a normal human psychology and its contemporary environment. This being our pre-supposition, we tend to approve the Antiochene school for its realistic exegesis of New Testament texts referring to the human weakness, progress, experience, finite knowledge, temptation and conflict of the Christ. Correspondingly, we criticise the Alexandrian Fathers for their unnatural exegesis, based, we instinctively feel, upon a form of docetism, however sophisticated.[1] How justifiable is this attitude? It is not the purpose of this paper to minimise the difficulties involved in the Alexandrian position, but the following suggestions may lead to a more sympathetic view of Alexandrian thinking.

The Alexandrian Christology is a remarkably clear and consistent construction, especially when viewed within its soteriological context.

The tradition represented by Cyril of Alexandria, and later by the Monophysites, derives from Athanasius's polemic on behalf of Nicene orthodoxy.[2] Anti-Arian and anti-Nestorian arguments are based on the same presupposition, namely, the soteriological position expounded in the *De Incarnatione*.

The basis of Athanasius's position was the idea that if man had not fallen, he would have lived ὡς θεός.[3] Because of his disobedience, man ceased to participate in the Logos of God. In the first place, this meant the loss of the principle of life, making men susceptible to corruption and death. So the Logos took a human body capable of dying; through the offering of that body to death, he conquered death, and through its resurrection, he

---

[1] E.g. my 'Christological Ideas in the Greek Commentaries on the Epistle to the Hebrews', *J.T.S.*, N.S. xx (1969), 150-63.
[2] For Monophysite dependence on Cyril, see J. Lebon, *Le Monophysisme Sévérien*, Louvain 1909; for Cyril's dependence on Athanasius, see J. Liébaert, *La Doctrine Christologique de S. Cyrille d'Alexandrie avant la querelle Nestorienne*, Lille 1951.
[3] *De Incarnat.*, iv. 6.

103

re-created humanity and restored in man the eternal life of the Logos.[1] Secondly, it meant that by squandering his share in the Logos, man perverted his intelligence and turned to idolatry, worshipping the creature instead of the Creator. Only a renewal of participation in the Logos could regain proper knowledge of God; this was accomplished by the Logos dwelling in a man.[2] Athanasius summarises the work of Christ in the words: Αὐτὸς γὰρ ἐνηνθρώπησεν, ἵνα ἡμεῖς ἐθεοποιηθῶμεν.[3] The vital principle was that only God could save, because only God could restore and guarantee the presence of his image in man. Since the Christological theories of the Arians undercut this soteriological principle, Athanasius was driven to his lifelong fight against their position.[4] The Logos, he maintained, is not a creature, but is ὁμοούσιος τῷ Πατρί; in the context of the Incarnation, he appears as a fallible creature in order that we, fallible creatures, may be saved, but he is not so in reality. Only by the establishment of this fact can our salvation be guaranteed.

This soteriological theory was not only threatened by the Arians, but also by the dualistic Christology of the Antiochene school. The opposition to Nestorianism felt at a later date by Cyril and his anti-Chalcedonian successors, was fired by a desire to guarantee salvation by attributing it, not to the efforts of a fallible humanity, but to the unchangeable, invincible power of God, restoring humanity to its true self.[5] It was no mere accident of Church politics that Nestorius hesitated to condemn the Pelagians. The theological parallel between the Christological debate in the East and the contemporary Pelagian controversy in the West should not be overlooked. One side in each case emphasised the human effort required for salvation, the other attributed all to God. The principle that neither the race nor the individual could save itself was fundamental to Augustine and to the Alexandrians.

This insistence on the role of God as the sole source of salvation produced the characteristic emphasis on the role of the incarnate Logos found in Alexandrian theology from Athanasius to the Monophysites. It was essential that the presence of the Logos should re-create human nature: so they did not speak of two distinct natures, but of the Logos prior to the Incarnation and the Logos in the incarnate state.[6] This emphasis gave rise to the problems and difficulties of their position. Against Arius, they insisted that the Logos was unchangeable, as indeed their Antiochene opponents did; yet, for them, this same Logos had to be the subject of the incarnate experiences. It would not do to separate the Logos from the

---

[1] De Incarnat., xi–xvi; cf. C. Arianos, i. 44, 45, 59, 60; ii. 14, 16, 55, 61, 66, 67, 68, 70; iii. 4, 31, 33, 38, 53.

[2] De Incarnat., xi–xvi; cf. C. Arianos, i. 9, 12, 16, 21, 35, 39, 43, 59, 61; ii. 16, 17, 22, 24, 54, 80, 81, 82; iii. 3–7, 11, 14, 16, 46.

[3] De Incarnat., liv. 3; cf. C. Arianos, i. 37–50; ii. 41, 47, 53, 61, 65, 70, 75, iii. 33.

[4] See preceding notes for use of the same ideas in the work against the Arians.

[5] E.g., Cyril's comments on Heb. ii. 16–18: P.G., lxxiv. 964A–9A; P. E. Pusey, Cyrilli in Joannem, 1872, iii. 463–6. For discussion see my article in J.T.S., N.S. xx. 152-3.

[6] See my article in J.T.S., N.S. xx. 152; cf. J. Lebon, op. cit., 205, 287.

104

experiences of his humanity. Inevitably, this led the Alexandrians into paradox—ἀπαθῶς ἔπαθεν—for it is impossible to conceive of changeless experience of or involvement in the human condition. In particular, their treatment of psychological weaknesses and fallibility in the Christ was bound to be unsatisfactory, and their exegesis of texts referring to the Saviour's increase in knowledge and grace, of his feelings of fear, grief and desertion by God, could not help but seem artifical and docetic in tendency.[1] Yet, it must be admitted that, viewed within its soteriological context, their position is consistent and religiously compelling. The Logos himself took our flesh, shared our experiences, and overcame our weaknesses and sin by his divine power. This was their faith and their Gospel.

Cyril and the Monophysites claimed that the unity of Christ, who is Logos and flesh, could be envisaged by analogy with the unity of body and soul in a human person.

If we regard Apollinarianism as the extreme form of the Alexandrian position, then inevitably we tend to think of this as a dangerous analogy, implying that the human soul was replaced by the Logos in the unique case of Jesus Christ. It may well be the case that the use of this analogy was encouraged by its presence in Apollinarian literature which was mistakenly attributed in the fifth century to Athanasius,[2] but, even so, this criticism is not entirely fair. There are three reasons for this.

(i) The Alexandrians were aware of the problems involved in using analogies. Cyril recognised that the force of analogies is weak and falls short of truth, merely introducing into the mind a trace, an appearance of the reality, which helps one to rise to what is inexpressible.[3] One of his Monophysite successors warned his readers not to push to extremes analogies which only correspond in one or two points.[4]

(ii) The analogy in question was not only used by the Alexandrians. It appeared in the writings of the opposing Antiochenes and Chalcedonians; it was the only illustration to appear in the Athanasian creed;[5] it was used by St. Augustine.[6] In other words, it was common currency and was not confined to the school which is so often regarded as crypto-Apollinarian.

(iii) Athanasius, it seems, would have felt unhappy with the use of this analogy,[7] but it became particularly prominent in the writings of Cyril and the Monophysites. It was used in the same way as other analogies to show that the union in Christ did not admit of any separation, and yet did not

[1] For discussion of such passages see (i) on Athanasius, M. Richard, 'S. Athanase et la psychologie du Christ selon les Ariens', in *Mélanges de Science Religieuse*, iv (1947) 5-54; (ii) on Cyril, J. Liébaert, op. cit.; (iii) on the Monophysites, J. Lebon, op. cit.
[2] J. Lebon, op. cit., 227, 232.
[3] *Quod unus sit Christus*, P.G., lxxv. 1357C.
[4] Philoxenus, quoted by Lebon, op. cit., 222.
[5] For this point I am indebted to M. F. Wiles, 'Psychological Analogies in the Fathers', to appear in *Studia Patristica* xi, in *Texte und Untersuchungen zur Geschichte der altchristlichen Literatur* (Berlin).
[6] *Tractatus in Joannem*, xlvii. 12.
[7] *De Incarnat.*, xvii.

105

imply change or mixing. Examples are many: light and eye, word and voice, thought and mind, scent and flowers, a ray of the sun and air, the male semen and the female blood which together create an infant. Even the Eucharist provided an analogy: the body is not *in* the bread, but *is* the bread; the blood is not *in* the wine, but *is* the wine; so in the Incarnation, the Word was not *in* man, but *was* man.[1] The union is a mystery, but it is a natural and inseparable union.[2] The analogy in question meant no more. Soul and body are different entities, yet in our experience of being human they are inseparable; there is no such thing as humanity without one or the other. There is one perfect nature and hypostasis of man by the union of soul and body.[3] Human existence, interpreted by the universally accepted soul-body analysis, provided a particularly illuminating analogy of the union of humanity and divinity in the Christ. Its potential can be appreciated even more when we notice statements like the following, which appears in Nemesius's treatise on the nature of man: the soul preserves its own independent unity of being, yet modifies that which it indwells in accordance with its own life, while itself receiving no reciprocal change.[4] This is very close to the sort of thing everyone was trying to say about the relationship between Logos and humanity in Christ.[5] It was a good *analogy*. It should not be taken as an analysis of the relationship and, therefore, be interpreted in Apollinarian terms.

However, while constantly using this analogy, Cyril and the Monophysites did feel obliged to see that it was accompanied by the repeated assertion that the *sarx* assumed by the Logos was a man with a soul and a mind, thus safeguarding themselves from the condemnation of heresy.[6] Modern studies of Athanasius and Cyril have emphasised the problems involved in their account of Christ's humanity.[7] Were the Alexandrians, then, attempting to have it both ways? Was their Christology an imperceptible acceptance of Apollinarianism while openly rejecting it?

It must be admitted that the Alexandrian tradition did not, on the whole, make any positive use of the idea of Christ's human soul. In the drama of salvation it had no active part to play. To this extent their Christological theory was indeed Apollinarian in tendency. The only subject of the incarnate experiences was the Logos. In replying to the Arian appeal to scriptural texts implying change or weakness in the Saviour, Athanasius attributed all weaknesses to the flesh, and made no use of the idea of a fallible human soul to account for Christ's psychological conflicts. Christ's progress, he explains, was not an improvement of the Logos, but a progressive revelation of the Logos through the maturing human body.

[1] Lebon, op. cit., 221-5.
[2] Ibid., 205, 217, 231, etc.
[3] Philoxenus, quoted by Lebon, op. cit., 229.
[4] Nemesius, *De Natura Hominis*, iii. 20: P.G., xl. 597.
[5] M. F. Wiles, art. cit.
[6] My art. cit., 153.
[7] E.g. M. Richard, art. cit; J. Liébaert, op. cit.

106

His tears, his fear of death, his ignorance, were, like his hunger and thirst, a means of displaying the reality of the Incarnation, a proof of the fact that he had assumed the weaknesses of human flesh for our salvation; but the changeless Logos could not in fact suffer these weaknesses. Athanasius is driven to claiming a pretence of fear, to admitting that the Logos is open to the charge of having lied when Jesus claimed to be ignorant, even to saying τὰ ἡμῶν ἐμιμήσατο.[1] The humanity of Christ according to Athanasius seems to lack conviction. It is almost as though it has been allegorised away like the references to divine emotion in the Old Testament, an analogy which Athanasius actually uses to excuse his position.[2]

Cyril's position is no different. His anti-Arian polemic follows that of Athanasius almost exactly; he makes no use of the idea of a fallible human soul to counter Arian arguments; in fact, he has been accused of failing to take account of Apollinarianism, at least in the period before the Nestorian controversy.[3] In spite of his frequent assertion that the *sarx* assumed by the Logos was a man with a soul and a mind (that is, a *totus homo*), it is suggested that he has not fully grasped the implications of the condemnation of Apollinarius.[4] In spite of his making ἀνθρωπότης the subject of Christ's passions rather than his flesh or body; in spite of showing a greater preference for discussing Christ's psychological rather than his physical weaknesses; he is accused of not having integrated the soul into his Christology,[5] and his exegesis gives adequate ground for this accusation.

Yet there are a number of reasons for suggesting that within the terms of their soteriological and anthropological outlook, a positive use of the idea of Christ's human soul was unnecessary, and its absence did not imply an inadequate or docetic interpretation of the Incarnation.

(i) Apology is often made on Athanasius's behalf by pointing to the Platonist conception of human nature as a spirit trapped in flesh.[6] According to Athanasius's early works, it is through the soul that man, however imperfectly, images God.[7] The image was lost in the Fall, and in the Incarnation it was restored by the true image of God, the Logos, taking flesh. An ordinary man is spirit (or *logos*) clothed in flesh; Christ is *the* Logos clothed in flesh. This explanation is helpful: all weaknesses can be attributed to the flesh because it is the flesh which drags a man down, and from which the soul, according to the Platonist view, seeks escape. Furthermore, the *Logos-sarx* picture of the Incarnation is not essentially docetic. The experience of being human is the experience of being trapped in the weaknesses of the flesh; for most of us it involves our succumbing to its

---

[1] For Athanasius's discussion of these problems, see C. Arianos, iii. 26–58; for an interpretation, see M. Richard, art. cit., 26–46.

[2] C. Arianos, iii. 50. For a similar use in Cyril, see J. Liébaert, op. cit., 123.

[3] Liébaert, op. cit.

[4] My art. cit., 153.

[5] Liébaert, op. cit., 117, 172 ff., 179.

[6] Richard, art. cit.; Liébaert, op. cit., 148–50.

[7] W. J. Burghardt, *The Image of God in Man according to Cyril of Alexandria*, Washington 957, 13; ref. C. Gentes, 34.

107

downward drag. The Logos had the experience of being human because he, like us, was trapped in flesh and, like us, was tempted through it. However, the subject of this experience was the Logos and this made the difference; the Logos, because of his very nature, did not in the process succumb to sin. But this does not mean that he did not really and fully share our experience, excepting only the experience of guilt and sinfulness. Rather it means that our human experience is redeemed from the necessity of succumbing to sin. If this was Athanasius's Christology, it is perfectly consistent with its underlying soteriology (as outlined earlier). The question whether a human soul was involved in the situation was irrelevant, and this does not mean that a purely docetic charade was envisaged. A real Incarnation was essential for Athanasius's soteriology, and this was how he understood a real Incarnation.

(ii) Apology is also made on Athanasius's behalf by appealing to the fact that the majority of his writings are prior to the period when Apollinarius's theories had made the question of the human soul of Jesus paramount. Indeed, there was a mistrust of the idea resulting from aversion to the ideas of Paul of Samosata, an aversion which was deeply felt throughout the Eastern Church.[1] Attention has been drawn to the fact that Athanasius did point out, even in the *C. Arianos*, that in the language of scripture 'flesh' regularly means 'man'.[2] Elsewhere in Athanasius's writings, it is claimed, man implies a being composed of soul and body. Therefore, flesh is simply a scriptural synonym for human nature, including the human soul; and this implicit acceptance of the human soul in Jesus became explicit at the synod of Alexandria in 362.[3] It is certainly possible that at the end of his life, even if not before, Athanasius did recognise the need to assert that the Christ had a human soul,[4] though the text is capable of an alternative interpretation. Perhaps Athanasius meant by the formula οὐ σῶμα ἄψυχον... a body animated and made intelligent by the presence of the Logos himself.[5] Whatever he thought he meant, he did accept the soteriological principle promoted by the Paulinians. It is true that he did not use the idea of Christ's human soul positively even after this, but he had recognised that 'it was not possible when the Lord became man for us that his body should be without intelligence', and he recognised it on the grounds that the 'salvation effected in the Word himself was a salvation not of body only, but also of soul.'[6] Soteriology was basic to Athanasius's theology. If there was any way of winning his support, it was by appeal to soteriological principles. The Logos must be ἄτρεπτος to save, but he must truly enter the realm of the τρέπτα, for that is what needs saving. A real Incarnation is essential for

[1] M. F. Wiles, 'The Nature of the Early Debate about Christ's Human Soul', in this JOURNAL, xvi (1965), 139–51.

[2] *C. Arianos*, iii. 30.

[3] P. Galtier, 'S. Athanase et l'âme humaine du Christ', in *Gregorianum*, xxxvi (1955), 553–89

[4] M. Richard, art. cit.

[5] J. N. D. Kelly, *Early Christian Doctrines*, 2nd ed., London 1960, 288–9.

[6] *Tomus ad Antiochenos*, 7.

108

the salvation of men, their souls and bodies.[1] Docetism is out of the question, however the Incarnation was envisaged.[2]

(iii) Whatever Athanasius thought, theologians in the same basic Christological tradition did condemn Apollinarius, and they did so on soteriological grounds. Gregory of Nazianzus, author of the classic anti-Apollinarian statement, 'What is not assumed, cannot be saved', worked within the traditional *Logos-sarx* pattern of thought, and even he failed to make use of the presence of the human soul in Jesus to expound realistically the New Testament passages referring to his progress in knowledge, ignorance, etc.[3] He, therefore, has many of the same weaknesses with regard to the Saviour's human psychology as Athanasius and Cyril, and yet no-one could accuse him of being crypto-Apollinarian.

Even those more obviously close to the Alexandrian tradition were not unable to assimilate the idea of a human soul into their Christology. In a passage attributed to Cyril's *Commentary on John*,[4] it is argued that being troubled by the thought of peril is as much a passion of the ψυχὴ λογική as hunger is an experience of the weakness of human flesh. The writer continues by pointing out that the Saviour said his soul was troubled, not his flesh, and argues on these grounds that the Divine Logos was united with the whole nature of man in order to save the whole man. This passage may in fact derive from Didymus the Blind,[5] and if so, this use of the human soul is explained by his dependence on Origen at this point. The interesting thing, however, is that the context is the traditional Alexandrian soteriology, whereby the power of the Logos recreates human nature. It is explained that in Christ human nature was raised to new life and the feeling of fear was transformed by his power.

Likewise, in the papyrus *Commentary on the Psalms* discovered at Tura in 1941, again in all probability to be ascribed to Didymus,[6] the author affirms the existence of Christ's human soul, and uses it to account for the fallibility and psychological weaknesses of Jesus as reported in the Gospels. This document enables us to see an explicit description of Christ's nature and work which is close to the outline of Athanasius's thought suggested earlier, and yet includes the presence of the human soul in a positive way. God created the human soul in his image, and the human soul of Jesus was alone in not succumbing to temptation. Its sinlessness meant that it was a human soul perfectly conforming to the plan of the Creator. He was like us in everything except sin, and so his soul, not needing salvation itself, became the instrument of our salvation.[7]

---

[1] *Ad Epictetum*, 7.
[2] See the discussion in J. Roldanus, *Le Christ et l'homme dans le théologie d'Athanase d'Alexandrie*, Leiden 1968, 252–76.
[3] See J. N. D. Kelly, op. cit., 297–8.
[4] P. E. Pusey, *Cyrilli in Joannem*, ii. 315–18.
[5] Liébaert, op. cit., 131 ff.
[6] A. Gesché, 'L'âme humaine de Jesus dans la Christologie du IVᵉ siècle', in *R.H.E.*, liv (1959), 385.
[7] Ibid., 398–9.

109

Cyril and the Monophysites recognised the soteriological grounds for asserting the existence of Christ's human soul, and were definitely opposed to the Apollinarian position. Granted that Cyril follows Athanasius's pattern of thought very closely, granted that the human soul of Jesus is not given an active role to play, it is, nevertheless, frequently asserted in his writings, and not merely to avoid condemnation as an Apollinarian. It is asserted because of the recognised soteriological necessity of its presence. The same soteriological presuppositions colour Cyril's approach: death is not abolished if he had not died, fear is not abolished if he had not been afraid.[1] Hence the *sarx* assumed by the Logos was a man with a soul and a mind. 'He makes his own all that belongs, as to his own body, so to the soul, for he had to be shown to be like us through every circumstance both physical and mental, and we consist of rational soul and body: and as there are times when in the Incarnation he permitted his own flesh to experience its own proper affections, so again he permitted the soul to experience its proper affections, and he observed the scale of the κένωσις in every respect'. Apollinarianism is repudiated because it placed the human mind outside the Logos's saving influence.[2] The Monophysites were definite on this point, and their greatest authority was Cyril: 'He was truly made man ... without leaving aside any circumstance in which our humanity finds itself. He was united hypostatically without change, to a flesh consubstantial with ours and passible like ours, animated by an intelligent and reasonable soul, and was like us in all things excepting sin'. 'He lacked nothing for our redemption; according to the foolish Apollinarius, he was deprived of the principal requirement for our salvation'.[3]

(iv) Granted that the presence of the human soul in Jesus was recognised on soteriological grounds, the accusation is made that no positive use was made of it. The psychological weaknesses of the Saviour, especially the ignorance attributed to him, are still in the main expounded in docetic terms, because it is the Logos alone who is the subject of the incarnate experiences. The human soul, it is claimed, is given a purely passive role, and this implies not merely that its presence is not really assimilated into the Christological picture, but even that its soteriological role is minimised. 'In the case of the Antiochenes, the role of the human soul was an active one; in the case of the Alexandrians it was almost wholly passive. While for the former the temptations and emotional struggles of Jesus show his human soul emerging unscathed and victoriously triumphant, for the latter they show the divine Logos effecting a divine conquest in the sphere of our human weakness'.[4] All this is true, but it does not mean that the humanity of Christ in the Alexandrian tradition is so truncated as to be unrecog-

---

[1] *Thesauras*: P.G., lxxv. 396–7.
[2] *De Recte Fide*: P.G., lxxvi. 413. For other passages in Cyril, see R. V. Sellers, *Two Ancient Christologies*, London 1940, 102 n.5.
[3] Theodosius of Alexandria and the διάθεσις presented to Justinian; quoted by Lebon, op. cit., 202.
[4] M. F. Wiles, 'The Nature of the Early Debate about Christ's Human Soul', in this JOURNAL, xvi (1965), 150.

110

nisable or irrelevant to the human situation, especially in the context of their presuppositions about human psychology. 'Didymus', as we have seen, spoke of Christ's human soul as an instrument of salvation.[1] This was a traditional expression found in Athanasius, though there it is the flesh which is the ὄργανον used by the Logos to effect redemption.[2] Whatever the actual analysis of Christ's humanity, the Alexandrian tradition clung to the concept of a human nature that was merely an instrument in the hands of the Logos, a human nature capable of such perfect response to the Logos in the unique situation of the Incarnation that there was no possibility of distinguishing an independent or opposing human subject. This responsiveness constituted sinlessness, and in the flesh, the Logos assumed all weaknesses apart from sin, that is, the refusal to respond. The flesh of the Logos was an instrument of salvation by being entirely receptive of his re-creating presence.[3] The discussion of Christ's human soul is irrelevant; it could perfectly well be accepted into the Alexandrian Christology, provided it presented no challenge to the unity of the Christ or the receptivity of the human nature assumed by the Logos. For Apollinarius, the human *ego* was inevitably active against the influence of the Logos; Incarnation implied schizophrenia unless the Logos replaced the warped mind of the human individual. For the Antiochenes, the human *ego* needed saving, and being characterised by αὐτεξουσία, had to be seen as a separate nature within the mediating Saviour, an active participant in the victory over evil. In the Alexandrian tradition, however, it was conceivable that man should be entirely receptive to the Logos; indeed, that was man's true being.

Ἀπαθῶς ἔπαθεν—in spite of apparent paradox, the Alexandrians were not inconsistent in maintaining the unity of Christ's person while accepting the impossibility of the Logos suffering on the Cross.

The Antiochenes, it must be admitted, did succeed in emphasising the exemplary nature of Christ's sufferings by making a rigid distinction between the two natures; for them, the man, Jesus, conquered human weakness, temptation and suffering as the pioneer of the way his followers should take, while the Logos remained unaffected. However, it was at the cost of failing to give any account at all of the Incarnation. Besides, they did not have a monopoly of this theme; it was common to all the Fathers. Too rigid a distinction between the suffering, conquering man and the Logos who remained ἀπαθής was not necessary within the commonly accepted framework of thought, especially when we remember the constant use of the analogy discussed above.

It has been suggested that Cyril's failure to use the idea of the presence of a human soul in the Saviour to account for his psychological weakness is

---

[1] See above, 109.
[2] That Christ's humanity was no more than an instrument used by the Logos who is the sole source of salvation in Athanasius's writings, is emphasised by Roldanus, op. cit., 212 et passim.
[3] Ibid., 268-74.

the result of his understanding of the human soul as being ἀπαθής.[1] In its own being the soul has no share in παθή or the experiences imposed on the body by external causes. But the properties of the body belong also to the soul, and when the body is stirred to desire, then, on account of the union, the soul united to the body participates in the sensation. Like the divine, the human soul is in itself impassible, since it is incorporeal; yet it is said to suffer when the body suffers. Cyril uses this analogy to elucidate the problem of how the Logos, though ἀπαθής, can still be said to have suffered, modifying the idea of participation, however, to impassible awareness of his flesh's sufferings, in order more radically to preserve the Logos's impassibility.[2]

Cyril was far from being an innovator in this description of the relationship between soul and body. It was current Neoplatonist teaching. Plotinus called the sufferings of the soul ἀπαθῆ πάθη.[3] Nemesius tells us that most learned authors took the view that the body was the sole sufferer, and even though the body derived its capacity to feel pain from the soul, the soul itself remained impassible. He, like Cyril, drew the parallel with the union of Logos and manhood, making the same proviso, that whereas the soul seemed to suffer with the body, sometimes mastering it and sometimes being mastered by it, the divine Word suffered no alteration from the fellowship which he had with the body and the soul.[4] Nemesius was Antiochene in his Christology. He and Cyril both accepted the assumptions of the best religious philosophy current at the time.

This outlook was not merely a theoretical position reached in the schools. The practical implications of it were ingrained into the moral philosophy of many different religious and philosophical sects. The ethical ideal towards which strove the philosopher and the wise man, the martyr, monk and mystic, was ἀπάθεια. To rise above the changes and chances of life, the sufferings and sins of the world and the flesh, was the way of salvation. The spirit trapped in flesh sought to overcome the downward drag, the distractions of the flesh.[5] This alone constituted true worship. According to Porphyry, the supreme God could only be worshipped by pure silence, holy sacrifice being offered to him simply by close contact with him and being transformed to his likeness, until the offering was perfected by achieving ἀπάθεια of soul and θεωρία of God.[6] From Clement of Alex-

---

[1] For the argument of this paragraph, I am indebted to G. Jouassard, 'Un problème d'anthropologie et de Christologie chez S. Cyrille d'Alexandrie', in *Recherches de Science Religieuse*, xlviii (1955), 366 ff.; and H. Chadwick, 'Eucharist and Christology in the Nestorian Controversy', in *J.T.S.*, N.S. ii (1951), 145.

[2] That Cyril did recognise some sense in which the soul had its own proper passions is shown by the passage quoted above, p. 110. Clearly he is not entirely consistent, and he wanted to claim that the Logos was ἀπαθής to a greater degree than the soul, while using the analogy to explain his Christological position. The analogy merely helps one to rise to what is inexpressible (see above, 105).

[3] *Enneads*, iii. 6. 1, quoted by H. Chadwick, op. cit.

[4] *De Nat. Hom.*, iii. 22; P.G., xl. 601.

[5] See above, 107 ff.

[6] *De Abstinentia*, ii. 34–5.

112

andria onwards, this type of thought and idealism prevailed in Christian circles, as elsewhere in the contemporary religious scene. The only sacrifice worthy of God, who needs nothing, is the offering of oneself purified from sin and in a state of ἀπάθεια;[1] this is true gnostic perfection and one who has achieved it is equal to the angels and is clothed in the divine image. God is ἀπαθής and the restoration of his image in man meant the moderation of human passions.[2] This constituted the *imitatio Christi*. The martyrs strove to attain the state in which their souls were unaffected by the torments of the flesh.[3] The wise man did not feel the cutting and burning of his tortured body.[4] The ideal of ἀπάθεια received its greatest development in the ethics of those for whom martydom was replaced by asceticism, for example, in the mystical writings of Gregory of Nyssa.[5] The idea frequently occurs in Palladius's *Lausiac History*.[6] In the light of this type of outlook, it was surely not unreasonable to speak of Christ's flesh suffering on the Cross while the Logos remained unaffected by, though intimately aware of, the experience.

The Alexandrian tradition insisted throughout that the Logos was the sole subject of the incarnate experiences; this alone could be called a real Incarnation of the Logos. In spite of docetic tendencies in their attempts to do justice to this belief, the Alexandrines in fact, gave a better account of traditional Christian belief than the Antiochene school, which divided the natures and failed to expound their unity in the Incarnation. Incarnation, as Cyril understood it, meant that the Logos subjected himself to the limitations, physical and psychological, of human existence.[7] This view was successfully maintained by treating the humanity of the Saviour as being entirely receptive of the Logos, a mere instrument in his hands. Thus the humanity was given a purely passive role, whether or not the presence of a human soul was recognised.

Our difficulty with this Christological picture hinges on the question of will. We, like the Antiochenes, do not perceive a satisfactory human psychology in the Christ unless there is present a human will which is at least theoretically capable of opposing the Logos. But what can we envisage as a proper human psychology in the unique context of the Incarnation? The very uniqueness of the situation makes this question hard to answer,

---

[1] Clement, *Strom.*, vii. 14, 31, 33, cf., v. 1.

[2] Ibid., iv. 22, vi. 13.

[3] Augustine, *In Psalmos*, 26. ii. 21. E. E. Malone (*The Monk and the Martyr*, Washington 1950) claims that this idea entered Christian asceticism from the Stoics via Philo, and continues, 'The doctrine of ἀπάθεια does not seem to have had any particular application in the case of the martyrs'. If not, it was certainly read back into their situation, as in this passage from Augustine.

[4] Eusebius, *Dem. Evang.*, iv. 13. 7: G.C.S., 172.

[5] E.g. P.G., xliv. 364; xlv. 40–1; xlvi. 285 et passim. See Daniélou's introduction to H. Musurillo's translation of some of Gregory's mystical writings entitled *From Glory to Glory*.

[6] Ed. C. Butler (Texts and Studies vi), Cambridge 1898; e.g. Prologue (p. 12, l.3); viii (p. 28, l.4); xxxvii (p. 116, l.4); etc.

[7] G. L. Prestige, *Fathers and Heretics*, London 1940, 159 ff.

and if we are true to Christian tradition, account must be taken of that uniqueness.

The passive role of the human nature of the Saviour is not only closer to traditional affirmations about the Incarnation, but is also more consistent with the account of sin and salvation traditional in Christian thinking, especially where the influence of Paul is felt. Human sin, according to this view, is a failure to be receptive; it is rebellion and the selfish activity of the *ego*. Sinlessness is receiving grace rather than deliberately doing good, an activity which so easily degenerates into a Pharisaic boast. Augustine claimed that we are only truly free when we are freed from slavery to sin to serve the living God.[1] The object of asceticism was to subdue one's will and allow the Logos to take over the self; this was expressed pictorially in the belief that the monk became the battleground fought over by the Logos and the devils. In the true ascetic, the human subject is submerged as the receptive instrument of the Logos:[2] 'This was Antony's first triumph against the devil—or rather the first triumph of the Saviour in Antony'.[3] In terms of this outlook on the nature of man, sin and salvation, the Alexandrian Christology was not basically docetic, though its confused exegesis sometimes was. Receptivity is man's proper characteristic. Christ in his human nature was alone truly receptive of grace; he alone was entirely sinless, and in this uniqueness he was more truly human than any of us. It is hardly out of tune with some modern approaches to begin with a human being uniquely responsive to the ultimate ground of being, in other words, the Logos. The Alexandrians would not have emphasised the man, Jesus, so strongly, but their ideas were not inconsistent with this approach.

[1] E.g. *Retractiones*, i. 9. 4. Cf. Anti-Pelagian literature, passim.

[2] J. Roldanus, op. cit., 309 ff., 328, 336; E. E. Malone, op. cit., 106–7, who also traces this back to the martyr literature: the martyrs did not feel pain because it was really Christ fighting in them; he refers to Perpetua and Felicitas, Polycarp and the martyrs of Lyons and Vienne.

[3] *Vita Antonii*, 7; P.G., xxvi. 852A.

114

THE ANTIOCHENE CHRISTOLOGY OF
DIODORE OF TARSUS

DR. ALOYS GRILLMEIER's book, *Christ in Christian Tradition*,[1] presents the argument that by the fourth century two
christological frameworks can be discerned. The one, represented in various ways by Apollinaris, Arius, and Athanasius, he calls
'Logos–sarx'; the other, to be found chiefly in Theodore and Nestorius
and reflected in the Chalcedonian definition, he calls 'Logos–anthropos'.
It may seem presumptuous to dispute conclusions which are carefully
argued and provide a splendid thread of Ariadne for the labyrinth of
fourth- and fifth-century christology. However, I propose to question
the validity of Grillmeier's thesis only on the basis of his treatment of
Diodore of Tarsus. My aim is not so much refutation as that of raising
the question how far the sort of schematization proposed by Grillmeier
is helpful. In the case of Diodore, he admits that Theodore's teacher
has affinities with the Logos–anthropos camp; but he is anxious to show
that there is a considerable difference of emphasis in Diodore and that,
in fact, the 'christological framework upon which he builds up his theology of "distinction", or even "division"' is a Logos–sarx one.[2] This
judgement springs from the fact that Diodore often uses 'flesh' to refer
to the humanity of Christ. According to Grillmeier, this and several
other features of Diodore's christology betray his failure to make the
soul of Jesus a theological factor in his christology and imply a Logos–
sarx framework for it. Historically, the influence is probably traceable
to Eusebius of Emesa and to Diodore's defence of Christ's divinity
against the attacks of the Emperor Julian. The usual description of
Diodore's christology as 'Antiochene' fails to take account of these
factors, while the categories Logos–sarx and Logos–anthropos provide
a way of describing the contrary tendencies in his thought. We must
examine this assessment and can begin, as against Grillmeier, by presenting the Logos–anthropos framework of Diodore's christology. It will
be argued that this framework rather than that of Logos–sarx is primary
for Diodore. We shall then be able to turn to other areas of his christology in order to examine their suitability to the framework.

---

[1] Mowbray, London, 1965. The book is a fuller rendering of Grillmeier's
monograph in *Das Konzil von Chalkedon, Band I* (Echter-Verlag, Würzburg,
1951), pp. 5–202. The section on Diodore has been altered in the English edition
only by the addition of some half-dozen sentences on p. 266.

[2] Ibid., p. 264; German ed., p. 138.

[Journal of Theological Studies, N.S., Vol. XVII, Pt. 2, October 1966]

It must, of course, be realized that the evidence for Diodore's theology is quite fragmentary and possesses the additional difficulty of existing largely in Syriac translation. Provided, however, one does not expect a fully developed system, the bare bones of Diodore's christology can be found. Let us start with an examination of language which seems to imply a Logos–anthropos christology. Unlike Theodore, who adopts the technical term 'assumed man' for the humanity of Christ, Diodore apparently has no fixed terminology. He does, nevertheless, make considerable use of personal and relative pronouns:[1]

I myself have heard them say that he who was conceived in Mary's womb and was born of her is also the Creator of everything that exists.

Diodore uses 'he who' to introduce a clause describing attributes of the humanity of Christ; and it is clear from the polemical tone of the passage that 'he who' is a subject of attribution to be clearly distinguished from the Word, the 'Creator of all'. The same construction is used elsewhere to attribute to the human subject being 'under the Law,' circumcision, being raised as a Jew, death, burial, and resurrection.[2] It is as though Diodore wished to distinguish two subjects for the verbs in credal statements about Christ. The one who was conceived, born, died, was buried, and rose again is not to be directly identified with the One born before the ages. This pronominal construction pervades the fragments of Diodore's dogmatic works. In addition, the personal pronoun is sometimes replaced by a noun:[3]

Therefore, the infant who was conceived by Mary and born of her was the seed of Abraham and David and the flower of the root of Jesse.

In precisely the same way reference can be made to 'the son born of Mary'.[4]

In the same spirit and yet more important is Diodore's use of 'Man' in these constructions:[5]

But if anyone wishes to be quite sure whether the Apostle says this (Gal. iv) about the man born of Mary, let him take Paul here as before for his teacher in what he wishes to learn. . . . Who, then, is he who 'was under the Law'? Who is he who was circumcised? Who is he who was brought up as a Jew? Was it not the man born of Mary?

Once, more, Diodore distinguishes two subjects in Christ's person—

---

[1] British Museum Codex add. 12156, ed. and tr. M. Brière, *Revue de l'Orient chrétien*, vol. 10 (1946), fragment 4. The translations are my own, but I should wish to acknowledge the careful advice of Dr. R. A. Norris.

[2] Brière, fragments 13 and 16. [3] Id., fragment 19.
[4] Id., fragment 22.
[5] Id., fragment 13.

God the Word and the 'man born of Mary'. In one instance, Diodore refers to the human subject quite simply as 'the man':[1]

Now if these events at the time of the Crucifixion show that God the Word suffered, and if they will not concede that they occurred for the sake of the man, then neither did the events in the days of Moses occur for the sake of the race of Abraham. . . .

It is this terminology that Theodore develops in his christology; his teacher's very language anticipates his technical term 'assumed man'. If one defines a Logos–anthropos christology solely on the evidence of terminology, then Diodore's failure to use 'man' of the human subject more consistently does tend to dissociate him from the Logos–anthropos framework. On the other hand, it is surely impossible to consider the formulae of a christology in isolation from their meaning in the total theological picture of a writer's work. Despite his sparing use of the characteristic Antiochene term, there can be no doubt that Diodore wishes to posit two subjects of attribution in Christ's person. This double predication is a far better touchstone for a Logos–anthropos christology than the terminology *per se*. Moreover, the key to understanding the Logos–sarx christology lies in realizing that all attribution is made to a single subject, viz. God the Word. The mere frequency with which a writer employs 'man' or 'flesh' is not necessarily decisive in relegating him to one camp or the other. We must, then, endeavour to show that the terminology reflects a thorough-going double predication. Two areas demand consideration—the exegetical basis of Diodore's christology and his philosophical presuppositions. Both require him to posit a duality of subjects in Christ's person. And this requirement, in turn, raises the fundamental problem of Antiochene christology, how to describe the union of subjects so as to define convincingly one Christ.

It need hardly be said that Diodore, as all patristic writers, believed that theology was no more than an attempt to expound scripture as clearly as possible. Scriptural statements are made with extreme care and, if examined honestly and intelligently, will yield an acceptable theology.[2] I am not concerned here with Diodore's exegetical method, but only with stating that he believed his theology to be scriptural. If it can be demonstrated that he regards the New Testament as containing a double predication for Christ's person, then it must be asserted that the duality of subjects he posits is rooted more deeply in his sytem than in the terminology alone. Three passages and Diodore's treatment

---

[1] Id., fragment 17. The word is *bar nasha*; Son of Man is *bareh d'nasha*.

[2] See *Collectio Palatina*, E. Schwartz, *A.C.O.* i. v, pp. 177–8 (ed. and tr. R. Abramowski, *Z.N.T.W.* 42 (1949), fragment 43, p. 57).

of them may be chosen for consideration—John ii. 19 ff., Phil. ii, and Matt. xxii. 41 ff. Diodore does not explicitly cite the first of these passages, but it is most probably the scriptural *locus* for his description of the human subject as the "Temple of God the Word'. The Johannine interpretation of Christ's word against the Temple is the only New Testament passage in which Christ (in John his 'body') is referred to as a temple. Diodore interprets the concept as follows:[1]

> Now he who is of David's seed from the time of his creation belonged to God the Word, for when he was created he was God the Word's. So, too, we first build a temple, then the one who dwells therein enters. Indeed, in the Virgin's womb the Indweller formed for Himself a Temple; and He was not far from it, but filled it with His own glory and wisdom.

The equation of 'he who is of David's seed' with the indwelt Temple is as easily made as that of the Word with the Indweller. Diodore is not identifying the Temple simply with Jesus' body; it is the complete human nature that is in question. In a sense, he has simply taken a biblical metaphor and redeveloped it in his own way to fit a presupposed christological framework. On the other hand, the passage never presented the Antiochenes with insuperable problems, and the division made in these verses between subject and object suited their distinction between the assuming Word and the assumed man. Although a direct link with the passage cannot be found in Diodore's extant writings, it is a reasonable assumption that he thought the passage provided the sort of double category upon which he built his christology. A more compelling example of the same treatment may be found in his use of Philippians ii:[2]

> Indeed, while He 'was in the form of God, He took the form of a servant'. He did not become a servant. 'And being found in fashion as a man' He was not a man, but as a man—He who was in the form of God, He who took the form of a servant. For a servant is certainly a human nature. Now the One who was hidden was as a man because of the one who was openly revealed.

The form of God and the form of a servant are distinguished as two subjects. Diodore reads the passage by underlining 'the likeness of men' and 'in fashion as a man'. The unity of subject in the passage proves no more than the unity of the subjects in Christ's person and does not remove their distinction in nature.

Diodore's treatment of these two passages may not strike the modern reader as fully satisfactory. And certainly the Alexandrians fulminated

---

[1] Severus of Antioch, *Contra Impium Grammaticum*, ed. and tr. J. Lebon, *Orat.* iii. 15 (*C.S.C.O.* 94 (1929), p. 178).
[2] Brière, fragment 14.

for a century at the notion that such texts implied a double predication. Nevertheless, Diodore is perfectly serious in his conviction that they implied his particular christological view. In this sense, his exegesis of Matt. xxii. 41 ff. is no different from that of John ii and Philippians ii; yet it seems the strongest weapon in his arsenal. He explains the passage as follows:[1]

And besides, consider the witness of our Lord's disciples, the Evangelists. If they knew that our Lord no longer wished to be called Son of David after the flesh, and that for this reason he cited the words of David to the Jews, they would not confess him to be the Son of David and Abraham, and would not teach others this. But the fact of the matter is that they knew with certainty that it is God the Word who is Lord of David and that He is not the one who is confessed as David's son.

The Gospel tells us that the Jews believed the Christ to be the Son of David, but were unable to explain how David in the psalm could call his son 'Lord'. Diodore's explanation is that Christ in the Gospel is demonstrating that he is both David's son *qua* man and David's Lord *qua* the Word and in so far as the man receives the title by his union with the Word. The two subjects are distinct and the humanity must not be suppressed.[2] David's son is a title that can pertain only to the human subject. Diodore's interpretation of the title David's Lord is fortunately preserved for us. It belongs by nature to the Word, as we learn in the passage just cited. But it is also attributed to the man in the following way:[3]

This is the reason that David calls his son Lord: not because he is from Mary, nor because he was conceived in her womb and born of her. Rather he confesses him as Lord in respect of honour. . . . Now he is, first, the one who is David's Lord in virtue of the fact that in the flesh, he is the Anointed One. . . . Then, too, our Lord is not chief over David because, as a matter of fact, he is his son (and I mean according to the flesh), but because he is the Temple of God the Word and was formed without intercourse, not by the law of nature, but by the operation of the power of God, who is David's Lord.

The title Lord properly belongs to God, but by grace is bestowed upon David's son. The human subject is David's son by nature; his Lord, by grace. 'The name above every name' has been given him. The biblical categories Temple, seed of Abraham, seed of David, and servant are identified with the one who was assumed, the man born of Mary.[4]

[1] Id., fragment 21.
[2] An allusion to Rom. i. 3 may be suspected in the phrase 'Son of David after the flesh'. Cf. 2 Tim. ii. 8. Both passages contribute to Diodore's exegesis of Matt. xxii.   [3] Brière, fragment 3.
[4] See Severus of Antioch, op. cit., *Orat.* iii. 25 (*C.S.C.O.* 102 (1933), pp. 33–34).

The New Testament provides not only the categories, but also, in Diodore's view, the double judgement concerning Christ which lies at the heart of his christology.[1]

Reason, as well as scripture, compels Diodore to adopt a double predication. It is, however, difficult to describe his philosophical assumptions, partly because of insufficient evidence, but partly because his concern is far more biblical than philosophical. Only in his rejection of Apollinaris' body–soul analogy does he discuss any of the major philosophical issues of his time. Preliminary to discussion of this rejection, we must try to ascertain Diodore's teaching concerning human nature. Despite its being inextricably bound up with his christology, certain of the fundamental tenets of his anthropology are easily found. The following passage defines the humanity of Christ, but would do equally well as a definition of man:[2]

Moreover, the son of Mary behaved like a man: he grew tired and wore clothes; he was hungry and thirsty; he was crucified; his side was pierced, and blood and water flowed forth; those who crucified him divided his garments; and he died and was buried; and when he rose, he showed himself to his disciples because he had flesh and bones—though, of course, impassible and immortal; and for forty days he ate and drank with his disciples; and he was taken up on a cloud in the sight of his disciples.

The two adjectives which most clearly characterize man are passible and mortal; man suffers change and must die. Diodore depends upon the general Greek notion that man is finite; he is *genetos*. At the same time, it must be noted that he simply adopts a popular and semi-philosophical concept. His doctrine is not presented philosophically. A second point to be made about this passage is that after the resurrection Christ's humanity is 'impassible and immortal'. The divine attributes are bestowed upon the human nature. We must beware of thinking that Diodore means Christ to be an exceptional case. The explicit teaching of Theodore that all men, once saved, will become immutable, impassible, and immortal in the Second Age is implicit in Diodore's thought:[3]

Now if those spirit-filled men were not mistaken in confessing that the body of Mary's son was corruptible and passible right up to his death on

---

[1] Certain passages (e.g., 1 Cor. ii. 8, John iii. 13 and viii. 58, Rom. viii. 32) provide Diodore with considerable difficulty. He refuses, however, to take them at their surface value and explains them by saying that the attribution is not made by nature, but only by virtue of the union. His exegetical gymnastics betray the depth of his conviction that Scripture assumes a double predication. Cf. Brière, fragments 15, 24, 25.

[2] Id., fragment 19.   [3] Id., fragment 21.

the cross, and that it was a creature even after our Saviour's ascension into heaven, then those who do not receive this apostolic witness despise the Lord of the Apostles.

The incorruptibility and impassibility of Christ's humanity after his exaltation must not be allowed to obscure the fact that he remains a creature.

In what we have noted thus far, Diodore defines human nature in terms of those functions which can be attributed to the body. With respect to his christology, this fact, combined with his use of 'flesh' and 'body' to describe the human nature, leads Grillmeier to assert that Diodore neglects to make the soul of Christ a 'theological factor'. I should dispute this judgement on three grounds. First, Diodore's definition of man depends more upon regarding him as a creature than upon an analysis of his body and soul and their relationship. This much is implicit in what has been said above. Second, his treatment of human nature in general and of Christ's in particular includes man's participation in God's grace and his becoming worthy of that grace—a process more suitably ascribed to soul than body.[1] It is such participation in grace that accounts for the exceptional character of Christ's humanity; we shall be obliged to return to the point. Third, it is not true to say that the soul of Christ 'does not become a central point of discussion even in the controversy with Apollinarianism'.[2] The last of these three points demands a certain amount of elaboration. Diodore sees the body-soul analogy as the fundamental error of the Apollinarians. He explicitly denies that the union of God the Word and the Son of David is comparable to that of body and soul:[3]

Why do you use the analogy of the ruling powers of the soul and the body? For the soul does not reign by itself, nor does the body reign by itself. But God the Word reigns before (the existence of) the flesh. Thus, the relationship of the soul and the body is not like that of God the Word and the flesh.

In the union of body and soul there is but one 'reigning power', that is, one subject. It would seem that Diodore identifies this subject with the whole man considered as a creature. Even if this be not admitted, it is clear that his rejection of the body–soul analogy depends upon his assertion of two subjects of attribution in the christological union. That

[1] See *Collectio Palatina*, *A.C.O.* I. v, p. 178 (Abramowski, *Z.N.T.W.* 42 (1949), fragment 38a, p. 53).

[2] Grillmeier, p. 264; German ed., p. 138. If Diodore does not discuss the soul of Christ more fully and explicitly, it is simply because he assumes that as a man Christ must have a human soul. By virtue of the double predication this assertion presents no problem to him; the onus is on those positing a single predication.

[3] Severus of Antioch, op. cit., *Orat.* iii. 26 (*C.S.C.O.* 102 (1933), p. 45).

union, therefore, is of a completely different order from the union of body and soul. These conclusions are obscured by Diodore's use of 'the flesh' to refer to Christ's humanity; but the terminology must be interpreted in terms of his system as a whole.

The interpretation offered above is substantiated in two anti-Apollinarian passages in which Diodore presents a polemical assessment of Apollinarian belief. In one of these Diodore notes that the more intelligent Apollinarians assert the immutability of the Word and admit that no human passions can be directly attributed to Him:[1]

> But they are unwilling to admit that the latter be called 'the one from above' and the former 'the one from below', or the former 'the Son of David' or the latter 'the Son of God'. Rather they confess that the same one is of God before the ages and of David in the last times—of God as to his divinity, of David as to his humanity. They confess that the same one is impassible and passible, the former in virtue of the Spirit, the latter in virtue of the flesh. They confess that the same one hungered and gave nourishment, suffered and did not suffer. . . .

The Apollinarian justification for saying that the Word 'suffered impassibly' and for making Him in some sense the subject of Christ's human attributes is found in the body–soul analogy. The Apollinarians reason that certain statements pertain by nature to the body and certain others to the soul, but 'we attribute to the whole everything which is by nature attributable to only one of these constituents'.[1] In the same way, certain things are predicated of Christ's humanity; certain others, of his divinity. Diodore rejects the analogy; it implies a limitation and alteration of the Word. He anticipates Nestorius' distinction between complete and incomplete natures. The soul of a man is an incomplete nature; God the Word, a complete nature. And the analogy breaks down on this basis. Diodore, at least in his extant writings, is less sophisticated. Nevertheless, although he has not given us a satisfactory philosophical basis for his rejection, he clearly denies any unity which would imply a natural identification of the Word with the Son of David.

The other anti-Apollinarian passage is rather difficult to translate. The paratactic nature of Syriac and the ambiguous use of relative words almost eliminate clarity.[2] The entire passage deserves to be translated afresh:[3]

> What are they trying to convince us of? To teach that the One from heaven and the one from the earth are one and the same, just as if he were,

---

[1] Brière, fragment 26.

[2] Because of this, Grillmeier mistakenly assumes that the passage presents Diodore's own view. See p. 265, n. 2; German ed., p. 140, n. 34. Cf. Richard's discussion in *Mélanges de sc. relig.* ii (1945), pp. 13 f.

[3] Brière, fragment 2.

so to speak, a single human being, immortal in respect of his soul, but mortal in respect of his body. So, they say, this one and the same being is before the ages and of the seed of David. He is from God and in the manger. He is everywhere, both upon the cross and in heaven. He suffered, and yet was not crucified and did not receive the nails. He is before Abraham and after Abraham, Creator of the earth and a creature who died and rose again. Nevertheless, some things must be attributed to the flesh and others to the divinity, and this is the sense in which he is one and the same being. There are not two different beings (*allos kai allos?*), but one composite being (*syntheton?*), as was stated previously: one Son brought to perfection in the two, the body and God the Word. Moreover, there is not a superior Son and an inferior, nor one Son by nature and another by grace; for Holy Scripture speaks of one Son and not two, that is, one from above and one from below. Nor does it speak of an impassible Son who is before the ages and of a passible Son who appeared in the last days, but of one and the same Son who is found both before the ages and in the last days. Indeed, those among them who are fond of learning hold this opinion, and they cannot say that we have misrepresented them.

Throughout the passage Diodore is attempting to give a fair statement of Apollinarian teaching. The implication is that by doing so he can show the absurdity of their position. No identification is possible between the divine and the human subjects. Such direct identification makes nonsense not only of Scripture, but also of a proper philosophical account of God's nature. The body–soul analogy is ruled out of court and the Apollinarians are left with no philosophical basis for their *syntheton*. To conclude this part of the argument, it is submitted that Diodore's philosophical presuppositions, though somewhat uncritical and certainly not fully elucidated, demand that he assert a double predication in Christ's person. In this sense, his christology is built upon a Logos–anthropos framework.

Our argument has been concerned with showing that a double predication and, hence, a Logos–anthropos framework, are essential to Diodore's christology and are deeply rooted in his exegesis and his philosophical assumptions. We must now turn to what Grillmeier considers proof of a Logos–sarx framework—Diodore's use of 'flesh' to refer to the humanity and his apparent assertion of a *communicatio idiomatum*. It will be argued that, far from implying a Logos–sarx christology, these factors can be assimilated to the Logos–anthropos framework described above. 'Flesh' for Diodore is simply an uncritical term for the man born of Mary; Diodore's *communicatio idiomatum* must not be confused with the Alexandrian doctrine and simply reflects his attempts to define the unity of Christ's person. Having stated the thesis in this dual fashion, let us present the evidence upon which it is based.

At the outset it must be admitted that Diodore's use of 'flesh' does present difficulty; at one level there is no way of avoiding the fact that he *speaks* of a Logos–sarx christology. Nevertheless, the phenomenon, we submit, is a surface feature and cannot obscure the fundamental tendency of Diodore's christology. The following passage presents the difficulty in its acutest form:[1]

Since the flesh was from Mary, while it was yet unassumed, it was from the earth and differed in no way from other flesh.

What does Diodore mean by 'the flesh'? His exegesis of Galatians iv. 4 provides us with something of an answer:[2]

Moreover, Paul does not require that God the Word, when He became flesh and was fashioned, should be the child born of Mary. Rather he speaks of the man who was born of Mary, who was sent for our salvation. For God did not send His Son to be born, but He did send the one who was born for our salvation. Paul's statement has to do with the one who was born of Mary.

It is difficult to see any distinction in the passage between 'flesh' and 'the man born of Mary'. God the Word became flesh in that He became the son of Mary, but this 'becoming' is not to be ascribed to nature. The first sentence could as easily be read: '. . . Paul does not require that God the Word, when He became the child born of Mary and was fashioned, should be flesh.' Our ears are slightly jarred only because 'becoming flesh' has a formulaic ring about it which makes it seem more authentic and traditional.

Let me suggest that Diodore means 'flesh' to equal the 'man born of Mary' and that the reason he uses the term is that it is firmly embedded in the universal tradition of the Church. His terminology is, in any case, rather loose and fluid; and there is no compelling reason to doubt that he could simply adopt uncritically the usual way of speaking of the Incarnation, a way which ultimately derives from John i. 14. If this be so, we should expect to find 'flesh' in Diodore's anti-Apollinarian discussions as well as in his exposition of his own christology; and we should expect the word in his exegetical passages when flesh occurs in the Scriptural texts he is expounding. This is, in fact, the case; and the majority of the occurrences of 'flesh' appear in such passages.[3] In short, Diodore uses 'flesh' in a traditional and non-technical way. Theodore alone of the Antiochenes eschews the word and replaces it with his more fixed terminology. Chrysostom often uses 'flesh', and Nestorius can

---

[1] Severus of Antioch, op. cit., *Orat.* ii. 21 (*C.S.C.O.* 112 (1938), p. 142).
[2] Brière, fragment 12.
[3] Id., fragments 1, 2, 3, 6, 7, 8, 17, 21, 26.

refer to the human prosopon in Christ's person as 'the body'. Indeed, even Theodore nowhere explicitly rejects the use of 'flesh'. His treatment of the Pauline spirit–flesh dualism found in Rom. vii. 5 leads him to say:[1]

Holy Scripture sometimes means by 'flesh' the nature itself, but sometimes not simply the nature, but the nature in so far as it is mortal.

The passage, read in its entirety, suggests that by 'nature' Theodore means human nature. Biblical and Jewish usage identified 'flesh and blood' with humanity and creaturehood. The traditional term 'flesh' is interpreted biblically rather than philosophically. And, I should argue, Diodore's use of 'flesh' must be read against a biblical rather than a philosophical background.

Our argument has been that no far-reaching conclusions can be drawn from Diodore's use of the word 'flesh' in opposition to the Word; the terms do not imply a Logos–sarx framework. They may serve to obscure the expression of his christology, but are by no means contradictory to it. In approaching Diodore's apparent teaching of a *communicatio idiomatum*, we must adopt a rather different line. The communion he describes is not one of nature, but of honour, worship, and grace. It, therefore, reflects not a Logos–sarx but a Logos–anthropos framework and retains the double predication. It is in this area of his thought that we may discover Diodore's closest approach to a consideration of the problem of the unity of Christ's person. Far from contradicting the Logos–anthropos foundation of his christology, it serves the essential purpose of defining the union between Word and man. 'Honour' is an important category used by Diodore to describe the union:[2]

... the Lord, when he was in the Virgin's womb—and in point of essence —did not possess the honour of the Sonship. But when he was fashioned and became the Temple of God the Word, by virtue of receiving the Only Begotten, he received the honour of the name, and participated in His honour.

The union is not of essence, but of honour; nevertheless, it implies that the human and divine titles are in some sense interchangeable. The Lord of David, for example, is by nature God; but David's son may be called Lord 'not because he is from Mary', but 'in respect of honour'.[3] Because of his being the Anointed One and because of the union in one

---

[1] Migne, *P.G.* 66. 805c. Cf. Theodore, *In Epistolas B. Pauli Commentarii*, ed. H. B. Swete (Cambridge, 1880/2), vol. i, pp. 35 n., 94 n., and 99 n., and vol. ii, p. 282.

[2] Severus of Antioch, op. cit., *Orat.* ii. 21 (*C.S.C.O.* 112 (1938), p. 142).

[3] Brière, fragment 3.

honour of the man with the Word, 'Lord' applies to the man. The concept of honour may possibly derive from such passages as John v. 23 and Heb. ii. 7, but its meaning is not strictly exegetical. It is rather to be identified with worship:[1]

> We worship the purple because of the one who wears it, the Temple because of the one who indwells it, the form of a servant because of the form of God, the lamb because of the High Priest, the one who was assumed because of the One who assumed, the one who was fashioned in the Virgin's womb because of the Creator of all. Confess the true facts of the matter, and, then, attribute a single honour. A single worship is not blasphemous if the facts of the matter are confessed. You say that there is one worship, but by means of this one worship you introduce blasphemy —if the singleness of worship is understood as a singleness of essence.

There is but one worship addressed to Christ. The unity of worship does not imply the blasphemous worship of a man, since the man is worshipped because of his union with the Word. On the other hand, the unity of worship does not imply a unity of essence. The human and the divine essences remain distinct.

Honour and worship provide Diodore with labels appropriate to his conception of the union, but these categories do not supply him a way of describing how the union is effected, nor do they present a convincing account of the reality of the union. It is in the area of God's grace that Diodore looks for the solution to this fundamental problem of his christology. Like Theodore, his pupil, he refuses to adopt any kind of strictly metaphysical or substantial solution, and regards the union as most profoundly explicable in terms of the gracious activity of God. He nowhere defines grace, but in christological contexts he thinks of it as the bestowal of gifts upon the man by God. The reason that the divine titles of the Word can be attributed by honour to the man is that they are graciously given him:[2]

> Therefore, we do not say that there are two sons of one Father, but one who is by nature Son of God, God the Word. And we say that the one born of Mary is by nature David's son, but by grace the Son of God. Moreover, let it be granted: the two are one son, and let what is impossible be repudiated explicitly.

The union is not by nature and the christological titles retain their reference to one or the other of the subjects of attribution. In the area of grace, however, the two are one; and the divine titles are appropriate to the man by grace. At this level, the *communicatio idiomatum* is a purely external one in that it is a sharing of one honour and worship.

[1] Severus of Antioch, op. cit., *Orat.* iii. 25 (*C.S.C.O.* 102 (1933), pp. 33–34).
[2] Brière, fragment 30; cf. fragments 31 and 33.

Nevertheless, the operation of grace effects more than a mere conjunction of the two subjects, and the communion is not merely external. We have seen that the divine attributes of immutability and immortality are thought to be conferred upon the man at his exaltation. Furthermore, during his mortal existence God's grace bestows upon him divine power and wisdom:[1]

For 'Jesus increased in stature and wisdom'. (Cf. Luke ii. 40.) Now this statement cannot be made in virtue of God the Word; for God is generated as Perfect from Perfect, Wisdom from Wisdom, Power from Power; therefore, He does not increase, for He is not imperfect so as to increase to a state of perfection. Rather the one who increases in 'stature and wisdom' is the flesh.

Just as the man grew physically, so by God's grace he grew in wisdom and power. The human life of the man is considered a growth towards perfection and manifests the perfect co-operation of the man's free will with God's grace. The view so elaborately developed by Theodore is adumbrated in Diodore's too succinct remarks. Certain attributes of God, but not His nature, are given the man by grace. The *communicatio idiomatum* involves no complete sharing of natural properties, and from the Alexandrian point of view this deficiency is decisive. The communion extends to the attributes of the man, but not directly to the human subject of attribution. Since Diodore assumes that a distinction between the man as a creature and the Word as Creator must always be maintained, the communion he describes is the only possible one. It preserves the man's response to grace and makes the union explicable on the analogy of God's gracious operation in the prophets and the saints. The analogy is implied; but, like Theodore, Diodore is aware of the danger of making Jesus' development totally parallel to that of any good man:[2]

God the Word dwelt in the one from David's seed in a different way than He did in the prophets. For they enjoyed a certain share and a particular portion of the grace of the Holy Spirit; but he remained united with those qualities which were present only from time to time in them, and was so filled with the glory of the Word and with Wisdom that he could be understood as the Son, though without doubt he was different from Him and existed in his own right.

[1] Severus of Antioch, op. cit., *Orat.* iii. 23 (*C.S.C.O.* 102 (1933), p. 9). Grillmeier expresses surprise that Diodore makes the Word the 'direct source' of the increase in wisdom and power (p. 265; German ed., p. 139). This is surprising only if one identifies Antiochene theology with adoptionism. This is impossible; and Theodore is equally insistent upon the primacy of God's grace, describing its effects upon the man in the same way.
[2] *Collectio Palatina, A.C.O.* i. v, p. 178 (Abramowski, *Z.N.T.W.* 42 (1949), fragment 38a, p. 53).

It is the perfection of God's grace which marks the man as unique. Since he is *the* man of God's own choosing, he can be called the Son. We have a hint of Theodore's christological formula: the indwelling of the Word in the assumed man by good pleasure as in (a) Son.

The *communicatio idiomatum*, then, is one of honour and worship and must be described in terms of God's gracious activity. Since the effect of this activity upon the man is a largely neglected aspect of Antiochene christology, perhaps some elaboration of the point is in order. Grace informs but does not alter the nature of the man; that is, it changes the attributes of the man in certain respects, but it does not change the human subject of attribution. This informing process, however, does give the son of Mary power and wisdom. The gifts of power are discussed by Diodore in several curious passages.[1] Although we cannot be sure, says Diodore, Jesus after the resurrection could have entered the room where his disciples were hiding without opening the doors. During his ministry he often escaped his enemies unnoticed 'by inflicting hallucinations upon them'. The natural miracles that occurred at the Passion happened because of the man. Diodore argues *a fortiori* (or *kal wahomer*) that if Moses, Joshua, and Elisha could perform wonders, how much more must *the* man of God's choice have done so. Moreover, Jesus possesses in an exceptional degree not only power, but also wisdom and knowledge:[2]

That cry of 'My God, my God, why hast Thou forsaken me!' not only does not befit God the Word, but I at any rate should decline to affirm that it befits the body in any sense which would suggest one who cries out because he is forsaken. Why, then, did he cry out as though he were forsaken? Did he not foresee his resurrection and glorification? . . . Did the man born of Mary not know that it was for this reason that he was born of the Virgin—namely, that with his own blood he might purify the human race?

The passage ends at this point so that Diodore's explanation is lost. Nevertheless, the rhetorical questions clearly demand an affirmation of Jesus' knowledge. At first, we seem to find a strangely Johannine and un-Antiochene Christ. But Christ's knowledge is treated in very much the same way by both Chrysostom and Theodore. It is not, however, to be attributed directly to the omniscience of the Word, but rather to the effect of the Word's gracious operation upon the man. What seems to be a discordant element in Diodore's thought is really nothing but a logical consequence of his understanding of grace and his determination to define the union as one of grace and not nature. That he takes the union seriously is demonstrated not only by his statements to that effect, but

[1] Brière, fragments 9, 10, 17, and 18.   [2] Id., fragment 18.

also by his realization that the union does demand Christ to be distinguished from other men. He simply draws the line at saying this distinction is one of nature. In terms of the *communicatio idiomatum*, Diodore accepts a communion of honour, worship, and grace. For him it is the most significant kind of communion; for the Alexandrians it fails to assert any communion within the metaphysical essences of God and man.

In conclusion, I have sought to show that Diodore's christology quite consistently builds upon a double predication; it is a Logos–anthropos christology. This is so both in its terminology and in its biblical and philosophical orientation. Elements that might on first sight contradict this verdict can be seen to contribute to it and in large measure reflect Diodore's attempts to solve the problem of asserting the christological union in a satisfactory fashion. By 'flesh' Diodore simply means the human subject. His treatment of the union implies a kind of *communicatio idiomatum*, but one of honour, worship, and grace rather than of nature. The union is defined in terms of grace and effects certain changes in the man, but these are by way of gifts of power and wisdom rather than by way of an alteration of nature. On this basis, I should wish to dispute Grillmeier's treatment of Diodore, and deny that Diodore builds upon a Logos–sarx framework.[1] It seems to me that Grillmeier's argument depends upon a series of questionable assumptions. He apparently regards the anti-Apollinarian fragment (cited above, p. 335), as representing Diodore's own view and has been misled by Brière's translation. He puts undue weight upon Diodore's strictly terminological use of 'flesh'. He misreads Diodore's *communicatio idiomatum* as implying a natural union of some kind, and, consequently, misinterprets Diodore's descriptions of Christ's remarkable powers. Finally, his attempt to orient Diodore's christology to a defence of Christ's divinity against the Emperor Julian rather than to the Apollinarian controversy seems quite gratuitous. These criticisms may seem over-weighted, but the reader must remember I am but a gadfly worrying a colossus. One may surely use Grillmeier's schematizations with profit. However, I submit that a reassessment of Diodore's position as regards Grillmeier's two categories must be made. And I should wish to end with a recalcitrant appeal to reclassify him as a true Antiochene.

ROWAN A. GREER

[1] There is some indication in the English edition of Grillmeier's work that he has modified his view. A sentence that does not appear in the German edition (p. 266; cf. German ed., p. 141) reads: 'Nor do we deny that in Diodore's writings the majority of expressions are taken from the "Word-man" framework.' The revision is slight and serves only to muddy the waters.

NESTORIUS WAS ORTHODOX

MILTON V. ANASTOS

Dedicated to the memory of my mother, Stella Anastos, who died on January 26, 1962.

Αἰωνία ἡ μνήμη

194

I. Prefatory Remarks on Nestorius and Cyril[1]

JUST as all thinking people are said to be either Platonists or Aristotelians, most theologians favor either Nestorius or Cyril. Both have their admirers, who usually assume, with championship of one of the two, an intense dislike for the other. Tradition and the Church (except, of course, for the Nestorians) have handed down a judgment adverse to Nestorius. This is unfortunate, not because Nestorius was always right, as he was not, but rather because both he and Cyril, when measured by the standard of the Fourth Oecumenical Council (held at Chalcedon in 451) and its Creed, which is the major criterion of Christological orthodoxy, have similar—or reciprocal defects. It should be noted carefully that my dogmatic definitions and the case for Nestorius are based upon the Chalcedonian Symbol and Cyril's *Second Letter to Nestorius*. Except for a brief reference (at note 66 *infra*), I do not discuss the question of the relationship between Nestorius' Christology and that of Cyril's *Third Letter* (with its *Twelve Anathemas*), which did not achieve oecu-

---

[1] I had completed this article before reading Aloys Grillmeier's admirable paper (see *infra*), with which I am in essential agreement. The major difference between us is that I take Nestorius to have been *completely* orthodox, whether judged on the criterion of the Chalcedonian Symbol or from the point of view of speculative theology, whereas he has some reservations. Excellent also is the book (see *infra*) of R. V. Sellers, who argues that Nestorius and Cyril were in reality seeking the same theological goals. His results are very similar to mine except that my method and purpose differ from his.

For the earlier bibliography on Nestorius, see Johannes Quasten, *Patrology*, 3, *The Golden Age of Greek Patristic Literature from the Council of Nicaea to the Council of Chalcedon* (Utrecht-Antwerp-Westminster, 1960), 514–19; Berthold Altaner, *Patrologie*, 5th ed. (Freiburg im Breisgau, 1958), § 72; Eng. transl., Hilda C. Graef (*ibid.*, 1960). See especially Aloys Grillmeier, "Das Scandalum oecumenicum des Nestorius in kirchlich-dogmatischer und theologiegeschichtlicher Sicht," *Scholastik*, 36 (1961), 321–56; Helmut Ristow, "Der Begriff πρόσωπον in der Theologie des Nestorius," *Aus der byzantinistischen Arbeit der deutschen demokratischen Republik* (*Berliner byzantinistische Arbeiten*, 5 [Berlin, 1957]), 218–36, who makes little use of the *Bazaar*; Luigi I. Scipioni, *Ricerche sulla Cristologia del "Libro di Eraclide" di Nestorio* (*Paradosis*, 11 [Freiburg, Switzerland, 1956]), is ecclesiastically committed to the traditional condemnation of N., though his approach to N.'s "metaphysics" is fresh and original; Chrysostomus Baur, "Drei unedierte Festpredigten aus der Zeit der nestorianischen Streitigkeiten," *Traditio*, 9 (1953), 101–26; texts with an "Antiochene" Christology; Thomas Camelot, "De Nestorius à Eutychès," *Das Konzil von Chalkedon*, edd. Aloys Grillmeier and Heinrich Bacht, 1 (Würzburg, 1951), 213–42; Henry Chadwick, "Eucharist and Christology in the Nestorian Controversy," *Journal of Theological Studies*, N.S. 2 (1951), 145–64; Aubrey R. Vine, *An Approach to Christology* (London, 1948); G. L. Prestige, *Fathers and Heretics* (London, 1940), 120–79; R. V. Sellers, *Two Ancient Christologies* (London, 1940); É. Amann, "Nestorius," *Dictionnaire de théologie catholique*, 11, 1 (Paris, 1931), 76–157; Friedrich Loofs, *Nestorius and His Place in the History of Christian Doctrine* (Cambridge, 1914); J. F. Bethune-Baker, *Nestorius and His Teaching* (Cambridge, 1908). On the philosophical implications of "Nestorianism," see Harry A. Wolfson, *The Philosophy of the Church Fathers*, 1 (Cambridge, Mass., 1956), 451–63. See special note at the bottom of p. 140.

The sources on which this paper is based are: Paul Bedjan, ed., *Nestorius, Le Livre d'Héraclide de Damas* (Leipzig-Paris, 1910), a critical edition of the Syriac version, against which I have verified the principal texts quoted *infra*; all of the English translations have been taken verbatim from G. R. Driver and Leonard Hodgson, *Nestorius, the Bazaar of Heracleides, newly translated from the Syriac* (Oxford, 1925). Cf. F. Nau, *Nestorius d'après les sources orientales* (Paris, 1911); Friedrich Loofs, *Nestoriana, Die Fragmente des Nestorius* (Halle a. S., 1905); and the immensely learned, extremely detailed, but massively unusable work of Ignaz Rucker, *Studien zum Concilium Ephesinum*, A. *Orientierende Quellenkunde*; B. *Zur Dogmengeschichte nach dem syrischen Liber Heraclidis*, ed. Bedjan, 1910 (1930–35), outlined by the author in B, IV, a, b, c, *Das Dogma von der Persönlichkeit Christi* (Oxenbronn bei Günzburg a. D., 1934), and *idem*, A, III, *Ephesinische Konzilsakten in syrischer Überlieferung* (*ibid.*, 1935).

menical sanction until 553 (see note 8 *infra*), and is therefore irrelevant to the subject of this paper.

Nestorius was condemned at Chalcedon (as also in 431 at Ephesus by the Third Oecumenical Council) for dividing Christ into two separate persons, although he always claimed that he was not guilty of making such a division, and continually affirmed his belief in the oneness of Christ. On the other hand, Cyril, who was enthusiastically acclaimed at both Ephesus and Chalcedon, formulated a Christology which many deem to be in direct conflict with that of 451. He repeatedly declares Christ to have been both divine and human, God and man. But his critics complain that, in his advocacy of the "hypostatic union" and the Apollinarian Christological formula, μία φύσις τοῦ Θεοῦ Λόγου σεσαρκωμένη ("one incarnate nature of God the Word"), which he mistakenly took to be Athanasian in origin, he lost sight of Christ's human nature. Curiously, in the appraisal of Nestorius and Cyril, it can be shown that the case for each rests mainly upon his understanding and use of a single word, to which he assigned contradictory meanings. The decisive term for Nestorius was πρόσωπον (person), which he used in two different senses; and Cyril[2] had similar difficulty with φύσις (nature).

Both were guilty of flagrant inconsistency. But both obviously meant to be what we call orthodox; and the more this question is studied, the more it appears that the conflict between them was not primarily theological in character, but largely personal, ecclesiastico-political, and terminological. If Nestorius and Cyril could have been compelled to discuss their differences calmly and to define their terms with precision, under the supervision of a strict and impartial arbiter who could have kept them under control until they had explained themselves clearly, there is little doubt that they would have found themselves in substantial agreement theologically, though separated *toto caelo* as far as the prestige of their respective archiepiscopal sees was concerned. Being Archbishop of Constantinople (428–31) and champion of the theological tradition of the city of Antioch, in which he had begun his career, Nestorius resented the intervention of Cyril, the Archbishop of Alexandria (412–44), who determined to humble the clergy of the capital city and gain dominion over the entire Eastern Church.

In discussing Nestorius, I have for obvious reasons disregarded almost entirely the remarks attributed to him by his opponents, and have relied heavily upon his own book, the so-called *Bazaar of Heracleides*, which he

---

[2] For the bibliography on Cyril, see A. Spindeler, "Kyrillos," *Lexikon für Theologie und Kirche*, 6, 2nd ed. by Josef Höfer and Karl Rahner (Freiburg im Br., 1961), 706–9; Quasten, *Patrology*, 3, 116–42; Altaner, *Patrologie*, § 56. In my forthcoming book, *The Mind of Byzantium*, I discuss Cyril's position and the Emperor Justinian I's espousal of the Cyrillian theology in separate chapters. For the Apollinarian origin of Cyril's Christological formula, see Hans Lietzmann, *Apollinaris von Laodicea und seine Schule*, 1 (Tübingen, 1904), 108 ff., 133 f., 185 ff., 251.1 ff.; *Contra fraudes Apollinaristarum*, P.G., 86, 2, 1948–76 (authorship unknown). Cf. Joseph van den Dries, *The Formula of Saint Cyril of Alexandria, mia physis tu Theu Logu sesarkomene* (Rome, 1939). In 532, Hypatius of Ephesus, a strict Chalcedonian, denounced the Apollinarian forgeries. He refused to believe that the highly revered Cyril could ever have been duped by them and preferred to regard the frequent appearance of the Apollinarian formula in Cyril's works as the result of interpolation by heretics: *Acta conciliorum oecumenicorum*, ed. Eduard Schwartz (cited *infra* as *ACO*), 4, 2 (Berlin, 1914), 171.40–173.2, 179.38–180.3; cf. note 8 *infra*.

completed in exile *ca.* 451. Unfortunately, the Greek text of this work has disappeared, but there is a Syriac translation dating from the sixth century which seems to be reliable, notwithstanding an initial error of the translator, who misunderstood the word πραγματεία ("treatise") in the original title, and incorrectly rendered it by *Bazaar*. The Heracleides in question was a man of high repute, whose name Nestorius deliberately substituted for his own, as we learn from the preface to the Syriac version, in order to attract readers, since, he feared, the pious would have been repelled by that of a notoriously heretical author.

It may be, as some object, that the *Bazaar* represents a Nestorius who had had twenty years since his condemnation in 431 to repent of his errors and make essential emendations. Even if this be true, it remains legitimate to allow him to be judged by his own latest and most mature efforts.

2. NESTORIUS GETS INTO TROUBLE

Theodore of Mopsuestia,[3] the leading theologian of the School of Antioch, vigorously attacked the Apollinarian formula, *one incarnate nature of God the Word*; and his antipathy for this description of the relation of the two natures in Jesus Christ was shared by Nestorius, who had been transferred to Constantinople in 428, the year of Theodore's death. Nestorius first provoked[4] the ire of conservative theologians when he espoused the view of a Constantinopolitan presbyter by the name of Anastasius that Mary the Virgin should not be described as Θεοτόκος ("she who bore God" or "Mother of God"). It was proper to speak of Mary as Χριστοτόκος ("Mother of Christ"), or, with the appropriate reservations, as Ἀνθρωποτόκος ("Mother of man"), or even possibly as Θεοδόχος ("God-receiving"), Nestorius said, but impious to suggest that a mortal woman could have been the Mother of God.

The designation Theotokos for Mary had been current at least since the beginning of the fourth century,[5] and meant that Mary, the mother of Jesus

[3] On Theodore of Mopsuestia, see the works cited in notes 1f. *supra*, s.v. In my paper, "The Immutability of Christ, and Justinian's Condemnation of Theodore of Mopsuestia," *Dumbarton Oaks Papers*, 6 (1951), 125-60, I show that Theodore's Christology was heretical because of his misuse of the term τρεπτός as defined by the First Council of Nicaea in 325. This seems to me to be a simpler and more decisive solution of the problem of Theodore's Christology than the erudite but complicated analyses to be found in the numerous books and monographs that have been written on this subject. The literature is collected by Luise Abramowski, "Zur Theologie Theodors von Mopsuestia," *Zeitschrift für Kirchengeschichte*, 4.F. 10 = 72 (1961), 263-93; Quasten, Altaner, etc., *op. cit.*, s.v.
[4] Socrates, *H. E.*, 7, 32, P.G., 67, 808ff.; cf. note 6 *infra*.
[5] First occurence, ed. Hans-Georg Opitz, *Athanasius Werke*, 3, 1, 1 (Berlin-Leipzig, 1934), 28.15f. (P. G. 18, 568C): a letter written in 324 by Bishop Alexander of Alexandria to the homonymous bishop of Thessalonike. Socrates, *H. E.*, 7, 32, 17, says that Origen wrote a long dissertation on the suitability of this designation for Mary in his *Commentary on Romans*, but the term cannot be found in the extant text or in the other early authors who are often cited (see works listed *infra*).
On the Virgin Mary, see Georges Jouassard, "Marie à travers la patristique," ed. Hubert du Manoir, *Maria, études sur la sainte Vierge*, 1 (Paris, 1949), 70ff., n.b. 85ff.; Antoine Wenger, "Foi et piété mariales à Byzance," *ibid.*, 5 (1958), 923-81; idem, *L'assomption de la T. S. Vierge dans la tradition byzantine du vi^e au xe siècle* (Paris, 1955); Carlo Cecchelli, *Mater Christi*, 4 vols. (Rome, 1946-54); Mauricius Gordillo, *Mariologia orientalis (Orientalia Christiana Analecta*, 141 [Rome, 1954]); Martin Jugie, *L'immaculée conception dans l'Écriture Sainte et dans la tradition orientale* (Rome, 1952); idem, *La mort et l'assomption de la Sainte Vierge* (Studi e Testi, 114 [Vatican City, 1944]); V. Schweitzer,

Christ, was in a strict sense the mother of the humanity of Jesus, which had been united in her womb with the divine nature of the eternal Logos. No one ever suggested that Mary was the mother of the divine nature, but only that the divine Logos had joined himself to the human nature of Jesus at the moment of conception, and that, by reason of the closeness of the union between the divine and human natures in Christ (the *communicatio idiomatum*, on which see notes 56-70 *infra*), she might then be *called* the Mother of God (see note 65 *infra*). For, all agreed, the flesh to which she gave birth was that of the divine Logos, and the Jesus Christ she bore was God as well as man.

Nestorius concedes that the epithet Theotokos was innocuous if properly explained in this fashion.[6] But, with rare exceptions, he refuses to use it by itself, as Cyril constantly did, without adequate qualification. Even apart from his strictures on this term, however, which was sanctioned by the universal Church at the Fourth Oecumenical Council in 451 (see note 9 *infra*), Nestorius was accused of other theological irregularities, and stands officially condemned as a heretic.

But he still has his champions.[7] The Christians of Persia, who seceded from the Byzantine imperial Church in 424, before the Nestorian question had arisen, and their descendants, the "Nestorians" of later times, revere his authority. In addition, a host of modern writers have taken up the cudgels in his defence.

"Alter des Titels Θεοτόκος," *Der Katholik*, Ser. 3, 27 (1903), 97–113. Cf. also Georges Jouassard, "Deux chefs de file en théologie mariale dans la seconde moitié du ivᵉᵐᵉ siècle: saint Epiphane et saint Ambroise," *Gregorianum*, 42 (1961), 5–36; Daniel Stiernon, "Bulletin de théologie mariale byzantine," *Revue des études byzantines*, 17 (1959), 201–50; *Lexikon der Marienkunde*, edd. Konrad Algermissen, Ludwig Böer, Georg Engelhardt, Michael Schmaus, Julius Tyciak (Regensburg, 1957–); René Laurentin, *Court traité de théologie mariale*, 4th ed. (Paris, 1959); Sergius S. Fedyniak, *Mariologia apud pp. orientales (Basilium M., Gregorium Naz., Gregorium Nys.)* (Rome, 1958).

[6] My references to the *Bazaar of Heracleides* are to the pages of the translation of Driver and Hodgson. See on this point pp. 99f., 148ff., 185, 193f., 293f., 295ff., 387 (fr. 271); Loofs, *Nestoriana*, index C, s.vv. ἀνθρωποτόκος, χριστοτόκος, Maria (p. 402), θεοδόχος. N. b. 177.11f., 263.12, 276.3-5, 277.20; Nestorius' *Second homily on the temptations of Jesus*, ed. F. Nau, *op. cit.* (note 1 supra), 345.7f., in which he uses θεοτόκος without exegesis; cf. Loofs, *op. cit.*, 191.6, 19f., 272.13–273.1.

[7] See especially note 1 *supra*: Grillmeier, Vine, Sellers, Loofs, Bethune-Baker, *op. cit.* Of these, Sellers is the most favorable to Nestorius. On the Persian Council of 424, see J. B. Chabot, *Synodicon orientale ou recueil de synodes nestoriens (Notices et extraits des manuscrits de la Bibliothèque Nationale et autres bibliothèques*, 37 [Paris, 1902]), 43–53, 285–98. Cf. Ignacio Ortiz de Urbina, "Storia e cause dello scisma della Chiesa di Persia," *Orientalia Christiana Periodica*, 3 (1937), 456–85; J. Labourt, *Le christianisme dans l'empire perse sous la dynastie sassanide, 224–632* (Paris, 1904), 121–25.

On the Nestorians, see J. Joseph, *The Nestorians and their Muslim Neighbors* (Princeton, 1961) (modern only); Bertold Spuler, "Die nestorianische Kirche," *Handbuch der Orientalistik*, 1. Abt., Bd. 8, Abschn. 2 (Leiden, 1961), 120–69; Raymond Janin, *Les églises orientales et les rites orientaux*, 4th ed. (Paris, 1955), 409–29; Wilhelm de Vries, *Der Kirchenbegriff der von Rom getrennten Syrer (Orientalia Christiana Analecta*, 145 [Rome, 1955]); *idem, Sakramententheologie bei den Nestorianern (Orientalia Christiana Analecta*, 133 [Rome, 1947]); A. C. Moule, *Nestorians in China* (London, 1940); Aubrey R. Vine, *The Nestorian Churches, a Concise History of Nestorian Christianity from the Persian Schism to the Modern Assyrians* (London, 1937): a popular survey; Martin Jugie, *Theologia dogmatica christianorum orientalium ab ecclesia catholica dissidentium*, 5 (Paris, 1935), 9–347; E. Tisserant, "L'église nestorienne," *Dictionnaire de théologie catholique*, 11, 1 (Paris, 1931), 157–323; Konrad Lübeck, *Die altpersische Missionskirche (Abhandlungen aus Missionskunde und Missionsgeschichte*, 15 [Aachen, 1919]): has references to sources. Cf. also Juan Mateos, *Lelya-Ṣapra, essai d'interprétation des matines chaldéennes (Orientalia Christiana Analecta*, 156 [Rome, 1959]); Henri Bernard, *La découverte de nestoriens mongols aux Ordos et l'histoire ancienne du Christianisme en Extrême-Orient* (Tientsin, 1935); George P. Badger, *The Nestorians and Their Rituals*, 2 vols. (London, 1852): erudite travelogue with translations from the liturgy.

Some argue that the action of the Council of Ephesus in 431 was ambiguous and cannot be regarded as a valid oecumenical condemnation of Nestorius. They point out, also, that the Letter of Cyril (the Third) most damaging to Nestorius, was not approved by the Church until 553.[8] Others contend, in a variety of ways, that Nestorius has been misrepresented or misunderstood and never was guilty of the dogmatic lapses that have been attributed to him.

But in general not even the most favorably disposed among his defenders have said much more in his behalf than that he was almost or nearly orthodox. In dogmatic theology, however, such an apologia is meaningless, and is very much like saying of an egg that "it is partly fresh" or that "parts of it are excellent." A doctrine is either heretical or it is not, and only a slight defect, no larger than the letter iota, which was all that separated the orthodox from the heretics in the matter of ὁμοούσιος, is sufficient to invalidate an entire system.

My own thesis is that Nestorius was not only thoroughly and indubitably orthodox, but also in many respects the profoundest and most brilliant theologian of the fifth century. It must be admitted that his style is often turgid and confusing. The repetitiousness of his great theological treatise, the *Bazaar of Heracleides*, is frustrating, wearisome, and painful. It would have been vastly more effective if some expert rhetorician had pruned it of tautology, eliminated contradictions, added the necessary logical definitions, which Nestorius unhappily eschewed, and reduced its length by a half or three quarters. Still, even in a morass of verbiage, the *Bazaar* is a document that merits careful consideration. The first book, which is devoted to a metaphysical analysis of Nestorius' first principles, is altogether unique, and constitutes the subtlest and most penetrating study of the mystery of the incarnation in the whole of patristic literature.

3. Terminological Complexities and Ambiguities

Nestorius fell into disrepute primarily because of his theory of the elements that made up the person of Jesus Christ, who was both perfect God and perfect man. The view authorized at Chalcedon in 451 was that in Jesus Christ there

---

[8] Cf. note 2 *supra*. The Council of Ephesus deliberately, it seems, withheld approval from Cyril's *Third Letter to Nestorius*: *ACO* (see note 2 *supra*), 1, 1, 1 (Berlin-Leipzig, 1927-30), 33-42; *ibid.*, 1, 2 (*ibid.*, 1925-26), 45-51; 1, 3 (*ibid.*, 1929), 26-35; P.G., 77, 105 ff. As Joseph Hefele-H. Leclercq, *Histoire des conciles*, 2, 1 (Paris, 1908), 301 note 2, say, there is no record that the letter was acclaimed or approved at Ephesus. According to *ACO*, 1, 2, 51.34, it was merely incorporated into the *Acta*. Bishop Hypatius of Ephesus pointed out at a conference held in Constantinople in 532, that the Council of Chalcedon had expressly withheld approval from Cyril's *Twelve anathemas* (which form an appendix to the *Third Letter*): *ACO*, 4, 2, 169-84; n.b. 173.18 ff., 21-29; 175.33-38; 177.10-17. On Hypatius, see Charles Moeller, "Le chalcédonisme et le néo-chalcédonisme en Orient de 451 à la fin du vi⁰ siècle," *Das Konzil von Chalkedon*, 1 (cited in note 1 *supra*), 661; Marcel Richard, "Le néo-chalcédonisme," *Mélanges de science religieuse*, 3 (1946), 158 f. For the literature on the twelve anathemas, see Quasten, *Patrology*, 3, 134. Jean Gouillard, "Hypatios d'Éphèse ou du Pseudo-Denys à Théodore Studite," *Revue des études byzantines*, 19 (*Mélanges Raymond Janin*) (Paris, 1961), 63-75, and the literature there cited deal with other aspects of Hypatius' activity, not with the problem at issue here.

Diepen, *Douze dialogues* (see note 66 *infra*), 49-126, makes a valiant but unsuccessful attempt to prove, against just about all of the major authorities, that the *Twelve Anathemas* (and Cyril's *Third Letter to Nestorius* as a whole) had received oecumenical endorsement at Ephesus and Chalcedon. He has found no evidence prior to 553 which indicates that these texts were used as oecumenically valid criteria of Christological orthodoxy.

were two natures, one divine and one human, which together formed one hypostasis or person (prosopon).[9] Nestorius granted that there were two natures in Christ. But he held that each nature (physis) implied an οὐσία (substance or essence), an ὑπόστασις (hypostasis),[10] and a prosopon, so that there were in Christ two natures, two substances (or essences), two hypostases (which he often omits), and two prosopa.[11] Cyril and his school admitted that each nature involved a substance, for these terms were synonymous in the Christological usage of the fifth century;[12] and they agreed that each nature had an hypostasis and a prosopon.

[9] The text of the Creed of 451 is to be found in *ACO*, 2, 1, 2, 129 [325]f.; J. B. Mansi, *Sacrorum conciliorum nova et amplissima collectio*, 7 (Florence, 1762), 116ABC, or in any of the numerous editions of H. Denzinger-I. B. Umberg, *Enchiridion symbolorum*, e.g., ed. 28 (Freiburg im Br., 1947), no. 148, p. 70f.; T. Herbert Bindley, *The Oecumenical Documents of the Faith*, 4th ed. by F. W. Green (London, 1950), 183–99, with introduction, translation, and notes. For commentary, see J. N. D. Kelly, *Early Christian doctrines*, 2nd ed. (London, 1960), 338–43; R. V. Sellers, *The Council of Chalcedon* (London, 1953); Aloys Grillmeier, "Die theologische und sprachliche Vorbereitung der christologischen Formel von Chalkedon," *Das Konzil von Chalkedon*, 1 (cited in note 1 *supra*), 1, 5–202; Ignacio Ortiz de Urbina, "Das Symbol von Chalkedon, sein Text, sein Werden, seine dogmatische Bedeutung," *ibid.*, 1, 389–418; Wilhelm de Vries, "Die syrisch-nestorianische Haltung zu Chalkedon," *ibid.*, 1, 603–35. In the text which follows I reproduce Schwartz's edition, *loc. cit.*, except that after the second ὁμοούσιον I read τὸν αὐτὸν ἡμῖν instead of ἡμῖν τὸν αὐτόν.

Ἑπόμενοι τοίνυν τοῖς ἁγίοις πατράσιν ἕνα καὶ τὸν αὐτὸν ὁμολογεῖν υἱὸν τὸν κύριον ἡμῶν Ἰησοῦν Χριστὸν συμφώνως ἅπαντες ἐκδιδάσκομεν, τέλειον τὸν αὐτὸν ἐν θεότητι καὶ τέλειον τὸν αὐτὸν ἐν ἀνθρωπότητι, θεὸν ἀληθῶς καὶ ἄνθρωπον ἀληθῶς τὸν αὐτόν, ἐκ ψυχῆς λογικῆς καὶ σώματος, ὁμοούσιον τῷ πατρὶ κατὰ τὴν θεότητα, καὶ ὁμοούσιον τὸν αὐτὸν ἡμῖν κατὰ τὴν ἀνθρωπότητα, κατὰ πάντα ὅμοιον ἡμῖν χωρὶς ἁμαρτίας· πρὸ αἰώνων μὲν ἐκ τοῦ πατρὸς γεννηθέντα κατὰ τὴν θεότητα, ἐπ᾽ ἐσχάτων δὲ τῶν ἡμερῶν τὸν αὐτὸν δι᾽ ἡμᾶς καὶ διὰ τὴν ἡμετέραν σωτηρίαν ἐκ Μαρίας τῆς παρθένου τῆς θεοτόκου κατὰ τὴν ἀνθρωπότητα, ἕνα καὶ τὸν αὐτὸν Χριστόν, υἱόν, κύριον, μονογενῆ, ἐν δύο φύσεσιν, ἀσυγχύτως, ἀτρέπτως, ἀδιαιρέτως, ἀχωρίστως γνωριζόμενον· οὐδαμοῦ τῆς τῶν φύσεων διαφορᾶς ἀνῃρημένης διὰ τὴν ἕνωσιν, σῳζομένης δὲ μᾶλλον τῆς ἰδιότητος ἑκατέρας φύσεως καὶ εἰς ἓν πρόσωπον καὶ μίαν ὑπόστασιν συντρεχούσης, οὐκ εἰς δύο πρόσωπα μεριζόμενον ἢ διαιρούμενον, ἀλλ᾽ ἕνα καὶ τὸν αὐτὸν υἱὸν μονογενῆ θεὸν λόγον κύριον Ἰησοῦν Χριστόν, καθάπερ ἄνωθεν οἱ προφῆται περὶ αὐτοῦ καὶ αὐτὸς ἡμᾶς Ἰησοῦς Χριστὸς ἐξεπαίδευσεν καὶ τὸ τῶν πατέρων ἡμῖν παραδέδωκε σύμβολον.

[10] Nestorius uses this term less frequently than he does the others, but he links it with them: *Bazaar*, 163, 208, 218f., 228.

[11] *Ibid.*, 163, 170, 218f., 262.

[12] On the history and development of this technical vocabulary, see Ernst Hammerschmidt, "Ursprung philosophisch-theologischer Termini und deren Übernahme in die altkirchliche Theologie," *Ostkirchliche Studien*, 8 (1959), 202–20; *idem*, "Eine Definition von 'Hypostasis' und 'Ousia' während des 7. allgemeinen Konzils: Nikaia II 787," *ibid.*, 5 (1956), 52–55; *idem*, "Hypostasis und verwandte Begriffe in den Bekenntnisschriften des Gennadios II. von Konstantinopel und des Metrophanes Kritopulos," *Oriens Christianus*, 40 = 4. S. 4 (1956), 78–93; *idem*, "Die Begriffsentwicklung in der altkirchlichen Theologie zwischen dem ersten allgemeinen Konzil von Nizäa (325) und dem zweiten allgemeinen Konzil von Konstantinopel (381)," *Theologische Revue*, 51 (1955), 145–54; *idem*, "Einige philosophisch-theologische Grundbegriffe bei Leontios von Byzanz, Johannes von Damaskus und Theodor Abū Qurra," *Ostkirchliche Studien*, 4 (1955), 78–93; Heinrich Dörrie, *Hypostasis, Wort- und Bedeutungsgeschichte, Nachrichten*, Göttingen, 1, Philologisch-hist. Kl. (1955), Nr. 3: concentrates on ancient, but does not neglect Christian, usage; contains references to texts but not to literature; G. L. Prestige, *God in Patristic Thought*, 2nd ed. (London, 1952), see index; Juan L. Oreja, "Terminología patrística de la Encarnación," *Helmantica*, 2 (Salamanca, 1951), 129–60; M. Nédoncelle, "Prosopon et persona dans l'antiquité classique," *Revue des sciences religieuses*, 22 (1948), 277–99; Marcel Richard, "L'introduction du mot 'hypostase' dans la théologie de l'incarnation," *Mélanges de science religieuse*, 2 (1945), 5–32, 243–70; A. Grandsire, "Nature et hypostases divines dans saint Basile," *Recherches de science religieuse*, 13 (1923), 130–52; A. Michel, "Hypostase," *Dictionnaire de théologie catholique*, 7, 1 (Paris, 1921), 369–437; Louis Rougier, "Le sens des termes οὐσία, ὑπόστασις et πρόσωπον dans les controverses trinitaires post-nicéennes," *Revue de l'histoire des religions*, 74 (1916), 48–63; 133–89; J. Tixeront, "Essais et notices: des concepts de 'nature' et de 'personne' dans les Pères et les écrivains ecclésiastiques des ve et vi^e siècles," *Revue d'histoire et de littérature religieuses*, 8 (1903), 582–92; T. B. Strong, "The History of the Theological Term 'Substance'," *Journal of Theological Studies*, 2 (1901), 224–35; 3 (1902), 22–40; 4 (1903), 28–45.

On the Latin use of these terms, cf. my "Some Aspects of Byzantine Influence on Latin Thought," *Twelfth Century Europe and the Foundations of Modern Society*, edd. Marshall Clagett, Gaines Post, and Robert H. Reynolds (Madison, 1961), 133, 165 note 11, 182 note 97.

But they differed radically from Nestorius in the Christological formula to which this logic led them, and attacked him because they thought that, when he spoke of two natures, he divided Christ into two, and was accordingly making the monstrous error of introducing a fourth member into the Trinity. Therefore, they felt bound to deny, not without equivocation, that there were two natures in Jesus Christ, and taught that there was "only one incarnate nature [or hypostasis] of God the Word." In so doing, they were making physis the equivalent of what the Chalcedonian Symbol called a prosopon or hypostasis, and alleged that this "one *incarnate* nature of God the Word" necessarily implied the two natures. Nestorius was puzzled by this terminology for many reasons, but in part because he himself followed the fathers of the Nicene period, who had treated hypostasis, usia, and physis as synonyms.

4. NESTORIUS' METAPHYSICAL AND CHRISTOLOGICAL PRESUPPOSITIONS

As stated *supra*, Nestorius' Christology appears to be diametrically opposed to Cyril's. But we shall not be able to evaluate it without determining carefully what Nestorius meant by the terminology he used. It should be noted at the outset that, in the first Book of the *Bazaar*, and frequently thereafter, he denounces the Jews, the Manichaeans, the Arians, the Sabellians, and the Apollinarians. In addition, he expressly condemns Paul of Samosata and the notion that there were two sons.

He based his theological system on the hypothesis that every independently existing object, thing, animal, or person, including man and God the Logos, has a substance or essence (usia)[13] of its own, as the indispensable underlying factor, from which it derives life or existence. The usia, which is invisible, is what the object is in itself, in its inmost being, apart from being perceived. Each usia, in turn, he thought, has a distinctive nature (physis), i.e., the totality of qualities, features, attributes, and peculiarities (both positive and negative) which give it its individual stamp or character. Every nature is founded upon its own usia; there is no nature without an usia; and no usia without a nature. Thus, usia and nature are correlative terms, each of which implies and requires the other.

But neither the usia nor the nature is fully present or effective without a third equally indispensable element, the prosopon. None of the three can be

[13] For the definition of these terms, see *Bazaar*, 10–86. I am greatly indebted to A. R. Vine's *An Approach to Christology* and to Luigi I. Scipioni's *Ricerche* (cited in note 1 *supra*) for valuable assistance in the study of Nestorius' terminology. The latter is prevented on ecclesiastical grounds from rehabilitating Nestorius. The former comes closer to my position, although he is convinced that Nestorius was not really orthodox. Vine would have exerted a greater influence had it not been for the occasional austerity of his style in passages like (p. 171): "The quasi-prosopon of the syntax in the case of a voluntary syntactic unity which includes a dominating animate nature is necessarily identical with the allogenous prosopon of that dominating animate nature. In the case of the syntax Jesus Christ the dominating animate nature is God the Word. Jesus Christ, then, is the allogenous prosopon of God the Word, and holds a place in the continuity of His durative prosopon. Indeed, during the duration of the syntax Jesus Christ, God the Word remained continuously in that syntax, so that for that entire period His prosopon was an allogenous prosopon, the quasi-prosopon of the syntax Jesus Christ. Jesus Christ, therefore, may be regarded as a syntax with a quasi-prosopon, or as the allogenous prosopon of God the Word during a certain period. Anything or anyone of which God the Word made use as an allogenous prosopon would similarly be a syntax with a quasi-prosopon which was also the allogenous prosopon of the God the Word ...."

separated from the other two, nor can the usia and the nature be recognized externally apart from the prosopon (see § 5 *infra*), which reveals them.[14] No ordinary entity or individual being has more than one each of these three components, nor does any one of the three have more than one each of the other two.

From this metaphysical structure, which may have been influenced in part by Stoicism, presumably via the Cappadocian fathers,[15] Nestorius derives his fundamental presupposition that the substance of God the Word and that of the manhood of Christ were both complete in themselves. They were "whole" natures, because the human could have become man by the creative power of God, without union with the divinity, and the latter was altogether independent of the former. On this account, he rejects Cyril's comparison of the union of God and man in Christ with that of body and soul in man. For soul and body are brought together in man, Nestorius says, by constraint, by an act of divine creation, whereas God and man in Christ joined in a union that was voluntary on the part of both participants. On the other hand, when body and soul are united, each is complemented by the other, since "the body has need of the soul that it may live, for it lives not of itself, and the soul has need of the body that it may perceive."[16]

It is not improbable, of course, that the tension between Nestorius and Cyril affected the former's attitude in this matter to some extent. Nevertheless, Nestorius' definition of usia and physis lay at the foundation of his Christological theorem that neither God the Word nor the human nature of Christ was combined with the other in its own nature or usia. They were mutually exclusive, or "alien to one another,"[17] so that neither could have served as the basis of union for the other. Hence, it was impossible for them to be joined together except through a third medium, the prosopon. For, according to him, this was the only vehicle of union[18] that was capable of preserving the properties of the two usiai and natures of Christ inviolate. This was for him essential, since otherwise Christ could not have been both perfect God and perfect man.

His proof of the unsuitability of the two natures (or usiai) as centers for the union illustrates the theory that lay behind his doctrine of the prosopic union. Natures (or usiai) cannot be combined, or changed in any way, he claims, without serious damage[19] to one or the other of them. For, either the one will be

---

[14] *Bazaar*, 158. There is no external prosopon which lacks an usia and a nature of its own: *ibid.*, 208 f., 220, 245–247, 228, 231; cf. 163, 170, 174, 216, 218 f., 261 f., 309, 322.

[15] Grillmeier, "Das Scandalum," cited in note 1 *supra*, 339 ff., would trace the Stoic elements in Nestorius' metaphysics to the Cappadocians. See also Scipioni, *Ricerche* (note 1 *supra*), 15–24, 31–44, 98–109, 133–37; Endre Ivánka, *Hellenisches und christliches im frühbyzantinischen Geistesleben* (Vienna, 1948), 84 ff.; R. Arnou, "Nestorianisme et néoplatonisme," *Gregorianum*, 17 (1936), 116–31.

[16] *Bazaar*, 304, 161. On the union between the divine and human as voluntary, see *ibid.*, 37 f., 47, 85, 90 f., 163, 179, 182, 184, 304. For Cyril's comparison of the incarnation to the union of body and soul in man, see P.G., 77, 225 B; cf. Hubert du Manoir de Juaye, *Dogme et spiritualité chez saint Cyrille d'Alexandrie* (Paris, 1944), 138 ff.

[17] *Bazaar*, 298 f.

[18] *Ibid.*, 23, 53 f., 89, 143 f., 145. 17 f., 147, 157–59, 160 f., 166 f., 170, 174, 189–91, 196, 206 f., 214–16, 219–20, 231, 240 f., 246 f., 262, 299, 308 f., 310 f., 313 f., 319–20. Cf. 33 ff., 37–39.

[19] *Ibid.*, 27.6–8, 28–36.

absorbed by the other, or the result of their combination will be some third nature that is different from both of them.

If, for example, God should take flesh into his own usia, he would not truly become man because he is "not of the nature of men."[20] Still worse, since the Godhead is characterized by lack of body or flesh, if God were to admit flesh or body into his usia, he would cease to be God.[21] Similarly, if Christ's manhood were to take God into its usia, there would be no incarnation of God,[22] but rather the obliteration of the human nature, the deification of man, and the addition of alien matter to the Trinity. That is, as he puts it, things which are changed from their original usia possess only the nature into which they have been changed, and cease to be what they formerly had been.[23] He enunciates this principle also in dealing with Moses' miracle of changing the water of the Nile into blood. In that case, he was of the opinion that the Nile had become blood in usia for the Egyptians, but had been changed back into water for the Hebrews when they used it.[24]

Normally, however, and especially with regard to the divine and the human usiai in Christ, he took such changes of usia to be impossible since "there are no means whereby the usia which was should cease to be, nor whereby that which was made should become unmade, ... nor again whereby a nature which was not should come into being, nor whereby that which is not eternal should become eternal either by a change of nature or by confusion or by mixture; or whereby from the usia of the eternal should come into being that which is not eternal."[25] Therefore, he concludes, the uncreated God the Word, who is eternal, cannot be transformed into that which is created (body), nor can the human body of Christ be changed into the usia of God the Word. On these premises, also, he rejects Cyril's formula of a "natural union" or "hypostatic union" in Christ, both of which, in his estimation, involved a mixture and confusion of natures or hypostases, and consequently an impairment of their integrity that would have been fatal to both the divine and human natures of Christ (cf. notes 19 ff., 46 f.).

5. THE PROSOPIC UNION

So, when he says that God the Word became man, he means that the manhood of Jesus formed a distinct usia alongside the usia of God, and that the two were joined together in the prosopon.[26] But he never even suggested that there were two persons in Christ, as his enemies allege, and, hence, four (a quaternity) in what tradition called a Trinity. This charge he spiritedly repudiates, and reiterates many times that

[20] Ibid., 20–23.
[21] Ibid., 14.
[22] Ibid., 23–26; cf. note 25 infra.
[23] Ibid., 17 f.
[24] Ibid., 18 f.
[25] Ibid., 26 f., 36 f., 80 f., 182, 220.
[26] Ibid., 1, 1, 27 and 29, cf. 18, pp. 20, 21 f., 22 f., 15; 55, 166, 210, 233, 236, 247.

"no one else than he who was in the bosom of his Father came and became flesh and dwelt among us; and he is in the bosom of his Father and with us, in that he is what the Father is, and he has expounded unto us what he is in the bosom of his Father...."[27]

Such texts abound and, he confesses, in conformity with the Creed of 451,

"in one Christ two natures without confusion. By one nature on the one hand, that is [by that] of the divinity, he was born of God the Father; by the other, on the other hand, that is, [by that] of the humanity, [he was born] of the holy virgin."[28]

In view of these express and unambiguous declarations, there can be no doubt that Nestorius firmly believed "that there is of the divinity and of the humanity one Christ and one Lord and one Son ...," and that "there both exists and is named one Christ, the two of them [i.e., the natures] being united, he who was born of the Father in the divinity, and of the holy virgin in the humanity, for there was a union of the two natures."[29]

He frequently refers to this union of the two natures[30] in the one prosopon of Jesus Christ, and denies that it should be described as a union of prosopa.[31] Most significantly of all, he envisaged this union in impeccably orthodox fashion. What he says[32] is that the human Jesus "received his prosopon as something created, in such wise as not originally to be man but at the same time Man-God by the incarnation [ἐνανθρώπησις] of God ...." This is an extremely subtle description of the oneness of Jesus Christ, and shows that Nestorius conceived the Man-God to have been the divine Logos, plus what would have become the separate individual man Jesus, if the Logos had not been united with him from the moment of conception. For the child born of the Virgin was at no time, Nestorius states, a separate man but "at the same time Man-God."

In addition, in the very next sentence he adds, "He [i.e., the Man-God] indeed was the Maker of all, the law-giver, ... the glory, the honour and the power; he was also the second man [the 'New Adam,' as in Romans 5:14ff.; I Cor. 15:22 and 45, i.e., Jesus] with qualities complete and whole, so that God was his prosopon while he was in God." This is a favorite subject with him, and he repeatedly gives utterance to his conviction that in Jesus Christ God and man were one (cf. notes 27f., 34, 41, 43), as when he argues that the "child [the human Jesus] and the Lord of the child [the divine Logos] are the same."[33]

---

[27] *Ibid.*, 50; cf. 53, 192f.
[28] *Ibid.*, 296.
[29] *Ibid.*, 295f. Nestorius' meaning is more clearly expressed in the translation by F. Nau, *op. cit.*, note 1 *supra*, 262: "Il y a et on reconnaît un seul Christ, les deux (natures) étant unies, lequel est né du Père selon la divinité et de la Vierge sainte selon l'humanité, car il y a eu union des deux natures."
[30] *Ibid.*, 58, 79f., 89, 143, 148, 156f., 161, 163, 172, 182, 295ff., 300–302, 308, 310, 314f.
[31] *Ibid.*, 156, 172, 224.
[32] *Ibid.*, 1, 1, 64, p. 60; cf. 92.1f., 237, 304. Although Nestorius frequently refers to what seems to be the *assumptus homo* (as *ibid.*, 237f.), the texts cited show that he understood by the "man assumed" nothing more than the human nature of Christ. See also following note.
[33] *Ibid.*, 230ff. N. b. 45 ("he who judges and is judged is the judge .... Who is it who has accepted the offering for all men, when it is he who accepts and he who is offered?"); 200 ("he who descended is the same whom the Father has sanctified and sent into the world"); 207 (the "taker" and the "taken"

Such texts are re-inforced by his statement, "We say not one and another, for there is one prosopon of both natures," by which Nestorius gives sanction to the orthodox doctrine that the divine and human in Jesus Christ should not be taken to be masculine in gender, ἄλλος καὶ ἄλλος, or ἕτερος καὶ ἕτερος, or *alius* and *alius*, as of two separate persons, but neuter, ἄλλο and ἄλλο, or *aliud* and *aliud*, of the two separate "things," i.e., natures or usiai, which were united in Jesus Christ.

Had his critics taken these passages into account, they could not have persisted in denouncing him as a heretic, especially in the face of his oft-repeated and passionate denial[34] that there were two Sons or Lords or Christs. Nor could they have accused him of having been committed to the doctrine that the human prosopon assumed by the divine Logos constituted a separate man, the *assumptus homo*, who lived by the side of the Logos during the incarnation—and therefore amounted to a second Son and a "fourth member of the Trinity."

Nevertheless, in order to do full justice to both sides, let us examine the objections that have been made against Nestorius, even if they must be regarded as deprived of all substance not only by the text quoted above but also by the emphasis he lays upon the union of the two natures and the oneness of Jesus Christ, as at notes 27-29 above and elsewhere.

Hostility towards Nestorius arises because, although he describes the union as taking place only in the prosopon, which he defines innumerable times as one in number (see note 43), he also makes reference to two prosopa (that of the divine nature and that of the human) and occasionally also to a "union of the prosopa."[35] Even when he does so, however, he immediately explains, in the same context, that the latter "took place for the prosopon" and that there was only "one prosopon of the two natures."

Such explanations demonstrate both that Nestorius did not conceive of the two prosopa which he mentions as in any way compromising the unity or oneness of Jesus Christ, and that he uses the word prosopon in two different senses. According to one usage (*sense A*), prosopon—i.e., what may be called the natural or external prosopon, means the exterior aspect or appearance of a thing, not opposed to its genuine character, but, in the words of a modern critic, "as an objectively real element in its being..., without which, or if it were other than it is, the thing would not be what it is."[36] This is the more general significance of the word (see notes 12 and 14 *supra*). When applied to the two natures in Jesus Christ it indicates, not that each nature had a separate,

---

are one, not two); 233. Nestorius' denial that there were in Christ "one and another" (masculine) is to be found *ibid.*, 200-201 (n.b. the Greek text Nestorius had in mind in quoting these words), 209, 224, 237. On the orthodox affirmation of the same principle, see Eduard Weigl, *Christologie vom Tode des Athanasius bis zum Ausbruch des nestorianischen Streites, 373-429* (*Münchener Studien zur historischen Theologie*, 4 [Munich, 1925]), 45, 47, 57 f., 108 f., 112, 152; J. N. D. Kelly, *Early Christian doctrines*, 297; Sellers, *Two Ancient Christologies*, 72 f.; cf. my "Some aspects of Byzantine influence on Latin thought," *Twelfth Century Europe* (see note 12 *supra*), 161 f.

[34] *Bazaar*, 47-50, 146, 160, 189-91, 196, 209 f., 215, 224 f., 227, 237 f., 295-302, 314, 317.
[35] *Ibid.*, 218-20; cf. 163, 246, 252, 261 f., 302, 309; and note 40 *infra*.
[36] *Ibid.*, 414-16. Cf. the texts cited in notes 11 and 14 *supra*.

independent existence (as a person), but that each had a substantive reality, recognizable in its distinctive qualities, which remained undiminished after the union. Hence, prosopon in *sense A* is to be understood as nothing but another aspect of physis or usia, to which, as we have seen (notes 12-14 *supra*), it is inextricably bound.

The other kind of prosopon (*sense B*) is an approximate equivalent of our word "person" and occurs in the *Bazaar of Heracleides* as the designation for Jesus Christ, "the common prosopon of the two natures."[37]

Let us now see how Nestorius applies these definitions to the union. "Man," he says, taking prosopon in *sense A* as above defined, "is known by the human prosopon, that is, by the *schema* [outward form] of the body and by the likeness, but God by the name which is more excellent than all names, and by the adoration of all creation and by the confession [of him] as God."[38] That is, every individual man is identified as such and distinguished from his fellows by the physical characteristics of his appearance. These constitute his prosopon (*sense A*). But the prosopon (*sense A*) of God, who is invisible, is recognized in a different way—by his glorious name and by the fact that he is acknowledged to be God. More specifically, to refer to one of the most significant paragraphs in the *Bazaar* (see note 32 *supra*), the prosopon of the divine nature (*sense A*) was God the Logos himself.

On the basis of these definitions, Nestorius maintains that, as a result of the union, a transfer of attributes (*communicatio idiomatum*: see § 6 *infra*) took place. God the Logos (understood as the prosopon in *sense A* of the divine nature) became the prosopon of Jesus Christ's human nature (note 32 *supra*). Nestorius sets forth the same idea somewhat differently when he says, citing Philippians 2: 9–11, that the divine Word of God gave the human nature of Jesus Christ his name so that, "at the name of Jesus every knee should bow which is in heaven and on the earth, and every tongue should confess that Jesus is the Lord."[39] Likewise as a consequence of the union, the Logos united with his divine nature the flesh—the body and appearance (i.e., the prosopon in *sense A* of the human nature). Or, to adopt one of Nestorius' favorite expressions, "the divinity makes use of the prosopon of the humanity, and the humanity of that of the divinity."[40]

These two prosopa (*sense A*), which, it will be remembered, were intimately connected, but not identical, with the two natures themselves, fulfilled the functions assigned them by Nestorius (see notes 14 and 36 *supra*). For they were the characteristic or visible elements by which the divine and human natures, respectively, were made apparent to the observer in all of their aspects. Hence, Nestorius was enabled to define the union of the two natures in the one prosopon (*sense B*) of Jesus Christ, the incarnate divine Logos,

[37] *Ibid.*, 319, 58, 148, 166, 170f., 220.
[38] *Ibid.*, 1, 1, 66, p. 61; *ibid.*, 64f., 67, pp. 60–62. Cf. pp. 55, 58f., 70, 89, 165–67, 246–49, 312–15. Hodgson, *ibid.*, 415f., ingeniously explains that the union of the prosopa is of two natures and usiai, "which nevertheless are identical in appearance," so that the "appearances overlap." But this would be an illusion, not the true union which Nestorius had in mind.
[39] *Ibid.*, 1, 1, 65, p. 61.
[40] *Ibid.*, 58, 207, 220, 240f. (quotation).

in terms of their external revelation through their prosopa (*sense A*). In addition, the two prosopa (*sense A*) served as media for the *communicatio idiomatum*. But in no respect did they connote a division or bifurcation into two separate persons. For Nestorius carefully adds (see note 40) so as to avoid "Nestorian" implications: "and thus we say one prosopon [i.e., in *sense B*] in both of them. Thus God appears whole, since his nature is not damaged in aught owing to the union; and thus, too, man [is] whole, falling short of naught of the activity and of the sufferings of his own nature owing to the union."

The last sentence indicates that Nestorius had not fallen into the error of supposing that the union of God and man in Jesus Christ, the *one* common prosopon (in *sense B*), which unites the two usiai and natures, was in any way illusory or involved a diminution of the fullness and perfection of either the divine or the human nature. This is a point to which he frequently returns, as when he says[41] of Jesus Christ, "He is truly God, ... in naught falling short of the nature of the Father; and we confess that the man is truly man, completely in his nature, in naught falling short of the nature of men, neither in body nor in soul nor in intelligence ...." Likewise, he adds elsewhere, "God indeed remained God and was made man, and man remained man and was made God; for they took the prosopon of one another, and not the natures."

Similarly (cf. notes 27-32 *supra*), in the language of the Creed of 325 Nestorius unequivocally identifies the one Lord Jesus Christ, "the only-begotten Son of God, that is, from the ousia of God the Father. God from God and Light of Light, Very God of Very God, born and not made, consubstantial with the Father, by whom all that is in heaven and in earth was made," with the same one Lord Jesus Christ, who "on account of us men and on account of our salvation came down and was made flesh of the Holy Spirit and of the Virgin Mary, who also was made man..., suffered and rose on the third day and ascended into heaven and will come to judge the living and the dead"—he who is "consubstantial with the Father" and "consubstantial with the mother, one Lord Jesus Christ."

At the same time, the quotations at notes 32–34, 37-40 show that Nestorius kept well within the permissible limits of orthodox theology in describing the difference between the two natures in Christ. The incarnation is a mystery, and cannot be made comprehensible in purely logical terms. But it would be difficult to conceive of a description that is, under the circumstances, more explicit or more orthodox than Nestorius'.

This point can best be proved by a brief review of his analysis of the unity of the two natures and usiai in one prosopon, the prosopon of union (*sense B*), Jesus Christ,[42] to the oneness of which he testifies uncompromisingly.[43] The prosopon of the human nature (*sense A*) was the visible manhood of Jesus, not merely his outward physical features, and signified the whole of his human individuality, with all the qualities that go to make up a perfect man. The

[41] *Ibid.*, 233, 220. For Nestorius' treatment of the Nicene Creed, see *ibid.*, 144 f.; cf. note 70 *infra*.
[42] *Ibid.*, 23, 53, 55, 58, 64, 66, 89, 143, 145-49, 156-59, 161, 164 f., 166 f., 174, 182 f., 189, 196, 201 f., 207, 214, 216, 220, 227, 230 ff., 235 f., 246 f., 252 ff., 258, 260 ff., 299, 301, 308 ff., 313 f., 315, 318, 319.
[43] *Ibid.*, 58, 148, 166, 170 f., 220, 236, 240, 246, 252, 310, 319.

prosopon of the manhood, thus understood, revealed by Christ's miracles the invisible divine nature of the eternal God the Word, who has neither physical form nor shape, but was fully present in the common prosopon (*sense B*) Jesus Christ, and manifested himself behind the cloak of flesh through his prosopon (in *sense A*), by the exertion of divine power.

Consequently, in Nestorius' system, the prosopon (*sense A*) of the divine nature, which was actually God the Logos himself, as we have seen, was recognized by the performance of divine acts and the manifestation of omnipotence, as we should say, or as he himself expresses it (note 38f.), by the name of God, "the adoration of all creation," and "confession of him as God." This language was intended, it would seem, to emphasize the immateriality of God and to explain how the divine Logos could be united with the humanity of Jesus without any objection able duality of person. But, it must be emphasized, this is only Nestorius' way of defining the indefinable prosopon of God the Logos in Christ, whom he represents consistently (see *supra*, notes 27–29, 41, *infra*, 51 ff.) as no mere external power or spirit, but truly the divine, eternal Logos, who descended from heaven and was joined with the human nature in the womb of the Virgin.

Thus, to the one prosopon,[44] the "common prosopon of our Lord Jesus Christ, the only-begotten Son of God," Nestorius referred "all the [properties] of God the Word whose nature is impassible and is immortal and eternal, and all the [properties] of the humanity, which are a nature mortal and passible and created, and those of the union and of the incarnation. ..." For[45] in Jesus Christ "the earthly and the heavenly, the visible and the invisible, the limited and the unlimitable are the same." These formulations, which vie with the Oecumenical Creeds in lucidity and exactitude, can apply only to what we should call a single person, the God-Man Jesus Christ, who is simultaneously perfect God and perfect man—the divine Logos, who became man and was known on earth through the prosopa (*sense A*) described *supra*.

According to Nestorius, therefore, Jesus Christ was the divine Logos incarnate, the Son of God in the flesh,[45a] the Lord whom his disciples knew as a man but recognized to be God. The unity of his "personality" was further guaranteed by the fact that it was the Logos who both "gave" his prosopon (*sense A*) to the human nature and "took" that of the human for his own. Moreover, the human will of Christ (see notes 51–55a *infra*) was always obedient to the divine, so that there never was any conflict or division between the two.

This analysis is a legitimate summary of Nestorius' Christology, which he himself, however, never presents systematically. Nor does he ever differentiate the "common prosopon" of Jesus Christ from the two prosopa (*sense A*), except by his constant emphasis upon its oneness or indivisibility and upon its having been the vehicle of the union of the two natures or the "common prosopon of the two natures" (*supra*, notes 30f., 37, 42f.). He obviously felt that

[44] *Ibid.*, 171.
[45] *Ibid.*, 230f.
[45a] *Ibid.*, 60f., 191, 193, 196–8, 200–1, 237. On the Logos' "giving" and "taking," see *ibid.*, 55, 61, 69, 165, 225.

these distinctions were in themselves decisive, and he would have been astounded by the hypersubtlety of the scholars (cf. note 13 *supra*) who have tried to speak for him in this matter—in language that he would have found utterly incomprehensible.

It is hardly necessary to add that his failure to attempt a more fully articulated metaphysical analysis of the "common prosopon of Jesus Christ" (*sense B*) is neither surprising nor in the slightest degree heretical. The Chalcedonian Symbol (see note 9 *supra*) merely affirms the oneness of the prosopon or hypostasis and denies that it was divided into two. Nestorius is far more explicit than his contemporaries, none of whom expounds the incarnation so fully as he does, or lays greater stress upon the oneness and unity of Jesus Christ.

Nestorius' deep personal commitment to the unity of Christ is demonstrated also by his acceptance of the Cyrillian idea of the hypostatic union, if hypostasis be defined as a synonym for prosopon and not for usia.[46] On this basis he could indorse the Cappadocian Trinitarian formula, one usia in three hypostases, although he himself preferred to speak of one usia in three prosopa.[47]

In addition, the quotation at note 32 above constitutes a powerful refutation of the Cyrillian taunt that Nestorius had an inadequate conception of the union of the two natures in Christ, and separated the one from the other spatially. Scorning Nestorius' specific denials that he ever divided or isolated the natures from each other, Cyril attacks him for saying, "I separate the natures but unite the adoration,"[48] as if Nestorius meant that, notwithstanding the absence of a real union of the natures, the separate man Jesus deserved to be worshipped because of his close association with the Logos. The verb "separate" ($\chi\omega\rho\iota\zeta\omega$), which Cyril finds offensive, was banned at Chalcedon. But Nestorius replies that he intended it to refer to the distinction between the two natures, since one was divine and the other human, not to any physical or spatial separation between them. Never, Nestorius protests, did he distinguish God the Word from "him that is visible,"[49] i.e., he never made a division in Jesus Christ as if between the Logos and the man Jesus. Nor did he say that there were two adorations, as if the divine Logos and the human nature of Jesus formed separate persons, and each received worship of his own. On the contrary,[50] he contends, the adoration in question, like the prosopon of Jesus Christ, was singular in number, though it was quite proper to conceive of the human nature (not a separate man) as being adored together with the divine, with which it was joined in the one prosopon of Jesus Christ.

It was the unity of Christ, furthermore, which made it possible for Nestorius to understand how it was that the will and purpose of Jesus Christ's human

---

[46] *Ibid.*, 156f. but cf. 208, 218.

[47] *Ibid.*, 247.

[48] *Ibid.*, 311 ff. See also the texts cited in notes 49–55 *infra*. Cf. Sellers, *op. cit.* (note 1 *supra*), 91–95, 190–200.

[49] *Ibid.*, 314.

[50] *Ibid.*, 188 f., 196, 202, 207, 227, 237 f., 314. For proof of the orthodoxy of Nestorius' doctrine of the adoration of the human nature of Jesus together with the Word, see Paul Galtier, *De incarnatione et redemptione* (Paris, 1947), §§ 288 ff.

nature were identical with those of God the Word.[51] This identity might have led to the "Nestorian" or adoptionist interpretation that the divinity of Jesus Christ consisted of nothing but his extraordinary submission to the divine will, which won for him the title of Son of God by way of reward or honor, and that the divine in Christ was comparable to the indwelling of God in Moses, the prophets, and the saints.

But Nestorius was not attracted by these notions, and insists that the union in Christ was not merely "moral" but truly metaphysical (see note 55). He does not fail on this account, however, to record the human traits[52] of Christ as recorded in the Gospels: his birth, low estate, swaddling clothes, "increase in stature and in wisdom with God and with men," suffering, death, and resurrection. Throughout, stress is laid on the Son's obedience, despite travail and temptation, and on his freedom of the will.[53] But Nestorius refrains from drawing "Nestorian" conclusions therefrom, rejects the notion that Christ achieved Sonship "as a consequence of moral progress" or by degrees (by adoption after proving his merit)[54] and traces the identity between the will of Christ's humanity and that of God the Logos to the union of their natures, that is, as he expressly states, to the very moment of Christ's conception.[55]

These pronouncements of Nestorius deserve close scrutiny. He understood by the identity of the divine and human wills in Christ, it should be noted, that the two were in complete harmony with each other, not that the two natures had only a single will between them or that the one had absorbed or obliterated the other. There were two wills, but they made identical decisions. The human will, despite its independence of the divine will, was always actively and deliberately obedient to it, through every trial and vicissitude. Nestorius argues (whether rightly or wrongly it is not my purpose to determine in this paper) that Cyril's treatment of this topic was unsatisfactory. The latter does not, of course, deny that the humanity of Jesus Christ was perfect, and included a human rational faculty, which was endowed with freedom of the will. But, Nestorius charges,[55a] Cyril ascribes Christ's moral and spiritual victories to the activity and power of the divine Logos, rather than to the free exercize of his human volition. Unless his human will had faced a real moral choice, Nestorius holds, and had responded thereto in genuinely human fashion, Christ could not have had a truly human nature. Nor could his humanity have otherwise been the model, vehicle, and assurance of immortality for all mankind. This conception was basic for Nestorius' soteri-

---

[51] On identity of the wills: *Bazaar*, 57 (end), 59, 62–68, 70, 163; God was *truly* in Christ, not just as in the saints: 44–46, 203–6, 227; cf. notes 48–55, especially note 50.

[52] *Ibid.*, 91 ff., 205 f., and *passim*.

[53] *Ibid.*, 62–66, 93 f.

[54] *Ibid.*, 57 (end) f., 59 f., 72, 252 f., cf. 314.

[55] *Ibid.*, 60.3 ff., 314; cf. 72 (end) and note 50 *supra*.

[55a] *Ibid.*, 91 ff., 210–12, 240, 247 f. For the argument of Cyril reprehended by Nestorius, see *Sancti Patris Nostri Cyrilli Archiepiscopi Alexandrini in D. Joannis Evangelium*, ed. Philip E. Pusey, 1 (Oxford, 1872), 487. 16–23 (on John 6:38 f.); *ibid.*, 2 (Oxford, 1872), 316-8–317.7, 320.13–23 (on John 12:27 f.); P. G., 73, 532 AB; P. G. 74, 88D–89A, 92D. Cf. Sellers, *op. cit.* (note 1 *supra*), 104 ff. The latter of these texts is deemed not to have been written by Cyril: Liébaert, *op. cit.* (note 66 *infra*), 131–37.

ology. It also serves to illustrate his understanding of the unity of Christ's personality, which, according to him, never experienced dissension or discord since the human will always followed the divine.

6. THEOTOKOS AND THE *Communicatio Idiomatum*

On the basis of the foregoing analysis, we are justified in clearing Nestorius of the charge of "Nestorianism," and can pronounce his theology to be unobjectionable when measured by Chalcedonian criteria. But, some urge, his unwillingness to designate Mary the Virgin as Theotokos without qualification indicates that he failed to comprehend fully the implications of the *communicatio idiomatum* (ἀντίδοσις τῶν ἰδιωμάτων or ὀνομάτων).

This phenomenon, the transfer or exchange of attributes, as defined by the Council of Chalcedon, notably in the Tome of Bishop Leo I (440–61) of Rome (see note 71 *infra*), is exhibited by the two natures of Jesus Christ (the divine and the human). According to orthodox doctrine, these natures are united "without confusion, change, separation, or division" (see note 9 *supra*), and retain all of their properties, which in the union of God and man are distinct from each other but not separate. The difference between the natures had given rise to two appellations of Jesus Christ, who, on account of his divine nature, is Son of God (the divine Logos) and also, at the same time, by virtue of his human nature, the Son of man (Jesus). Whatever the designation, reference is always to one and the same person, Jesus Christ. Strictly speaking, the divine characteristics are attributable to the divine nature and the human to the human. Nevertheless, as a result of the union of the two in one person, it is deemed possible to ascribe the experiences of Jesus Christ in respect of his divine nature to the Son of man, and those which Jesus Christ underwent because of his human nature to the Son of God. Consequently, it was theologically permissible to teach that the "Son of God" (see note 65f. *infra* for further extension of this idea) underwent death, to which the divine nature was not subject, and that the "Son of man" received worship, which is accorded only to God.

Neither the Council of Chalcedon nor Bishop Leo of Rome was less ambiguous or more positive about this doctrine than Nestorius. Like them, he says,[56] "we name the man God indeed on account of the union of the divinity but man in nature; yet similarly once more also God the Word is God indeed in nature, but we call God man by reason of the union of the prosopon of the humanity."

In support of this proposition, he cites Athanasius[57] approvingly to the same effect: "Now that the Word has become man and has made the properties of the flesh his own, the same are no longer imputed to the body because the Word has come to be in it." From this, like Athanasius, he concludes that in the union the Logos acquired the characteristics of man, and the human in Christ, in turn,

---

[56] *Ibid.*, 248; cf. 180, 228, 233.
[57] *Ibid.*, 221.

those of God. He specifically states[58] that he agrees with the orthodox who assign "the [properties] of the humanity to the divinity and those of the divinity to the humanity, and this is said of the one and that of the other, as concerning natures whole and united, united indeed without confusion and making use of the prosopa of one another."

He does not mean of course that such an exchange was actually effected between the two natures, but rather between God the Logos and the human in Christ, through their prosopa. His formula for this transfer is the sentence, "the divinity makes use of the prosopon of the humanity and the humanity of that of the divinity," which recurs repeatedly in the *Bazaar*, in one form or another, and must be ranked high among patristic attempts to define this central mystery of the incarnation.

This was his way of safeguarding the divinity and integrity of the divine nature of the Logos. For it enabled him to attach Jesus Christ's human experiences and agony, which God the Word assumed,[59] not to the divine nature, but to the human prosopon (*sense A*) which the Logos "used." Hence, in the kenosis[60] (the "emptingy" by which God humiliated himself and took on human form: Philippians 2: 6–11), the Logos endured "death upon the cross, in that he made use of the prosopon of him who died and was crucified as his own prosopon, and [i.e., as a consequence] in his own prosopon he made use of the things which appertained unto him who died and was crucified and was exalted."

Accordingly, he does not question the validity of such traditional affirmations as "God suffered" and "God died," if correctly understood as applying to the human prosopon the divine Logos took, not to his nature. Thus, he recognizes Jesus Christ's two generations (note 28f. *supra*) and confesses[61] of the Logos that "nothing is his own apart from the human humiliation; but while remaining God in all things, [he is] that which the man was by his nature in sufferings, even in impassibility." Or, in other words, the Logos "is impassible in a passible body"[62] and "truly...came to be in the body and was not distinguished from the body."

He was, however, far more persistent than Cyril in pointing out that God the Logos did not undergo the human process in his own nature. For, he shows,[63] in the New Testament death and suffering are never associated with God but only with Christ, the Son, or the Lord, since these names are "indicative of two natures

[58] *Ibid.*, 240f.; see also 81, 174, 182f., 191, 233. For Nestorius' formula for the *communicatio idiomatum*, see *ibid.*, 240, 190, 207, 219f., 233 ("the one is the other and the other the one"), 238; cf. 66, 69, 81, 159, 163, 167, 172, 183, 252, 261, 320.

[59] *Ibid.*, 174.

[60] *Ibid.*, 58; cf. 138 ("the Only-begotten Son of God created and was created; the Son of God suffered and suffered not, the same but not in the same [*ousia*]; for [some] of these things are in the nature of the divinity and [others] of them in the nature of the humanity. He suffered all human things in the humanity, and all divine things in the divinity ...."), 165, 170, 179, 191, 193, 221. On the kenosis, see Paul Henry, "Kénose," *Dictionnaire de la Bible, Supplément*, 5 (Paris, 1957), 7–161.

N. b. that Nestorius' analysis on this point (cf. note 63 *infra*) was accepted by Cyril and the Council of Chalcedon (note 72[a] *infra*).

[61] *Bazaar*, 70.

[62] *Ibid.*, 237.

[63] *Ibid.*, 256f.

and indicate sometimes the divinity, but sometimes the humanity and sometimes both of them." Cyril was to be censured, therefore, he felt,[64] for failing to appreciate adequately the impassibility of the divine nature.

Basically, as Nestorius in part understood, Cyril really was in agreement with him on this point. In his *Second Letter to Nestorius,*[65] for example, which received oecumenical indorsement at the Councils of Ephesus and Chalcedon, Cyril declared that the Logos, though begotten of the Father before the ages and in no need of a second birth, is *said* (λέγεται) to have been born in the flesh (σαρκικῶς) because he had united himself with human nature. In this sense, the Virgin Mary, who was in no wise, Cyril concedes, the mother or source of God the Word himself or his divine nature, could be regarded as Theotokos, since she gave birth to the flesh to which the Logos was joined in hypostatic union. Likewise, the Logos, who is in his own nature incorporeal, impassible, incorruptible, and immortal, is *said* to have suffered, died, and risen from the dead, because of his union with a human body which underwent these experiences. By this process of reasoning, Cyril evolved a formula,[66] according to which the Logos submitted to birth, suffering, and death *in the flesh* (σαρκί) or according to the flesh (κατὰ σάρκα). His treatment of the Word's relation to passibility is eminently reasonable, and closely resembles what Nestorius has to say on this subject (see note 72[a] *infra*).

Unhappily, the latter, out of the same contrariety which led Cyril to contradict him at every turn, repudiates[67] Cyril's solution of the problem, and objects[68] that Cyril referred the qualities of both the human and the divine natures to the eternal Logos but failed to attribute those of God the Word to Christ's manhood. As a consequence, he complains, Cyril was guilty of the Manichaean error of reducing Christ's flesh to an illusion. This is not the place to analyze Cyril's position on these matters. But Nestorius' animadversions, however unjustified, prove once again that he thoroughly understood the *communicatio idiomatum*, and realized that there could have been no true union of the divine Logos and

---

[64] *Ibid.*, 91–94, 136ff., 141–51, 174, 176, 181 ff., 188, 191–206, 247, 252–62, 295 ff., 323, 362, 364 ff., 367 f.

[65] Nestorius insists that Cyril at times agrees with him on the impassibility of the divine nature: *ibid.*, 145, 150, 174, 191, 195, 221 f., 232 252, 260, 262, 265 f., 296 f. For the text of Cyril's Second Letter to Nestorius, see *ACO*, I, I, I, 25. 23–28. 26; P.G., 77, 44 ff.; Bindley, *op. cit.* (note 9 *supra*), 94 ff., 209 ff.

[66] See previous note and Cyril's *Third Letter to Nestorius, ACO*, I, I, I, 33–42; P.G., 77, 105–21; ed. and trans. with commentary by Bindley, *op. cit.*, (note 9 *supra*), 106–37, 212–19; n.b. 111.149, 165 f.; 113.253–70, and the twelfth anathema in this letter. On Cyril's view of the *communicatio idiomatum*, see Georges Jouassard, "Impassibilité du Logos et impassibilité de l'âme humaine chez saint Cyrille d'Alexandrie," *Recherches de science religieuse*, 45 (1957), 209–44, and other articles by him, listed in Quasten, *Patrology*, 3, 141. A warm and erudite defense of Cyril, along with an attack on the theology of the *assumptus homo*, is made by H. M. Diepen, *Douze dialogues de christologie ancienne* (Rome, 1960); *idem, La théologie de l'Emmanuel* (n. p., 1960); *idem, Aux origines de l'anthropologie de saint Cyrille d'Alexandrie* (n. p., 1957), who directs his fire mostly against Déodat de Basly (see my "Immutability" [note 3 *supra*], 138, note 52). Cf. Paul Galtier, "Saint Cyrille et Apollinaire," *Gregorianum*, 37 (1956), 584–609; Jouassard, *loc. cit.*; and Jacques Liébaert, *La doctrine christologique de saint Cyrille d'Alexandrie avant la querelle nestorienne* (*Mémoires et travaux publiés par les professeurs des facultés catholiques de Lille*, 58 [Lille, 1951]), with all three of whom I agree against Diepen. A precise summary of Cyril's position is to be found in Hubert du Manoir de Juaye, *op. cit.* (note 16 *supra*), 145–50.

[67] *Bazaar*, 150 f.

[68] *Ibid.*, 146, 219, 225, 239, 240 f., 245–48, 260.

138   MILTON V. ANASTOS

the human nature in Jesus Christ unless the qualities of the one were deemed applicable to the other and *vice versa*.

Actually, the fundamental difference between Nestorius and Cyril in interpreting the results of the *communicatio idiomatum* stems from their disagreement concerning the subject of the God-man's career and experience. Cyril, as Nestorius remarks,[69] preferred to begin with the divine Logos ("the maker of the natures"), and habitually speaks of the Logos as saying, doing, suffering, dying, and rising from the dead. Nestorius, on the other hand, associates all these activities with "the prosopon of the union" (the Jesus Christ of the Gospels). In defence of his position, he appeals to the New Testament (see note 63 *supra*) and the Creed of Nicaea.[70] The latter, he contends, in a rebuttal of Cyril, ascribes the incarnation, death, and resurrection to Jesus Christ, not to the divine Logos. It should be added, also, that the Symbol of Chalcedon follows the same pattern (see note 9 *supra*), and qualifies the terrestrial generation of Jesus Christ exactly as Nestorius does, stating that he "was born of Mary the Virgin Theotokos, *according to the manhood.*" We cannot censure him for expressing himself with similar circumspection, and there is no doubt that he would have subscribed unreservedly to this Creed and to the Tome of Leo, as one of his followers claims.[71]

[69] *Ibid.*, 143–146, 153 and *passim*.
[70] *Ibid.*, 141 ff., 144 ff., and *passim*. For the text of the Creed of 325, see *ACO*, 2, 1, 2, 79 [275]. 16 ff. Other versions and the so-called Creed of 381: *ACO*, 1, 1, 1, 12.32–13.5, 35.1–11; *ACO*, 1, 1, 2, 12.29–13.7; *ACO*, 1, 1, 3, 39.1–11; *ACO*, 1, 1, 7, 65 f.; *ACO*, 2, 1, 1, 90.30 ff.; *ACO*, 2, 1, 2, 127 [323] f.; *ACO*, 3, 4.24–5.11; Mansi, *op. cit.* (note 9 *supra*), 7, 110–12. Apart from minor variants in punctuation, I reproduce the text of *ACO*, 2, 1, 2, 79.16, except for ἢ κτιστὸν in the last sentence, which occurs in Athanasius' recension and seems to be an essential element of the Creed: *De decretis Nicaenae Synodi*, 37, 2, ed. Hans-Georg Opitz, *Athanasius Werke*, 2, 1 (Berlin-Leipzig, 1935), 36.33–37.2. For the formation and meaning of the Creed, see J. N. D. Kelly, *Early Christian Creeds* (London, 1951), 215 ff., and the literature set forth in *Dumbarton Oaks Papers*, 6 (1951), 141 note 60.

πιστεύομεν εἰς ἕνα θεὸν πατέρα παντοκράτορα, πάντων ὁρατῶν τε καὶ ἀοράτων ποιητήν. καὶ εἰς ἕνα κύριον Ἰησοῦν Χριστόν, τὸν υἱὸν τοῦ θεοῦ, γεννηθέντα ἐκ τοῦ πατρὸς μονογενῆ. τουτέστιν ἐκ τῆς οὐσίας τοῦ πατρός, θεὸν ἐκ θεοῦ, φῶς ἐκ φωτός, θεὸν ἀληθινὸν ἐκ θεοῦ ἀληθινοῦ, γεννηθέντα οὐ ποιηθέντα, ὁμοούσιον τῷ πατρί· δι' οὗ τὰ πάντα ἐγένετο, τά τε ἐν τῷ οὐρανῷ καὶ τὰ ἐν τῇ γῇ, τὸν δι' ἡμᾶς τοὺς ἀνθρώπους καὶ διὰ τὴν ἡμετέραν σωτηρίαν κατελθόντα καὶ σαρκωθέντα καὶ ἐνανθρωπήσαντα, παθόντα καὶ ἀναστάντα τῇ τρίτῃ ἡμέρᾳ, ἀνελθόντα εἰς τοὺς οὐρανούς, καὶ ἐρχόμενον κρῖναι ζῶντας καὶ νεκρούς. καὶ εἰς τὸ ἅγιον πνεῦμα. τοὺς δὲ λέγοντας, ἦν ποτε ὅτε οὐκ ἦν, καὶ πρὶν γεννηθῆναι οὐκ ἦν, καὶ ὅτι ἐξ οὐκ ὄντων ἐγένετο, ἢ ἐξ ἑτέρας ὑποστάσεως ἢ οὐσίας φάσκοντας εἶναι, ἢ κτιστὸν ἢ τρεπτὸν ἢ ἀλλοιωτὸν τὸν υἱὸν τοῦ θεοῦ [τούτους] ἀναθεματίζει ἡ καθολικὴ καὶ ἀποστολικὴ ἐκκλησία.

The so-called Creed of 381, which first appears as such in the Acts of the Council of Chalcedon is taken from *ACO*, 2, 1, 2, 80 [276]:

Πιστεύομεν εἰς ἕνα θεὸν πατέρα παντοκράτορα, ποιητὴν οὐρανοῦ καὶ γῆς, ὁρατῶν τε πάντων καὶ ἀοράτων. καὶ εἰς ἕνα κύριον Ἰησοῦν Χριστόν, τὸν υἱὸν τοῦ θεοῦ τὸν μονογενῆ, τὸν ἐκ τοῦ πατρὸς γεννηθέντα πρὸ πάντων τῶν αἰώνων, φῶς ἐκ φωτός, θεὸν ἀληθινὸν ἐκ θεοῦ ἀληθινοῦ, γεννηθέντα οὐ ποιηθέντα, ὁμοούσιον τῷ πατρί, δι' οὗ τὰ πάντα ἐγένετο, τὸν δι' ἡμᾶς τοὺς ἀνθρώπους καὶ διὰ τὴν ἡμετέραν σωτηρίαν κατελθόντα ἐκ τῶν οὐρανῶν καὶ σαρκωθέντα ἐκ πνεύματος ἁγίου καὶ Μαρίας τῆς παρθένου καὶ ἐνανθρωπήσαντα, σταυρωθέντα τε ὑπὲρ ἡμῶν ἐπὶ Ποντίου Πιλάτου, καὶ παθόντα καὶ ταφέντα, καὶ ἀναστάντα τῇ τρίτῃ ἡμέρᾳ κατὰ τὰς γραφάς, καὶ ἀνελθόντα εἰς τοὺς οὐρανούς, καὶ καθεζόμενον ἐν δεξιᾷ τοῦ πατρός. καὶ πάλιν ἐρχόμενον μετὰ δόξης κρῖναι ζῶντας καὶ νεκρούς· οὗ τῆς βασιλείας οὐκ ἔσται τέλος. καὶ εἰς τὸ πνεῦμα τὸ ἅγιον, τὸ κύριον καὶ ζωοποιόν, τὸ ἐκ τοῦ πατρὸς ἐκπορευόμενον, τὸ σὺν πατρὶ καὶ υἱῷ συμπροσκυνούμενον καὶ συνδοξαζόμενον, τὸ λαλῆσαν διὰ τῶν προφητῶν· εἰς μίαν ἁγίαν καθολικὴν καὶ ἀποστολικὴν ἐκκλησίαν. ὁμολογοῦμεν ἓν βάπτισμα εἰς ἄφεσιν ἁμαρτιῶν· προσδοκῶμεν ἀνάστασιν νεκρῶν καὶ ζωὴν τοῦ μέλλοντος αἰῶνος.

[71] *Bazaar*, frag. 308, p. 388 f., cf. *ibid.*, ix f., xxix f., 241, 369 ff., 374 f., 378. For the text of the Tome of Leo (Ep. 28), see *ACO*, 2, 2, 1, 24–33 (Latin); 2, 1, 1, 10–20 (Greek version); C. Silva-Tarouca, S. *Leonis Magni Tomus ad Flavianum Episc. Constantinopolitanum (Textus et documenta*, Series theologica, 9 [Rome, 1932]). For exegesis, etc.: Hugo Rahner, "Leo der Grosse, der Papst des Konzils," *Das Konzil von Chalkedon*, 1 (see note 1), 323–39; Paul Galtier, "Saint Cyrille d'Alexandrie et Saint Léon le

Still, since Cyril is universally esteemed in the Church as a Chalcedonian before Chalcedon, the Christology of Nestorius, if orthodox, should be reconcilable, notwithstanding angry denials on both sides, with Cyril's. In truth, it must be admitted, the line which separates them on this, as on all other issues, is either very thin or nonexistent. Both agreed that the qualities of the two natures were referable to the one person, Jesus Christ. They defined this entity somewhat differently, but it is obvious that Cyril's "one prosopon, ... the one incarnate hypostasis of God the Logos,"[72] and Nestorius' "one prosopon of Jesus Christ" (notes 37, 42 f.) were both intended to define the Jesus Christ of the Gospels. Moreover, Cyril's characteristic notion that "the Logos suffered in the flesh" is theologically the exact equivalent of Nestorius' dogma that the Logos suffered in the prosopon of the manhood which he took for his own. For, as we have seen (note 38 ff.), the prosopon of the manhood is the *schema* or the flesh and body of Jesus Christ.

Nevertheless, Nestorius was always offended by Cyril's constant preoccupation with the paradox that God the Logos suffered, died, and was raised from the dead—*in the flesh*—although he recognized (notes 57-62) the validity of the proposition stated in this form. His unwillingness to do so without the necessary restrictions, however, and his insistence that the human experiences should in a strict sense be attributed to Jesus Christ, or to his human nature (or, as he preferred to put it, to the human prosopon [*sense A*] which the Logos appropriated for himself), rather than to the divine nature of the Logos, are by no means to be regarded as idiosyncrasies of "Nestorianism." On the contrary, Cyril himself made similar qualifications, as in his letter to John of Antioch, in which he quotes with approval the compromise Creed of 433. A passage in this document, whose orthodoxy received oecumenical confirmation at the Council of Chalcedon in 451, corresponds exactly with what Nestorius had to say on the same topic (see quotations in notes 60 and 63 *supra*): "With regard to the evangelical and apostolic texts concerning the Lord, we know that the theologians make some common as referring to one person, and distinguish others, as referring to two natures, assigning those appropriate to God to the divinity of Christ, and the humble ones to his humanity."[72a]

At the same time, granting Nestorius to have been technically correct on all these matters, we can be sure that the Chalcedonians would have been bewildered by his strange view[73] that God only "passed through the holy virgin, the

Grand à Chalcédoine," *ibid.*, 1, 345-87; Trevor Jalland, *The Life and Times of St. Leo the Great* (London, 1941), 451 ff., the best general book on Leo. Cf. Altaner, *Patrologie*, § 78,11 for further bibliography.

[72] *ACO*, 1, 1, 1, 38.21 ff.; Bindley, *op. cit.*, (note 9 *supra*), 112.205-7; P.G., 77, 116 C: ἐνὶ τοιγαροῦν προσώπῳ τὰς ἐν τοῖς εὐαγγελίοις πάσας ἀναθετέον φωνάς, ὑποστάσει μιᾷ τῇ τοῦ Λόγου σεσαρκωμένῃ. Κύριος γὰρ εἰς Ἰησοῦς Χριστός, κατὰ τὰς γραφάς. Cf. du Manoir de Juaye, *loc. cit.* (note 66 *supra*).

[72a] *ACO*, 1, 1, 4, 17. 17-20; P.G., 77, 177 AB; Bindley, *op. cit.* (note 9 *supra*), 142.61 ff.: τὰς δὲ εὐαγγελικὰς καὶ ἀποστολικὰς περὶ τοῦ Κυρίου φωνάς, ἴσμεν τοὺς θεολόγους ἄνδρας, τὰς μὲν κοινοποιοῦντας, ὡς ἐφ' ἐνὸς προσώπου, τὰς δὲ διαιροῦντας, ὡς ἐπὶ δύο φύσεων· καὶ τὰς μὲν θεοπρεπεῖς κατὰ τὴν θεότητα τοῦ Χριστοῦ, τὰς δὲ ταπεινὰς κατὰ τὴν ἀνθρωπότητα παραδιδόντας.

Approval by Chalcedon: *ACO*, 2, 1, 2, 81 [277]. 1-13. When the Illyrian and Palestinian bishops expressed doubts as to the orthodoxy of expressions of this sort, other passages were quoted from Cyril's writings to the same effect: *ibid.*, 82 [278]. 4-36; Mansi, 6, 972D. See Galtier, *loc. cit.* (note 50 *supra*), 355 f.; Sellers, *op. cit.* (note 1 *supra*), 90-95; Nestorius, *Bazaar*, 314 ff.

[73] *Bazaar*, 296. Gregory of Nazianzus had opposed this view: P.G., 37, 177C f.

'mother of Christ'," but was not born of her. They agreed with him that God did not derive the origin of his being from Mary, but they expressed this idea differently (see the Creed of 451 in note 9 *supra*). In strict justice, Nestorius can be vindicated on this point also, and he definitely avoided the Gnostic and Manichaean implications of this peculiar description of the relation of the Godhead to Mary. For the Gnostic doctrine that "Jesus passed through Mary like water through a pipe"[74] was directed against Christ's assumption of a truly human nature, which Nestorius always championed.

It is not correct, however, to say, as many do, that he was primarily concerned with the human nature of Jesus. He does, of course, lay great stress upon Christ's manhood. But he by no means neglects the divine nature. Indeed, his theory that neither of the two usiai could be mixed with the other or combined with it in its own usia was intended, among other things, to preserve the impassibility of the divine nature (see notes 59-64 *supra*). Actually, Nestorius' Christology is not characterized by preoccupation with either one of the two natures to the exclusion or detriment of the other, but rather by uncompromising insistence upon the union of both of them in Christ, in their full totality, and unimpaired.

He was the dyophysite *par excellence*, and, more than any other theologian, except possibly Theodoret of Cyrus (d. 466),[75] his friend and ally, devoted his energies to demonstrating that Jesus Christ was equally and in full measure both God and man, both human and divine. No one else championed this principle more vigorously than he, or was more forceful in denouncing the slightest deviation from it.

In view of the great merit of his theological ideas, it is all the more regrettable that he was not able to present them more skilfully. The obscurity and prolixity of his style are major defects, from which he cannot be exculpated, and explain in part why he failed to hold the favor of Emperor Theodosius II (408-50), and spent the last years of his life (from 431-*ca.* 451)[76] in agonizing exile.

[74] Irenaeus, *Against Heresies*, 3, 11, 8, ed. W. W. Harvey, *Sancti Irenaei episcopi lugdunensis libros quinque adversus haereses*, 2 (Cambridge, 1857), 42.

[75] On Theodoret, see Quasten, *Patrology*, 3, 536–54; Altaner, *Patrologie*, § 73.

[76] For the chronology, see, in addition to the works cited in note 1 *supra*, B. J. Kidd, *A History of the Church to A.D. 461*, 3 (Oxford, 1922), 267 f.; J. F. Bethune-Baker, "The Date of the Death of Nestorius," *Journal of Theological Studies*, 9 (1907-8), 601-5: Nestorius was alive at the time of the Council of Chalcedon.

Note: Special tribute should be paid to G. R. Driver, Leonard Hodgson, and François Nau (see note 1 *supra*) for their meticulous translations of the *Bazaar*, without which this essay would never have been undertaken. In my quotations therefrom, I have used square brackets to indicate words added by the translators or my own exegesis of the text.

JUSTINIAN AND THE THREE CHAPTERS CONTROVERSY

By The Rev. DEMETRIOS J. CONSTANTELOS

INTRODUCTION TO JUSTINIAN'S RELIGIOUS POLICY

Justinian was a very ambitious man. He had a diversity of interests and his plans were vast. Political strength, artistic achievements and religious fervor and learning characterized his reign.

Upon his enthronement as Emperor of the Byzantine Empire he expressed his dynamic personality through various laws and edicts of great scope and dimension that were indicative of his ambitions and interests. He dreamed of restoring the Empire to its ancient glory. But for this to be accomplished, he required and demanded unity in both the political and the religious realms. His costly wars against the Persians, Goths, Vandals and other contemporary barbarians were aimed at making the Empire as strong as it was in past centuries and at preserving its ancient prestige and might.

Notwithstanding his political ambitions, he was also very much interested in religious and ecclesiastical affairs. He was a student of the Christian Holy Scriptures[1] and as a man of his age, Justinian was absorbed in theological discussion and controversy.

Procopius, his contemporary historian, says that Justinian 'was devoting his time for the most part to the doctrines of the Christians, seeking eagerly and with great determination to make a satisfactory settlement of the questions disputed among them.'[2]

But in addition to Procopius' testimony, Justinian's *codices* and *novellæ* concerning religious and ecclesiastical matters constitute sufficient evidence.[3] A devout and sincere Orthodox Christian,

---

[1] Procopius, *The Gothic War*, VII.xxxii.9, ed. with an English translation by H. B. Dewing, Vol. 4 (Loeb Classical Library, London MCMXXIV), p. 422. Cf. A.A. Vasiliev, *History of the Byzantine Empire* (Madison, Wis., 1952), p. 149.

[2] *Wars*, 7.35.11; cf. *Wars*, 7.32.9; cf. K. Krumbacher, *History of the Byzantine Literature*, tr. from the German by G. Sotiriades, Vol. 1 (Athens, 1939), p. 89.

[3] *Vid.* Justinian's *Novellæ, Corpus Juris Civilis*, ed. by Rudolfus Schoell, Vol. 3rd (Berlin, MCMIV), Nos. III, V, VI, VII, CXXXI, pp. 18-24, 28-64, 654-676 *et al.* "33 Novels are devoted to ecclesiastical laws," J. B. Bury, *History of the Later Roman Empire*, Vol. 2 (New York, 1958), p. 361, note 4.

71

Justinian was eager to see religious unity in the Empire. It was his Christian zeal that led him to his proseletyzing activities — converting pagans to Christianity or finding means by which schismatics or heretics were brought back to the fold of the established church. He desired to bring religious uniformity to the Empire and 'finding that the belief in God was, before his time, straying into errors and being forced to go in many directions, he completely destroyed all the paths leading to such errors, and brought it about that it stood on the firm foundation of a single faith.'[4] In his edict concerning the faith of the Empire, he urged that his subjects 'should gather into one and the same church, being unanimous concerning the true belief of Christians, and withdrawing from such as affirm or entertain contrary opinions.'[5]

Justinian's notion of religious unity was not new. The Imperial policy from Constantius down advocated religious unity. 'For him the *imperium romanum* was identified with the Christian *œkoumene,* and the triumph of Christianity was as sacred a mission as the restoration of Roman supremacy.'[6] In order to bring religious unity in the Empire Justinian turned first against all forms of paganism. Since Hellenism, which was identified with paganism, was still exerting a considerable influence in learning and culture, Justinian made extensive efforts to root out paganism and he went as far as closing down even the University of Athens and restricted the teaching of 'all the impieties of the Hellenic religion.'[7] He not only proclaimed the Christian faith, urging all to embrace it as 'true faith,' but, in addition, he issued edicts condemning the instruction 'of every subject taught by teachers who suffer with the mania of the impious Hellenes.'[8]

---

[4] Procopius, *Buildings,* I.i.9. Cf. Bury, *op. cit.,* p. 361.

[5] Evagrius, *Ecclesiastical History,* ed. by J. Bidez and L. Parmentier (London, 1898), p. 198. The present translation is from Samuel Bagster's edition of *The Greek Ecclesiastical Historians,* Vol. 6 (London, MDCCXLVI), p. 249.

[6] George Ostrogorsky, *History of the Byzantine State* (New Brunswick, N. J., 1957), pp. 70-71. Also cf. Bury, *op. cit.,* p. 364.

[7] Codex Justinianus, *Corpus Juris Civilis,* ed. by Paulus Krueger, Vol. 2, 8th ed. (Berlin, MCMVI), pp. 63-64, «πάντα τὰ τῆς Ἑλληνικῆς θρησκείας ἀσεβήματα». Cf. G. Downey, 'Justinian's View of Christianity and the Greek Classics,' *Anglican Theological Review* (Jan., 1958), pp. 17-19.

[8] Codex Justinianus, *op. cit.,* p. 64, «πᾶν μάθημα παρὰ τῶν νοσούντων τὴν τῶν ἀνοσίων Ἑλλήνων μανίαν διδάσκεσθαι».

But the heathens of non-Hellenic affiliation were not in any better position. Up to the fifth century, pagans of various beliefs could still believe in their religions as long as there was no open scandal or anti-Christian propaganda. Now under Justinian they faced a new situation, for he was resolved that in his Empire there should be no diversity in religious faith. More than once he 'decided to tear them down.'[9]

In his religious policy Justinian was especially severe against the Manichæans, the Samaritans and the Montanists. In one of his codices against the Manichæans he states that 'a Manichæan should be subject to the most extreme punishment wherever he may be found upon the earth.'[10] Justinian considered them as enemies of humanity and of the state, and singled them out for severe punishment.[11] The Samaritans likewise were subject to the same treatment. Their synagogues were destroyed and together with the non-orthodox, they were deprived of various political and social rights. He writes that 'the synagogues of the Samaritans are to be destroyed and if they attempt to erect new ones they are to be punished.'[12] The Montanists and other religious confessions did not fare any better. The anti-pagan laws were applied with equal severity against them. Thus 'whatever we have already ruled against the Samaritans must be held against the Montanists, Tascodrougois and Ofitas as well.'[13]

Christian heretics and schismatics were also included in Justinian's determined plans for religious uniformity. They had proved to be more disturbing elements in the Empire than even the pagans. The Christological controversies which began in the first half of the fourth century were still feverish and the cause of much turmoil in the Christian world.

Through decrees and edicts Justinian attempted more than once to bring the heretics back into union with the Orthodox

---

[9] Procopius, *The Persian War*, 1.xix.36. Cf. John of Ephesus, *Ecclesiastical History*, Third Part, tr. by R. Payne Smith (Oxford, 1860), pp. 209, 223-229 *et al.*

[10] Codex, in *op. cit.*, p. 53, «ταῖς εἰς ἔσχατον τιμωρίαις ὑπάγεσθαι τὸν ὁπουδὴ γῆς φαινόμενον Μανιχαῖον». Cf. Bury, *op. cit.*, p. 364.

[11] A. A. Vasiliev, *Justin the First* (Cambridge, 1950), p. 246.

[12] *Ibid.*, p. 56, «αἱ τῶν Σαμαρειτῶν συναγωγαὶ καθαιροῦνται καί, ἐὰν ἄλλας ἐπιχειρήσωσι ποιῆσαι τιμωροῦνται».

[13] *Ibid.*, p. 56, «ἃ ... περὶ τῶν Σαμαρειτῶν ἐτύχομεν ἤδη νομοθετήσαντες, κρατεῖν καὶ ἐπὶ τοῖς Μοντανισταῖς καὶ Τασκοδρούγοις καὶ 'Οφίταις θεσπίζομεν».

church. In one of his encyclicals he writes that 'we have thought it pious by the present edict to warn those heretics, not only to abandon their heretical mania and so not destroy the souls of others through heresy, but also rather themselves to return to the holy Church of God where the true doctrines are taught.'[14]

When the heretics refused to return to the Orthodox church, Justinian, asserting his pontifical authority, anathematized them[15] and he even used violent means to accomplish his end. John of Ephesus mentions that Justinian persecuted the Arians[16] although the persecution was not as severe as in other cases. Justinian was extremely severe against the heresiarchs Nestorius, Eutyches and Apollinarius. Namely, he declares that 'we anathematize every heresy, even more so [we anathematize] Nestorius the worshiper of man . . . not only him but Eutyches the mentally disturbed as well . . . in a similar way [we anathematize] Apollinarius the destroyer of souls.'[17]

While Justinian was co-emperor with his uncle Justin, and still in the beginning of his reign, he also persecuted the most powerful heresy, the Monophysite. Following the Council of Chalcedon, the Monophysites exerted a great influence and attracted an ever-increasing number of followers. Justinian wrote a caustic tractate against them which indicates his early attitude.[18] It is in his later years that he inaugurates a more lenient policy toward Monophysitism. But his general religious policy is an eloquent testimony that he was against pagans and heretics alike.

The age of Justinian was a transitional age. The fifth and sixth centuries were marked by events which required that Justinian

---

[14] *Novellæ*, in *op. cit.*, p. 665, «εὐσεβὲς ἡγησάμεθα διὰ τοῦ παρόντος ἡμῶν ἰδίκτου παραινέσαι τοῖς τοιούτοις, ἐφ' ᾧ καὶ αὐτοὺς ἀποστῆναι τῆς αἱρετικῆς μανίας καὶ μηδὲ τὰς ἑτέρων ψυχὰς δι' ἀπάτης ἀπολλύναι, ἀλλὰ μᾶλλον προδραμεῖν τῇ ἁγίᾳ τοῦ Θεοῦ 'Εκκλησίᾳ ἐν ᾗ τὰ ὀρθὰ πρεσβεύεται δόγματα». Cf., Codex, *op. cit.*, p. 6. Cf. C. I. Amantos, *History of the Byzantine State*, 2nd ed., in Greek, Vol. I (Athens, 1953), pp. 226-227.

[15] *MPG*, Vol. 86, 1, pp. 1015-1019.

[16] John of Ephesus, *op. cit.*, p. 354.

[17] Codex, *op. cit.*, pp. 6-7 *et al.* «ἀναθεματίζομεν πᾶσαν αἵρεσιν, ἐξαιρέτως δὲ Νεστόριον τὸν ἀνθρωπολάτρην . . . οὐ μὴν ἀλλὰ καὶ Εὐτυχέα τὸν φρενοβλαβῆ . . . τὸν αὐτὸν δὲ τρόπον καὶ 'Απολλινάριον τὸν ψυχοφθόρον».

[18] The anti-Monophysite tractate is preserved in *MPG*, Vol. XXXVI, pp. 1103 sqq. Also it was edited in Angelo Mai, *Scriptorum Veterum Nova Collectio*, E. Vaticanis Codicibus, Vol. VII (Romæ, MDCCCXXXII), pp. 292-313.

take a firm stand in both external and internal affairs in order to preserve the stability and the survival of the Empire. The invasion of various barbaric tribes upon the Empire and the esoteric crisis of the Christian religion disturbed all the years of his dominion. Confronted with such a situation, Justinian took measures regarding the great religious diversity in the state which were not altogether without justification. His internal policy was aimed often toward the esoteric peace and unity of the Empire. Internal peace was prerequisite to successful campaigns against external hostile powers and barbarians.

As the supreme head of the Empire, Justinian's preoccupation was not confined to theoretical religious controversies, but also with the practical aspects of the state religion. The administration of ecclesiastical property, the election of bishops, the rights of the clergy, the monastic life, the episcopal jurisdiction, and other administrative problems of the church were also of vital interest to him.

It is very important that we take all these points into consideration if we are to do justice to the man when studying his stand on major theological and ecclesiastical issues such as 'The Three Chapters.'

One of his major tasks was to bring unity between the two primary Ecclesiastical Sees, Constantinople and Rome. A schism was created between these two Sees lasting 36 years as a result of Zeno's *Henoticon*.[19] Although this friction had come to an end in 518 when Justin I ascended the throne,[20] the relations between Constantinople and Rome were still very cool. Justinian renewed friendly relations with Rome and other dissatisfied parties.

But the fundamental problem that he had to resolve was to pacify and resume friendly relations with the Monophysite movement which became very powerful following the decisions of the 4th Œcumenical Council of Chalcedon. The followers of the Monophysite sect were increasing, and they were threatening the unity of the Empire. In the later years of his administration he recognized that his earlier persecutions of the Monophysites,[21] following the example of his uncle Justin, had embittered the

[19] Evagrius, Bidez-Parmentier, pp. 111-114.
[20] Vasiliev, *History of the Byzantine Empire, op. cit.,* p. 109.
[21] Bury, *op. cit.,* pp. 372-373.

people of vast regions and provinces which were of vital importance to the economic well being of the Empire.

Justinian was now eager to modify his stand leaving the door
open for their return to the fold of the one established Orthodox
church. This however could not be done at the expense of the
authority and decisions of the Council of Chalcedon. For it
would have been contrary to his own religious convictions and
at the same time would alienate the rest of Christendom which
had accepted the Council. But he did not despair of finding a
way in which he would reconcile the Monophysites with the Council of Chalcedon.

The formula Justinian utilized to ultimately bring the Monophysites into the Church was an edict of three propositions or
chapters. Fundamentally this was a camouflaged attack against
Nestorianism, the rival movement of Monophysitism. Nestorianism and Monophysitism were two Christological teachings which,
next to Arianism, disturbed the Eastern Empire for more than two
hundred years.

A. The Background of 'The Three Chapters'
Controversy

One of the first measures that Justinian undertook to establish
peaceful relations with the Monophysites was to permit the Monophysite bishops who were exiled by his uncle Justin, to return to
their sees.[22] He invited them to table talks and gave quarters
to monks of their sect in Constantinople. He addressed letters of
reconciliation to various Monophysite bishops, including the
Patriarch of Alexandria.[23]

All these attempts at compromise on the part of Justinian
were of no avail. The Monophysites refused to cooperate and
come back to the Church on the grounds that she had fallen in
heresy by embracing Nestorianism. But Nestorianism had already
been condemned by the Third Œcumenical Council. When this
fact was pointed out to them, the Monophysites answered that
the condemnation of the Council of Ephesus was not satisfactory
since it had not touched upon the theories of Nestorianism. The
Monophysites did not consider Nestorius alone as the father of

---

[22] Cf. Vasiliev, *op. cit.*, p. 151.
[23] Vasilios Stephanides, *Ecclesiastical History*, in Greek (Athens,
1948), pp. 210-211. Bury, *op. cit.*, p. 377.

Nestorianism. His teacher, Theodore of Mopsuestia, was the target of the Monophysites and, according to them, the originator of their rival heresy, namely Nestorianism.

Nestorianism was the theological controversy which took its name from Nestorius, Patriarch of Constantinople. Following the Antiochian school of theological thought and especially his teacher Theodore of Mopsuestia,[24] Nestorius taught that Christ, the eternal Logos and Son of God, was twofold in persons. Christ the God and Christ the man. Christ the man was born as a man and not as the Logos of God. Therefore, Mary, the mother of Christ the man, cannot be called Theotokos,[25] for she did not give birth to God. She is only *Christotokos*, that is, she gave birth to the man known as Christ. This teaching drew a clear distinction between the two persons in Christ and created much confusion and, what is worse, bloodshed during the fifth and sixth centuries.

According to the established teaching of the Orthodox Catholic Church, Christ the God and Christ the man were not two independent persons but one person with two natures united into a harmonious entity. Therefore, Mary rightly can be called Theotokos, for she gave birth to the God-man. The emphasis of the Orthodox was in the unity of the divine and human natures united in the one person of Christ. The relation of these two natures was that the one nature was sharing in the peculiar attributes of the other, and *vice versa*. Nevertheless, the people had been confused and divided into two groups 'some maintaining that Mary ought to be called mother of man and others mother of God.'[26] The reaction primarily came from Alexandria, the rival See of Constantinople. Whether for political or ecclesiastical reasons is still disputed.

Against this sect rose a movement of the opposite extreme known as Monophysitism. This heresy, which appeared very vigorous during the fifth and sixth centuries, chronologically is older than Nestorianism. Its seeds are found in the teaching of Apollinarius, bishop of Laodicia, in the last quarter of the fourth century. But the real champion of this heresy was Eutyches. The

---

[24] Evagrius, *op. cit.*, p. 7.
[25] *Ibid.*, p. 7.
[26] Evagrius, *op. cit.*, p. 12, «καὶ τῶν μὲν λεγόντων ἀνθρωποτόκον δεῖν τὴν Μαρίαν ὀνομάζεσθαι, τῶν δὲ θεοτόκον». Cf. Codex Justinianus, *op. cit.*, pp. 6-7.

Council of Chalcedon in 453 condemned Eutyches and Monophysitism. It is with the decisions of the Chalcedonian Council that Monophysitism revolves into the greatest religious controversy in the early Christendom.

The dogmatical formulation of Monophysitism is very comprehensively expressed by Eutyches who says: 'I proclaim that our Lord was composed of two natures before the union, but I proclaim only one nature after the union.'[27] This confession of faith claimed that before the conception of Christ in the womb of Mary, there were two natures in Him, the divine and the human. But following the conception, the human nature was assimilated by the divine, thus there was left only a divine nature in Christ. This is the main tenet of Monophysitism. There are numerous sects which were soon developed from this specific one.

The Orthodox Church condemned Monophysitism and decreed that Jesus Christ was perfect God and perfect man . . . of one substance with the Father as touching His Godhead, of one substance with us as touching His manhood . . . in two natures without confusion, without change, without distinction, without separation.[28]

Monophysitism was consolidated as a strong body with a great following in Egypt and Syria. Orthodox Christians complained that the Monophysites were more numerous than any other group, including the Orthodox Church. 'These men [the Monophysites] gather in large meetings and celebrate the communion and baptism in greater numbers than the catholic church, even if you add to it all the heresies . . .'[29] Monophysitism is of special significance for the additional reason that it attracted to its fold persons of high positions and influence in the Empire.

Justinian had the difficult task of dealing with these three factions, the Nestorians, the Monophysites and the Orthodox. We have already pointed out that he was an avowed Orthodox himself who turned practically against every form of paganism

---

[27] Evagrius, *op. cit.*, p. 17, «ὁμολογῶ ἐκ δύο φύσεων γεγενῆσθαι τὸν Κύριον ἡμῶν πρὸ τῆς ἑνώσεως, μετὰ δὲ τὴν ἕνωσιν μίαν φύσιν ὁμολογῶ».

[28] *Vide*, C. J. Hefele, *A History of the Councils of the Church*, tr. by W. R. Clark, Vol. 4 (Edinburgh, 1895), pp. 334-335. Stephanides, *op. cit.*, p. 205, and Milton Anastos, 'The Immutability of Christ and Justinian's Condemnation of Theodore of Mopsuestia,' *Dumbarton Oaks Papers*, No. 6 (Cambridge, Mass., 1951), p. 125.

[29] John of Ephesus, *op. cit.*, p. 359.

and heresy. As late as 533, he 'issued a series of bulls, addressed to the Patriarch of Constantinople and the people of all great cities of the Empire, destined to establish the truth of the true faith of Christianity against the "folie" of Nestorius and Eutyches.'[30] That is, by 533 Justinian was equally severe against all pagans and heretics. But circumstances required a change of policy. A few years later, in 546, he issued an Edict which was destined to create much dissention and frustration on many parts.

B. The Edict

The edict Justinian promulgated is known to history as the Edict of Three Chapters. This is generally understood as three propositions drawn up in the form of anathematisms. In subsequent years the edict was perverted to mean the condemned opinions.[31]

Following the Council of Chalcedon and the condemnation of Monophysitism, revolt broke out in Palestine. The people of Egypt and Syria had risen in protest to its decisions and the powerful monks in Palestine were uncompromising. Cappadocian protests were made and dissatisfaction had spread against Constantinople.[32]

Justinian inherited this situation which was getting worse because of the ever increasing numbers of Monophysites. But it was imperative that these peoples be satisfied. They constituted the frontier of the Empire and their countries were the producers of grain and food for the State. He issued the Three Chapters in the hope of satisfying them, thus preserving the internal unity. But Justinian was not the architect of this edict. He was manipulated into issuing it.

1. The Persons Behind the Edict

Theodore Ascidas, bishop of Cæsarea in Cappadocia, and Empress Theodora were two persons who exerted a great influ-

---

[30] Charles Diehl, *Justinien et la Civilisation Byzantine au VI° Siècle* (Paris, 1901), p. 335. Cf. H. S. Alivisatos, 'Die Kirchliche Gesetzgebung des Kaisers Justinian I,' *Neu Studien zur Geschichte der Theologie und der Kirche*, Vols. 17-19 (Berlin, 1913), p. 25.

[31] Hefele, *op. cit.,* p. 231; Bury, *op. cit.,* p. 384.

[32] Louis Duchesne, *Early History of the Christian Church,* tr. by C. Jenking, Vol. 3 (London, 1924), pp. 324-329.

ence upon Justinian.[33] Both wanted Justinian to take a stand against those who were opposed to the Monophysites. They thought that the condemnation of the rivals of Monophysitism, such as Nestorianism and Origenism, would bring peace to the Empire and satisfy their party.

Theodore Ascidas was an Origenist and secretly a Monophysite of the *akephalos* sect.[34] But the mood of the times was against Origen and his teachings. Justinian himself was an anti-Origenist and had written very caustically against Origen.[35] Under the advice of ecclesiastical dignitaries and through personal investigation, Justinian took action and in 543 he issued a decree condemning Origen and his theology. This edict gratified all the Patriarchs including the Pope of Rome, except Bishop Ascidas and his party. He was placed in a difficult position. His influence in the palace would be terminated and probably he would have lost his position had he refused to accept the anti-Origen edict.

Thus Ascidas invented or revived a theological question which would gratify the Monophysites and at the same time it would avert Justinian's preoccupation with Origen.[36]

Theodora warmly approved of Ascidas' plan. She herself was a Monophysite. It was her ambition to promote Monophysitism and to protect its adherents from the consequences of Justinian's anti-heretic laws. She procured the election of a Monophysite Patriarch and had another living in concealment in her own palace.[37]

Ascidas, with the consent and assistance of Theodora, persuaded Justinian that the Monophysite problem could be dealt with on other lines. Unity of the Church and satisfaction of the Monophysites in Egypt, Syria and Cappadocia could be accomplished by anathematizing for Nestorianism Theodore of Mopsuestia, whose writings were more offensive to the Monophysites than anything else. He was esteemed as the theorist of Nestori-

---

[33] Evagrius, *op. cit.*, p. 187. Cf. Procopius, *The Persian War*, 11.xxv. 4-5.

[34] Hefele, *op. cit.*, p. 241. Cf. W. G. Holmes, *The Age of Justinian and Theodora*, Vol. 2 (London, 1907), p. 679.

[35] *MPG*, Vol. 86.1, pp. 946-991.

[36] W. H. Hutton, *The Church of the Sixth Century* (London, 1897), pp. 163-164. Cf. B. J. Kidd, *The Churches of Eastern Christendom* (London, 1927), p. 42.

[37] Bury, *op. cit.*, p. 377.

anism. But in addition to Theodore, certain writings of Theodoret of Cyrrhus and a letter addressed to Maris by Ibas, bishop of Edessa were included in the items of condemnation.[38] Evagrius says that while others '. . . mooted the question relating to Origen . . . Theodore of Cappadocia, with a view to divert them from this point, introduces the subject of Theodore of Mopsuestia, Theodoret, and Ibas . . .'[39] Justinian followed the advice of Ascidas and his protegé Empress Theodora and promulgated the Edict of Three Chapters against (1) Theodore of Mopsuestia and his writings, (2) Specified works of Theodoretus of Cyrrhus, and (3) The letter of Ibas.

The edict has not been preserved except three fractions of it, but another edict of 551 contains a similar text but in a different form.[40] It may read as follows: '. . . we condemn and anathematize (a) Theodore, styled bishop of Mopsuestia, and his impious writings; also (b) whatever has been impiously written by Theodoret against the right faith, against the twelve chapters of the Sainted Cyril, and against the first holy Synod at Ephesus and all that he has written in defense of Theodore [Mopsuestia] and Nestorius. We further anathematize (c) the impious epistle said to have been written by Ibas to Maris the Persian . . .'[41]

2. The Persons Involved

The persons involved in the religious controversy under discussion belong to the Antiochian School of theological thought. Antioch and Alexandria were two of the predominant centers of letters and theological opinion and there was a kind of antagonism between the two.[42] In regards to Christology, suffice it to say that these schools opposed each other. While the Antiochian theologians were interested in proving that in the person of Christ there were two natures, the Alexandrians worked to show that in Christ there was only one person.[43]

---

[38] Amantos, op. cit., p. 231.

[39] Evagrius, Bidez-Parmentier, p. 187, «. . . τὰ κατὰ 'Ωριγένην πρωτοτύπως ἐκίνουν . . . Θεόδωρος δὲ ὁ Καππαδόκης, ἑτέρωθεν τούτους ἀφέλκειν ἐθέλων, ἐπεισάγει τὰ κατὰ Θεόδωρον τὸν Μοψουεστίας καὶ Θεοδώρητον καὶ "Ιβαν». Together with Theodore Ascidas and Theodora, Anthimos, Patriarch of Constantinople, favored Monophysitism but he was removed from the See of Constantinople soon.

[40] Stephanides, op. cit., p. 215, note 13.

[41] MPG, Vol. 86.1, p. 1041; Evagrius, op. cit., p. 188.

[42] R. V. Sellers, The Council of Chalcedon (London, 1953), p. 3.

[43] Stephanides, op. cit., p. 194.

a. Theodore of Mopsuestia (350-428)

This man was the target of the Origenists and the Monophysites alike. His teachings became the real foundation of Nestorianism, thus the explanation why the Monophysites had a special reason to hate him. In fact, Theodore was the head of the Antiochian School of theological thought.[44] As a close friend of John Chrysostom and a man with vast education,[45] he attracted the attention of Theodosios II and came to exercise a great influence in the Imperial court and in Byzantine letters in general. He died in peace with the church and his memory was respected for a while.

The denunciation of Theodore[46] begins with the exposition of the Nestorian doctrine. Although Nestorius did not expound an original theory, it was he who drew first the attention of the church about the duophysitic dogma. Around 438 Cyril of Alexandria took issue with Nestorius but he condemned Theodore, his teacher, as the real theorist of Nestorianism.[47] When Nestorius was accused of heresy he very proudly retorted that Theodore of Mopsuestia was his chief doctor, pointing especially to the fact that he had never been condemned.[48]

Theodore's doctrinal position is summed up in his own words as follows: 'We declare that the nature of the God Logos is perfect and perfect is his personality, likewise we declare that both his human nature and human personality are perfect.'[49] That is, two perfect natures in two perfect persons, in God the Logos. The Monophysites, however, following the Platonic doctrine about the nature of man, claimed that 'two perfect natures cannot be united into one.'[50] Thus the friction.

---

[44] J. Tixeront, *A Handbook of Patrology*, tr. by S. A. Raemers (London, 1957), pp. 197-198. For Theodore's Christology *vide*, Anastos, *op. cit.*, pp. 132 ff. and H. M. Diepen, *Les Trois Chapitres au Concile de Chalcedoine* (Oosterhout, 1953), pp. 20-30.

[45] Hefele, *op. cit.*, p. 233.

[46] Earliest reliable information about Theodore is found in two letters, *Ad Theodorum lapsum*, MPG, lxvii, pp. 277-316.

[47] Cf. Tixeront, *op. cit.*, p. 198.

[48] Hutton, *op. cit.*, p. 164.

[49] Stephanides, *op. cit.*, p. 194.

[50] Stephanides, *op. cit.*, p. 191. The Orthodox teaching was that «τὸν ἄνθρωπον ἐκ ψυχῆς νοερᾶς καὶ σώματος ἄριστα κατεσκευάσθαι». Nemesius, MPG, Vol. 40, p. 504. For a fresh discussion of Theodore's Christology see, John S. Romanides, 'Highlights in the Debate over Theodore Mopsu-

Nevertheless, Justinian condemned Theodore not exclusively on the basis of his Nestorianism but because of Ascidas' influence upon him. Theodore was hated by the Origenists and Ascidas disliked him and his writings.

b. Theodoretus of Cyrrhus (393-457?)

Theodoretus is described as the most learned man of the Antiochian School of theology. Nestorius was his fellow student and probably Theodore of Mopsuestia was his master. He was one of the staunchest supporters of Nestorius during the Third Œcumenical Council, and a vehement opponent to Cyril of Alexandria and the Christology of Alexandrian theology. In 438 he undertook to defend the memory and writings of Theodore of Mopsuestia against the attacks of Cyril. Though Theodoretus had anathematized Nestorius[51] in the Council of Chalcedon and had died in peace with the church, the Monophysites and especially Ascidas brought the attention of Justinian upon him because of his 12 anathematisms against Cyril. The latter was considered a champion of the Orthodox faith and all written against Cyril deserved anathema.

In the 'Three Chapters' the condemnation is confined on the writings of Theodoret against Cyril, his writings for Nestorius and against the Synod of Ephesus.[52]

c. Ibas of Edessa (— d. 457)

Ibas' name was mentioned in the Three Chapter controversy because in Syria he was one of the most influential persons. He was associated with the Antiochian School of theology and he was an admirer and follower of Theodore of Mopsuestia and Nestorius. The Monophysites in Syria disliked Ibas[53] on account of his associations and his ideas and, in addition, for Ibas' zeal in spreading the Nestorian heresy in all the Orient by means of the

estia's Christology and Some Suggestions for a Fresh Approach,' *The Greek Orthodox Theological Review*, Vol. v, No. 2, pp. 140-185.

[51] Hefele, *op. cit.*, p. 236.

[52] N. Bonwetsch, 'Theodoret,' *The New Schaff-Herzog Encyclopedia of Religious Knowledge, op. cit.*, p. 324 and Hefele, *op. cit.*, p. 232. For Theodoretus' role in the Christological controversies, see Diepen, *op. cit.*, pp. 75-90.

[53] For more information about Ibas' role in the Monophysite-Nestorian controversy, see Sellers, *op. cit.*, pp. 49-56 and Diepen, *op. cit.*, pp. 90-106.

writings of Theodore Mopsuestia, which he translated into
Syriac.[54]

Ibas wrote a letter to Maris in which the history of Nestorianism and the views of the author about it are developed.[55] He
used unfavorable language of Cyril and because of its importance
the letter was included by the Monophysites in the works for
condemnation.[56]

It is evident that all three persons involved in this controversy
belong to the school of Antioch, which was especially obnoxious
to the Monophysites. All three, however, had died in peace with
the church and the decisive Council of Chalcedon did not condemn the memory or the name of any one. And yet, under the
circumstances Justinian issued the Three Chapter Edict in the
hope that the chief stumbling-block that the Monophysites found
in the Council of Chalcedon would be removed.

3. The Motives Behind the Edict

But what were Justinian's own motives for issuing the Three
Chapters edict? Were they simply political or at the same time
religious? Certain historians emphasize the political aspect with
practically no room for religious consideration.

Justinian, they argue, desired to retain the powerful Monophysites in the Empire. Above all he was an Emperor, willing to
do anything in order to preserve the unity of the Empire. Egypt
and Syria at this time were extremely important to the Empire;
to let them go just because of a religious controversy already 150
years old seemed unwise. Therefore, with haste he promulgated
the edict with the prospect of winning the Monophysite party over
to his side. These historians explain history on economic bases
only. They claim that what really mattered was the financial wel-
fare of the State and the preservation of the sources of food and
wealth such as Syria, Egypt and Armenia. Vasiliev observes that
'the historians who emphasize the political side of Justinian's
activities claim that the chief motive in his Cæsaropapism was a
desire to make secure his political power, to strengthen the government, and to find religious support for the throne which he had

---

[54] E. Nestle, 'Ibas,' The New Schaff-Herzog Encyclopedia of Religious
Knowledge, op. cit., Vol. v, p. 435.
[55] It is preserved in Mansi, Concilia, vii, p. 241.
[56] Cf. Duchesne, op. cit., p. 309.

procured by chance.'[57] These historians fail to see that Justinian was truly a religious man, fond of participating in religious discussions and hyperbolically anxious to establish Orthodox Christianity throughout his vast State.

On the one hand, Justinian promoted good relations, and he even flattered the popes of Rome, in order to have them subservient to his political ambitions. On the other hand, his political plans in the Eastern borders of the Empire required the pacification of the disturbed Monophysites and their satisfaction with the Court. Thus the emphasis on the political motives of the edict.[58]

Political motives alone cannot be accepted as the sole basis for the issuance of the Three Chapters edict. This would be acceptable without any reservation if Justinian were not a religious man. It is beyond doubt, as we point out in the introduction of the present paper, that he was a religious man by conviction. His theological interests, his religious life, his ecclesiastical legislation prove beyond dispute his religious character. In fact, one of his early duties, upon his elevation to the throne, was to uphold the disputed synod of Chalcedon 'and what was put forth by it.'[59] His tone in his religious discourses sounds like that of a zealous Christian who is convinced that 'Christ our Lord' was the eternal Logos and the Saviour of man.

It is difficult to disassociate a man of such a religious character from religious motives in a dispute like the Three Chapters. Justinian, indeed, had political reasons to preserve the unity of the Empire, but he also had religious motives to secure the unity of the established church. Religious unity was of primary concern to Justinian. The persecutions against pagans and heretics, though they cannot be sanctioned, indicate his endeavors to bring religious conformity. Ostrogorsky comments that 'he was . . . a Christian ruler filled with the consciousness of the Divine source of his imperial authority. His strivings towards the achievement of a universal Empire were based on Christian, as well as on Roman, conceptions . . . the triumph of Christianity was as sacred a mission as the restoration of Roman supremacy.[60]

He intervened in the affairs of the church with extreme meas-

---

[57] Vasiliev, *op. cit.*, p. 150. Cf. Stephanides, *op. cit.*, p. 210; *ibid.*, p. 194.
[58] Cf. Krumbacher, *op. cit.*, p. 89.
[59] Evagrius, *op. cit.*, p. 160.
[60] Ostrogorsky, *op. cit.*, pp. 70-71.

ures. Nevertheless, he was sincere in his idea of unity in the Christian religion,[61] according to which Orthodoxy was the only salvation not only for the individual but for the State as well.[62] He specifically states that: 'We believe the true and immaculate Christian faith to be the first and greatest gift that men can enjoy.'[63]

While he had religious motives to hold fast the religious unity of the Empire, he nevertheless used religion to promote his political goals. His religious convictions led him to encourage the spread of Christianity among the neighboring barbarians but with the additional motive of acquiring their friendship and securing peace.

Thus political expediency went hand in hand with religious motives. This combination was in accordance with his character and Cæsaropapistic convictions. Under this light we ought to understand his stand against the persons or the writings involved in the edict of the Three Chapters.

Like previous edicts, the Three Chapters was issued with no due consultation of any Synod.[64] The opinion of religious dignitaries was requested following the issuance. This caused much dissatisfaction among the religious leaders.

C. REACTION FROM THE CHURCH

The Church both in the East and the West found in the person of Justinian a protector as well as a master, 'for though Christian, he remained a Roman to whom the conception of any autonomy in the religious sphere was alien.'[65] Consistent with his convictions, Justinian treated both Patriarchs and Popes as his subordinates and often he would act arbitrarily in ecclesiastical matters without consulting either one. He followed this tactic, too, at the issuance of the Three Chapters.

---

[61] D. A. Zakynthinos, *Byzantion, State and Society: A Historical Review*, in Greek (Athens, 1951) pp. 84-85.

[62] Cf. Amantos, *op. cit., p.* 224.

[63] Novel 132, *op. cit.,* p. 665, «πρῶτον εἶναι καὶ μέγιστον ἀγαθὸν πᾶσιν ἀνθρώποις πιστεύομεν τὴν τῆς ἀληθοῦς καὶ ἀμωμήτου τῶν Χριστιανῶν πίστεως ὀρθὴν ὁμολογίαν».

[64] Amantos, *op. cit.,* p. 231. Cf. Francis Dvornik, 'Emperors, Popes, and General Councils,' *Dumbarton Oaks Papers,* No. 6 (Cambridge, Mass., 1951), p. 21.

[65] Ostrogorsky, *op. cit.,* p. 71.

Nevertheless, Justinian met with opposition from the Church. His condemnation of Theodore and his writings, as well as his censorship of the other two parties under discussion, meant a challenge and a repudiation of the Council of Chalcedon which did not take any condemnatory action against them. Thus his demand that the Three Chapters edict be signed by all Patriarchs, including the Pope of Rome, and other bishops, could not be accomplished easily.

The ecclesiastical leaders on previous occasions had accepted Justinian's edicts, such as that against Origen in 543,[66] without opposition but now they refused to sign the Three Chapters. They were aware of the implications involved in such a move. The Council of Chalcedon had been well received by the public. It is safe to say that, in general, the edict did not receive recognition by the Church. The reaction came from both East and West.

1. Reaction from the East

Menas, Patriarch of Constantinople, was unwilling to accept or sign the edict. An act of consent and acceptance of the edict was contrary to his Chalcedonian principles. He refused to reopen any question which could weaken the authority of the Chalcedonian Council. Furthermore, it would vindicate the position of the Monophysites and imply that even the previous councils could be disputed. In addition, it was unprecedented in the history of the church to condemn the dead who could not speak and defend themselves. Thus at first Menas refused to cooperate.[67]

It was the crafty policy of Justinian that eventually induced Menas to sign it. He was promised by the Emperor that all bishops and patriarchs would follow, including the bishop of Rome. Menas was careful not to do anything which would bring another schism in the church. Justinian seemed to favor the Church of Rome and the Patriarch was careful not to give an opportunity for friction with the Pope which could put him in an unfavorable position.[68]

---

[66] Cf. Stephanides, op. cit., pp. 212-214 and Bury, op. cit., p. 383.

[67] Vasiliev is arbitrary and fails to present concrete evidence in support of his assertion that 'the eastern church was willing to accept the decree and condemn the Three Chapters,' op. cit., p. 152.

[68] Cf. James Bryce, 'Justinianus,' A Dictionary of Christian Biography, ed. by W. Smith and H. Wace, Vol. 3 (London, 1882), p. 547.

The Patriarchs Zoilus of Alexandria, Ephraim of Antioch and Peter of Jerusalem were strong Chalcedonians and certainly they did not want to take a course contrary to Chalcedon. At first, they refused to subscribe to the edict but eventually they followed the example of Menas. The evidence points to the fact that they succumbed under threats of deposition and the cunning ways of Justinian.

There are data which indicate that these Patriarchs accepted the edict and signed it because they were wholly dependent on the State. They were men of wealth and rich sees and, therefore, unwilling to sacrifice them under the threats of Justinian. Nevertheless, we must be hesitant and cautious not to draw any conclusions as to their motives because the data are given by hostile sources, Facundus, the African bishop of Ermione.

Following the example of the four leading Eastern Patriarchs, many bishops in Syria, Egypt, Greece, Asia Minor, etc., fell into Justinian's trap.[69]

2. Reaction in the West

The West was moving slowly but steadily away from the East. Following the Acacian Schism, relations between East and West were still cool and the Church of Rome was not so much under the direct interference and influence of Justinian and the court.[70] Thus the spirit of compliance was less. The bishops of Italy, Gaul and Dalmatia resisted the edict. Vigilius, the newly elected Pope of Rome, refused to accept it on the grounds that he was not consulted about it.[71] Justinian commanded him to come to Constantinople, for he was determined to have all bishops sign it. Vigilius refused to go to Constantinople. But whether willingly or by force, he went to the capital around 547,[72] having spent nearly a year in Sicily on his way. He received a cordial welcome by Justinian and took up residence in the Placidia palace.

---

[69] Modern historians agree that all the Eastern Patriarchs at first were unwilling to subscribe to the Three Chapters. *Vide*, Hefele, *op. cit.*, pp. 244-245; Hutton, *op. cit.*, p. 167; Bury, *op. cit.*, p. 384; Stephanides, *op. cit.*, p. 215.

[70] Cf. Bryce, *op. cit.*, p. 547.

[71] Amantos, *op. cit.*, p. 231.

[72] Procopius, B. G. 111, 16.1. He arrived μηνὶ φεβρουαρίῳ according to Malalas, not on January as Bury says, *op. cit.*, p. 345, note 2. *Vide*, Ioannes Malalas, *Chronographia*, ed by B. G. Niebuhr, *Corpus Scriptorum Historiæ Byzantinai* (Bonn, MDCCCXXXIC), p. 483.

Almost one year later, Vigilius was manipulated by the pressure of Justinian and Theodora to issue his Judicatum wherein he deliberately condemned Theodore and his writings together with the other writings mentioned in the Three Chapters. He was cautious, however, not to diminish the authority of Chalcedon.

Vigilius created consternation, and the ecclesiastical opinion of the West turned against him.

From the very beginning the bishops of Africa led the opposition to the edict. Facundus, Bishop of Hermione, Dacius, Archbishop of Milan, were strong opponents. Facundus published a treatise *Pro defensione trium capitulorum*,[73] in which he attacked Justinian's edict. Being mostly Chalcedonians, the African bishops convened in a Synod and condemned Vigilius, dissolving communion with him.

The African attitude as well as that of his own jurisdiction in the West confused Vigilius even more. His was a difficult part to play. For while he was pressed by and afraid of the Emperor, he was deeply concerned about the western opinion. This explains why his behavior was inconsistent as he tried to please both parties. Under the pressure of the western opinion he recalled his condemnatory Judicatum in order to avert a schism with the West.

But the Pope took a more definite position against the Emperor when Justinian issued another edict in 551 against the three Christian teachers. This was addressed to the whole Christian world under the title of Confession of Faith.[74] Vigilius refused to subscribe to it and to avoid the consequences of Justinian's wrath took refuge in a church.

The dissensions that were created at the issuance of the second edict persuaded Justinian that the summoning of a general council was the only solution. He called the Fifth Œcumenical Council in 553 without consulting the Patriarchs or any ecclesiastical leader. Invitations were extended to bishops of all parts of the Empire. But none came from the western regions of Gaul, Spain, Illyricum and Dalmatia.

---

[73] The treatise composed of twelve books has not been preserved except some fragments, Mansi, *op. cit.*, pp. 104-105, 181.

[74] It has been preserved as «Ὁμολογία πίστεως Ἰουστινιανοῦ Αὐτοκράτορος», Mansi, *op. cit.*, pp. 537-582. *Vide*, Hefele, *op. cit.*, pp. 269-278.

3. The Fifth Œcumenical Council

By the year 553 new faces had occupied the sees of the Eastern Patriarchates. Eutychius succeeded Menas on the throne of Constantinople, Apollinarius was the Patriarch of Alexandria, Domminus of Antioch and Eustochios of Jerusalem while Vigilius was still Pope of Rome.[75] In addition to 3 patriarchs, 162 bishops, 165 in all,[76] came to Constantinople for the Council. The Patriarch of Jerusalem was represented by three bishops. Vigilius refused to attend though 'he gave his assent in writing to the assembling of the Synod.'[77]

The Synod opened by the reading of a letter from the Emperor addressed to the convocation. It described the aim of Justinian at settling religious controversies following the example of previous Emperors.[78] He inquired of the bishops as to what was their opinion about Theodore and his writings, the twelve expressions of Theodoret against Cyril as well as the epistle of Ibas to Maris.[79]

Justinian succeeded in his purpose to confirm the essence of his Three Chapters edict.[80] Evagrius relates that 'after the reading of many passages of Theodore and Theodoret, and proof given that Theodore had been long ago condemned . . . they [the bishops] unanimously anathematize Theodore, and what had been advanced by Theodoret against the twelve chapters of Cyril and the right faith; as also the epistle of Ibas to Maris, the Persian . . .'[81]

Although the Synod dealt with other religious problems, such

---

[75] Evagrius, op. cit., book 4, ch. 38.

[76] Mansi, op. cit., v. 9, p. 656.

[77] Ibid., p. 239. Cf. Bury, op. cit., p. 389. Photius says that «παρὼν μὲν τῇ πόλει, οὐ παρὼν δὲ τῇ συνόδῳ, ὡς εἰ καὶ μὴ πρόθυμος εἰς τὴν συνδρομὴν τῆς ἱερᾶς ὁμηγύρεως κατέστη. 'Αλλ' οὐδὲν ἔλαττον ὅμως τὴν κοινὴν τῶν πατέρων πίστιν ἐπεκύρου λιβέλλῳ». Mansi, op. cit., v. 9, p. 656.

[78] Hefele, op. cit., p. 298.

[79] Evagrius, op. cit., p. 239; Bury, op. cit., p. 389.

[80] Amantos, op. cit., p. 232.

[81] Evagrius, op. cit., p. 239 and Mansi, where we read: «Εἴ τις ἀντιποιεῖται Θεοδώρου τοῦ ἀσεβοῦς τοῦ Μοψουεστίας ... καὶ τῶν ἀσεβῶν αὐτοῦ συγγραμμάτων ... εἴ τις ἀντιποιεῖται τῶν ἀσεβῶν συγγραμμάτων Θεοδωρήτου τῶν κατὰ τῆς ἀληθοῦς πίστεως ... εἴ τις ἀντιποιεῖται τῆς ἐπιστολῆς τῆς λεγομένης παρὰ "Ιβα γεγράφθαι πρὸς Μάριν τὸν Πέρσην ... ἀνάθεμα ἔστω». Op. cit., v. 9, pp. 348-388.

as the Origenists,[82] it can be concluded safely that it was summoned primarily to confirm Justinian's two edicts against the three Christian teachers.[83] His victory was indicative of his cæsaropapic power and proved that, indeed, he could exercise his claim that he was the guide of the church. He demanded that the decrees of this Synod be obligatory and he threatened the bishops who did not agree with the condemnation of the Three Chapters.

Pope Vigilius, upon his refusal to sign the proceedings of the Council, was exiled. But eventually he did sign the condemnation and was permitted to return to his see. He died on his way to Rome.

D. THE RESULTS OF THE CONDEMNATION

The question is whether Justinian succeeded in uniting the Monophysites with the Orthodox Church. He undertook a long and intense religious policy expecting 'to win the adherence of the heretics . . . to the Council of Chalcedon,'[84] but he did not succeed. The Fifth Œcumenical Council, which brought final condemnation upon Theodore and his writings, as well as the twelve propositions of Theodoret and the letter of Maris, caused a schism in the West and failed to unite the Monophysites with the State Church and bring peace in the East.

1. In the West

Vigilius was repudiated by the western bishops for his consenting to sign the condemnation. Consistent with their original attitude against Justinian's edict of the Three Chapters, the bishops of Africa, Italy and Illyricum broke off relations with the Church of Rome. They refused to accept the decrees of the Council and their separation from the Roman Church lasted until the end of the sixth century.[85] The leadership in Italy was taken by Milan and Aquileia which would know nothing of the decisions. Milan resumed communion with Rome for political reasons only while the diocese of Aquileia maintained its schism 'for more than a hundred and forty years.'[86] It was with Gregory the Great, around 600, that the Council of 553 was recognized in the West as an œcumenical council.[87]

---

[82] Evagrius, op. cit., pp. 240-241.
[83] Bury, op. cit., p. 392.
[84] Procopius, Anecdota, ed. by H. B. Dewing, xvii, 5.
[85] Vasiliev, op. cit., p. 153.
[86] Bury, op. cit., p. 391.
[87] Vasiliev, op. cit., p. 153.

2. In the East

Justinian seems to have been the loser all the way. In vain he initiated such an extensive religious struggle. The real cause of the Monophysite disatisfaction must be sought elsewhere. Their refusal to unite with the Church in the East sprung not from their hatred towards the three religious teachers but from other sources. Despite the great concessions by the Council of 553 on their behalf, the Monophysites did not seem satisfied. Thus both objects of Justinian's ecclesiastical policy, the maintenance of the doctrine of Chalcedon and the reconciliation of the Monophysites, failed in the East.[88]

The regions of Syria and Egypt were unhappy under the Byzantine banner. They were developing separatistic tendencies and were waiting for the opportunity to express their national hatred against the Empire. Religious dissensions offered an excellent opportunity to revive their national traditions and free themselves from Constantinople. 'The native population of Egypt was the bulwark of Monophysitism in that country. It understood none of the abtruse metaphysical tenets of that sect, but it found in it a useful instrument through which to express its nationalistic and anti-imperial tendencies.'[89] This was true at the reign of Zeno and Anastasius, and it could safely be true in Justinian's age,[90] approximately fifty years later.

CONCLUSION

It becomes evident that the Three Chapters Edict and the condemnation of three brilliant writers like Theodore, Theodoret and Ibas was a failure on the part of the Emperor, unwise and a grave mistake on the part of the Christian Church. Justinian apparently fell in the trap that Ascidas and Theodora had prepared for him. It was only very unfortunate that the Church, instead of guiding Justinian away from the scheme, was herself led by him into it.

Justinian and the Church failed to understand the real psychology of the masses of Syria and Egypt. The attitude of the natives

[88] Stephanides, *op. cit.*, p. 218.

[89] Peter Charanis, *Church and State in the Later Roman Empire* (Madison, Wis., 1939), p. 16.

[90] Cf. Amantos, *op. cit.*, p. 232 and Charles Diehl, *History of the Byzantine Empire*, tr. by G. B. Ives (Princeton, N. J., MCMXXV), p. 34.

of these lands towards the Greek and Roman world did not originate during the fifth or the sixt century. It had begun long before that. There are indications of a general revival of nationalism in Egypt with the beginnings of Christianity during the first century after Christ and even earlier under the Ptolemaic dynasty. The Greeks with their notion towards non-Greeks, considering them 'barbarians,' and the Romans with their 'favour shown . . . to Hellenic culture and the policy of differentiation between Greeks and Egyptians, by throwing the latter back upon their own separate way of life strengthened nationalist feeling'[91] and gave new life to the Egyptians long before Justinian's time.

Justinian was wrong in thinking that religion alone could close the gap that separated Egypt and Syria from the Empire. Dr. Downey advances the theory that 'lack of educational opportunity and effort may be the answer'[92] to the question of the gap between Egypt and the Empire. The natives were illiterate and could not understand theological and ambiguous terminology. Since the days of Anthony the Great and the other monks of the second and third centuries, the Egyptians had come to understand that they were the heirs of the simple faith of Christ. They participated with bitter passion in Christological issues with the feeling that they were preserving the true belief.

Thus the new terminology that was used by Leontius of Byzantium[93] and the Fifth Œcumenical Council under Justinian could not pacify them. Instead, an additional opportunity was presented to inflame nationalism and anti-Imperial policy. Monophysitism became, especially for the natives, a national creed and contributed to national solidarity.

The situation in Syria and Armenia bore similarity to that in Egypt. The dissatisfaction of Syria with the Empire did not begin with the condemnation of Monophysitism. In fact it had begun with the decisions of Ephesus and the condemnation of Nestorianism. Though Syria and Egypt stood apart theologically, now common hostility against Constantinople brought them together.

Like Egypt, Syria was anti-imperial in character and was de-

---

[91] H. Idris Bell, *Cults and Creeds in Græco-Roman Egypt* (Liverpool, 1953), p. 66.
[92] Glanville Downey, 'Coptic Culture in the Byzantine World: Nationalism and Religious Independence,' *Greek and Byzantine Studies* (October, 1958), p. 134.
[93] Cf. B. J. Kidd, *op. cit.,* p. 45.

veloping her own national and religious character.[94] Antioch, proud of its glorious past in Christian letters, was unwilling to yield to, and envious of, the leadership of Constantinople. Monophysitism was adopted also in Armenia as a means to defend its nationalism.

Thus nationalism, illiteracy, racial antagonisms and hostility against the Imperial government since earlier days, contributed to the failure of Justinian's attempts to reconcile the Monophysites of Egypt, Syria and Armenia and unite them with the established Orthodox Church. His attitude towards the persons identified as the Three Chapters is little to his credit and even less to the credit of the Church,[95] which proved subservient to Justinian's policies. The Three Chapters Edict perpetuated a superfluous and a harmful dispute which did not heal the breach, but, to the contrary, contributed to much dissatisfaction and more schisms.

---

[94] Cf. E. L. Woodward, *Christianity and Nationalism in the Later Roman Empire* (London, 1916), pp. 47-48.

[95] Cf. John S. Romanides, *op. cit.*, p. 185.

RUTGERS—THE STATE UNIVERSITY

The Origin of the Monophysite Church
in Syria and Mesopotamia

Arthur Vööbus

The earliest extant sources of Syrian Christianity reveal a powerful spirit of self-consciousness for independence. This desire is imprinted on every page of the historical records. That which stands at the very forefront of Tatian's thought[1] is profoundly instructive for our purposes: it is his dislike, nay more his hatred, fore everything bearing a Greek or Roman label. This spirit shows itself in whatever direction we look. Syrian gnosis is the least hellenized of all. The pattern of Christian life carries its own attributes of sovereignty in every respect. Autonomy is the hallmark of the early Syrian conception of the church. Theological thought travels along quite independent lines in accord with that genius—even in the works of Aphrahat[2] written decades after the Council of Nicea.

Later history of Christianity in Syria and Mesopotamia is comprehensible only if we take into account those factors which excited the stimuli for the development which ended with the nationalization of the church of the Syrians. The main elements concern the ethnic, cultural, religio-sociological and social areas —though this does not exhaust all the factors involved.

Ethnically we are confronted by a phenomenon stimulated by strong impulses to forge a route of its own. This passion is an essential ingredient in the Syrian psyche. It is an order of rapture which can be perceived in literary sources as well as in the frescoes of early Syrian provenance in which pictures of the screaming and over plus-dimensional figures of the Syrian deities are on view.[3] The flames of fury nearly scorch the parchment in the polemical writings of Ephrem, Ishaq, Rabbula and others. The fervor of fanaticism[4] leaps out of the hagiographical sources, and the searing lava of mortification of every conceivable kind virtually scalds the works in which such accounts are recorded.

In the cultural field we meet a constellation which can only evoke our admiration. The destiny of the idiom of Edessa, the metropolis of Mesopotamia, after it was adopted as the vehicle for the Christian community, is little short of amazing. Astounding is the élan of the Syriac language. As the idiom for the literary life, it had the power to absorb all other dialects; even a language like that of Palmyra—widely used in the third century—could not retain its identity in the face of this tongue. A steady and ambitious growth towards the stature of a literary language of the world marks this idiom.[5]

Allied with this was the surge of sources to enrich the literary life. Like

1. See A. Vööbus, *History of Asceticism in the Syrian Orient: A Contribution to the History of Culture in the Near East*, I (Louvain, 1958), CSCO Subsidia, 14, pp. 31ff.
2. See A. Vööbus, "Methodologisches zum Studium der Anweisungen Aphrahats," *Oriens Christianus*, 46 (1962), pp. 25ff.
3. See A. Vööbus, *History of Asceticism in the Syrian Orient*, II (Louvain, 1960), CSCO Subsidia, 17, pp. 314f.
4. *Ibid.*, pp. 256ff, 292ff.
5. It is with awe and pride that the Syrians at the high-water mark of this advance became convinced that God himself spoke Syriac.

Mr. Vööbus is professor of church history in the Lutheran School of Theology at Chicago.

an artesian well, they began to flow and that abundantly. It is astounding how eagerly the Syrians grasped hold of these works. They began to translate almost everything they could lay hold of with a zeal that is probably without parallel. Original creations were stimulated soon to join in the stream of works which fed and enriched the intellectual culture.[6] In turn, the national self-consciousness was excited by these new and positive stimuli.

The emergence of the loci of higher studies certainly gave added impetus to these endeavors. Once the torch of learning was ignited in Edessa, it impressed itself upon the intellectual and cultural climate throughout the Syrian Orient. A recent work on the School of Nisibis[7] describes the impact of this achievement in such areas as schooling, higher education, literary life, scholarly endeavors and mission work. Centers of higher education emerged in Edessa, Homs, Qenneshre, Tell Ade, Pesiltha, Mar Zakkai and elsewhere. This network delineates a most important milestone in the progressive advance in the intellectual arena. It is impossible to underestimate the impact of this development upon the Syrian self-consciousness.

We must also touch upon the religio-sociological area. This concerns the spectacular growth of monasticism in Syria and Mesopotamia during the fourth and fifth centuries. The rapidity of this advance spilling over from monasteries to caves and clefts in the mountains is truly surprising.[8] Special significance must accordingly be attached to this phenomenon in the history of Syrian spirituality.

The attendant consequences were far-reaching. In the light of the immense veneration of the ascetics and monks by the religious masses, it is not difficult to understand why the care of souls gradually fell into the hands of the monks. Indeed other sectors of the pastoral office also came under their control. The role which monasticism actually played in the religion of the Syrians is thus properly highlighted. It begins to dawn upon us that monasticism exercised extraordinary functions in that society.[9]

In view of such first-rate factors it suffices only to glance momentarily at the social conditions of the time as revealed by our sources. Abuse on the part of the administration was reckless. The peasantry particularly suffered very hard. Economic conditions, poor at best, were aggravated the more by additional hardships. The garrisons located in the communities and travelling functionaries caused endless bitterness with their exorbitant demands and chicanery in regard to food, lodging and so on. Abuse practiced freely by local administration caused deep resentment and affront not soon to be forgotten.

It is only when we take these factors into consideration that we begin to perceive the forces operative in the Syrian Orient embracing Monophysitism. These are the reasons why within a short time Monophysitism[10] was no longer merely a protest against the Chalcedonians but became a developed doctrine, a movement with its own content and a separate church which did not hope for anything from the Byzantine emperors nor from the Byzantine church.

If we are to understand the position of Christianity in Syria and Mesopotamia during the fateful period under the Emperor Justinian, we must take a look, however briefly, at the events leading up to and contemporaneous with

6. See A. Vööbus, *History of Syriac Literature*, I (in press).
7. A. Vööbus, *History of the School of Nisibis* (Louvain, 1965), CSCO Subsidia, 26.
8. See Vööbus, *History of Asceticism*. . . . . ., I, pp. 209ff; II, pp. 70ff.
9. See A. Vööbus, *Syrische Kanonessammlungen: Ein Beitrag zur Quellenkunde*. I: *Westsyrische Originalurkunden*, 1,A (Louvain, 1970), CSCO, 35, pp. 165ff.
10. See J. Lebon, *Le monophysisme sévérien* (Louvain, 1909).

that era. In other words, it is necessary to include a few words in the area of pre-history.

In the time of Emperor Justin (518-527), a synod was convened in July, 518 A.D., which rendered the fateful decision to condemn the Patriarch Severus.[11] Other synod meetings held in Jerusalem and Tyros quickly followed echoing the same decision.[12] The dark clouds on the horizon converged to rain destruction upon the Monophysites. Severus[13] was deposed and the patriarchal seat given to Paul. Save for hasty escape[14] to Egypt, Severus would have lost his life.

Heavier blows awaited. During the following year, a large wave of persecution swept through the patriarchate. Diocese after diocese was robbed of its bishop.[15] The bishops were deported or imprisoned. A few years later, either 521[16] or 525,[17] the tide of persecution welled up again to engulf the monks; they were driven from their monasteries. Many priests were so overwhelmed by the ferocity of these attacks that they lost their courage and switched to the Chalcedonian party.

The whole life of the communities was upset. The acute shortage of clergy became a life and death issue for virtually every Monophysite community.[18] Johannan of Ephesus paints a very sad picture of this tragic situation, basing his report on that of a man who himself had been ordained by the same Johannan. The terrified bishops hung on the horns of a dilemma. On the one hand, they were afraid to ordain;[19] on the other, the congregations bombarded them with requests and pleas for clergy. At conclaves of the bishops, one and all refused to ordain for fear of repercussion, if not also of reprisal. At this juncture, Johannan of Tella[20] volunteered to take the risk, provided his colleagues and the patriarch gave him the mandate to "ordain all expelled men".[21]

The superhuman efforts of this man who had been captivated by anchorite ideals and who now plunged into an ocean of limitless activity have been ex-

11. *Acta conciliorum oecumenicorum*, ed. E. Schwartz (Berolini et Lipsiae, 1914ff.), 3, pp. 76f.
12. *Ibid.*, 3, pp. 77ff.
13. About the discovery of a new source on Severus, see A. Vööbus, "Découverte d'un memra de Giwargi, évêque des arabes, sur Sévère d'Antioche," *Le Muséon*, 84 (1971), pp. 433ff. About the discovery of another new source on Severus, see A. Vööbus, "Ein Panegyrikus von Severus von Antiochein von Qyriaqos," *Jahrbuch für Liturgiewissenschaft*, 42 (in press).
14. About the discovery of a new important source, namely an unknown letter of Severus, see A. Vööbus, "Découverte d'une lettre de Sévère d'Antioche," *Revue des études byzantines*, 31 (in press). Among his letters this new document is of extraordinary character since it is autobiographical and gives a detailed account of his escape.
15. More than forty bishops were expelled from their sees (*Chronicon anonymum ad A.D. 846 pertinens*, ed. E. W. Brooks (Louvain, 1904), CSCO Syr. 5, pp. 225ff.
16. *Incerti auctoris chronicon anonymum Pseudo-Dionysianum vulgo dictum*, ed. J. B. Chabot (Louvain, 1933), CSCO, Syr. 53, p. 27.
17. Zacharias Rhetor, *Historia ecclesiastica*, ed. E. W. Brooks (Parisiis, 1924), CSCO, Syr. 39, p. 82.
18. Candidates from the Syrian Orient even went as far as Constantinople to obtain ordination; "and he would return perhaps after a year of days without gaining any satisfaction from his labor, as I saw happen to many" (John of Ephesus, *Lives of the Eastern Saints*, ed. E. W. Brooks, 2. *Patrologia Orientalis*, 18 (Paris, 1924), p. 522).
19. That they consecrated some of them secretly was of very little help in view of the situation (*ibid.*, pp. 515f.).
20. Regarding him see also the discovery of an unknown biography of Jaqob of Serug. A. Vööbus, *Handschriftliche Überlieferung der Mēmrē-Dichtung des Jacqōb von Serūg: Sammlungen*, 1 (Louvain, 1972), CSCO Subsidia 39, pp.5ff. He was banned in 521 (Eliya, *Vita Johannis episcopi Tellae*, ed. E. W. Brooks (Parisiis, 1907), CSCO, Syr. 7, pp. 80ff.). After this he resided for some time in the Monastery of Mar Zakkai near Callinicus.
21. John of Ephesus, *Lives of the Eastern Saints*, 2, pp. 516ff.

tolled in a monument by Johannan of Ephesus and also by his disciple, Eliya.[22] Johannan of Tella must have been a man of extraordinary stamina to brave the immense task before him. It took him on a marathon run from the Persian frontiers to Armenia, Cappadocia and Phoenicia,[23] encouraging, instructing, examining candidates and performing mass ordinations. Such heroic effort soon began to bear fruit. Depressed communities felt a quickening spirit; growing numbers of turncoats sought him out in order to be pardoned and received once more into the fold.[24] Candidates for ordination came to him "like a flood that is produced in a river by thick clouds"[25] wherever he appeared—in monasteries, on the road, even in the desert. His labors were risky but the communities and villages were provided with deacons and priests. The records he is reported to have kept are said to have contained thousands of names of ordained persons.[26] In addition, the epic efforts of this shepherd instilled courage, hardened determination and fanned the flames of the spirit of resistance. His example no doubt proved invaluable in establishing the essential premises for the upbuilding of life under the most severe of conditions.

The hurricane force of the persecutions sought to eradicate Monophysitism forever. But it failed to win the day; it brought opposite, latent powers to the fore. The Syrian Orient successfully withstood this first merciless test—an experience that gave it the muscle and iron to face the excruciating trials yet to come.

In 527 the imperial throne fell to Justinian (527-65) who thus came to the helm of the ship of state. This shift eased the furor, and monks quietly began to return to their monasteries.[27] The communities had been severely tried and tested and, though pressure was still applied, the enthronement of Justinian must have encompassed all these vexed ones with a surging emotion of relief. Johannan of Tella now prosecuted his work more openly and boldly, carrying out mass ordinations.[28] A graphic view of the situation in the year 529 is afforded us by one who himself experienced examination in a nightly gathering together with a contingent of monks at the hands of Johannan of Tella.[29] The vigor with which he fulfilled this program brought down upon him the wrath of the authorities and left him in a very precarious position.[30]

Nonetheless, much more could be attempted during this period; increasing attention was given to the upbuilding of life. The breach between the church bodies widened to include areas beyond those of doctrine alone. The foundation was laid for an indigenous canon law which was designed to regulate ecclesiastical practice in piety, worship, liturgy and church order. The Monophysite tradition began to take on definite form. Most valuable glimpses are allowed us when we examine the canons issued by Johannan of Tella. Search for new manuscript sources in the churches and monasteries in the Orient has led to the oldest

22. *Vita Johannis episcopi Tellae*, pp. 1ff.
23. John of Ephesus, *Lives of the Eastern Saints*, 2, p. 519.
24. *Ibid.*, pp. 519f.
25. *Ibid.*, p. 518.
26. The Oriental lightheartedness in dealing with numbers is shown by the figure given — 170,000! (*ibid.*, p. 522).
27. Mîka'êl, *Chronique*, ed. J. B. Chabot (Paris, 1910), 4, p. 270.
28. Eliya, *Vita Johannis episcopi Tellae*, pp. 23ff.
29. This company of about seventy monks came from the monasteries of Amid and its surroundings (John of Ephesus, *Lives of the Eastern Saints*, 2, p. 521).
30. *Ibid.*, p. 520.

and most valuable evidence of these documents.[31] They aim at complete separation of the Monophysite believers and affirm the readiness to suffer unto death for the sake of their creed.[32] The position and lot of the clergy is also dealt with, especially in respect to its qualifications and further training—certainly a not unnatural consequence of the mass ordinations.[33] They cast a singular light upon another facet of his endeavors: the institution of the deaconesses and its role in the organism of church life. Newly discovered sources exhibit the attention given by him to the nurture and strengthening of organized monasticism.[34] These years saw not only the growth in the number of Monophysites but also consolidation in the life of the church, due in great part to this tireless man. An atmosphere was created in which, for the first time, not only two separate churches consisting of the clergy and the communities but also two traditions faced one another.

During the summer of 531 the Emporor Justinian issued an order permitting the exiled monks to return.[35] Near the end of the year, a half-dozen bishops, also in exile, were given a royal invitation to present themselves at Constantinople.[36] They were understandaby enough nonplused at the turn of events.[37] What is more, in Constantinople these shepherds were allowed to submit a confession[38] to the emperor.[39]

The disposition of the Empress Theodora toward the Monophysites was as positive as it was gracious. She turned the Hormisda Palace over to oriental ascetics—to that company of men whose panoply of peculiar custom seemed so strange—to do with as they would.[40] The palace was converted into a huge monastic camp. A more conspicuous platform for the anti-Chalcedonian forces could hardly have been provided. It was this locus which provided the setting for a theological conference[41] with representatives of both parties in attendance.[42] The exact date is not known but it must have taken place either in 532[43] or 532/33.[44] The Monophysites were allowed to disseminate their propaganda[45] in complete freedom.[46] The appointment of the new patriarch Anthimus[47] was a

---

31. A. Vööbus, *Syrische Kanonessammlungen: Ein Beitrag zur Quellenkunde*, I, 1,A, pp. 156ff; 1,B (Louvain, 1971), pp. 263ff.
32. Canon I, *op. cit.*, 1,A, p. 158.
33. It was necessary to curb the wild and the exotic in ecclesiastical practice and to specify the qualifications of monks to make them eligible for the priesthood (see Canon XI). See *Syriac and Arabic Documents*, ed. A. Vööbus (Stockholm, 1960), p. 58.
34. See Vööbus, *Syrische Kanonessammlungen*, I, 1,A, pp. 156ff; 1,B, p. 267.
35. Zacharias Rhetor, *Historia ecclesiastica*, II, 6,2, p. 82.
36. They were able to stay there for more than a year.
37. At first they did not go; they wrote to the emperor and received a new invitation.
38. This document is preserved in Zacharias Rhetor, *Historia ecclesiastica*, 9.15, pp. 115ff.
39. *Inter alia* it rejects Eutyches on the one hand and the council of Chalcedon on the other.
40. Even cells were created in this place to satisfy the needs of the reclusi (see John of Ephesus, *Lives of the Eastern Saints*, 2, pp. 676ff).
41. Innocentius de Maronia, *Epistola de collatione cum Severianis habita*, *Acta conciliorum oecumenicorum*, 4.2, pp. 169ff.
42. Both parties were represented by a six-man delegation. The Monophysites were represented by Sargis of Cyrrhos, Thomas of Germanicia, Philoxenos of Doliche, Peter of Theodosiopolis, Johannan of Tella and Nonnos of Circesion.
43. See E. Stein, *Histoire du Bas-Empire* (Paris-Bruxelles-Amsterdam, 1949), 2, pp. 378 ff.
44. See Schwartz, *Acta conciliorum oecumenicorum*, 4.2, p. xxvi.
45. John of Ephesus, *Lives of the Eastern Saints*, 17, pp. 18ff. See *Acta conciliorum oecumenicorum*, 3, pp. 139, 148, 181.
46. In 553 they utilized the panic caused by an earthquake in order to stage a mass demonstration against the Chalcedonians (see *Chronicon paschale*, ed. L. Dindorf (Bonnae, 1832), p. 629).
47. Consecrated in June 535.

bold move, rather astonishing under the circumstances. On top of all this, the Patriarch Severus was invited to come to Constantinople. He was received and showered with great honor[48] and allowed to promote his cause.[49]

Did the Monophysites succumb to new hope in view of the emperor's new role—despite his known vacillation in ecclesiastical policy? Did they become so complacent about their activities that they dropped their guard?

Certainly Justianian's move drew Johannan of Tella away from his activities; he too had been invited to Constantinople.[50] But it is highly improbable that the leaders, who had been tested and tried, cherished any illusions about the new imperial policy. The reasons are obvious. The clergy and monks in Constantinople remained adamantly opposed to the new trend in the emperor's policy. The formation of an assault detachment of monks, their agitation,[51] maneuvers and intrigues[52] were well-known facts. Further, the web of intrigue had drawn Syria[53] into the controversy as the documents themselves prove.[54] Let it not go unnoticed that the mastermind of the intrigue, namely the pope, was in contact with circles in Syria. The symptoms of a tour de force to come were perceptible. Severus, who in 534 went to Constantinople and remained there for a year, told his friends with resignation: "Do not err, under this emperor the peace of the church is impossible".[55] Predictions of Johannan of Tella may also be mentioned here. In 529 when Johannan of Ephesus along with a large contingent of monks received ordination from Johannan of Tella, the latter's admonition was indelibly pressed upon the memory of those participating in the act of consecration: "Pray and cease not, for a time is coming when men to give a hand of ordination to believers shall be wanting and shall not be found".[56] The outlook was bleak.

Indeed, that which men like Severus and Johannan of Tella anticipated probably came about more quickly than expected. The intrigues intensified to a feverish pitch when Pope Agapetus personally took matters into his expert hands. Arriving in Constantinople in 536, he assumed the role of prosecutor, intervening in ecclesiastical matters at will. Justinian complied with the wishes of Agapetus in every respect,[57] indeed to such a point that the throne itself suffered humiliation.[58] The pope's campaign was executed at lightning speed. Anthimus,

48. In the year 535.
49. He was able to promote the cause of Monophysitism for one year. He also influenced the newly appointed patriarch, Anthimus.
50. He was invited to Constantinople to participate in the conference.
51. The man who organized the band of monks and who directed the agitation on a large scale was perhaps Menas whose merits earned the patriarchal seat. This has been suggested by E. Schwartz.
52. Monks in Constantinople, used as an assault detachment, sent a delegation to Rome (Acta conciliorum oecumenicorum, 3, p. 141).
53. Particularly Palestine and Syria II.
54. Zacharias Rhetor, Historia ecclesiastica, 9.19, pp. 135ff.
55. Ibid., 9.19, pp. 136ff.
56. John of Ephesus, Lives of the Eastern Saints, 2, p. 521. See also a letter written about 530 in R. Draquet, "Une pastorale anti-julianiste des environs de l'année 530," Le Muséon, 40 (1927), pp. 83ff. This addition rests on Ms. Br. Mus. Add. 14,663, which unfortunately has preserved only the first part of the document. A tireless search for new manuscript sources has revealed the only complete text preserved in Ms. Mardin Orth. 350. See A. Vööbus, Syriac Manuscripts from the Treasury of the Monastery of Mār Hananyā, or Deir Za'f arān (Stockholm) (in press).
57. Whether Justinian indeed did all this because he saw in the pope a help against Theodora (see E. Schwartz, Zur Kirchenpolitik Justinians (München, 1940), pp. 44f.) cannot be discussed here.
58. According to the official account of the Roman curia (Gesta pontificorum Romanorum, ed. T. Mommsen (Berolini, 1874), p. 142), the orthodox pope conquered the tyrannical heretic Justinian. This is a distortion; there was no resistance at all.

patriarch of Constantinople, was deposed. Menas was appointed his successor, consecrated by the pope.[59] The submission of a confession, Chalcedonian in theology, was required;[60] a synod was convened;[61] Monophysite leaders were anathematized;[62] and Severus thrown into prison.[63] The imperial decree followed;[64] the Monophysites were banished from the capital; the works of Severus were consigned to destruction;[65] and cruel punishment was established for everyone who copied Monophysite writings.[66]

A new vector in the zigzag course of Justinian's ecclesiastical policy had occurred. In consequence, the persecution which swept up the patriarchate of Antioch far exceeded the previous one in cruelty and severity. In the main, Patriarch Ephrem[67] himself carried it out, covering the territory[68] during the winter of 536/7.[69] He was accompanied by a detachment of soldiers[70] in order to ensure the submission of the Monophysites and to break their spirit.[71]

This persecution was carried out with savage fury which fed on inhuman cruelty and was coupled with the power of arrest, imprisonment and expulsion.[72] Many broke under the pressure.[73] Yet for all of that, the persecution failed to accomplish the objectives. The undaunted and the indomitable—particularly the monks—deprived of house and home, again became wanderers. Even nature itself, an extraordinarily cold winter, seemed to support the patriarch in his work of destruction.[74] Most of the shepherds, if not all, fell victim. Two years later, Johannan of Tella, having returned from Constantinople, was able to ordain only in Persia[75]—nowhere else! The hunt for him was on in the mountains of Shiggar.[76] This courageous figure was finally captured, imprisoned and killed.[77] Monophysitism had entered upon its most critical phase.

That the consequences were of the utmost gravity to the sufferers is clear. A process of strangulation was in effect. Overnight the problem of the clergy became extremely important. The situation suddenly experienced an utterly critical tremor, presenting as it did the end of all that had been built up at such enormous cost and effort. The moment had arrived, the moment which had

59. The consecration by the pope on March 13, 536, was itself an unheard-of event.
60. *Epistolae imperatorum, pontificum, aliorum*, ed. O. Günther (Vindobonae, 1895-98), *CSEL*, 35, pp. 338ff.
61. May 2 to June 4, 536.
62. *Acta conciliorum oecumenicorum*, 3, pp. 26ff.
63. This was regardless of the assurance of guarantee given to him. However, Theodora salvaged him from the worst and helped his escape.
64. August 6, 536, which sanctioned the decrees of the synod.
65. Novella XLII of August 6, 536.
66. For this crime his hand had to be chopped off.
67. Concerning this man, see J. Lebon, "Ephrem d'Amid, patriarche d'Antioche," *Mélanges Ch. Moeller* (Louvain, 1914), 1, pp. 197ff.; G. Downey, "Ephraemius, Patriarch of Antioch," *Church History*, 7 (1938), pp. 365ff.
68. Namely Aleppo, Qenneshrin, Mabbug, Serug, Edessa, Shura, Callinicus and the rest of the frontier area, Reshaina, Amid and Tella.
69. Zacharias Rhetor, *Historia ecclesiastica*, 10.1, p. 175.
70. *Ibid.*, 10.1, pp. 174ff.
71. See a moving account of the horrors and endless vexations of the monasteries of Amid in John of Ephesus, *Lives of the Eastern Saints*, pp. 607ff.
72. Some were burned alive (*ibid.*, p. 524). About Presbyter Qura of Amid, Zacharias Rhetor, *Historia ecclesiastica*, 10.3, p. 173.
73. *Ibid.*, 10.1, pp. 174f.
74. The extraordinarily cold winter multiplied the agony of the calamities, and many died (*ibid.*, 10.1, pp. 174f.).
75. Eliya, *Vita Johannis episcopi Tellae*, pp. 58ff.
76. He was detected by some functionaries with the aid of a "strangulator of the robbers" (Johannes Malalas, *Chronographia*, ed. L. Dindorf (Bonnae, 1831), p. 382).
77. He was dragged off to Antioch where he spent the remainder of his life in imprisonment and died on February 6, 538.

haunted the leaders—the flock in the Syrian Orient was without any shepherds. Philoxenos of Mabbug, Thomas of Marash, Thomas of Damascus, Thomas of Dara, Petros of Reshaina, Johannan of Tella and others were dead. Patriarch Anthimus, Patriarch Theodosius of Alexandria, Peter of Apamea and Johannan of Hephaistou were kept in confinement at a fortress. On top of all, the Patriarch Severus breathed his last in the year 538.

The situation was desperate beyond belief. Johannan of Hephaistou, a Syrian,[78] decided to do something about it. By a ruse,[79] he managed to slip out of interment at Constantinople. He made secret trips to accomplish his work, to confirm and strengthen the beseiged communities and to provide the flock with shepherds. Various clandestine journeys took him to Asia Minor, as far as Tarsus, Cilicia, Cyprus and Rhodes. The third such journey probably took place in 541. He also used literary means to strengthen his mission.[80]

Naturally, assistance to the congregations in the oriental communities was very limited despite such extraordinary efforts. It is certain that some from these communities travelled great distances at enormous risk in order to receive ordination. For the oriental provinces, the only opportunity available was to be found in Persia. But in that territory, only one bishop, Qyros, was left.[81] He carried out ordinations during the period 537/8-544/5 at which time, regrettably, the frontier was closed because of the war.[82]

Just when darkness and despair were at their deepest, there occurred an event which was entirely unpredictable—the genesis of the Monophysite church is rich in such dramatic moments! Hārith bar Gabala, King of the Arabs, suddenly appeared in Constantinople in 542/3. He was determined to create a closely knit Monophysite realm in his kingdom and demanded two or three bishops for Syria from Theodora. She complied. This was salvation from the very brink of the chasm. It must rank as one of the most decisive events in the history of the period when Patriarch Theodosius intoned the ceremony of episcopal consecration of two monks who were in Constantinople at that time: Theodorus of Arabia and Jaqob Burdana.[83] The first became bishop of the Arabs whose settlements consisted of tents.[84] Immense territory came under his jurisdiction: the entire desert, Arabia and Palestine up to Jerusalem[85]—an area which had been a place of refuge to the hunted. The second bishop, Jaqob, became bishop of Edessa, but his territory included all areas beyond the diocese of Theodorus. The advent of these two bishops meant not reprieve but rescue. They were aware of the tremendous burden laid upon them and their mission. As it turned out, a new leaf in the book of Monophysite history had been turned.

Bishop Jaqob, a monk garbed in a patchwork garment, was a thoroughly

---

78. About him see Vööbus, *Syrische Kanonessammlungen*, I, 1,A, p. 178ff.
79. Under the pretext of illness Johannan obtained permission from Theodora to live separately in a villa. From this base he slipped out on his secret mission tours (John of Ephesus, *Lives of the Eastern Saints*, 2, pp. 530ff.).
80. From Cyprus he sent a letter with the canons to the Syrian abbots in the Orient (see Vööbus, *Syrische Kanonessammlungen*, I, 1,A, pp. 175ff.).
81. Mīka'ēl, *Chronique*, 4, p. 309.
82. John of Ephesus, *Lives of the Eastern Saints*, 2, p. 522.
83. *Op. cit.* 3, pp. 153f., p. 228. About the discovery of new manuscript sources on Jaqob Burdana, see A. Vööbus, "Neue handschriftliche Funde über die Biographie des Ja'qōb Būrdᶜānā", *Ostkirchliche Studien*, 22 (1973).
84. Hirtha of the Arabs, *op. cit.*, 2, p. 693.
85. *Op. cit.*, 3, p. 154.

educated man,[86] having mastered Greek and Arabic in addition to Syriac. He undertook the enormous task of leadership within his immense[87] jurisdictional domain[88] and gave it all he had. A moving, vivid account of his heroic endeavors to encourage, comfort, strengthen and nurture the life of the communities under his care is given by Johannan of Ephesus.[89] Constantly harassed by pursuers, he moved from village to village; "he would complete all the work of his ministry in one night and perhaps one day, and would pass the next night 30 or 40 miles or more farther on."[90] The number of ordinations he performed in this necessarily clandestine fashion is reported in fantastic figures.[91] Unfortunately, documentation for the study of this period is studded with lacunae. The picture Johannan gives us is not adequate; his colorful and moving panegyric does not include substantial data so essential for the historian. Some information can be culled from the tradition and habits which lived on in ecclesiastical practice, as seen in the canonical literature produced by Jaqob of Edessa in particular.

Newly discovered documents have unearthed unknown important material which increases our knowledge.[92] These documents show us how difficult it was even at a later time to wean the monks from the practice of blessing the myron and from exercising priestly functions. They reflect with all desirable clarity the role which the contingent of monks once had played, that is, during the most critical period under discussion. Among the resolutions, one tells us something of the travelling priest on the way to serve the scattered flock—a real *conversatio viatorum;* it describes in striking fashion how a deacon, while on the way, can serve as an altar for the celebration of the eucharist. What a portrait of ecclesiastical life under emergency conditions, of the cultic life geared to meet the demands of being on the move in secrecy and in haste!

Back to Jaqob—it is a miracle that this man who was pursued, who had a price on his head, was never caught by church agents working for the orthodox cause. Two phases can be distinguished in Jaqob's activities[93] in building up his church. The records we have can only be interpreted properly to mean that Jaqob initially wished to confine himself to the accomplishment of the most urgent and vital tasks. To create a Monophysite hierarchy at the very beginning was to attempt too much. But the time for this was to come. When it did, Jaqob took the initiative.[94] The first step was to select two monks for metropolitan duty in Asia Minor.[95]

As to the exact date of this event, the sources offer no record. It is very difficult to fix the time Jaqob forged ahead in this new direction. One source,

---

86. He was from Tella and was educated in the Monastery of Phesiltha (*op. cit.*, 2, p. 690).
87. His territory extended from the Persian border to Constantinople (*ibid.*, p. 693).
88. *Op. cit.*, 3, p. 154.
89. *Op. cit.*, 2, p. 623.
90. *Ibid.*, p. 623.
91. John of Ephesus believes that 100,000 is not too high a figure for the number of his ordinations (*ibid.*, pp. 696f).
92. *The Synodicon in the West Syrian Tradition*, ed. A. Vööbus, CSCO (in press).
93. The time granted for his work was quite lengthy. He died on July 30, 578. About the bishops he consecrated, see E. Honigmann, *Évêques et évêchés monophysites d'Asie antérieure en VIe siècle* (Louvain, 1951), CSCO Subsidia, 2, pp. 178ff.
94. John of Ephesus, *Lives of the Eastern Saints*, 2, p. 697.
95. Eugenios of Isauria and Conon of Cilicia. The first became the metropolitan of Tarsus (*ibid.*, p. 697; see *op. cit.*, 2, pp. 155f.).

namely the chronicle of Ps. Dionysios with its obviously erroneous chronology,[96] has for some time been a source of confusion to scholars.[97] Assumptions about an early date for the consecration of the patriarch by Jaqob[98] have simply muddled matters so much the more. The ground is more secure when we take a different fact into consideration. Constantinus, the metropolitan of Laodicea, upon the death of the Patriarch Severus, was invested with the dignity of deputy.[99] It is known that he died in 553.[100] This fact becomes important as soon as we realize that his death left Jaqob free to act.[101] Confirmation seems likely from another angle—from the list of the bishops and archbishops consecrated by Jaqob. This list begins with Dimat, the successor of Constantinus in Laodicea.[102] His consecration must have taken place soon after 553. The impression given is that this prelate was the first to be consecrated by Jaqob.

If so, then more than a decade passed before Jaqob began to expand the hierarchy. The list just mentioned then provides us with further information on the framework of the first organization. In respect to the Syrian territories of the patriarchate of Antioch,[103] two metropolitans were appointed for Syria (Laodicea and Seleucia) and one for Mesopotamia (Amid). Of the three bishops consecrated for this area, one was assigned to Syria (Qenneshre), one to Osrhoene (Harran) and one for Euphratesia (Shura). In consecrating the Patriarch Sargis, Jaqob completed the highest degree in the Monophysite hierarchical ladder.[104] He had to repeat this act very soon.[105]

This list takes us to 566. At that time, the hierarchical network was well provided in respect to Syria I, with the patriarchal seat, two metropolitans and one bishop for Qenneshre. The further development and completion of the structure of the Monophysite hierarchy belong to a later epoch, even to the epoch following upon the Islamic conquest.

96. A large number of consecrated bishops appears in connection with the time of the great pest, Pseudo-Dionysios (*Historia ecclesiastica*, p. 110). It has been wrongly assumed that this section is simply a copy of the work of John of Ephesus.
97. About this question, see A. van Roey, "Les débuts de l'église jacobite," in A. Grillmeier-H Bacht, *Das Konzil von Chalkedon*, 2 (Würzburg, 1953).
98. The consecration of Sargis as patriarch of Antioch has been placed in 538 (A. Sanda in Johannes Philoponus, *Opuscula monophysitica* (Beryti Phoenicum, 1930), p. 6); about 547-50 according to A. Jülicher, "Zur Geschichte der Monophysitenkirche." *ZntW*, 19 (1925), p. 37. But this event actually took place later, about 557 (see E. W. Brooks, "The Patriarch Paul of Antioch and the Alexandrian Schism of 575," in *Byzantinische Zeitschrift*, 30 (1930), p. 469).
99. About this document and the newly unearthed manuscript sources, see Vööbus, *Syrische Kanonessammlungen*, I,1,A, pp. 167ff.
100. Mīka'ēl, *Chronique*, 4, p. 312.
101. See also Honigmann, *Évêques et évêchés monophysites*, pp. 171f.
102. John of Ephesus, *Lives of the Eastern Saints*, 3, pp. 156ff.
103. Jaqob consecrated bishops and archbishops also in Egypt, Asia Minor and the island of Chios.
104. When he consecrated his former fellow brother of the Monastery of Phesiltha is not clear. In any case this must have taken place about 558; shortly before that time Johannes Philoponos dedicated his work to him (Johannes Philoponos, *Opuscula monophysitica*, pp. 81ff.).
105. Sargis died about three years later. It was Theodosius, the former patriarch of Alexandria, who after a sedisvacance of three years wrote to Jaqob and asked to consecrate Paul to the vacant seat of Antioch (*Documenta ad origines monophysitarum illustrandas*, ed. J.B. Chabot (Parisiis, 1908), CSCO Syr. 18, pp. 89f).

ALASDAIR HERON

The Holy Spirit in Origen and Didymus the Blind: A Shift in Perspective From the Third to the Fourth Century

Among those fourth century theologians who inherited and built upon the foundations laid by Origen, a special place belongs to Didymus the Blind (313–398), the last outstanding head of the catechetical school in Alexandria. His position was uncompromisingly Nicene orthodox: in this he stands with Athanasius and the Cappadocians over against such other heirs of Origen as Eusebius of Caesarea. Eventually however the shadows which gathered around Origen's name clouded his reputation as well, and he (or at least some of his teachings) was included in the condemnation of Origen associated with the Fifth Ecumenical Council in 553. Partly no doubt as a result of this, the greater part of his writings was lost; the only major work to survive intact was Jerome's Latin translation of his De Spiritu Sancto[1]. A good number have fortunately been recovered in modern times, most notably, the various commentaries found among the Toura papyri. There are also grounds for regarding as his both the large work De Trinitate[2] first ascribed to him two hundred years ago by Mingarelli, and the fourth and fifth books of the Adversus Eunomium of Basil[3].

One reason for the eclipse of his reputation may well have been the fact that very shortly after his death his name was dragged into the bitter

[1] MPG 39, 1031–1086. On the MS tradition and variant readings see L. Doutreleau, Étude d'une Tradition Manuscrite: Le «De Spiritu Sancto» de Didyme, in P. Granfield/J. A. Jungmann (ed.), Kyriakon (Festschrift Johannes Quasten), Münster, 1970, vol. I, pp. 352–389.

[2] MPG 39, 269–992; also Didymus der Blinde: De trinitate, Buch I, herausgegeben und übersetzt von Jürgen Hönscheid, Beiträge zur Klassischen Philologie, Heft 44, Meisenheim am Glan, 1975. On the question of authorship may I refer to my 1972 Tübingen dissertation, Studies in the Trinitarian Writings of Didymus the Blind. His Authorship of the Adversus Eunomium IV–V and the De Trinitate.

[3] MPG 29, 671–768. The concluding section (768B–774) does not belong to Books IV–V.

personal battle between Jerome and Rufinus. Both men had known and admired him; Rufinus had studied with him for several years, and Jerome, in addition to translating the De Spiritu Sancto, had heaped fulsome praise upon him[4]. Didymus however had been a staunch defender of Origen's thought; and once Jerome came to launch his attack on Rufinus' translation of the De Principiis he accused Rufinus of drawing on Didymus' favourable reinterpretations of Origen to order to cover up sundry errors in it[5]. While Jerome was careful to insist that Didymus was orthodox, at least in respect of the Trinity[6], the charge that he was too favourable towards Origen seems most to have influenced subsequent attitudes to him.

These links between Origen, Didymus, Jerome and Rufinus suggest that it may be useful to consider some of the points of similarity and contrast between Didymus' De Spiritu Sancto as preserved for us by Jerome and the De Principiis, which is for the most part only available in Rufinus' translation. The chief aim in doing so is to ask how far Didymus may in fact have depended on Origen, and in what ways he may have departed from him. Beyond that, such a comparison may help to pave the way for further study of Didymus' own thought, and of the change in theological perspective from Origen to his fourth century successors, and even perhaps cast some light on Rufinus' handling of the De Principiis. To his end, I should like to focus on one particular (but central) feature of the De Spiritu Sancto: the way in which Didymus grasps and formulates the contrast between the being of God and that of creatures.

Divine and Creaturely Being in the De Spiritu Sancto

The fact that the De Spiritu Sancto survives only in Jerome's translation, which was completed ca. 387, raises two preliminary questions. First, how far is the translation reliable? Second, when was the original work composed? The first can be answered with reasonable confidence. Jerome appears to have been almost painfully precise in his rendering,

---

[4] E. g. in his preface to the De Spiritu Sancto; De Vir. Ill. 109; Ep. 68 ad Castrutium. Jerome's various references were collected by Mingarelli in his De Didymo Veterum Testimonia, reprinted in MPG 39: a clear change in tone can be observed after the controversy with Rufinus, though Jerome continued to mention Didymus with (critical) respect.

[5] See especially Adv. Rufinum II 16, which says of Didymus: et in ipsius περὶ ἀρχῶν, quos tu interpretatus es, libros breves dictavit commentariolos, quibus non negaret ab Origene scripta, quae scripta sunt; sed nos simplices homines non posse intelligere quae dicuntur; et quo sensu in bonam partem accipi debeant, persuadere conatur. Hoc duntaxat de Filio et Spiritu Sancto . . .; from Adv. Ruf. I 6 and II 11, Jerome suspected that Rufinus had actually used some of this material.

[6] Adv. Ruf. II 16: . . . pro Didymo, qui certe in Trinitate catholicus est.

anxious to reproduce the Greek as accurately as possible, even including explanatory comments where it might have been easier to paraphrase (1044C; 1048A; 1075D), retaining Greek terms (1069D; 1081D), and generally using the most literal Latin equivalents throughout. Moreover he makes it clear in his preface that his noble motive was to show how other Latin writers (and by this he means Ambrose in particular) had made unacknowledged borrowings from Greeks, and that his work is to be taken as a translation, not as something of his own. It is also perhaps significant that although Jerome made great play with the inaccuracies of Rufinus' work on the De Principiis, Rufinus does not seem to have felt able to hurl the same charge back at him in respect of the De Spiritu Sancto. (He did claim in his preface to the De Principiis that he had followed Jerome's example in improving minor blemishes in Origen; but that is a different matter!) Given Jerome's brilliance as a translator, his avowed motive, and the internal evidence of the text, we may feel confident that it is reliable[7].

The question of the original date of writing is more difficult. It has commonly been estimated as in the 370s, and so as being roughly midway between Athanasius' Letters to Serapion and the Council of Constantinople (358/9 and 380/1 respectively), and perhaps a little earlier than Basil's De Spiritu Sancto (ca. 375). More recently the suggestion has been advanced that it should be placed much earlier, even before the Letters to Serapion[8]. In that event it would claim to rank as the first full-scale defence of the divinity of the Holy Spirit; and this in turn would demand a re-evaluation of Didymus' originality and significance. The arguments in favour of this redating are not however very strong[9], and on balance the period around 370 seems more probable. At any rate, the immediate context is the debate about the Holy Spirit which followed hard on the heels of the Arian controversy.

The central theme of the work is that the qualities and nature of the Holy Spirit are identical with those of the Father and the Son, and differ toto caelo from those of all created beings. Didymus' conception of the character of this contrast between divine and creaturely being is thus fundamental to the entire argument. It is expressed by him in a variety of

---

[7] See the detailed analysis of E. Stolz, 'Didymus, Ambrosius, Hieronymus', ThQ 87 (1905), pp. 371–401.

[8] E. Staimer, Die Schrift „De Spiritu Sancto" von Didymus dem Blinden von Alexandrien, Diss., Munich, 1960, pp. 118–133.

[9] My reasons for abandoning Staimer's early dating, which I had earlier accepted, are given in my paper, Zur Theologie der „Tropici" in den Serapionbriefen des hl. Athanasius: Amos 4.13 als pneumatologische Belegstelle presented at the Kyrios Athanasios-Tagung in Berlin in 1973, ~~but unfortunately not yet~~ and published, in Kyrios 14 (1974), pp. 3-24.

ways; and this, together with the fact that he never pauses to give a single, fully systematic exposition of it, can at first sight obscure what is in fact a remarkably unified and coherent pattern of thought. On closer examination, however, the pieces fall neatly into place and combine to supply a structured framework within which he is able to work out his case. This framework is one which he himself patently accepts without question, and to which he appeals without hesitation; it supplies what may be called his metaphysical frame of reference, and is constitutive for his theology. While a full account of his positions and arguments would have to look at other aspects as well – most notably his use of Scripture and the dogmatic issues under debate – this pattern presents us with at least one of the bases for his thought. In a nutshell, he emphasises an absolute contrast between God and creatures; but on the ground of that contrast he also sketches a kind of correlation in which the divine fullness of being fills those creatures who participate in God. The different aspects of this contrast and correlation must be laid out in more detail to bring out its particular character.

Underlying all that Didymus says is first of all a twofold contrast between the being of God and that of creatures. God 'is simple and of an uncompounded and spiritual nature, and has neither ears nor organs with which he sends forth a voice, but is a unique and incomprehensible substance, not composed of members or parts.' (1064B) This does not apply to any created being, not even the invisible (1037A). Similarly, God is infinite, whereas all created beings have a nature which is circumscribed and limited, the visible by place and the invisible by the nature of their being (1037C). There is thus a distinction among creatures between the visible and the invisible (1035C); but more radical still is the ultimate ontological contrast between God and creatures of all kinds. From the nature of this fundamental contrast follow three other differences which he specially emphasises.

(a) God *is* by his very nature goodness, holiness, wisdom and so on. What he has, he is by definition: there is no room in his 'simplicity' for any attribute or quality which is not inherent in his own being, not simply an aspect of himself. God 'makes those good to whom he imparts himself, himself not having been made good by another, but subsisting (sc. as good)' (1036D). The Son 'is sanctity' (1038C), 'is himself . . . the fullness of all good things' (1077C). The Holy Spirit is 'the fullness of the gifts of God', 'substantially good', 'the substance of sanctification' (1036A). Creatures on the other hand do not possess holiness, goodness or wisdom out of their own substance or nature, but 'through communication' from another (1038C; 1052A). Even 'the angels are holy by participation in the Holy Spirit and by the indwelling of the Only-begotten Son of God, who is holiness and the communication of the Father . . . not of their own substance ... but by participation in the Holy Trinity' (1038C).

(b) Because God possesses his attributes by his very nature, he cannot lose them or be deprived of them: they belong to him immutably and unchangeably. Any being on the other hand which must receive qualities from elsewhere – and such are all creatures – is necessarily capable of change and alteration (1035C). What is unchangeable is eternal; what is mutable, creaturely; and so no creature is unchangeable or eternal (1044Df). What can be altered must also have been made and have a beginning, whereas what is incorruptible is also eternal (1083Df). So Didymus repeatedly asserts of all three divine persons that they are incorruptible, immutable, unalterable (e.g. 1035C; 1036C; 1041A; 1055C; 1077C; 1080B), while every creature is by nature mutable (1036C). This was indeed the reason why the devil could fall (1083C), while the angels who did not remained loyal through obedience, not because of inherent incapacity to change (1044Df).

(c) A third point of difference, closely bound up with the preceding ones, is, in Jerome's terminology, that the nature of God is capabilis, that of creatures is capax. Jerome himself seems to have felt that these expressions would be less than transparent to his Latin readers, for he added a word of explanation at 1044C.D: 'He calls capabilis a substance which is received by several others, and gives them a part in itself; and capax one which is filled through the communication of another substance, and which, receiving another substance (sc. into itself) is itself not received (sc. by another).' From another of his comments at 1083D it appears that the Greek word rendered as capabilis was μετοχικός: 'that which can be participated in'. It may be that in the De Spiritu Sancto Didymus also used the very similar term μεθεκτός; for at least two passages in the work are closely paralleled by statements in the De Trinitate in which μεθεκτός is used[10]. In either case, what is being spoken of is the concept of μέθεξις, of 'participation' in the Platonist sense. The link between the capax/capabilis distinction and the others we have indicated is brought out by Didymus at 1036Df:

'Everything which is capax of any good thing from outside itself is distinct from that (sc. divine) substance; and such are all the creatures. But God, since he is good, is the fountain and source of all good things. Thus

---

[10] Cf. especially De Spiritu Sancto 1044D: Capabili quippe statim inconvertibile, et inconvertibili aeternum est consequens with De Trinitate 369B: ἕπεται γὰρ τῷ μεθεκτῷ τὸ ἄτρεπτον· καὶ τούτῳ τὸ ἄκτιστον, ὅ ἐστιν καὶ ἄναρχον; also the (less close) parallel between De Spir. S. 1082C and De Trin. 529A. The De Spiritu Sancto was manifestly used as a source for the De Trinitate (whether or not Didymus was the author of the latter) and there are so many parallels that it would be possible to attempt a partial reconstruction of at least some passages in the original Greek by drawing upon the De Trinitate.

he makes good those to whom he imparts himself, himself not having been made good by another, but subsisting (sc. as good). Hence he is capabilis, but not capax. So too the Only-begotten Son . . . is capabilis, but not capax . . . the invisible creation . . . is not capabilis, but capax; for if it were capabilis it would not be capax of any good thing, but would subsist by itself as simple, but (sc. in fact) it is in receipt of goodness from elsewhere.'

Similarly he argues that the Holy Spirit is not capax (1036A) but capabilis – and therefore uncreated (1044C).

The capax/capabilis distinction in effect sums up and focuses all the other differences between divine and creaturely being and is indeed pivotal in Didymus' entire argument. It also shows that his concern was not merely to contrast the being of God and of creatures, but also to establish a connexion between them. Because the nature of the Father, Son and Holy Spirit is capabilis, creatures, who are by contrast capaces, may receive and participate in the divine being itself, and so share in the qualities which are inherent in God, but which they must receive from without themselves. This connexion in no way blurs or diminishes the distinction between God and creature; rather it reflects the character of the distinction, which accordingly has a positive rather than a merely negative function. The positive connexion is brought out by Didymus in a variety of ways. The metaphors of 'fountain' (1036A; 1036D; 1073C) and 'fullness' (1036A; 1040BC; 1077C) applied to the divine persons implicitly underline the fact that created beings are in and by themselves 'empty', but that the divine gifts overflow to them from the being of God. A whole range of verbs and verbal nouns is employed to stress the positive action and initiative of God in bestowing these gifts – e.g. attributor bonorum, sanctificationis attributor et creator, sanctificator, all applied to the Holy Spirit in 1035Df. In particular facere (1036D; 1037A; 1037B; 1052A) and compounds (efficere – 1040BC; 1052A; 1078A; perficere – 1038C; 1078A; effector – 1035C) and capere (1040C; 1044D; 1078C) and compounds (accipere – 1036A; 1051Df; 1052A; 1052B; receptatrix – 1037A) serve to emphasize the very different respective roles of God and of creatures who must be *made* holy, good and wise by him.

This making holy, good and wise is not simply a matter of some external operation of God upon creatures, nor of the mere infusion of qualities into them. It is a genuine participation in God, enabled by a genuine communication of himself, a real 'indwelling' in created beings. The angels 'are holy by participation in the Holy Spirit, and by the indwelling of the Son of God, who is sanctity and the communication of the Father . . . through participation in the Holy Trinity.' (1038C); and the same language of communication, participation, filling and indwelling is used throughout the work of created beings in general (e.g. 1035C;

1039C; 1040BC; 1054C; 1055C; 1078A; 1078C). God who is capabilis can be really and substantially present in his creatures. That is itself a mark of his divinity, and in particular of the divinity of the Holy Spirit (1054Cf), who shares with the Father and the Son this ability to 'indwell the soul and mind of man' (1082C). The weight placed by Didymus upon this point is indirectly shown by the fact that at 1082Cf he takes up an objection apparently made by a hearer to his previous development of the argument at 1054Cf. Does not Scripture say that the devil too enters into the hearts of creatures? He goes to some lengths to demonstrate that any devilish 'indwelling' is purely metaphorical; that of the Father, Son and Holy Spirit by contrast is to be taken literally.

This presence and indwelling of God is not automatic, nor, once given, is it impossible to lose it. Creatures are mutable, and can fall away; this was the reason for the fall of the devil and his angels (1083C). So too of men: 'The Holy Spirit is only put into those who turn away from their faults and follow after the choir of virtues and live according to these virtues, and through them by faith in Christ. But if then through gradual negligence they begin to turn to what is worse, then they stir up the indwelling Holy Spirit against themselves, and turn him who gave him to enmity.' (1075C) There is a certain vagueness here as to whether the gift of the Spirit or the turning away from faults comes first, and that vagueness is characteristic of Didymus. He can speak sometimes as if the mortification of the flesh (1069C) or the overcoming of mental 'perturbations' (1061C.D) are preconditions for the gift of the Spirit; but he can also ascribe mortification (1070B) or the conquering of perturbation (1068B) to the Spirit himself. Nor is clarity greatly increased when he comments that 'those who have often received the benefits of God know that they have achieved them more by his grace and mercy than by their own efforts' (1071C)! But Didymus is not in fact concerned with the issues which would only arise sharply with Pelagius; he is describing the dynamic of an ongoing interaction rather than the priorities in its beginnings. In that context, he gives special prominence to two motifs: the *pure heart* and *being worthy,* which appear repeatedly (e.g. 1042B; 1055A; 1056A; 1058C; 1063BC; 1064A). 1066AB brings them both out very clearly:

'The Spirit glorifies the Son, presenting him and making him openly known to those who are worthy to recognise and see him with a pure heart, and so to know him as the splendour of the substance and the Image of the invisible God. Again, the Image shows himself to pure minds, and glorifies the Father . . . The Father too reveals the Son to those who have deserved to attain the goal of knowledge . . . the Son himself gives the Holy Spirit to those who have prepared themselves to be worthy of his gift.'

The ultimate goal of this participation in the Trinity is 'blessed and eternal life among the sons of God' (1070BC), but it also brings a host of different gifts adapted to the individual (1041A). A whole catalogue of these gifts could be compiled from the De Spiritu Sancto's numerous references not only to virtue, benefits and good things in general, but also more specifically to such as sanctification, goodness, love, faith, grace, justice, fortitude, prophecy and ministry. Two in particular seem however to lie especially close to Didymus' heart: knowledge of divine truth, and the peace and joy which that knowledge brings. Sapientia, scientia and veritas are mentioned frequently, and the resultant peace and gladness are several times described. One passage from 1068B illustrates both:

'Just as it is the fault of the fleshly to be wise about the things of the flesh, to think about those things which are corporeal, so by contrast it is the strength of the spiritual always to think upon the things which are heavenly and eternal, and to speak of those things which are of the Spirit. But the wisdom of the flesh . . . kills . . . whereas the wisdom of the Spirit gives tranquillity of mind, and peace, and life eternal to all who possess it. When they have received it they will have all perturbations and all kinds of faults, and the very demons themselves . . . beneath their feet.'

Similarly, in a passage as near to purple as he ever comes in praising the gift of salvation, the note of knowledge is once more predominant (1073Df):

'"He himself redeemed them, and bore them up, and exalted them." (Isa. 63,9) For he bears up and exalts the saved, and raises the redeemed on high upon the wings of virtue, and through erudition and knowledge of the truth. Not only for one day or two, but for all the days of eternity he dwells in them and with them, giving them life to the very end of the age, being himself the author of their salvation. Enlightening their hearts all the days of the age, he does not allow them to wander in the darkness of ignorance and error.'

This knowledge, however, is not something merely intellectual or theoretical in an abstract sense. It is rather a fruit of the divine indwelling, a participation in him in whom knowledge itself subsists (1061Bf):

'The Holy Spirit, who comes in the name of the Son, sent by the Father, will teach everything to those who are complete in the faith of Christ – everything which is spiritual and intellectual, and in brief all the mysteries of truth and of wisdom. He will teach, not like a teacher or the master of a discipline which he himself has learnt from elsewhere . . . but being himself, so to speak, the art and doctrine and wisdom, and the Spirit of truth, he invisibly insinuates into the mind the knowledge of divine things.'

20 Kerygma und Logos

So we are brought back to the starting-point. Truth and, we may add, reality, subsist in God and are ultimately identical with him. The goal set before created beings is participation in that truth and reality in which their being is grounded and their destiny to be discovered. And it is because the Holy Spirit is himself the indwelling substance of divine truth that his own divine status is to be affirmed.

Didymus and Origen

This brief survey of the pattern of Didymus' thought may serve to show the extent of his debt to the concepts and categories of Hellenistic philosophy, especially those of the Platonist traditions. The comparison and distinction between levels of being, the emphasis on knowledge and truth, above all the centrality of the concept of participation by which the gulf between time and eternity is bridged – all these are manifestations of that Greek spirit which, in Harnack's words, conceived and constructed Christian dogma on the ground of the Gospel. But this is only one side of the story: the other is the extent to which Christian thinkers, Didymus among them, modified and adapted the fruits of Hellenism in order to build a distinctively Christian theology. The character of this two-way interaction as illustrated by Didymus' work can best be seen by comparing him with Origen, who represents not only an earlier stage in the same process, but also the primary source for Didymus' own thought.

The resemblances between Didymus and Origen are both numerous and striking. Almost every point that we have quoted from Didymus can be paralleled from Origen, and a detailed study of the whole of the De Spiritu Sancto in the light of Origen's works could certainly uncover many more similarities. It is not possible within the limited space of this paper to demonstrate this in detail; but for the sake of example these points may be noticed from the De Principiis:

The being of God is 'simple' (I 1.6).

The Father, Son and Holy Spirit possess their attributes substantially, whereas creatures only receive good qualities as 'accidents' (I 8.3).

All creatures are accordingly changeable (I 2.4), whereas the Father, Son and Holy Spirit are not (I 3.4).

Creatures are all capax of good and evil (I 7.2) whereas the Father, Son and Holy Spirit do not receive anything from without (I 8.3).

The reception of good gifts by creatures is enabled by the presence of God himself. Holiness is given by participation in the Spirit (I 1.3); the Father and the Son indwell those who are capaces of them (I 1.2); participation in holiness, wisdom and divinity – i.e. in the Trinity – is full blessedness (I 6.2).

This participation is granted only to the 'worthy' and may be withdrawn if they prove 'unworthy' (I 3.7).

Among the gifts specially emphasized are those of 'spiritual' as opposed to 'mortal' knowledge (I 1.9), and of gladness and peace (II 7.4).

It is apparent that Didymus has inherited from Origen not only specific points of detail, but the whole framework of thought which we have outlined. He has not, however, adopted the whole of Origen's teaching on the Trinity and the Holy Spirit, but only one side of it. For Origen combined this perspective with others which were to some degree in tension with it. Didymus has in effect constructed a complete system out of one part of Origen's, and so eliminated these tensions.

The tensions in Origen's teaching are well known, and need only the most summary mention here. Along with the line of thought just sketched, which draws a sharp line between the Trinity and all other reality, there is another which also distinguished gradations of being and of reality within the Trinity itself: the Father alone is absolutely good, while the Son is the image of that goodness, but not himself good *simpliciter* or absolutely (Justinian, Ep. ad Menam; cf. De Princ. I 2.13; where Rufinus seems drastically to have altered the meaning); the Spirit may even have been created through the Son (De Princ. I 3.3). Here it seems that the model of 'participation' is being applied by Origen to the relations between the divine persons[11], though not in quite the same fashion as when he deals with the connexion between any or all of them and creatures. Consonant with this, he also seems to have distinguished different kinds or degrees of 'participation' in the Father, Son and Holy Spirit by different levels of created being. In the schema outlined in De Princ. I 3.5, the Father ist the source of *all* being, the Son of *rational* being, and the Spirit as acting only in those 'who are turning to better things and entering upon the ways of Christ Jesus'. As the following chapters show, participation in the Holy Spirit then leads on to a higher degree of participation in the Son, and so ultimately in the Father. Rufinus again seems to have softened the subordinationist implications in his translation, but they are faithfully expressed by Justinian (ibid.): '. . . so then according to this, the power of the Father is greater than the Son and the Holy Spirit, and the Son's than the Holy Spirit . . .' To complicate matters further, two other places in Rufinus' translation seem to contradict this restriction of the Spirit's sphere of operation by saying that 'every

---

[11] Cf. D. L. Balás, 'The Idea of Participation in the Structure of Origen's Thought. Christian Transposition of a Theme of the Platonic Tradition', in H. Crouzel/G. Lomiento/J. Rius-Camps (ed.), Origeniana (record of the 1973 Origen colloquium at Montserrat) = Quaderni di "Vetera Christianorum" 12, Bari, 1975, pp. 257–275.

earthly and corporeal being' (I 3.4) or 'every rational creature' (II 7.2) participates in him.

In Didymus, these other perspectives have effectively disappeared. Certainly, occasional traces of them can still be found. At 1055A he remarks that 'in another place (sc. in Scripture) the nature of every rational creature is said to be the habitation of the Saviour.' But this is not in line with his general approach, nor even with the particular context; for the argument here (from 1054Cf) is that *the whole Trinity* dwells *in believers*. Again, an echo of Origen's understanding of the relations between the divine persons may perhaps be heard when he says at 1065Cf: 'The Son is said to receive from the Father those things in which he himself subsists. For the Son is nothing other than those things which are given to him by the Father, and the Spirit is no other substance than that which is given to him by the Son.' There too, however, the context makes it clear that what is meant is the opposite of any subordinationism: giving and receiving in the Trinity do not involve either diminution or change, but the sharing of the one divine substance. Throughout, Didymus' concern is not to *distinguish* but to *equate* both the gifts brought by and the indwelling of all three persons, to insist that where one is, all are, and that to participate in one is to share in all, as he emphasizes at 1069BC:

'Wherever the Holy Spirit may be, there too is Christ, and from wherever the Spirit of Christ should depart, from there Christ also departs . . . If one wished to express the converse one might say: If anyone is Christ's so that Christ is in him, then the Spirit of God is in him. And this must also be taken in the same way about God the Father. If anyone does not possess the Spirit of God, he is not God's. Again, if one wished to express the converse, one might say: If anyone is God's, the Spirit of God is in him . . . All of these prove the inseparable and indivisible substance of the Trinity.'

Here the distinctions drawn by Origen between the different levels of divine being and spheres of divine action have been wiped out; the concept of participation has been restricted in scope to the relation between the Trinity and created beings; the hierarchical cosmology, pivoting on the Logos/Son, which is fundamental to Origen's system, has been quietly left aside; pneumatology, which in Origen was a secondary or even tertiary sub-centre, has been brought into the very heart of the doctrine of God, and the understanding of the Trinity re-minted on that basis. Another stage has been reached in the modification and adaptation of the heritage of Hellenism in working out the implications of the Gospel. This could not be achieved without a price; there is no comparison for depth or range between Didymus' theology and Origen's. Others, more creative than Didymus, were perhaps able to preserve more of the richness of Origen in the reconstruction of dogmatic theology. In his own way, however, Didymus provides us with a clear illustration of the way in which thought moved, and had to move, from Origen into the fourth century.

In conclusion I would like to hazard two suggestions. The first has to do with Didymus' motive in departing so far from Origen while yet in other ways remaining so close to him. It is of course true that by Didymus' day the Arian controversy had rendered some of the elements in Origen's system suspect and unusable. This does not seem to me, however, to be a sufficient explanation, though it is part of the answer. It does not adequately take account of the fact that Didymus himself seems to have believed that he was loyally following Origen, and that Origen's teaching was defensible[12]. It seems to me more probable, though it may appear paradoxical, that the key to Didymus' departure from Origen lies precisely in his dependence upon him. He built on that aspect of Origen's thought which he himself found most congenial, and interpreted Origen from that standpoint. By drawing on Origen's understanding of the Holy Spirit as the indwelling master, the source and power of divine sanctification, and making that the starting-point for his own reflection, he came to emphasize in a way that Origen could not have done the divinity of the Spirit and the equality of the Trinity. Should we wish to probe further into his reasons for taking this approach, the clue may lie in another respect in which he seems to have abandoned the teaching of his predecessor. Origen believed that all spiritual beings, apart from the pre-existent soul of Christ, were involved in the primordial fall (De Princ. I 8.1). Didymus by contrast believed that the blessed angels stood fast in loyal obedience to the Trinity (1045Af). Some light on this may be cast by De Trinitate 588Bf, which makes it clear both that the cult of the angels was widespread in Egypt, and that the author (whom I believe to have been Didymus himself) venerated them and indeed prayed to them. While he is careful to draw a sharp distinction between the Holy Spirit and the angels – that indeed is the theme and occasion of the prayer – may it not be that in both angelology and pneumatology for him, as for so many others in so many areas, lex orandi was lex credendi? that a spirituality centred and focused on the Holy Spirit was what led this heir of Origen to the recognition that in the Spirit is nothing less than the truth and reality of God himself?

My second suggestion must be more briefly and even more tentatively formulated. In view of the similarities and differences we have seen between Didymus and Origen, and in view also of some of Jerome's hints that material from Didymus found its way into Rufinus' translation of the De Principiis, in addition to what we already know about the weaknesses

---

[12] Cf. Jerome, Adv. Ruf. II 16 (quoted supra, n. 5).

of Rufinus' work[13], it might seem appropriate to look in that translation not only for general 'orthodox improvements' of Origen's thought, but quite specifically for points which may echo the voice of Didymus himself. Particularly in the areas of the Trinity and the Holy Spirit, it would not be surprising if such were to be found[14].

---

[13] Two recent studies which supplement work done earlier, especially that of Robinson, Koetschau and Bardy, are included in Origeniana: J. M. Rist, The Greek and Latin Texts of the Discussion on Free Will in De Principiis, Book III (pp. 97–111), and H. Crouzel, Comparaisons précises entre les Fragments du Peri Archon selon la Philocalie et la Traduction de Rufin (pp. 113–121). For Jerome's hints that Rufinus used Didymus' reinterpretations, cf. supra, n. 5.

[14] The apparent widening of the possibilities of participation in the Holy Spirit at I 3.4 and II 7.2 is at least *prima facie* suspicious. Both statements are rather vague, so that whatever else we have here, it is most probably not a clear statement of Origen's original meaning. All that II 7.2 can in fact mean, if one looks at the rest of the sentence, is that every rational creature is *potentially capable* of participating in the Spirit, not that all in reality *do:* cf. I 8.3., where the problems of accurate speech about this are discussed. But more than mere clumsy translation may have been going on. Such an extending of the Spirit's activity, however, would scarcely be in line with the way in which Didymus appears to have transposed Origen's thought, at least so far as the De Spiritu Sancto suggests. More likely candidates might be passages such as I 3.4, which speaks of the Holy Spirit belonging in unitate trinitatis, id est patris inconvertibilis et filii eius because et ipse semper erat spiritus sanctus. Could a little gentle Procrustean pressure have been applied here to an originally less enthusiastically trinitarian text? If so, it may be that some of the points of similarity between 'Origen' and Didymus reflect not so much Origen's influence on Didymus as Didymus' on Rufinus. The possibility should at least be kept in mind!

THE ICONS BEFORE ICONOCLASM

NORMAN H. BAYNES

London

"THE FEELING against ikon-worship suddenly burst out in the earlier part of the eighth century when the iconoclastic (ikon-smashing) emperors of Constantinople tried to suppress the practice by force." So wrote Edwyn Bevan in an admirable essay on Idolatry.[1] And from modern accounts of the iconoclast movement one does generally get the impression that after the violent challenge of Epiphanius in the fourth century — when he tore down a pictured curtain which hung in a church [2] — the East Roman world had accepted without protest and without question the widespread cult of the icon, while the policy of iconoclast emperors appears as a sudden breach with a universally recognized tradition. But is such an impression justified? When we put together such fragmentary pieces of evidence as we possess is it not rather probable that there was a continuous questioning of the legitimacy of the cult? May not the part played by the icon in the life and religious usage of the Byzantine world have been subjected to the constant criticism of pagans, Jews and even of Christians? And if this is so, it may help us to understand somewhat more clearly the primary motives which inspired the policy of the iconoclast rulers. It may be worth while to consider the evidence afresh since it has been increased by two recent publications.

In 1938 Franz Diekamp published [3] a fragment from the σύμμικτα ζητήματα — the "Vermischte Untersuchungen" — of Hypatius of Ephesus contained in the Codex Parisinus 1115 ann. 1276. fol. 254ᵛ–255ᵛ. These "Mixed Enquiries" were addressed to Julian, bishop of Atramution (in western Asia Minor), a suf-

[1] The Edinburgh Review, vol. 243, No. 496 (April 1926), pp. 253–272.

[2] I accept the authenticity of the Epiphanian documents. For a criticism of the argument of G. Ostrogorsky, Studien zur Geschichte des byzantinischen Bilderstreites (Historische Untersuchungen, Heft 5) Breslau, 1929 see Franz Dölger, Göttingische gelehrte Anzeigen, August 1929, pp. 353–372.

[3] In his Analecta Patristica (Orientalia Christiana Analecta 117), Rome, Pont. Inst. Orientalium Studiorum, 1938, pp. 109–153, text at pp. 127–129.

fragan bishopric of Ephesus. This fragment is from chapter 5 of
the first book of the work and concerns τὰ ἐν τοῖς ἁγίοις οἴκοις —
"the things in the holy churches." This text has not, apparently,
attracted any attention from scholars, yet it is of considerable
interest since Hypatius of Ephesus was a prominent champion
of Chalcedonian orthodoxy in the reign of Justinian. Julian of
Atramution was troubled by the scriptural prohibition of the
making of images and by the command to destroy such images
when they had been made. He will allow representations (γραφάς)
in the churches but none on wood or stone and no sculpture.
These γραφάι may be on the door-curtains (ἐπὶ θύραις: I suppose
this is how the words must be translated), but no more is permissible. In his reply Hypatius urges that we must consider the
reason for the Old Testament prohibition, and at the same time
we must seek to understand why the making of sacred things
(τὰ ἱερά) is allowed as it is at present. Since some, as sacred
Scripture says, thought that the Godhead (τὸ θεῖον) was like gold
and silver and stones and graven works of art, and since they
made according to their own pleasure material gods and worshipped the creature rather than the creator, God rejected their
altars and their idols (Hypatius quotes Romans 1[25], Deut. 7[5],
4[15-16], Ps. 71[19]), for nothing of all the things that are is like or
equal to or the same as the holy Trinity and the Maker and
Cause of all things. But we direct that the unspeakable and
incomprehensible "philanthropy" (φιλανθρωπία) of God towards
us and the sacred images of the saints shall be glorified in sacred
representations (γράμμασι), though we ourselves have no pleasure at all in anything formed (πλάσει) or any representation
(γραφῇ). But we allow simpler and immature folk to have these
as being fitted to their natural development, that thus they may
learn through the eye by means adapted to their comprehension.
For we have found that often and in many cases both old and new
divine commands have made concessions to the weak to secure
their salvation. Hypatius instances the hierophant Moses who
at God's prompting had been his people's legislator and yet had
been bidden to make the images of the Cherubim. "And in many
other cases we see the divine wisdom (τὴν θεολογίαν) with "philanthropy" (φιλανθρωπίᾳ) for man's salvation releasing the strict-

ness of the law to benefit the souls of those who still need to be led by the hand." It is the care which guided the magi by a star and which led Israel away from idolatrous sacrifices to sacrifice to God. Therefore we, too, allow material ornament in our churches, not as though we thought that God was a god of gold and silver and silken vestments and vessels adorned with precious stones but making a concession so that each order of the faithful may be led by the hand in a way which is proper to itself and so brought to the Godhead. Thus of these, too, some will be led by the hand to spiritual beauty (ἐπὶ τὴν νοητὴν εὐπρέπειαν) and from the many lights in our churches to the spiritual and immaterial light.

And some of those who have studied the higher life (τὴν ὑψηλο-τέραν ζωὴν φιλοσοφησάντων) have learned that worship in the spirit can be offered in every place and that it is holy souls which are God's temples. . . . So then we in our churches do not re-move the sacred objects, but to the immature we stretch out a helping hand; we do not allow them to remain untaught concern-ing the more perfect doctrines, but them, too, we hold in the knowledge that the Godhead is not the same as any created thing nor is it equal or like to any such thing.

"As for ourselves we have no delight in the icons" — did that sixth century view persist among the bishops of Asia Minor? And if it did, it can readily be understood that any general cult of the icons in such extreme forms as later appear in the apologies of the iconodules would seem dangerous and a wrongful use of a practice which was tolerated only in the interest of the weaker members of the church. Here is an attitude which may help to explain the action of those bishops of Asia Minor who in the eighth century inaugurated the iconoclast movement.[4]

Through the sixth century protest of Julian of Atramution we can observe the Christian criticism of the place taken by the icons in the service of the church. We tend, however, to forget that not all the East Romans had been converted to the imperial faith. And in a fragment from St. Symeon's work on the Sacred Images [5]

[4] See G. Ostrogorsky, Les Débuts de la Querelle des Images, Mélanges Charles Diehl, vol. i, pp. 235–255.

[5] P.G. 86b col. 3220 (P.G. = Migne, Patrologia Graeca).

we find the pagan argument that the Christians, too, through their obeisance to the icons were praying to lifeless idols. It could not have been easy for the Christians to refute the charge. The pagans, it is said, traduced the Christians and gave birth to heresies; [6] what those heresies were we are not told; did pagan criticism lead to the rejection of the use of the icons? A passage from the work of John, Bishop of Salonica [7] is in its argument unexpected. The Christians, says the bishop, do not give corporeal forms to powers which have no body; the icons of Christ through the effect of the Incarnation represent God as seen on earth "and not as He is conceived in His divine nature" (καὶ οὐχ ὡς νοεῖται φύσει θεός). This the pagans — surely surprisingly — were prepared to admit; granted, they said, that you can represent One made Man, what of the angels pictured on the icons as human beings though the Christians regarded them as spiritual and incorporeal (νοεροὺς καὶ ἀσωμάτους)? And to this objection the Christians replied that the angels were not completely incorporeal (ἀσώματοι) as the pagans contended, they are of the air or of fire and their bodies are very fine. Angels are localized, they have appeared in bodily form to those whose eyes God opened and are therefore rightly so painted as spiritual created beings and ministers of God (κτίσματα νοερὰ καὶ λειτουργοὶ θεοῦ). It would seem that the essential point for the pagans was to establish that the Christian use of the icons was idolatrous: the Christian reverencing the Cross was a worshipper of a wooden god; if he worshipped the Cross he ought to worship asses. The Christian replied that no demon trembled when he saw asses.[8] And under Justinian pagans were given a short shrift: they were arrested and carried in public procession, their books were burned and so were their "icons and images of their foul Gods" (εἰκόνες τῶν μυσαρῶν θεῶν καὶ ἀγάλματα).[9] Did pagan criticism of the icons raise doubts of their legitimacy in the minds of the Christians? Our fragmentary sources give us no answer to such a question.

[6] Byzantion 17 (1944–45), p. 66.
[7] Mansi, vol. 13, col. 164–65.
[8] Pseudo-Athanasios P.G. 28, col. 621–624.
[9] Malalas (Bonn ed.), p. 491 [19-20]

It is strange that, so far as I know, no study has appeared of the appeal of Leontius, Bishop of Neapolis in Cyprus, directed to the Jews who charged the Christians with having introduced idolatry into the Church. That appeal we possess only in fragmentary form,[10] but it is of great interest as giving us the defence of the icons as it was formulated in the early years of the seventh century. Leontius knew Egypt well, he wrote the biography of the Patriarch St. John the Almsgiver; [11] and from the first many Jews had settled in Alexandria. It may well have been in Alexandria that Leontius composed his apology against the Jews (ἀπολογία κατὰ 'Ιουδαίων). We have in the Pratum Spirituale of John Moschus an account of Cosmas, a scholasticus of Alexandria, who possessed a large library — he was πολύβιβλος ὑπὲρ πάντας τοὺς ἐν Ἀλεξανδρείᾳ ὄντας (Pratum Spirituale ch. 172, P.G. 87, 3, col. 3040 D) and generously lent his books to all who wished to read them. John Moschus went to see him daily and always found him either reading or writing against the Jews, for he was passionately desirous to convert them to the truth, "And he often sent me to the Jews that I might discuss with them on the evidence of the Scripture." This is the background which must be kept in mind as one reads the appeal of Leontius. A summary of that appeal (so far as we possess it) is the simplest way of illustrating its significance.[12]

The Jews took their stand upon the God-given Law, and for the Christians also that Law formed part of their sacred scriptures since they had laid claim to the Old Testament as their own and refused to follow Marcion in rejecting the earlier revelation. And that Law had expressly ordained "Thou shalt not make unto thee any graven image or likeness of any thing that is in heaven above or that is in the earth beneath or that is in the water under the earth, thou shalt not bow down thyself to them nor serve them" (Exodus 20$^{4-5}$). "You shall make you no idols nor graven image . . . neither shall ye set up any image of stone in your land to bow down unto it" (Levit. 26^1; cf. Deut. 5^8).

---

[10] I do not understand the relation between the text cited from Mansi vol. 13, P.G. 93, col. 1597–1609 and the extracts quoted by John of Damascus P.G. 94.

[11] Translated in E. Dawes and N. H. Baynes, Three Byzantine Saints, Blackwell, Oxford, 1948.

[12] P.G. 93, col. 1597–1609.

Such was the tradition; but, Leontius argued, there was another legal tradition: God had said to Moses that he should fashion two Cherubim [13] graven in gold (Exodus 25[18]), while God showed to Ezekiel a temple with forms of palms and lions and men and with Cherubim from pavement to roof (Ezekiel 41[18]). Thus had God revoked his own ordinance. "If you wish to condemn me," wrote Leontius, "on account of images (εἰκόνες), then you must condemn God for ordering them to be made." [14] And though God gave no instructions concerning the adornment of His temple yet on the legal precedent of God's command to Moses (ἐκ νόμου λαβὼν τὸν τύπον) [15] Solomon filled the building with lions and bulls and palm-trees and men in bronze and with carved and molten images. It was important for Leontius to prove that the Christians were not innovators, they were but maintaining a tradition derived from the scriptures which were sacred alike to Jew and Christian; [16] elsewhere in a passage cited by John of Damascus (P.G. 94 col. 1273) he meets an objection that might be raised by the Jews. "It may be objected," Leontius writes, "that all those things which were in the tent of witness God ordered to be placed there and I reply that Solomon made many different things in the temple, carved and molten things which God had not ordered him to make nor were they amongst the things which were in the tent of witness nor were they in the temple which God showed to Ezekiel, but Solomon was not condemned for this, for he made these shapes to the glory of God just as we do." [17]

Others, it may be noted, carried the argument still further. Thus Hieronymus, a presbyter of Jerusalem, suggested that God had allowed each nation (ἔθνος) to worship its own gods through things made by man in order that no one might be able to raise objection to the Christian use of the Cross and the Christian obeisance (προσκύνησις) before the icons. So the Jews made their obeisance (προσκύνησις) before the ark of the covenant,

[13] For the argument derived from God's direction concerning the Cherubim see P. — supra.

[14] Cf. P.G. 94, col. 1384 A–B.

[15] Cf. John of Damascus De Imaginibus Oratio, III, P.G. 94, col. 1384 A–B quoting Leontius: Solomon ἐκ νόμου λαβὼν τὸ τύπωμα.

[16] Cf. ibid., col. 1381 s.f. νομικὴ γὰρ αὕτη ἡ παράδοσις καὶ οὐχ ἡμετέρα.

[17] Cf. Byzantion 17(1944–45), p. 59 "Et Dieu ne désapprouva pas et il l'appela le temple de son nom."

the Cherubim and the tables of the Law, although Moses was nowhere bidden to do obeisance to or to reverence (προσκυνεῖν or ἀσπάζεσθαι) these things (P.G. 40 col. 865) and the same view is expressed in a fragment cited in a note, ibid.

The reply of the Jew was that these images, permitted to be made by God, were not to be adored as gods but served only to remind us. "Well said," responded the Christian, "the same is true of our icons." [18] Elsewhere Leontius states that the godless (πανάθεοι) call the Christians idolaters and worshippers of wooden gods (ξυλοθέους). In P.G. 94 col. 1384 B he rejects the charge with scorn: "We do not make obeisance to the nature of the wood but we revere and do obeisance to Him who was crucified on the Cross" ibid. 1384 D. "We do not say to the Cross nor to the icons of the saints 'You are my God.' For they are not our gods, but opened books to remind us of God and to His honour set in the churches and adored" ibid. col. 1276 A. "If we worshipped the wood of the image, we should not burn the icon when the representation grew faint. When the two beams of the Cross are joined together I adore the figure because of the Christ who on the Cross was crucified, but if the beams are separated, I throw them away and burn them." This argument is adopted by other writers.[19]

One who receives an order from the Emperor and kisses the seal does not honor the paper but gives to the Emperor his obeisance and respect; [20] and in the same way, when we see the representation of Christ, through it we hail and do obeisance to the Crucified. Just as children, if their father is away, cherish his staff or his chair so we cherish the places which Christ visited, Nazareth or the Jordan, and remember his friends, the saints

---

[18] This theme of the function of the icons to keep alive men's memory is constant, cf. e.g., the citations of Leontius in P.G. 94 col. 1276 A ἀνάμνησις and in ibid., 1385 A; ὑπάμνησις in 1384 B and P.G. 28 col. 621 D. John Bishop of Thessalonica in Mansi 13 col. 164 on the icons of the saints εἰς τὸ μεμνῆσθαι αὐτῶν καὶ τιμᾶν αὐτοὺς . . . ὡς γνησίους δούλους καὶ φίλους θεοῦ καὶ παρρησίαν ἔχοντας πρεσβεύειν ὑπὲρ ἡμῶν. Of the icons we read in Quaestiones; ad Antiochum, Ducem P.G. 28 col. 621 οὕσπερ δι' ὑπόμνησιν καὶ μόνον ἐντυποῦμεν καὶ οὐ δι'ἕτερον τρόπον cf. Stephen of Bostra P.G. 94 col. 1376 B–D.

[19] Cf. Les Trophées de Damas, ed. G. Bardy, Patrologia Orientalis Tome 15, Fasc. 2, Paris 1920, p. 245 (75) — Isaiah 44[14-17] quoted; Quaestiones ad Antiochum Ducem P.G. 28 col. 621 B and the fragment ibid. col. 709 A.

[20] Cf. P.G. 94 col. 1384 D.

and the martyrs. And on account of Christ and of those things which are Christ's we figure his sufferings in our churches and houses, in our market places and on our garments — everywhere — so that through seeing them constantly we may be warned that we should not forget. Then turning to the Jew, Leontius says:

"You do obeisance to the book of the Law, but you do not make obeisance to parchments and ink but to the words of God contained therein. And it is thus that I do obeisance to the icon of God, for when I hold the lifeless representation of Christ in my hands [21] through it I seem to hold and to do obeisance to the Christ. As Jacob kissed the bloody coat of Joseph and felt that he held him in his arms, so Christians think that holding the image they hold Christ or His apostles and martyrs.

You say that there must be no obeisance paid to anything made by human hands or created. But haven't you, when wife or children have died, taken some garment or ornament of theirs and kissed it and shed tears over it and were not condemned for doing so? You did not do obeisance to the garments as to God; through your kisses you did but show your longing for those who once had worn them. Fathers and children, sinners and created beings as they are, we often greet them and no one condemns us, for we do not greet them as gods, but through our kisses we express our natural love for them. As I have said many times, in every greeting and every obeisance it is the purpose of the action which is in question.[22] And if you accuse me of doing obeisance to the wood of the Cross as though it were God why do you not say the same of the staff of Joseph? [23] Abraham did obeisance to infamous men who sold a sepulchre, and went on his knees before them, but not as though they were gods. Jacob blessed the idolater Pharaoh and did obeisance to Esau, but not as though they were gods. Do you see how many salutations and obeisances I have adduced out of the Scriptures and all without blame?"

"You call us idolaters when it was Christian saints and martyrs who destroyed the temples of the idolaters." [24] Leontius accuses the Jews of blindness because they fail to realize that through the relics of the

---

[21] Cf. τῇ σαρκί P.G. ibid. 1385 B and the fragment P.G. 28 col. 709.

[22] Cf. P.G. 94 col. 1385 B ὁ σκοπὸς ἐξετάζεται.

[23] P.G. 93 col. 1601 διὰ τί οὐκ ἐγκαλεῖς τῷ Ἰακὼβ προσκυνήσαντι ἐπὶ τὸ ἄκρον τῆς ῥάβδου τοῦ Ἰωσήφ. Jacob did not make obeisance to the wood but through the wood to Joseph. Hebrews, 11,21. Cf. F. Nau, La Didaskalie de Jacob, Patrologia Orientalis vol. 8, fasc. 5 p. 740 (30), Quaestiones ad Antiochum Ducem P.G. 28 col. 621.

[24] Cf. P.G. 94 col. 1385 D.

martyrs and through the icons demons are put to flight, and yet foul men pervert and mock and laugh at such things as these. Often blood will gush forth from the icons and from the relics of the martyrs and foolish folk, though they see this, are not persuaded; they treat the miracles as myths and fables. As Leontius writes in another fragment "If the bones of the just are impure, how was it that the bones of Jacob and Joseph were carried back with all honour from Egypt? How was it that a dead man touching the bones of Elisha straightway stood up? And if God works miracles through bones, it is clear that he can do the same through icons and stones and many other things." [25]

With this belief in the cogency of the argument from miracle may be compared a passage from the Quaestiones ad Antiochum Ducem: "Let those who refuse to do obeisance to the Cross and the icons explain how it is that the holy icons have often poured forth streams of myrrh by the power of the Lord, and how it is that a lifeless stele when it has received a blow has miraculously given forth blood as though it were a living body. Let them say how it is that from tombs and relics and icons demons are often driven howling away." [26] In Les Trophées de Damas it is stated that the sick whether they be believers or unbelievers take their seat beside the coffins of the saints and are healed.[27]

And daily, Leontius continues, almost throughout the inhabited world unholy and lawless men, idolaters and murderers, adulterers and robbers are suddenly smitten in their consciences through Christ and His Cross, say farewell to the whole world and give themselves to the practice of virtue. Tell me, how can we be idolaters who pay our homage ($\pi\rho o\sigma\kappa\upsilon\nu\epsilon\hat{\iota}\nu$) and do honor to the bones, the dust, the clothes, the blood and the tombs of those who refused to sacrifice to idols?

The Christian brings to the Creator, the Lord and Maker of all things, his adoration and worship through heaven and earth and sea, through stone and wood, through relics and churches, through the Cross, through angels and through mankind. For creation cannot itself directly worship its Maker, but through me the heavens declare the glory of God, through me the moon

[25] P.G. 94 col. 1272 C–D.
[26] P.G. 28 col. 621 C. For a story of a demon and the icon of the Virgin ibid.
[27] Les Trophées de Damas, ed Bardy. Patrologia Orientalis vol. 15, Fasc. 2 p. 273 (103) and cf. ibid. p. 272 (102).

worships God, through me the stars, through me the waters, the showers and the dew, through me all creation worship and glorify God.

When a good king has made for himself a rich and elaborate crown all those who are truly loyal to the king pay their respect and honor to the crown, but it is not the gold or the pearls that they honor but the head of the king and his skilful hands which have fashioned the crown. So with the Christians: whenever they pay their respects to the representations of the Cross and to icons it is not to wood or stone, not to gold or the perishable icon, not to the coffin or the relics that they bring their worship, but through these they bring their respect and their worship. For the honor paid to His saints courses back (ἀνατρέχει) to Himself. Thus it is that men destroying or insulting icons of the Emperor are punished with extreme severity as having insulted the Emperor himself and not merely the painted board. Man made after God's image is God's icon indwelt by the Holy Spirit. It is right therefore that I should honor and make obeisance (προσκυνεῖν) to the icon of the servants of God and glorify the dwelling of the Holy Spirit.

If the Jews accuse the Christians of idolatry they should be covered with shame, for they did obeisance to their own kings and the kings of other nations. Everywhere the Christians have armed themselves against the idols: against the idols we sing our hymns, against the idols we write, against the idols and the demons we pray. Supposing that an idolater had come into your temple and seen the two sculptured Cherubim and had blamed the Jews as being themselves idolaters what, asks Leontius, could you reply? For the Christian the Cross and the icons are not gods: they remind us of Christ and His saints that we should do them honor: they are there to beautify our churches; and he who pays his worship to Christ's Mother carries the honor to Him and he who honors the apostle honors Him who sent him forth.[28]

If then prophets and righteous men bowed to the earth before idolaters because of services rendered why do you blame me when I bow before the Cross and before representations of the saints through whom from God I receive ten thousand good things?

[28] Cf. P.G. 94 col. 1276 A.

On this appeal of Leontius Dr. E. J. Martin writes (A History of the Iconoclastic Controversy, p. 141) "The views . . . are so complete an anticipation of the Iconoclastic struggle and its very arguments that the authenticity of all the passages attributed to Leontius must be gravely suspect." He conjectures that Leontius is really the champion of orthodoxy, George of Cyprus. This judgment seems to me perverse. I am struck by the great skill with which Leontius presents his case: the whole argument is based throughout on the Old Testament, the common ground of Jew and Christian. Leontius may have known the theological justification, deduced from the Incarnation, of the icons of Christ, but he makes no use of it: it would have had no cogency for the Jews. "The principle stands that we must either not argue with a man at all or we must argue on his grounds and not ours." [29] Leontius knows St. Basil's doctrine that the honor paid to the icon passes to the prototype (ἡ τῆς εἰκόνος τιμὴ ἐπὶ τὸ πρωτότυπον διαβαίνει); he may well have known that key-text, but nowhere in the fragments which we possess does he cite a Christian Father of the Church. The only distinctively Christian argument which he employs is the evidence of those miracles performed through the icons for which the Jew was in duty bound to furnish an explanation, since Leontius was persuaded that the fact of miracle was incontrovertibly established. The plea of Leontius is thus widely different from the later Iconodule propaganda and deserves close study.[30] Indeed it may be suggested that the repetition, in a series of works against the Jews, of the arguments of Leontius in defence of the icons was indirectly intended to meet the scruples of Christians impressed by the Jewish contention. It is to be observed that it is a Christian who asks Antiochus for a justification of the disregard of the Old Testament prohibition of images.[31]

It is not necessary to consider in detail that series of works against the Jews, since the argument concerning the icons for the most part does but reproduce the plea of Leontius. Thus in

[29] G. K. Chesterton, St. Thomas Aquinas, 1933, p. 110.
[30] It would, for example, be of interest to know whether there are parallels to the view of Leontius that the world of nature needs the help of man before it can worship its Creator.
[31] P.G. 28 col. 621.

Les Trophées de Damas the Jewish charge of idolatry is repeated — the Christians are falling back into old pagan practices (τῇ παλαιᾷ ὑμῶν τῶν ἐθνῶν συνηθείᾳ),[32] they do obeisance to things made by human hands (χειροποίητα καὶ κτιστὰ πράγματα). The Christian in reply points to the ark of the covenant, to Moses and the (second) tables of the Law and to the Cherubim. The book of the Law is brought from the synagogue and the Jews do obeisance to it and so prove the Christian's argument.

A. C. McGiffert's edition of the Dialogue of Papiscus and Philo [33] (Marburg, 1889) is not accessible to me, but the text of the curious brief section on the Cross and the icons is cited by F. Nau in his edition of the Didascalia of Jacob.[34] This, again, only repeats arguments which we have met with previously: the Jew asking why the order which was given by God forbidding to do obeisance to things made of wood (μὴ προσκυνεῖν ξύλοις) was disregarded by the Christians in their use of the Cross and of icons, and the Christian replying Why do you do obeisance to the book of the Law and why did Jacob do obeisance on the top of Joseph's staff (ἐπὶ τοῦ ἄκρου τῆς ῥάβδου τοῦ Ἰωσήφ)? In respect of the book of the Law the Jew answers that he does not do obeisance to the nature of the skins but to the meaning of the words of the Law, while Jacob did not do obeisance to the wood of the staff, but he honored Joseph who held it.

In the summary of Leontius' argument references have been given to parallels in the Pseudo-Athanasian Quaestiones ad Antiochum Ducem P.G. 28, Quaestio 39, col. 621; there is no fresh development. A fragment added to the Quaestiones ibid. col. 709 does but give a variant to the text of Leontius: "For if Christ is not present to my lips in His body, nevertheless with heart and mind I am present with Christ in the spirit." It is interesting in such passages as this to catch an echo of the emotion which inspired the cult of the icon: in the Quaestiones ad Antiochum Ducem: "We make our obeisance to express the attitude and the love of our souls (τὴν σχέσιν καὶ τὴν ἀγάπην τῆς ψυχῆς ἡμῶν) for

[32] Les Trophées de Damas, ed. G. Bardy, Patrologia Orientalis vol. 15, p. 245.
[33] On this dialogue see A. Lukyn Williams, Adversus Judaeos, Cambridge, 1935, pp. 169–174.
[34] La Didascalie de Jacob, Patrologia Orientalis vol. 8, 5, p. 740.

those represented in the icon,[35] or "to show our longing ($\pi \acute{o} \theta o s$) for them just as we greet fathers and friends; [36] through the Cross we express the true attitude of our souls ($\tau \grave{\eta} \nu \ \tau \hat{\eta} s \ \psi \nu \chi \hat{\eta} s$ $\dot{\eta} \mu \hat{\omega} \nu \ \gamma \nu \eta \sigma \acute{\iota} a \nu \ \delta \iota \acute{a} \theta \epsilon \sigma \iota \nu$) towards the Crucified.[37] The very simplicity of the wording seems to carry with it an assurance of genuine feeling.

There remain to be considered two documents recently translated from the Armenian, a seventh century apology for the icons and a letter of the vardapet John Mayragometsi taken from the history of Moses Kaghankavatsi.[38] The apology begins on lines which must have become traditional: the Old Testament prohibition of images is met with references to the Cherubim, and to Solomon's Temple — God did not disapprove Solomon's initiative, He called the Temple the Temple of His name. The Christian paintings are not the true God, but we paint them in the name of God "tel qu'il apparut" — a precise parallel to the passage quoted from John, bishop of Salonica (supra p. 96). The writer of the apology is addressing Christians and therefore he can proceed to quote from John Chrysostom, Severian of Gabala and Gregory the Illuminator, and can translate from Eusebius his account of the statue of the woman with an issue of blood at Paneas. Heretics consider the icons to be idle, for they can neither speak nor understand: "What of the ark," is the reply, "when it overturned Dagon?" And the Cross raised the dead in the Holy City and still performs numberless miracles down to our own day — the Cross which is the pride of angels, the salvation of men and the terror of the demons. But the special interest of this apology lies in the statement that in Armenia two monks are preaching the destruction of the icons — "l'impie et l'égaré Thaddée et Isaïe et leurs compagnons qui entraînèrent à leur

[35] P.G. 28 col. 621 B.
[36] Ibid.
[37] P.G. 40 col. 865. It may be noted that the cult of the Cross was not extended to embrace other objects connected with the passion — the ass, the holy lance, the sponge, the reed — and when Christians asked the reason for this $\mathring{a} \gamma \iota a \ \gamma \grave{a} \rho \ \epsilon \mathring{\iota} \sigma \iota$ $\kappa a \grave{\iota} \ \tau a \mathring{v} \tau a \ \kappa a \theta \grave{a} \ \kappa a \grave{\iota} \ \mathring{o} \ \sigma \tau a \upsilon \rho \acute{o} s$ it was not easy to find a satisfactory answer, see P.G. 28 col. 624, Trophées de Damas p. 249.

[38] Sirarpie der Nersessian, Une Apologie des Images du septième Siècle, Byzantion 17 (1944-45), pp. 58-87. By her translation of these texts and her fully documented commentary Miss der Nersessian has rendered a great service to those of us who cannot read Armenian works.

suite un grand nombre de personnes," and from the letter we learn that when the leaders of the movement were arrested and were asked why they refused to accept the image of the incarnate God they replied that that was alien to the commandments "et c'est l'oeuvre des idolâtres qui adorent toutes les créatures; quant à nous nous ne nous prosternons pas devant les images car nous n'en avons pas reçu l'ordre des saintes écritures. Alors, leur ayant parlé des images de l'autel de Moïse, des diverses sculptures du temple de Salomon, et expliqué que nous représentons les mêmes choses dans nos églises; leur ayant donc dit ceci, et d'autres paroles semblables, nous corrigeâmes leur erreur."

Thus the story which begins with the scruples of Julian ends with an active Iconoclast movement in Armenia and Albania. I would suggest that too little attention has been paid to this evidence as forming the background of imperial policy. Need we doubt that Iconoclasm was primarily religious in its inspiration? Is there any reason to believe that "Iconoclasm was but an outgrowth and indeed the climax of the caesaropapistic theory and practice of the State as represented by some of the most successful Byzantine Emperors"? [39]

[39] So Gerhart B. Ladner, Origin and Significance of the Byzantine Iconoclastic Controversy, Mediaeval Studies 2 (1940), Pontifical Institute of Mediaeval Studies, pp. 127–149. I prefer Louis Brehier's summing up of Les caractères généraux et la portée de la réforme iconoclaste, Revue des Cours et Conférences for 11 April 1901, pp. 226–235.

THE CONCEPT OF THE IMAGE
IN THE GREEK FATHERS
AND THE
BYZANTINE ICONOCLASTIC CONTROVERSY

Gerhart B. Ladner

Except for the notes, this article is substantially identical with a paper read at the Symposium on Byzantine Iconoclasm held at the Dumbarton Oaks Research Library and Collection in April 1951.

THE honor rendered to the image passes to the prototype," to the model or original: ʽH τῆς εἰκόνος τιμὴ ἐπὶ τὸ πρωτότυπον διαβαίνει. This is the *locus classicus* of the defenders of the images in the Byzantine Iconoclastic Controversy, and it is the first of three patristic quotations chosen to introduce this paper. The sentence just cited is taken from St. Basil's late fourth century anti-Arian treatise *On the Holy Spirit*,[1] where it had served to illustrate the unifying image relation of the Son to the Father in the Divine Trinity, a relation first expressed by St. Paul when he said that Christ was the Image of God.[2]

The second text is from the book *On the Making of Man* by Basil's younger brother, St. Gregory of Nyssa. It was used by St. John of Damascus in his *First Oration on the Images* written not long after the outbreak of iconoclasm in the Byzantine Empire in the second quarter of the eighth century. "As . . . painters transfer the human forms to their pictures by means of certain colours, applying to their work of imitation (μίμημα) the proper and corresponding tints, so that the archetypal beauty may be transferred exactly to the likeness (ὁμοίωσις), thus it would seem to me that our Maker also, with certain tints as it were, by putting on virtues, paints the image" — that means the divine image in us — "with various colours according to His own beauty."[3] The words image and likeness may already have made it clear what the point of reference of this metaphor is: verses 26 and 27 of the first chapter of the Book of Genesis: "Let us make man to our image and likeness . . . And God created man to His own image: to the image of God He created him. . ."

The third patristic passage to be quoted is again from St. Basil, from his Twenty-Fourth Homily, directed against Sabellians and Arians. For the sake of brevity, I shall slightly paraphrase the lengthy text.[4] Basil says that "the Son" (i.e., Christ) "is from the Father by generation (γεννητῶς) and expresses in Himself the Father by nature (φυσικῶς); as an image He is absolutely without difference, as generated He preserves the same essence as the Father. . ." Now, if even an "Emperor's image is the Emperor" — for the image does not cause two emperors to exist — Christ all the more is the supreme Emperor, that is, God. For in the case of an imperial image, it is "wood, wax, colors and the art of the painter" which "make up a corruptible image, an imitation of something corruptible," in the case of Christ, He as an image is "the splendor of the glory" of God.

This text does not seem to have been utilized during the Byzantine

Iconoclastic Controversy, but the same idea and similar terms also occur in the chapter of the treatise *On the Holy Spirit* which has the famous passage mentioned earlier [5] and was often quoted by the Byzantine iconophiles. The distinction of an image by nature ($\phi v \sigma \iota \kappa \hat{\omega} s$) or generation ($\gamma \epsilon v v \eta \tau \hat{\omega} s$) — as in the Father-Son relationship — from an image as $\mu \iota \mu \eta \mu a$, as an imitation by art, is noteworthy. For a similar distinction of images $\kappa a \tau \grave{a} \mu \iota \mu \eta \sigma \iota v$ or $\kappa a \tau \grave{a} \theta \acute{\epsilon} \sigma \iota v$ or $\kappa a \tau \grave{a} \tau \acute{\epsilon} \chi \nu \eta v$ (imitative or conventional or art images) from images $\kappa a \tau \grave{a} \phi \acute{v} \sigma \iota v$ (natural images) was one of the principal *topoi* of the image doctrines of John Damascene, of the Fathers of the Second Nicaenum, and of Theodore of Studion. In order to trace the origin of this distinction — and it has never been traced — it will, however, be necessary to go back far beyond St. Basil to Aristotle and Plato.

The three texts so far discussed are characteristic of the whole relationship between orthodox Byzantine image doctrine and patristic thought. They deal with images in the proper sense in an accidental manner only, and are primarily concerned with Trinitarian, Christological, and anthropological doctrine. The Fathers of the Second Council of Nicaea and the Byzantine theologians of the eighth and ninth centuries in general cannot, of course, have failed to realize that such patristic texts were not written either to approve or disapprove of the use or veneration of images in the Church. In fact, they also made numerous patristic excerpts of a quite different kind in which the paedagogic-religious value or the miraculous effect of actual images of art was stressed: they referred, for instance, to a text from Gregory of Nyssa (not otherwise surviving?) according to which the saint had said that he had never seen a certain pictorial representation of Abraham's sacrifice of Isaac without being moved to tears; [6] or to St. Nile of Ancyra's story of a captive monk who was liberated through the dream appearance and intervention of a saint whom he recognized from having seen his image in the past.[7] Nevertheless, the orthodox Byzantines used the writings of the Fathers as a storehouse not only of practical and didactic but also of doctrinal and speculative arguments. They must then have assumed that patristic utterances like the ones I have quoted in the beginning expressed a concept of the image favorable to them. Modern critics have either agreed or disagreed with them, but no full effort has, to my knowledge, ever been made to ascertain whether there is not an intrinsic and genetic connection between patristic ideas of what an image is and the image doctrine of the Byzantine iconophiles.[8] Nor has the double root, in Holy Scripture and Platonizing thought, of the patristic image concept itself been exactly investigated. The truth is that the Greek Christian concept of the image was elaborated, not in the sphere of art, but in close contact with the development of the most fundamental dogmas about God and man. Yet this is only one half of the truth: for the image metaphors which were used in the formulation of Trinitarian and anthropological doctrine presuppose pre-Christian views on the character of an image which were based in part on the naturalism of classical and Hellenistic art and in part on a spiritualization of the naturalistic image concept through Platonism. It is from these two hallowed sources — Christian theology and anthropology on the one hand and Platonistic metaphysics and mysticism on the other — that orthodox Byzantine speculation derived the aura of awesome and blissful sacredness which surrounds its idea of an image. Such origins make it easier to understand the vital role of the doctrine of the Holy Images in Byzantine religiousness, and even the majesty and beauty of Byzantine art itself.

The connection of their doctrine with the principal Christian dogmas must be all the more important to the iconophiles since — though they would not admit it — the attitude of the *early* Fathers had been anything but friendly toward the images of *art*. They had rejected their use by Christians and had held a quite derogatory view of religious imagery.[9] It was only in the age of the great Cappadocians, toward the end of the fourth century, when in religious literature and learning, too, the first phase of the fusion between Christianity and Hellenism was well-nigh completed, that religious imagery was no longer considered as idolatry by the leaders of Christian thought. But it remained for the era of the Iconoclastic Controversy to give a thorough theoretical foundation to the distinction between idols and icons.

Following the lead of my three introductory quotations, I shall now try to describe the principal trends of thought which resulted in the emergence of a doctrine of the image of art in Greek Christianity. This will be done with a view to a genetic explanation of orthodox Byzantine teaching on the images, and with only occasional reference to the doctrine of the iconoclasts.

The first of the relevant ideological developments may be defined as the transfer of the image concept from the sensible to the intellectual realm, a long process traceable in Hellenistic and Early Christian thought from Plato to Philo and St. Paul, and from Plotinus and Proclus to Pseudo-Dionysius the Areopagite and St. John of Damascus. The Divine Logos Himself becomes the Image of God, and even images of such an image participate in its divine character.

Plato himself, as is well known, used the concept of the image first of all to depreciate the world of sense experience and to distinguish it sharply from the world of ideas. When he says in the *Phaedrus*,[10] "There are few who going to the images behold in them that which the images express," he implies that the so-called real things are only images of their truly real forms or ideas. Now, art for Plato is an imitation of nature, and if the natural things themselves have only a secondary reality and dignity, it follows that works of art will stand even lower in the scale of true values. And since the artist copies not only things of nature but also things made by man, *mimesis* or imitation by art can be called thrice removed from truth: "The art of imitation is then an inferior who marries an inferior and has inferior offspring." This is Plato's standpoint in the tenth book of the *Republic*.[11]

Now if Plato had stopped here, he would, perhaps, have to be considered the forerunner of the Byzantine iconoclasts rather than of the iconophiles.[12] But it must always be remembered that Platonism has two sides. Even in Plato's own late dialogues one finds a conception of images, both natural and artistic, which is not altogether derogatory. This conception and its post-Platonic development were most important for the patristic foundations of orthodox Byzantine image doctrine which are the main subject of this paper.

In the *Timaeus*, Plato sees the whole natural *kosmos* as the perfect image of an eternal *paradigm*, no longer as a deficient, but as a wonderful, manifestation of the divine;[13] cosmic time itself — the measure of all change and decay — is a moving image of eternity.[14] In the *Laws* and in the *Sophist* standards are set up which define the qualities required to give true value even to artistic or imitative images. "Imitation is not to be judged of by pleasure and opinion . . . for, the equal is not equal or the symmetrical symmetrical because somebody thinks or likes something, but they are to be judged by the standard of truth."[15] Whoever wants to judge an artistic image, pictorial or otherwise, must, therefore, know first what the thing represented is; secondly, how true; and thirdly, how well executed the representation is.[16] Among the artists themselves, those are the best who keep to age-old divinely instituted patterns, as are those of Egyptian art,[17] or to pure mathematical forms and relations;[18] and those are the worst who in their works do not exactly represent the existent symmetries of the original, but change them into proportions which may give a mere illusion of reality and beauty.[19] Thus, through participation in, or imitation of, intellectual and intelligible principles like symmetry, number, and equality, even the images of art can according to Plato be somehow connected with the realm of ideas. For like the rest of the world, true images must be images of something truly real. And yet the intellectual and intelligible, the ideal spheres, remain for Plato far above all imagery — man can hope to reach the *noeton* only by leaving all images behind.[20]

It is not known with certainty when exactly in later Platonism the status of the term and concept *eikon*, image, was raised to join the company of intelligible essences so that, paradoxically enough, the Platonic ideas could be called incorporeal or invisible images. Some suggestions are made by Willms in his excellent book ΕΙΚΩΝ.[21]

It is Philo, the great Jewish Bible scholar and Platonist of the first century of the Christian era, who made the identification of the most sacred ideas (ἱερώταται ἰδέαι) with incorporeal images (εἰκόνες ἀσώματοι) an accomplished fact.[22] How was this possible? It was possible for two reasons: first, because in later Platonism the ideas were gradually changing from independent entities into thoughts of God,[23] and thus were no longer quite uppermost in the hierarchical order of beings. Secondly, because such an interpretation of the ideas fitted in with Philo's theology of the Divine Logos who is the supremely rational Word of God, the sum of God's powers and energies including the ideas of all things. The Divine Logos is, therefore, for Philo, a kind of second God, and is quite logically Himself called the image of God, ἡ εἰκὼν τοῦ Θεοῦ.

In his work *On the Creation of the World*, Philo explains that the intelligible world of invisible light, the κόσμος νοητός, is nothing but the Word of God which is the Divine Image.[24] Elsewhere the Logos is called the eldest or first Image of God.[25] What this means becomes clear when we read in the *Allegories to the Third Book of Genesis* that the Logos is God's Shadow "which He made use of like an instrument and so made the world," and that this Shadow and Image is the archetype of all other things. For just as God is the Pattern of the Image or Shadow, so this Image becomes the Pattern of other beings.[26]

It is clear then that Philo is an important link between Platonic and Christian thought on the image. The image quality of the Logos of God who dwells in the very center of divinity is here the reason for the image quality of the entire *kosmos*.

It is very probable that St. Paul, about a generation younger than Philo, knew his writings, and especially his Image-Logos doctrine, to which he, perhaps, makes a polemical reference in the First Epistle to the Corinthians (15:45 ff.).[27] It would appear, however, that Paul derived his own doctrine of Christ as the Image of God chiefly from his novel development of the Genesis account of the creation of man. For when he speaks of Christ as the Image of God it is in connection with the reformation of fallen *man* to and even beyond the state in which he had been created: like many of the

Fathers after him, the Apostle seems to interpret this condition as an image-likeness, not with the Creator directly, but with *the* Image of God, Christ.[28] However this may be, the doctrine of Christ as the Image of God formulated by St. Paul must, of course, remain a guiding principle of all Christian speculation, not only about the Son of God, but also about images.

It was especially in the Trinitarian controversies of the fourth century concerning the true divinity of Christ that the necessity arose to show that an image can be essentially the same as its original.

Even though by the fourth century much of Graeco-Roman naturalism had been given up in the practice of art, the theoretical conception of the image was still based, to a large extent, on the matter-of-fact naturalism or even illusionism of Plato's time and on the Platonic view that a true image reproduces its model faithfully.[29]

St. Athanasius, the great fighter for Christ's full divinity, was, perhaps, the first to use in this connection the simile of the Emperor's image which we have already met in St. Basil.[30] The Athanasian and Basilian formulations, and several patristic variants, were often quoted by the Byzantine iconodules.

Athanasius argues as follows: [31] "In the image there is the idea ($\epsilon\tilde{\iota}\delta o\varsigma$) and form ($\mu o\rho\phi\acute{\eta}$) of the emperor. . . The Emperor's likeness is unchanged in the image, so that who sees the image, sees the emperor in it, and again who sees the emperor, recognizes him to be the one in the image. . . The image might well say: 'I and the emperor are one,' 'I am in him and he is in me. . .'" — (an obvious parallelism to the Gospel of St. John: "I and the Father are one. . ." and "I am in the Father, and the Father in me.") [32] Athanasius continues: "Who, therefore, adores the image, adores in it also the emperor. For the image is the form of the latter and his idea."

Kindred examples could be multiplied. The underlying idea is always the same: that in so far as an image is similar to the original, it is *equal*, *identical*, with it.

It has often been observed that the image of Christ was the prime concern both of iconoclast and iconophile theory. The relationship between Trinitarian doctrine and the concept of the image as such helps in explaining this fact. Christ as the Image of God was the summit of a great hierarchy of images, expounded by John Damascene in the first and third of his *Orations on the Images*. One is introduced into a world of images which extends from Christ through the divine ideas, through man as image of God, through the symbols and types of Holy Scripture down to the memorials or monuments of literature and art.[33]

This, too, is Platonism, but a Platonism not only Christianized but also broken through a complex prism of Neoplatonic and Pseudo-Dionysian facets. Through Dionysius the Areopagite, some of the substance of Proclus and Plotinus entered Byzantine image doctrine. In one very important point, however, the image hierarchy of John of Damascus differs from the Neoplatonic system: John no longer calls *the non-human things of nature* images. While for Plato *these latter* had been the images *par excellence*, and for Philo, Plotinus, and Proclus, both intelligible *and* material natures were images, it was in the nature of Christian thought that material natural creatures should stand both above and below the dignity of images: above as creatures of God; below, if compared, for instance, with an image of Christ. For Plato — to use the famous example of the tenth book of the *Republic* — a material bed, as the image of the idea of a bed, is better than any art-image of a bed.[34] For Plotinus, corporeal things are images comparable to the images of art, and both classes of images have reality in so far as they are in contact with the intelligible images of the unimaginable supreme unity, the One.[35] For Proclus, *everything*, except the very highest intelligible and the very lowest material, can exist in its cause (potentially), in itself, and by participation in something higher in the manner of an image.[36] Even Origen was enough of a Platonist to think that not only man but also an animal or a plant may have been created according to some heavenly form or image.[37] But the Areopagite moved farther away from the genuinely Platonic relation between images and ideas. It is true that, at least once, he uses Plato's simile of the sun as the image of the highest Good.[38] Yet on the whole, Pseudo-Dionysius' celestial and ecclesiastical hierarchies are hierarchies of angels and men, of symbols and sacraments. It is typical also for the Dionysian transformation of the Platonistic doctrine of ideas and images that the Areopagite no longer makes use of the terms *idea* or *eidos*. The relational terms *paradigm* and *eikon* from Plato's *Timaeus* do occur,[39] but they are applied in a broader sense which corresponds to St. Paul's teaching that "the invisible things of Him [God] . . . are clearly seen, being understood by the things that are made."[40] Truly characteristic for Dionysius and for John of Damascus is the term *proorismos*, a noun related to the Paulinian verb προορίζειν,[41] which means "to mark out providentially." In the Areopagite[42] and in the Damascene,[43] it signifies God's foreknowledge and pre-definition of the things He was to create. It is then these *proorismoi* which are the ideas existent in the mind of God, and it is they which stand second in the *image* hierarchy of the Damascene, from which the things of a non-human nature themselves are conspicuously *absent*. For the Christian East, not only angels and men but also their symbols and images had gradually come to be incomparably more important than mere things of nature — and the victory of the orthodox image doctrine in the Iconoclastic Controversy completed this development. Contrary to the Augustinian and, generally speaking, the Western idea of knowing God even through his vestiges in non-human nature,[44] the Byzantines saw the things of nature only as accompanying symbols within a vast cosmic liturgy performed by Christ and by hierarchies of angels and men, and represented by the sacred icons.

In Greek patristic and Byzantine thought, then, the concept of the image refers to *God* Himself and His Incarnation and Revelation and to *man* himself and his inspired prophecy and sacred art. To the influence on Greek patristic and Byzantine image doctrine of the image-likeness of *man* with God, according to the Book of Genesis, I must now return.

The second text introducing this paper, taken from Gregory of Nyssa, compares the creation of man according to God's image and likeness to the painting of a picture. Such comparisons of the divine creation of man with the reproduction of man by art were another commonplace of patristic literature.

The principal scriptural data concerning the creation of man on which the Fathers could and must build contained three problems which demanded interrelated exegetical solutions. First, man was created only to or after the image, whereas Christ was Himself *the* Image of God. Second, according to Genesis 1:26 f., man was made to the image of God, but according to Genesis 2:7, he was molded from earth, and God breathed into him a living soul. Third, he was made not only in God's image but also in God's likeness or similitude (Genesis 1:26). The questions that thus arose all have a bearing on the development of the patristic image concept.

How could corporeal man be made after the image and likeness of an incorporeal God? One type of answer was given by St. Irenaeus of Lyons, at the end of the second century. He countered all anthropomorphic conceptions of God Himself by referring the image relation between God and man in advance, as it were, to God Incarnate, to Christ. For "when the Logos of God became flesh, He truly showed the image . . . Himself becoming that which His image, namely man, already was." [45] Irenaeus was followed in this respect by St. Methodius of Olympus, around 300, who in his dialogue *Symposium* or *On Virginity* said that Christ assumed a human body in order that man could imitate Him better: as if He had painted His picture for us so that we can imitate Him, its painter.[46] Methodius' prime concern was with the full reality of the Incarnation of Christ and the resurrection of all men according to the body or flesh. His metaphors from the realm of art, therefore, do not emphasize the equality between the representation in the image and the prototype represented, but the indestructible nature of the image's material. Just as a sculptor will melt down a bronze statue if he finds some blemish in it and then cast it anew, so God recreates man in death and resurrection. And just as the metal of the second statue is the same as that of the first, so our body will still be extant in the new life. It will be a spiritual body as St. Paul said, because desiring spiritual things only, but still a body, not some incorporeal substance, as Origen had assumed.[47] Irenaeus is not quoted by the Byzantine iconophiles of the eighth and ninth centuries, and Methodius only once by John of Damascus.[48] But their basic conception that man is an image of Christ *as man* does appear, though less explicitly and exclusively, in later patristic works and may have provided indirectly a fundamental Byzantine argument against iconoclasm: namely, that the image of Christ can and will reproduce Him as man only.

Even more important in itself, and for Byzantine image doctrine, was another approach to the exegesis of the Genesis accounts of the creation of man which is almost the opposite of the first. It is of Alexandrian origin, found in Philo, in Clement, in Origen, and in Athanasius, and it was to become the prevalent patristic interpretation. Here the image relation between God and man is transferred to an altogether different plane, raised to the realm of soul and spirit. We must remember that in patristic as well as in Platonistic thought a bipartite or a tripartite division of the *soul* — according to its reasonable and unreasonable or to its rational, spirited, and desirous-appetitive parts — [49] went along with the dichotomy according to soul and body. It is to his endowment with mind, in other words, to the higher parts of the soul, to reason, to free will, that the image of God in man is referred by most of the Fathers. Already for Philo,[50] man was an image *through his mind* of *the* Image of God, that is to say, of the Logos, the Divine Word and Reason. That the image-likeness was something spiritual-intellectual was to remain the almost unanimous opinion of the Fathers of the Church from the time of Clement of Alexandria [51] and Origen,[52] that is, from the third century.[53] The only exception I know of is Methodius, whose dependence upon Irenaeus and whose antagonism towards certain doctrines of Origen are also otherwise known.

A further patristic distinction was that between the divine image, *eikon*, and the divine similitude or likeness, *homoiosis*, in man. The image was identified with man's native reasonableness and spiritual freedom, similarity and assimilation to God with his efforts toward perfection, aided by God's grace. The origins of this distinction are found, in somewhat divergent forms, in the Valentinian Gnosis,[54] in St. Irenaeus,[55] and above all in Clement of Alexandria [56] and Origen.[57]

This whole trend of patristic anthropological exegesis was bound sooner or later to affect the development of the image concept. How could it be otherwise? Man's soul, under its highest intellectual and spiritual aspects, was a painting painted by Christ, the best painter — thus, for instance, Origen in the famous *Thirteenth Homily to Genesis*.[58] The performance of the liturgy, too, could be called a process of spiritual painting or repainting by the hands of Christ, and through the priest who is His pen — thus, for instance, the fifth-century Nestorian Narsai, in his liturgical homilies.[59] Again, according to Origen, the image could be covered through man's fault with wrong colors and become invisible by the accumulation of dirt [60] — this latter a Plotinian metaphor [61] which was taken up also by Athanasius [62] and Gregory of Nyssa.[63] But even so, the image could never be completely destroyed and, therefore, could be restored to its primitive splendor.[64] True, the divine image in man was only a copy made according to *the* Image of God, Christ, an image of the image, but even so it could be a faithful copy, large and skillfully made: "If I shall make the image of the image, that is my soul, great, and shall magnify it by work, thought, and word, then . . . the Lord Himself Whose image it is, will be magnified in our soul" — thus Origen's exegesis of the *Magnificat* in his *Eighth Homily to St. Luke*.[65] The image could, in fact, become as close to its archetype as the image in a cleansed and polished mirror — a favorite metaphor of Gregory of Nyssa [66] in which, as Cherniss has shown, he made use of Plato's *First Alcibiades* [67] and, perhaps, also of Plotinus' mirror similes.[68] Man's soul was finally a sculpture the form of which had to be separated from the rock of brute matter, carved out and smoothed until it conformed to the thought of the supreme artist — thus Gregory of Nyssa,[69] in the tracks of Plotinus' *First Ennead*.[70]

In all these comparisons *similarity* is the term of reference which links the man-God relation to the image-prototype relation. In both cases similarity is almost synonymous with perfection. Just as images can be better or worse, depending on the artist's skill and the subsequent similarity with their originals,[71] so — to quote Gregory of Nyssa — the definition (ὅρος) of human happiness is the greatest possible similarity with God.[72] Only of sin, because it is non-being or absence of being, there is no image with which it could be compared — thus Theodoret of Cyrus, or a later glossator, according to a fragment from, or scholion to, his lost *Commentary to Isaiah*.[73]

The whole conception of the image as a blend of like and unlike, same and other, is undoubtedly Platonistic. The remote ancestor of this conception is found in Plato's own dialogues, for instance at the end of the Sixth Book of the *Republic*,[74] in the *Statesman*,[75] and especially in the *Parmenides*[76] and in the *Sophist*.[77] Pseudo-Dionysius the Areopagite, for example, whose writings John Damascene and Theodore of Studion, of course, knew and who himself had used Proclus' *Commentary on the Parmenides*, if not the *Parmenides* itself,[78] had in fact given an exposition quite Platonic in spirit of the doctrine that God is similar to Himself and to nothing else, and yet gives the greatest possible similarity with Himself to those who turn to Him. "For," the Areopagite says, "things of the same order can have reciprocal similarity . . . but in the case of cause and effect He shall not admit mutual reciprocity."[79] In other words, we must try to become similar to God, but God will never be similar to us. St. Theodore of Studion[80] quotes another Dionysian text from the book *On the Ecclesiastical Hierarchy*, a text which, for the sake of a metaphor, applies this doctrine to the images of art: ". . . in sensible images, if the painter looks without interruption at the archetypal form, neither distracted by any other visible thing nor splitting his attention toward anything else, then he will, so to speak, duplicate the person painted and will show the true in the similitude, the archetype in the image, the one in the other except for their different essences [or natures]."[81]

It is obvious why Byzantine iconophiles quoted this text and many a similar one. They were thus enabled to bolster their ever recurring contention that the image of Christ in a work of art can be identical with Him in one way though not in another: identical as to the form of His humanity and even as to His divine-human hypostasis or person, not identical as to His divine, invisible essence.[82]

Similarity with God, with Christ, as a topic of patristic thought is derived then from a combination of Biblical and Hellenic ideas in which the Christian element, of course, was the dominant. Genesis 1:26–27, Christ's words "Follow me,"[83] St. John's "We shall be like to Him" (ὅμοιοι αὐτῷ ἐσόμεθα),[84] blend with phrases from Plato's *Theaetetus* about man's flight from earth to heaven through his becoming similar to God,[85] or from Plotinus' *First Ennead* where the soul's development toward goodness and beauty is called assimilation to God.[86] Clement of Alexandria[87] was probably the first who consciously harmonized the assimilation and followership doctrine of Plato's *Theaetetus* and *Laws*[88] with St. Paul's idea of μίμησις. In patristic thought the concept of *mimesis*, imitation, which had been accorded at best a relative dignity by Plato, can stand on the higher level of assimilation to and followership of God, because of St. Paul's designation of himself, and of the Christian in general, as μιμητὴς Χριστοῦ.[89] Origen, for instance, in distinguishing divine image and divine likeness in man, says expressly that similarity to God, lost by original sin, can be regained by imitating and following Him; [90] and Gregory of Nyssa asserts: "Christendom is imitation of the divine nature." [91]

Besides the Biblical and Platonistic tradition, so-called Pythagorean literature, the chronology of which unfortunately is so doubtful, may have influenced patristic ideas about image-likeness, assimilation, and imitation. A few examples will demonstrate the typical uncertainties as to the value of this literature for the knowledge of genuine Pythagorean thought, not to speak of the difficulty of deciding in what relationship some of these documents stand to Hellenic and Jewish-Christian thought, respectively. [92]

Clement of Alexandria in the third century quotes a pseudoepigraphic text, attributed to the Pythagorean Eurysus (meaning Eurytus?). [93] He quotes it as a pagan testimony for man's creation to the image of God. The Neoplatonist Jamblichus (about A.D. 300), in his *Life of Pythagoras*, speaks of followership of, and conformity with, God as of the principal tenet of Pythagorean doctrine. [94] Lucian who in the second century had written that, according to the best of philosophers, man was an image of God, [95] may well have had Pythagoras in mind. [96]

"Pythagorean" influence on the patristic doctrine of *man's* image-likeness with God can in any case hardly have been more than secondary. It has, nevertheless, been mentioned, because this source of patristic thought seems to have been very effective in the case of the ideology of the *ruler* as image of God (see below).

As for the continuity between patristic and Byzantine thought on man's image-likeness with, and imitation of, God, there is ample evidence for it. I mention as an example St. Maximus the Confessor, who carries on the distinction between image and similitude in the manner of Origen. [97] What is, perhaps, the earliest explicit use of the image-likeness doctrine in defense of Christian religious imagery is found in a fragment from the writings of Stephen of Bostra, about whom very little is known otherwise. He seems to have been a seventh- or early eighth-century Bishop of Bostra, that is to say, Bosra in Syria, and wrote a treatise against the Jews which contained anti-iconoclastic passages of considerable interest. [98] It seems that this work was composed at a time when the first distant rumbles of the great Byzantine iconoclastic outbreak of the eighth century could be heard. There is evidence of iconoclastic unrest in various eastern borderlands of the Byzantine Empire from the sixth century onward. [99] To quote one instance, the Younger Symeon the Stylite complained to the Emperor Justin II about the breaking of Christian images by the Samaritans. His letter was read at the Second

Nicaenum.[100] In the seventh century, such trends became more vigorous. It is doubtful whether Moslem influence played a role then. The existence of Jewish and Christian-heretical iconoclasm, however, is certain from historiographical testimony.[101] There also survive Jewish-Christian dialogues of that period, fictitious in their literary form, in which the controversial relation between Christian images and pagan idols is discussed.[102] Stephen of Bostra's work belonged to this genus of writings. We have only extracts from it in two versions: a shorter one in John of Damascus' *Third Image Oration*,[103] and a longer one found in a Codex of the Ambrosiana by Cardinal Mercati, more than half a century ago.[104] The latter is the more faithful, since it is identical with the quotation made by Pope Hadrian I in his letter to the Second Council of Nicaea which was read during the Second Session.[105] In the Ambrosiana excerpt Stephen says: "An image (εἰκών) is one thing, and an idol (ἄγαλμα or ζῴδιον) is another." Then he quotes Genesis 1:26, and continues: "Now is it idolatry and impiety that man is an image of God? Far from it. If Adam were an image of demons, he would be abject and inacceptable; but because he is an image of God, he is honorable and acceptable. . . And what is the honor rendered to the image if not just honor, as also we sinners do reverence (προσκυνοῦμεν) one another in accordance with honor and love?"[106] Stephen of Bostra thus establishes a clear distinction between an idol and an image which was to remain a constant and forceful argument of the eighth- and ninth-century defenders of the images. Adoration and salutation of images are not to be construed as idol-worship but as signs of respect and affection. It is interesting to see how in this respect, too, Christian argumentation incorporated certain elements of pagan thought where they seemed to fit.[107] I cannot enter upon the subtle difference between *eikon* and *eidolon* in Platonism.[108] Plotinus and Porphyry certainly wished to avoid the simple identification of the images of gods with the gods themselves.[109] Plotinus used the mirror simile in this connection,[110] and in a fragment from Porphyry's *Peri Agalmaton*, statues of gods are said to have human forms because man alone has an intellectual part (like the godhead itself).[111] Thus the elder Philostratus could claim that whosoever rejects images does an injustice to truth,[112] and Callistratus that in images the divine intelligible is produced by the material.[113] It is also worth while to recall that a late Platonist like Julian the Apostate defended the worshipping of divine images by a comparison with the affectionate or respectful reaction toward the images of emperors or parents,[114] just as some of the Fathers did [115] who were followed among the Byzantine iconodules, for instance, by the Patriarch Nicephorus.[116] Stephen of Bostra's direct parallel between the image-not-idol character of Adam and the image-not-idol character of religious art, perhaps, may have prompted John of Damascus to insert man as image of God in his hierarchy of images.[117] The same idea, finally, found its most convincing formulation in the *Third Antirrheticus* of St. Theodore of Studion: "The fact that man was made according to the image and likeness of God shows that in the making of an image its form or idea ($\tau\grave{o}$ $\epsilon\mathring{i}\delta o\varsigma$) is something divine." [118]

The form or idea of the image: this phrase expresses and compresses what were, perhaps, the most original thoughts within Greek Christian image speculation. Above,[119] the fact has been alluded to that for the Fathers and for the Byzantines, identity between image and original does not exist with respect to the former's matter ($\mathring{v}\lambda\eta$) or the latter's nature ($\phi\acute{v}\sigma\iota\varsigma$), which in the case of Christ is even the divine essence ($o\mathring{v}\sigma\acute{\iota}\alpha$). The identity is only a formal, an ideal, a relational one (according to $\sigma\chi\acute{\epsilon}\sigma\iota\varsigma$ or $\pi\rho\acute{o}\varsigma$ $\tau\iota$).[120] There can be no question of putting into a picture made of wood, colors, and the like, the *nature* or *essence* of either man or God. But on the other hand, the iconophiles, and most outspokenly Theodore of Studion, went so far as to hold that Christ's image is identical with Him $\kappa\alpha\theta'$ $\mathring{v}\pi\acute{o}\sigma\tau\alpha\sigma\iota\nu$.[121] This means that Christ's image was supposed to participate in, or imitate, however relatively, the Second Hypostasis or Person of the Holy Trinity, Christ, not only as man, but as God.[122] This was truly a high claim to make.

Does the influence of Neoplatonic emanationist ideas sufficiently explain such a claim? The truth is simpler and the influence less one-sided. When quoting from St. Basil's *Oration against the Arians and Sabellians* — the third introductory quotation of this paper — I suggested that there existed in the writings of John Damascene and his iconophile successors a distinction of images $\kappa\alpha\tau\grave{a}$ $\phi\acute{v}\sigma\iota\nu$ or $\gamma\acute{\epsilon}\nu\nu\eta\sigma\iota\nu$ from images $\kappa\alpha\tau\grave{a}$ $\tau\acute{\epsilon}\chi\nu\eta\nu$ or $\theta\acute{\epsilon}\sigma\iota\nu$ or $\mu\acute{\iota}\mu\eta\sigma\iota\nu$, which was part of a patristic tradition, itself founded on Platonic and Aristotelian elements. It is this distinction which really overarches all the other ones mentioned. Without it Byzantine image doctrine would be illogical as a system of Christian thought, in which Christ as the natural or essential image of God must be on a higher level than an imitative, a "thetic," that is to say, a "posited" or conventional, image of Christ, an image of art, made by man. In its application to the problems of the Iconoclastic Controversy the *physis-thesis* distinction first appears in John Damascene. It will, therefore, be sufficient to study it briefly in his writings and to trace its origin from there. But it does occur in various forms also in the Acts of the Second Council of Nicaea,[123] in the writings of St. Theodore of Studion,[124] and also in the early ninth-century *Commentary to the Gospel of St. John*, edited by Hansmann in 1930,[125] which contains numerous references to the problems of religious imagery and to the Iconoclastic Controversy itself.

In his *Third Oration on the Images*, John Damascene defines what an image is, and the first kind of image, he says, is the natural one (φυσική). "For in each thing that which is according to nature (κατὰ φύσιν) comes first, and only then τὸ κατὰ θέσιν καὶ μίμησιν, that which is according to convention or imitation." [126] Christ, therefore, is the natural Image of the Father, man is God's image by imitation,[127] and so are the images of art. John of Damascus, as everybody knows, was not only a defender of the images but the Byzantine systematizer of patristic thought. His greatest work is *The Fountain of Knowledge*, of which the first part is a *Dialectic*, largely dependent on Aristotelian logic. Chapter 53 in Lequien's edition is entitled Περὶ τοῦ κεῖσθαι.[128] Κεῖσθαι, "situation," is one of Aristotle's categories of thought.[129] The second paragraph of John Damascene's chapter of Περὶ τοῦ κεῖσθαι begins as follows: "Among the things which have a situation (κειμένων), some have it κατὰ φύσιν, thus the elements in their proper places, for instance, éarth, water, air, fire, etc.; others κατὰ θέσιν καὶ τέχνην, according to their being posited and by art, for instance, a statue, a column, and the like." [130] Now there is as far as I see nothing like this either in Aristotle's *Categories* or in Porphyry's Introduction to it, the famous *Eisagoge*. Yet the relevant terms do occur in Aristotle's *Physics*. In the second book [131] Aristotle speaks of those who see the nature or essence of a thing in its matter, for instance, the wood of a bed, or the bronze of a statue, and not in the normative arrangement and artistic procedure (τὴν κατὰ νόμον διάθεσιν καὶ τὴν τέχνην) according to which the bed or statue is made. Also, natural generation is contrasted with technological reproduction. In a later paragraph,[132] Aristotle says that art either completes what nature cannot attain or imitates nature. In these passages one finds all the terms which appear in the *physis-thesis* topos of patristic and Byzantine speculation; it is true that there their use is not strictly in accordance with Aristotle's thought. But this question is not of great concern here, nor the other one, which of the Aristotelian commentators the Damascene may have consulted. Perhaps it was John Philoponus, the Alexandrian Monophysite of the sixth century, of whose theological works John Damascene in his book *On Heresies* gives extracts.[133] Philoponus' *Commentary* on the *Physics* survives,[134] and his terminology does seem to form a link between Aristotle and the Damascene. So, when commenting on the Aristotelian passages just quoted, he uses θέσις in addition to the Aristotelian διάθεσις,[135] and elsewhere σχέσις to paraphrase the Aristotelian πρὸς ἡμᾶς: [136] both changes are akin to the use of these terms by John of Damascus. In any case there can hardly be much doubt that the latter's *physis-thesis* distinction is based on Aristotle or on Aristotelian commentaries and, in addition, perhaps, on Plato's *Cratylus* and Neoplatonic commentaries, such as that of Proclus, where the mutual relation of things and names is treated under the aspects of *physis* and *thesis-mimesis*.[137] Above all, however, John of Damascus rests on earlier patristic tradition in this as in all other points of his doctrine. From this tradition neither the *thesis-physis* nor the *techne-genesis* topos was absent. I mention only a few patristic examples besides the passages from St. Basil already quoted.[138] In one of the surviving fragments from the works of the early fourth-century Bishop Eustathius of Antioch, Christ as man is compared to an art-image made θέσει, Christ as God to an image generated φύσει.[139] Gregory Nazianzen, in a passage of his *Thirtieth Oration*,[140] says that while it is the nature of an ordinary image to be an imitation (μίμημα), Christ as an image of God is much more than that: he is a truer image of the Father even than Seth is of Adam — in Genesis 5:3, Seth is said to be begotten according to the idea and image of Adam — or than anything begotten is of its begetter.[141] This text, in part quoted by John Damascene,[142] seems to be dependent on a similar one in Origen, *De principiis*.[143] Also, the Fifth Ecumenical Council held at Constantinople in 553, in its twelfth anathematism condemned Theodore of Mopsuestia because he allegedly had too closely identified the relationship between an emperor and his image with that between God Father and Christ,[144] at the same time calling Christ Son by adoption, υἱοθεσία [145] — here, too, we have the contrast between the "thetic" and the natural image.[146] This anathematism is quoted by John Damascene without comment.[147]

The Platonic-Aristotelian-Patristic contrast between *thesis* and *physis*, between imitation by art and natural or supernatural generation, was consciously used as an anti-idolatrous safeguard by the masters of Byzantine image theory. At the same time, owing to the ambivalence of such terms as imitation and assimilation, they found it possible to derive from the very limitation which they imposed upon their own doctrine further support for it. For is imitation of, assimilation to, the divine not the highest duty and privilege, the true grace, of Christendom? Commenting on Exodus 15:11, Origen had said: "Nobody is similar to God, either potentially or by nature . . . only by grace. . ." For, "if an image is said to be similar to its model, this refers to the grace that can be seen in the picture, while the substances of image and model remain quite unlike."[148] A text from John Chrysostom's *Seventeenth Homily on the Epistle to the Hebrews*, used by John Damascene in a significant paraphrase, shows even more clearly how the images of art could be linked up with the grace of the new dispensation. Hebrews

10:1 reads: "For the Law [that is, the Old Testament], having a shadow of the good things to come, not the very image of the things . . ." To this John Chrysostom adds, ". . . not the truth itself. For as long as somebody traces the outlines as in a drawing, there results [only] a sort of shadow; but when he paints over it brilliant tints and lays on colors, then an image emerges." [149] John of Damascus, claiming to quote Chrysostom,[150] writes that Melchisedek was somehow an "image"[151] of Christ, but only in the sense in which somebody might call the painter's adumbration ($\sigma\kappa\acute{\iota}\alpha\sigma\mu\alpha$), that is, the underpainting which precedes the colored picture, the latter's "shadow": in other words, Melchisedek is not a true image (whereas an art image of Christ is). "Therefore the Law is called shadow, but Grace truth, and that which is to come [to come, that is, after the consummation of this world] is called things ($\pi\rho\acute{\alpha}\gamma\mu\alpha\tau\alpha$, i.e., reality). As the Law and Melchisedek are the preliminary adumbration ($\pi\rho\sigma\kappa\acute{\iota}\alpha\sigma\mu\alpha$) of the colored picture, so Grace and Truth are the colored picture, and so is that which is of the world to come, reality ($\pi\rho\acute{\alpha}\gamma\mu\alpha\tau\alpha$). Thus, the old dispensation is a figure ($\tau\acute{\upsilon}\pi\sigma\varsigma$) of a figure, and the new a figure of real things."[152] Here, the first theologian of the images has reached the aim of all Byzantine thought on the holy images. He has proved to his own satisfaction and with considerable effect upon following generations that images are *truthful* in so far as truth can be seen at all on this earth. And of Christ who is *the* Truth, there can be images, because of the Incarnation, because His divinity has assumed visible flesh. This coping stone of the edifice of iconophile thought had been anticipated also by the Fathers of the so-called Quinisextum. The famous eighty-second canon of this Constantinopolitan synod demanded that in the future the figure of the Lamb of God, the Saviour, pointed to by John the Baptist, should be replaced in pictures by the image of Christ in His humanity; for Grace and Truth are to be preferred to figures and shadows, to typology and symbolism.[153]

To the obvious question: Did men like John of Damascus or Nicephorus or Theodore of Studion really believe that Christ and the saints had looked just as they appeared in their images? one must reply: They did and they did not. Similarity in the sense of portrait likeness was rather taken for granted than claimed, but allowance was made for the existence of *more* or *less* similarity, depending on the painters' skill in copying the authentic types. Dobschütz in his valuable book *Christusbilder* has made the most thorough study of the so-called *acheiropoietoi*, images which were thought to have originated without the intermediary of human hands and were supposed to have received true likeness from the impression of the face itself or through other miraculous means. He has shown that the earlier interest in these acheiropoietic images slackened just at the time of the Iconoclastic Controversy. Eighth- and ninth-century image doctrine attributed comparatively little importance to the *acheiropoietoi* and to the claims of miraculous similarity made for them.[154] This fact has received further elucidation through André Grabar's book *Martyrium*. He has made it clear how from the seventh century onward the iconography of the *martyria*, which had been dominated by the memory and evocation of the Holy Places of Palestine and their pictorial decoration, was being replaced in Byzantium by iconographic programs of a different kind; how also, at the same time, icons began to take the place of relics in Byzantine religiousness.[155] It may, perhaps, be said that in the era which just preceded and accompanied the Iconoclastic Controversy, the Byzantine approach to religion and art changed from the historic to the speculative and that, therefore, also the problem of the similarity of the images was treated more in a philosophical than in a practical way. The faithfulness of the great art-types of Christ, the Mother of God, and the saints seemed assured, exactness in copying them was required, and it remained only to caution the faithful that an image was both like and unlike its original, and equal to the prototype only in so far as it *was* like. This John of Damascus, the Fathers of Nicaea, and the other great writers on images did abundantly, using their Platonic-Aristotelian and patristic learning not without skill.

That an image should be similar to its prototype was one point on which Byzantine iconoclasts and iconophiles agreed, though they drew very different conclusions from this demand. There was one other point of agreement between them. Neither the friends nor the enemies of the images in eighth- and ninth-century Byzantium questioned the use of imperial images or their adoration — adoration as *proskynesis timetike* only, of course, and as distinct from *proskynesis latreutike* which was reserved for God alone, even by the iconodules. A study of the patristic antecedents of Byzantine image doctrine — even in the few examples quoted — has shown a close connection between the conception of the imperial image and that of the image of Christ or the saints. From Origen to Theodore of Studion and beyond, examples taken from imperial imagery are over and over again used for the definition of the nature and scope of a religious image.[156] The development of the concept of the religious image cannot be fully understood without reference to the history of ruler worship, and in eastern Christendom even less than anywhere else.

I cannot here attempt to summarize this history, but only draw attention to some of its points of contact with the ideology of image-likeness and imitation. In the Neo-Pythagorean pseudoepigraphic *Treatises on Kingship* of Ecphantus, Diotogenes, and Sthenidas,[157] the idea of man's image-like-ness to God appears in a very significant transformation: not man as such, but the king, is here created after God as his model; it is he who is the imitator of God *par excellence*, while ordinary man is only the image of the royal archetype.[158] It seems that the famous verses of Genesis as well as Hellenic sources were blended into a monarchical ideology, the origins of which can be traced back at least to the orientalized Hellenistic monarchies of the Ptolemies and Seleucids.[159] Norman H. Baynes has made it probable that Eusebius of Caesarea knew these or similar works when he developed his somewhat imperfectly Christian conception of Constantine the Great as God's image, imitator, and vice-regent on earth.[160] The same may hold true for Synesius of Cyrene,[161] at the end of the fourth century, and his pagan contemporary Themistius.[162]

In this respect, too, then, Byzantium, which gradually was to Christian-ize the Neo-Pythagorean-Eusebian ideology more fully, stands within a long tradition of the Greek-speaking world. But a rather interesting observa-tion can be made. While in the development of patristic and Byzantine Trinitarian and image doctrine the *imperial image* served as an important simile, the concept of *the ruler himself as image* or imitator of God paralleled but did not overlap the ideological field of religious imagery. In other words, the relationship between God and ruler is never made use of in the theory of the religious image. True, a metaphor such as "the ruler as image" does not easily lend itself to further metaphorical use such as would be required in order to compare the emperor (as image of God) with a work of art as image of its prototype. Yet this cannot have been the only reason for not using the emperor-God relationship in such a way, for the simple man-God relationship served as just such a simile.[163] I believe that these facts rather tend to strengthen the growing realization that Byzantine religious life must not be seen as stifled by a supposedly all-pervading Caesaropapism. The deeper layers of doctrine and spirituality — and the holy icons very much belonged to them — were affected by the Emperor's position in the Church only under extraordinary circumstances, such as the rise of a new heresy, and for this iconoclasm itself is the best example. Christ's words, "Render therefore to Caesar the things that are Caesar's; and to God, the things that are God's," [164] remained a postulate also in eastern Christendom.

Origen, in so many respects the father of Byzantine thought, both orthodox and heterodox, gives a significant allegorical interpretation of this famous Gospel verse which has a definite bearing on the doctrine of the image.[165] He contrasts with one another the image of the emperor on the tribute coin and the image of God in the soul of man. "When [Christ] said 'Render therefore to Caesar the things that are Caesar's and to God the things that are God's' He meant . . . throw off the earthly image so that you can put on the person of the heavenly image [166] and thus render to God the things that are God's." In Origen's exegesis the imperial image as a symbol of this world has become an analogue to man molded from earth according to Genesis 2:7, and the man of the heavenly or divine image [167] is analogous to the image of Christ, which was not on the imperial coin — one might be tempted to add: not yet on the imperial coin. That Christ and the emperor *could* appear on Byzantine coins, first during the reigns of Justinian II (about 700) and then continuously from the end of the Iconoclastic Controversy to the end of the Empire [168] — this was in a sense a fulfillment of Origen's allegory and a realization of patristic image doctrine in general.

NOTES

1. *De Spiritu Sancto* XVIII, 45, Migne, *Patrologia Graeca* (hereafter *PG*) XXXII, 149 C: Ὅτι βασιλεὺς λέγεται καὶ ἡ τοῦ βασιλέως εἰκὼν καὶ οὐ δύο βασιλεῖς. Οὔτε γὰρ τὸ κράτος σχίζεται οὔτε ἡ δόξα διαμερίζεται. Ὡς γὰρ ἡ κρατοῦσα ἡμῶν ἀρχὴ καὶ ἡ ἐξουσία μία, οὕτω καὶ ἡ παρ' ἡμῶν δοξολογία μία καὶ οὐ πολλαί. διότι ἡ τῆς εἰκόνος τιμὴ ἐπὶ τὸ πρωτότυπον διαβαίνει.

2. Cf. 2 Corinthians 4:3; Colossians 1:15; etc.

3. Gregory of Nyssa, *De opificio hominis*, 5 *PG* XLIV, 137 A: Ὥσπερ τοίνυν τὰς ἀνθρωπίνας μορφὰς διὰ χρωμάτων τινῶν ἐπὶ τοὺς πίνακας οἱ γραφεῖς μεταφέρουσι τὰς οἰκείας τε καὶ καταλλήλους βαφὰς ἐπαλείφοντες τῷ μιμήματι ὡς ἂν δι'ἀκριβείας τὸ ἀρχέτυπον κάλλος μετενεχθείη πρὸς τὸ ὁμοίωμα, οὕτω μοι νόει καὶ τὸν ἡμέτερον πλάστην οἷόν τισι βαφαῖς τῇ τῶν ἀρετῶν ἐπιβολῇ πρὸς τὸ ἴδιον κάλλος τὴν εἰκόνα περιανθίσαντα. . . In part quoted by John Damascene, *De imaginibus*, oratio I, *PG* XCIV, 1269 A f. The text from St. Basil quoted in notes 1 and 5 is also found in John Damascene, *ibid*., 1261 D f.

4. *Homil.* XXIV, *Contra Sabellianos et Arium et Anomoeos*, *PG* XXXI, 607 A f.: Διότι γεννητῶς ὑπάρχων ἐκ τοῦ Πατρὸς ὁ Υἱὸς καὶ φυσικῶς ἐκτυπῶν ἐν ἑαυτῷ τὸν Πατέρα, ὡς μὲν εἰκὼν τὸ ἀπαράλλακτον ἔχει, ὡς δὲ γέννημα τὸ ὁμοούσιον διασώζει. Οὐδὲ γὰρ ὁ κατὰ τὴν ἀγορὰν τῇ βασιλικῇ εἰκόνι ἐνατενίζων καὶ βασιλέα λέγων τὸν ἐν τῷ πίνακι δύο βασιλέας ὁμολογεῖ, τήν τε εἰκόνα καὶ τὸν οὗ ἐστιν ἡ εἰκών. . . Εἰ γὰρ ἡ εἰκὼν βασιλεύς, πολλῷ δήπου εἰκὸς βασιλέα εἶναι τὸν τῇ εἰκόνι παρασχομένον τὴν αἰτίαν. Ἀλλ ἐνταῦθα μὲν ξύλα καὶ κηρὸς καὶ ζωγράφου τέχνη τὴν εἰκόνα ποιεῖ φθαρτὴν φθαρτοῦ μίμημα καὶ τεχνητὴν τοῦ ποιηθέντος· ἐκεῖ δὲ ὅταν ἀκούῃς εἰκόνα, ἀπαύγασμα νόει τῆς δόξης.

5. That passage continues as follows (*PG* XXXII, 149 C): Ὁ οὖν ἐστιν ἐνταῦθα μιμητικῶς ἡ εἰκών, τοῦτο ἐκεῖ φυσικῶς ὁ Υἱός. Καὶ ὥσπερ ἐπὶ τῶν τεχνικῶν κατὰ τὴν μορφὴν ἡ ὁμοίωσις, οὕτως ἐπὶ τῆς θείας καὶ ἀσυνθέτου ἐν τῇ κοινωνίᾳ τῆς θεότητός ἐστιν ἡ ἕνωσις.

6. Cf. John Damascene, *De imaginibus*, oratio I, *PG* XCIV, 1269 C, oratio III, *ibid*. 1361 C f.; the same text is cited in the *Acts of the Second Council of Nicaea*, Mansi, *Concil.* XIII, 9 C, XII, 1066 B.

7. *Epist*. IV, 62, *Heliodoro Silentario*, *PG* LXXIX, 580 f., also in the *Acts of the Second Nicaenum*, Mansi, *Concil.* XIII, 31 C ff.

8. The best study of patristic and early Byzantine concepts of the image is contained in the book of K. M. Setton, *Christian Attitude towards the Emperor in the Fourth Century* . . . (New York, 1941), especially 198 ff. Setton's material is in part identical with that used in this article, but the scope of the two studies is, of course, different. A fair number of patristic sources of the Byzantine iconophiles is arranged in convenient lists by E. J.

Martin, A History of the Iconoclastic Controversy (London, s.a.) 146 ff., 197 f. Cf. also V. Grumel, in Dictionnaire de théologie catholique VII/1 (Paris, 1927) 766 ff., s.v. Images (Culte des).

9. Cf. Hugo Koch, Die altchristliche Bilderfrage nach den literarischen Quellen (Forschungen zur Religion und Literatur des Alten und Neuen Testaments XXVII, 1917); W. Elliger, Die Stellung der alten Christen zu den Bildern in den ersten vier Jahrhunderten (Studien über christliche Denkmäler XX, 1930); id., Zur Entstehung und frühen Entwicklung der altchristlichen Bildkunst (ibid. XXIII, 1934).

10. Phaedrus 250 B.

11. Republic 597 E; 603 B.

12. In a very interesting article, "Origen, Eusebius and the Iconoclastic Controversy," Church History XIX (1950) 77 ff., Father George Florovsky, while not denying Platonistic elements in Byzantine iconophile doctrine, stresses the undeniable anti-iconic spiritualistic element in Platonism and Origenism as the main source of iconoclastic theology as well.

13. Timaeus 29 B.

14. Ibid. 37 C.

15. Laws 667 E f.

16. Ibid. 669 A–B.

17. Ibid. 656 D.

18. Cf. Philebus 51 C.

19. Sophist 235 D–236 A.

20. For a similar interpretation of Plato's attitude toward art, see, for instance, P.-M. Schuhl, Platon et l'art de son temps (Arts plastiques) (Paris, 1933).

21. H. Willms, ΕΙΚΩΝ (Münster, 1935).

22. See also H. A. Wolfson, Philo I (Cambridge, Mass., 1948) 238 f.

23. For the history of this change, and for its relation to the late-Platonistic tendency toward explaining the work of art by its idea in the artist's mind, cf. E. Panofsky, "Idea," (Studien der Bibliothek Warburg V, Leipzig, Berlin, 1924) 5 ff., 8 ff.; also W. Theiler, Die Vorbereitung des Neuplatonismus (Berlin, 1930) 15 ff.; E. Birmelin, "Die kunsttheoretischen Gedanken in Philostrats Apollonios," Philologus LXXXVIII (1933) 402 ff.; Willms, op. cit., 26 f.; F. Cayré, Initiation à la philosophie de Saint Augustin (Paris, 1947) 199 ff. F. Steckerl, "On the Problem: Antefact and Idea," Classical Philology XXXVII (1942) 288 ff.

24. De opificio mundi 24 f., 31. Philonis Alexandrini Opera . . . edd. L. Cohn and P. Wendland (Berlin, 1896 ff.) I, 7 f., 9.

25. De confusione linguarum 147 f., loc. cit. II, 247.

26. Legum Allegor. III, 96, loc. cit. I, 134.

27. See especially 1 Corinthians 15:49: "Therefore, as we have borne the image of the earthly, let us bear also the image of the heavenly." Did St. Paul, in insisting that the heavenly and spiritual comes after the earthly and physical (1 Corinthians 15:46 f.), also mean to reject Philo's preëxistent "ideal" man who was not clearly distinct from the Divine Logos, but explicit in the "generic" heavenly man (who together with the "generic" earthly man makes up the historical Adam)? The question is controversial. See B. A. Stegmann, O.S.B., Christ, the "Man from Heaven" (Washington, D.C., 1927); for Philo's conception of "genus" and "generic," also Wolfson, Philo I, 251 f.; furthermore, E.-B. Allo, Saint Paul: Première Epitre aux Corinthiens (Paris, 1935) 426 ff.

28. Cf. above all Colossians 3:9 f. For the doctrine of Christ as the Image of God and of man as created and reformed after the image of God, see the following recent works: R. Leys, L'image de Dieu chez Saint Grégoire de Nysse (Bruxelles, Paris, 1951), with references to similar studies on Clement of Alexandria, Origen, and Athanasius; W. Dürig, Imago: Ein Beitrag zur Terminologie und Theologie der Römischen Liturgie (München, 1952); D. Cairns, The Image of God in Man (New York, 1953); also G. Ladner, "Die mittelalterliche Reformidee und ihr Verhältnis zur Idee der Renaissance," Mitteilungen des Instituts für Österreich. Geschichtsforschung LX (1952) 31 ff.

29. Cf., for instance, Proclus, In Timaeum II, 81 B f. (to Timaeus 28 A f.), quoted by Panofsky, "Idea," note 63. For "Verismus" in the Graeco-Roman conception of the image,

see the excellent pages in K. Borinski, *Die Antike in Poetik und Kunsttheorie*, I (Leipzig, 1914) 1-21.

30. Professor A. M. Friend, Jr., draws my attention to the fact that according to Photius, *Bibliotheca*, Cod. 119, PG CIII, 400 B f., Pierius, late third-century head of the Catechetical School of Alexandria, had made some statement about the relation between image and prototype which Photius interpreted in the sense of Basil's famous sentence; see also O. Bardenhewer, *Geschichte der altkirchlichen Literatur* II ² (Freiburg i. B., 1914) 236. But it may well be that Pierius following Origen — cf. *Contra Celsum* VII, 66, *Die griechischen christlichen Schriftsteller der ersten drei Jahrhunderte*, ed. *Preussische Akademie der Wissenschaften* (hereafter quoted GCS), *Origenes*, II, 216, and VIII, 17 f., *ibid.* 235 f. — was speaking not of Christ as the Image of God but of man as made according to God's image and likeness.

31. *Oratio III contra Arianos* 5, PG XXVI, 332 A f.: Ἐν γὰρ τῇ εἰκόνι τὸ εἶδος καὶ ἡ μορφὴ τοῦ βασιλέως ἐστί· καὶ ἐν τῷ βασιλεῖ δὲ τὸ ἐν τῇ εἰκόνι εἶδός ἐστιν. Ἀπαράλλακτος γάρ ἐστιν ἡ ἐν τῇ εἰκόνι τοῦ βασιλέως ὁμοιότης· ὥστε τὸν ἐνορῶντα τῇ εἰκόνι ὁρᾶν ἐν αὐτῇ τὸν βασιλέα καὶ τὸν πάλιν ὁρῶντα τὸν βασιλέα ἐπιγιγνώσκειν ὅτι οὗτός ἐστιν ὁ ἐν τῇ εἰκόνι. ἐκ δὲ τοῦ μὴ διαλλάττειν τὴν ὁμοιότητα τῷ θέλοντι μετὰ τὴν εἰκόνα θεωρῆσαι τὸν βασιλέα εἴποι ἂν ἡ εἰκών· Ἐγὼ καὶ ὁ βασιλεὺς ἕν ἐσμεν. Ἐγὼ γὰρ ἐν ἐκείνῳ εἰμί, κἀκεῖνος ἐν ἐμοὶ καὶ ὃ ὁρᾶς ἐν ἐμοί, τοῦτο ἐν ἐκείνῳ βλέπεις, καὶ ὁ ἑώρακας ἐν ἐκείνῳ, τοῦτο βλέπεις ἐν ἐμοί. Ὁ γοῦν προσκυνῶν τὴν εἰκόνα ἐν αὐτῇ προσκυνεῖ καὶ τὸν βασιλέα· ἡ γὰρ ἐκείνου μορφὴ καὶ τὸ εἶδός ἐστιν ἡ εἰκών. This text is quoted with some slight variations, for instance, by John Damascene, *De imaginibus, oratio III*, PG XCIV, 1405 A, and in the *Acts of the Second Nicaenum*, Mansi, *Concil.* XIII, 69 B f.

32. John 10:30; 14:10.

33. John Damascene, *De imaginibus, oratio I*, 9 ff., PG XCIV, 1240 C ff.; *De imaginibus, oratio III*, 18 ff., *ibid.*, 1337 C ff.

34. *Republic* 597.

35. *Ennead* V, 9, 5; cf. V, 2, 1, V, 3, 7, V, 9, 11.

36. *The Elements of Theology*, Proposition 65, ed. E. R. Dodds (Oxford, 1933) 62 f., and Commentary 235 f. (see also the other Propositions referred to there).

37. *In Canticum Canticorum* II, 9, GCS, *Origenes*, VIII, 209: it may be that plants and animals "habeant . . . incorporalium rerum formas et imagines quibus doceri anima possit et instrui ad contemplanda etiam ea quae sunt invisibilia et caelestia . . ."

38. *De divinis nominibus* IV, 4, PG III, 697 B f.

39. *Op. cit.* V, 8, *ibid.* 824 C; *De coelesti hierarchia* 1, 3, *ibid.* 121 D; *Epist.* 10, *ad Johannem, ibid.* 1117 A f.

40. Romans 1:20.

41. Cf. Romans 8:29; 1 Corinthians 2:7; Ephesians 1:5; 1:11.

42. *De divinis nominibus* V, 8, PG III, 824 C.

43. Cf. *De imaginibus, oratio I*, 10, PG XCIV, 1240 D; *oratio III*, 19, *ibid.* 1340 C.

44. For St. Augustine, see E. Gilson, *Introduction à l'étude de Saint Augustin* ² (Paris, 1949) 275 ff. A secularized version of this conception can still be found in Shakespeare's famous verses in *As You Like It*, II, 1:

"... tongues in trees, books in the running brooks,
Sermons in stones, and good in every thing."

45. *Adversus Haereses* V, 16, 1, ed. W. W. Harvey, II (Cambridge, 1857) 368: As long as the Word according to the image of which man had been made was invisible, man lost the similitude easily. Ὁπότε δὲ σὰρξ ἐγένετο ὁ Λόγος τοῦ Θεοῦ, τὰ ἀμφότερα ἐπεκύρωσε· καὶ γὰρ καὶ τὴν εἰκόνα ἔδειξεν ἀληθῶς αὐτὸς τοῦτο γενόμενος ὅπερ ἦν ἡ εἰκὼν αὐτοῦ καὶ τὴν ὁμοίωσιν βεβαίως κατέστησε συνεξομοιώσας τὸν ἄνθρωπον τῷ ἀοράτῳ πατρὶ . . .

46. *Symposium* I, 4 (24), GCS, *Methodius* 13: Ταύτῃ γὰρ ᾑρετίσατο τὴν ἀνθρωπίνην ἐνδύσασθαι σάρκα θεὸς ὢν ὅπως ὥσπερ ἐν πίνακι θεῖον ἐκτύπωμα βίου βλέποντες ἔχωμεν καὶ ἡμεῖς τὸν γράψαντα μιμεῖσθαι. For the painter simile, see below, p. 12.

47. For all this, see Methodius, *De resurrectione* I, 35, 3-4 f.; 43, 2 ff.; II, 10, 7-12, 10; III, 6; 16, 9; *loc. cit.* 274 f.; 289 ff.; 352 ff.; 396 ff.; 413. See also N. Bonwetsch, "Die Theologie des Methodius von Olympus" *Abhandlungen der kgl. Gesellschaft der Wissen-*

schaften zu Göttingen, Philologisch-historische Klasse, Neue Folge, VII/1 (Berlin, 1903) 119, 123.

48. John Damascene, *De imaginibus, oratio III*, PG XCIV, 1420 B, quotes Methodius, *De resurrectione II*, 24 (GCS, *Methodius* 379 f.). Identical quotation in the *Sacra Parallela*, ed. K. Holl, *Fragmente vornicänischer Kirchenväter aus den Sacra Parallela (Texte und Untersuchungen zur Geschichte der altchristlichen Literatur, Neue Folge*, V/2, Leipzig, 1899) 183, no. 430.

49. Cf., for instance, H. F. Cherniss, *The Platonism of Gregory of Nyssa* (University of California Publications in Classical Philology, XI, Berkeley, 1934) 16 ff.

50. *De opificio mundi* I, 69, ed. Cohn and Wendland, *loc. cit.*, I, 23.

51. *Stromata* V, 14 (94, 5), GCS, *Clemens Alex.*, II, 388: Εἰκὼν μὲν γὰρ θεοῦ λόγος θεῖος καὶ βασιλικὸς ἄνθρωπος ἀπαθής, εἰκὼν δ' εἰκόνος ἀνθρώπινος νοῦς. See also *Stromata* II, 19 (102, 6), *ibid.* 169: Τῷ γὰρ ⟨⟨κατ' εἰκόνα καὶ ὁμοίωσιν⟩⟩ . . . οὐ τὸ κατὰ σῶμα μηνύεται . . . ἀλλ' ἡ κατὰ νοῦν καὶ λογισμὸν . . .

52. *De principiis* IV, 4, 10, GCS, *Origenes*, V, 363; *In Genesim homil.* I, 13, *ibid.* VI, 15: "Hunc sane hominem quem dicit 'ad imaginem Dei' factum, non intelligimus corporalem. Non enim corporis figmentum Dei imaginem continet . . . Is . . . qui 'ad imaginem Dei' factus est, interior homo noster est, invisibilis et incorporalis et incorruptus atque immortalis." Cf. *Contra Celsum* VI, 63, *ibid.*, II, 133; VII, 66, *ibid.* 216; *Selectiones in Genesim*, PG XII, 93 ff.; *In Canticum Canticorum*, Prologue, GCS, *Origenes*, VIII, 64.

53. See also Athanasius, *Oratio II contra Arianos* 78, PG XXVI, 312 B f. Man's dominion over the earth under God, his upright posture and royal quality, often referred to by the Fathers, hardly imply a corporeal conception of the image-likeness with God (*pace* Cairns, *op. cit.* above n. 28); see also below, note 163.

54. Cf. A. Struker, *Die Gottebenbildlichkeit des Menschen in der christlichen Literatur der ersten zwei Jahrhunderte* (Münster, 1913) 55 ff.

55. *Adversus Haereses* V, 6, 1, ed. Harvey, II 334 f.

56. *Stromata* II, 22 (131, 6), GCS, *Clemens Alex.*, II, 185.

57. *De principiis* III, 6, 1, GCS, *Origenes*, V, 280 f.; cf. *Commentar. in Joann.* XX, 22 (20), GCS, *Origenes*, IV, 355, lines 13 ff.

58. *In Genes. homil.* XIII, 4, GCS, *Origenes*, VI, 119: "Filius Dei est pictor huius imaginis [i.e., of the image of Genesis 1:26]. Et quia talis et tantus est pictor, imago eius obscurari per incuriam potest, deleri per malitiam non potest." Whether or not the idea is original with Origen (cf. *Acta Joannis* [saec. 2 ex.] 28 f., edd. R. A. Lipsius and M. Bonnet, *Acta Apostolorum Apocrypha* II, I [Leipzig, 1888] 166 f.), it is certainly part of an old tradition concerning God as artist (see Excursus XXI, "Gott als Bildner," in E. R. Curtius, *Europäische Literatur und Lateinisches Mittelalter* [Bern, 1948] 529 ff.), which goes back at least to the demiurge of Plato's Timaeus (cf. also Origen's contemporary, the elder Philostratus, *Life of Apollonius of Tyana*, II, 22, about God as painter), and which could blend with the conception of a divine effigy in the virtuous soul (for Origen, see note 71). Such ideas could be turned in an anti-iconic sense, so, for instance, by Eusebius in his famous letter to Constantia in which he blamed her for desiring an art image of Christ (the letter is quoted approvingly in the *Acts of the Second Nicaenum*, Mansi, *Concil*, XIII, 314; see also PG XX, 1545 ff.); cf. Florovsky, *op. cit.*, 85. Yet, at least from the later fourth century onward, the idea that the virtuous soul is the best image of Christ, the best painter, did not exclude the toleration and even positive evaluation of the Christian image of art by the majority of the theologians.

59. *Homil.* XII (B), ed. Dom R. H. Connolly, *The Liturgical Homilies of Narsai (Texts and Studies*, VIII/1, Cambridge, 1909) 33; *Homil.* XXI (C), *ibid.* 47, 55. I owe the knowledge of these interesting passages to Professor Ernst Kantorowicz; for further examples, see now his article quoted in note 138.

60. *In Genes. homil.* XIII, 4, *loc. cit.* 119 f.: "Haec [i.e., the image of God] in te videri non poterat, donec domus tua sordida erat immunditiis et ruderibus repleta. . . . Cum . . . te libido fuscaverit, induxisti unum colorem terrenum; si vero et avaritia aestuas, miscuisti et alium;" etc.

61. *Enneads* I, 6, 5: . . . οἷον εἰ τις δὶς εἰς πηλὸν ἢ βόρβορον τὸ μὲν ὑπερ εἶχε κάλλος

μηκέτι προφαίνοι, τοῦτο δὲ ὀρῷτο ὃ παρὰ τοῦ πηλοῦ ἢ βορβόρου ἀπεμίζατο. See note 63 for the very close parallelism between this text and a passage from Gregory of Nyssa, who must no doubt have used the Plotinian text. See also J. Daniélou, S.J., *Platonisme et théologie mystique: Essai sur la doctrine de Saint Grégoire de Nysse* (Paris, 1944) 224 ff.

62. *De incarnatione* 14, PG XXV, 120: Ὡς γὰρ τῆς γραψείσης ἐν ξύλῳ μορφῆς παραφανισθείσης ἐν τῶν ἔξωθεν ῥύπων πάλιν χρεία τούτον παραγενέσθαι οὗ καὶ ἔστιν ἡ μορφὴ ἵνα ἀνακαινισθῆναι ἡ εἰκών δυνηθῇ ἐν τῇ αὐτῇ ὕλῃ – διὰ γὰρ τὴν ἐκείνου γραφὴν ἡ αὐτὴ καὶ ὕλη ἐν ᾗ καὶ γέγραπται οὐκ ἐκβάλλεται, ἀλλ' ἐν αὐτῇ ἀνατυποῦται – κατὰ τοῦτο καὶ ὁ πανάγιος τοῦ Πατρὸς Υἱὸς εἰκὼν ὢν τοῦ Πατρὸς παρεγένετο ἐπὶ τοὺς ἡμετέρους τόπους ἵνα τὸν κατ' αὐτὸν πεποιημένον ἄνθρωπον ἀνακαινίσῃ . . .

63. *De virginitate* 12, PG XLVI, 372 B: . . . through sin τὸ θεοειδὲς ἐκεῖνο τῆς ψυχῆς κάλλος τὸ κατὰ μίμησιν τοῦ προτοτύπου γενόμενον, οἷόν τις σίδηρος κατεμελάνθη τῷ τῆς κακίας ἰῷ. . . οἷον πάσχουσιν οἱ ἐξ ὀλισθήματος ἐγκατενεγθέντες, βορβόρῳ καὶ τῷ πηλῷ τὴν μορφὴν ἑαυτῶν ἐξαλείψαντες ἀνεπίγνωστοι καὶ τοῖς συνήθεσι γίνονται, οὕτως κἀκεῖνος ἐμπεσὼν τῷ βορβόρῳ τῆς ἁμαρτίας ἀπώλεσε μὲν τὸ εἰκὼν εἶναι τοῦ ἀφθάρτου Θεοῦ. Cf. also *De beatitudinibus, Oratio VI, ibid.* XLIV, 1272 A f.

64. Cf. Origen, *In Genes. homil.* XIII, 4, *loc. cit.*: "Manet enim semper imago Dei, licet tu ipse superducas 'imaginem terreni' (1 Corinthians 15:49) . . . Et cum deleverit [i.e., God] omnes istos in te colores qui ex fucis malitiae sumpti sunt, tunc resplendet in te imago illa, quae a Deo creata est." See also Gregory of Nyssa, *loc. cit.* 373 A: The lost and sought-for drachma of Luke 15:9 means the image of God the King, τὴν οὐχὶ παντελῶς ἀπολλυμένην ἀλλὰ ὑποκεκρυμμένην τῇ κόπρῳ.

65. *In Lucam homil. VIII, GCS, Origenes,* IX, 56: "Si considerem Dominum Salvatorem 'imaginem esse invisibilis Dei' (Colossians 1:15), et videam animam meam factam 'ad imaginem conditoris' ut imago esset imaginis – neque enim anima mea specialiter imago est Dei, sed ad similitudinem imaginis prioris effecta est – tunc videbo quoniam in exemplum eorum qui solent imagines fingere et uno, verbi causa, vultu regis accepto ad principalem similitudinem exprimendam artis industriam commodare, unusquisque nostram ad imaginem Christi formans animam suam aut majorem aut minorem possit imaginem vel obsoletam vel sordidam aut claram atque lucentem et respondentem ad effigiem imaginis principalis. Quando igitur grandem fecero imaginem imaginis, id est animam meam, et magnificavero illam opere cogitatione sermone, tunc imago Dei grandis efficitur et ipse Dominus, cujus imago est, in nostra anima magnificatur." The Greek surviving fragments cover only part of this text as translated by St. Jerome; they do not essentially differ from it.

66. See *De beatitudinibus, oratio VI,* PG XLIV, 1272 B; *In Cantic. Cantic., homil.* XV, *ibid.* 1093 D: Καὶ οἷον ἐπὶ τοῦ κατόπτρου γίνεται, ὅταν τεχνικῶς τε καὶ καταλλήλως τῇ. χρείᾳ κατεσκευασμένον ᾖ, ἐν καθαρᾷ τῇ ἐπιφανείᾳ δὶ ἀκριβείας ἐν ἑαυτῷ δείξει τοῦ ἐπιφανέντος προσώπου τὸν χαρακτῆρα, οὕτως ἑαυτὴν ἡ ψυχὴ προσφόρως τῇ χρείᾳ κατασκευάσασα καὶ πᾶσαν ὑλικὴν ἀπορρίψαμένη κηλίδα καταρὸν τοῦ ἀκηράτου κάλλους ἐν ἑαυτῇ τὸ εἶδος ἀνετυπώσατο. See also *In Cantic. Cantic., homil.* III, *ibid.* 824 C; *homil.* IV, *ibid.* 833 B f.; *homil.* V, *ibid.* 868 C f.; *De mortuis, ibid.* XLVI, 509 C f.; *De vita Mosis, ibid.* XLIV, 340 A; *De hominis opificio* 12, *ibid.* 161 C; *De virginitate* 11, *ibid.* LXIV, 368 C f. Cf. Daniélou, *op. cit.*, 223 ff.

67. 132 f. Cf. Cherniss, *op. cit.*, 40.

68. See *Ennead,* IV, 3, 11; 5, 7; VI, 2, 22; cf. *Ennead* I, 6, 9.

69. *De opificio hominis* 30, PG XLIV, 253 C: Οἷον δὲ ἐπὶ τῶν λιθογλύφων ἐστὶν ἰδεῖν· Πρόκειται μὲν γὰρ τῷ τεχνίτῃ ζώου τινος εἶδος ἐν λίθῳ δεῖξαι· τοῦτο δὲ προθέμενος πρῶτον μὲν τὸν λίθον τῆς συμφυοῦς ὕλης ἀπέρρηξεν· εἶτα περικόψας αὐτοῦ τὰ περιττὰ προήγαγέ πως διὰ τοῦ πρώτου σχήματος τῇ μιμήσει τῇ κατὰ πρόθεσιν . . . πάλιν ἐπεγρασάμενος προσήγγισε πλέον τῇ ὁμοιότητι τοῦ σπουδαζομένου. Εἶτα τὸ τέλειον καὶ ἀκριβὲς εἶδος ἐγχειρουργήσας τῇ ὕλῃ εἰς πέρας τὴν τέχνην προήγαγε . . . See also the much longer exposition of the same thought in *In Psalmos*, c. 11, *ibid.* 541 D–544.

70. The dependence of Gregory on Plotinus has been clearly established by Daniélou, *op. cit.*, 46. Cf. *Ennead* I, 6, 9: Πῶς ἂν οὖν ἴδοις ψυχὴν ἀγαθὴν οἷον τὸ κάλλος ἔχει; Ἄναγε ἐπὶ σαυτὸν καὶ ἴδε· κἂν μήπω σαυτὸν ἴδῃς καλόν, οἷα ποιητὴς ἀγάλματος, ὃ δεῖ καλὸν γενέσθαι, τὸ μὲν ἀφαιρεῖ, τὸ δὲ ἀπέξεσε, τὸ δὲ λεῖον, τὸ δὲ καθαρὸν ἐποίησεν, ἕως ἔδειξε καλὸν ἐπὶ τῷ ἀγάλματι.

πρόσωπον, οὕτω καὶ σὺ ἀφαίρει ὅσα περιττὰ καὶ ἀπεύθυνε ὅσα σκολιά, ὅσα σκοτεινὰ καθαίρων, ἐργάζου εἶναι λαμπρὰ καὶ μὴ παύσῃ τεκταίνων τὸ σὸν ἄγαλμα, ἕως ἂν ἐκλάμψῃ σοι τῆς ἀρέτης ἡ θεοειδὴς ἀγλάια . . . For this text, see also Panofsky, "Idea," 14 f. Plotinus' concept of *aphairesis* is found in somewhat different expression (ἐξαιρεθέντων, περιαιρέσει) in Gregory of Nyssa, *In Psalmos* c. 11, *loc. cit.* 544 A f. K. Borinski, *Die Antike in Poetik und Kunsttheorie* I (Leipzig, 1914) 169 f., has noted that the Pseudo-Dionysian antithesis of *thesis* and *aphairesis*, used to circumscribe the nature of God who is above "positive" and "negative," above kataphatic and apophatic theology, is still based on the Plotinian artist metaphor (cf. *Theologia Mystica*, 2, PG III, 1025 B, also the scholia to *De divinis nominibus* II, 4 [*ibid.* 641 A; the scholia *ibid.* IV, 217 B–C], attributed to Maximus the Confessor but probably originating from John of Scythopolis; cf. H. U. v. Balthasar, S.J., "Das Scholienwerk des Johannes von Scythopolis," *Scholastik* XV [1940] 16 ff.). There is only a very slight logical and historical connection between the antithesis of *thesis* and *aphairesis* and that of *physis* and *thesis*, discussed below.

71. Origenes, *Contra Celsum VIII*, 17, GCS, *Origenes*, II, 235: Ὥσπερ δὲ καὶ ἐπὶ τῶν ἀγαλματοποιῶν οἱ μέν τινες εἰσὶ θαυμαστῶς κατορθοῦντες τὸ ἔργον, ὥσπερ εἰπεῖν Φειδίας ἢ Πολύκλειτος ἢ ζωγράφοι Ζεῦξις καὶ Ἀπελλῆς, ἕτεροι δὲ ἔλαττον τούτων ἀγαλματοποιοῦσι . . . καὶ ἀπαξαπλῶς πολλὴ διαφορά ἐστι τῆς σῶν ἀγαλμάτων καὶ εἰκόνων κατασκευῆς, thus do some men build up a better image of God in their souls than others — but in no case can even Phidias' Olympic Zeus be compared to man, made according to the image of his creator, not to speak of the image of the Father in our Saviour.

72. *In Psalmos* c. 1, PG XLIV, 433 C: . . . ὅρος ἐστὶ τῆς ἀνθρωπίνης μακαριότητος ἡ πρὸς τὸ Θεῖον ὁμοίωσις. Cf. also *De opificio hominis* 5, *ibid.* 137 A f.; *Oratio catechetica* 21, *ibid.* XLV, 57 D; *De professione christiana*, *ibid.* XLVI, 244 Cf.

73. *In Isaiam* 64, 6, PG LXXXI, 481 B: . . . οὐκ ἔχει γὰρ εἰκόνα παραβαλλομένη ἡ ἁμαρτία. See also Theodoret's *Quaestiones in Exodum*, *Interrogatio* 38, PG LXXX, 264 C, where the nothingness of an idol is contrasted with the similitude of an image. This is probably taken over from Origen, *Homil. in Exodum* VIII, 3, GCS, *Origenes*, VI, 221 f. Cf. Theodore of Studion, *Antirrheticus I*, 16, PG XCIX, 345 C ff.

74. 509 D ff.

75. 285 A.

76. 132 D; 148.

77. 259.

78. Cf. R. Klibansky, "Ein Proklos-Fund und seine Bedeutung," *Sitzungsberichte der Heidelberger Akademie der Wissenschaften, Philosophisch-historische Klasse* 1928–1929/5 (1929).

79. *De divinis nominibus* IX, 6, PG III, 913 C f. From the same Platonic premises Cicero (*De natura deorum* I, 17, I, 24, II, 16 ff.) had reached a similar result and, therefore, had criticized Epicurus' euhemerist conception of the gods. This analogy was noticed by Petavius, *Dogmata Theologica* III (Paris, Vivès, 1865) 197.

80. *Antirrheticus II*, 10, PG XCIX, 357 B f.; *Epist.* II, 199, PG XCIX, 1604 D; etc.

81. *De ecclesiastica hierarchia* IV, 3, PG III, 473 C.

82. See, for instance, Theodore of Studion, *Antirrheticus III*, 2, 12, PG XCIX, 425 B f. Cf. my articles, "Der Bilderstreit und die Kunstlehren der byzantinischen und abendländischen Theologie," *Zeitschrift für Kirchengeschichte*, Ser. III, I (1931) 1 ff., and "Origin and Significance of the Byzantine Iconoclastic Controversy," *Mediaeval Studies* II (1940) 144; also the excellent study by P. Lucas Koch, unknown to me until recently: "Zur Theologie der Christusikone," *Benediktinische Monatsschrift* XIX (1937) 375 ff., XX (1938) 32 ff., 168 ff., 281 ff., 437 ff. (especially 44 and 282 f.).

83. Matthew 8:22, 9:9, 19:21; Luke 18:22; John 1:43, 21:19; etc.

84. 1 John 3:2.

85. *Theaetetus* 176 A f.

86. *Ennead* I, 6, 6.

87. Cf. *Stromata II*, 22 (132, 1 f.), 136, 1), GCS, *Clemens Alex.*, II, 185 f., 188.

88. Cf. *Laws*, 716 C, 837 A; *Theaetetus* 176 A f.

89. See 1 Corinthians 11:1; Ephesians 5:1; etc.

90. ˙*De principiis* III, 6, 1, *GCS, Origenes*, V, 280; In *Genes, homil.* I, 13, *ibid.* VI, 18.

91. *De professione christiana*, PG XLVI, 244 f.

92. Cf. also L. Delatte, *Les Traités de la royauté d'Ecphante, Diotogène et Sthénidas* (*Bibliothèque de la Faculté de Philosophie et Lettres de l'Université de Liège* XCVII, Liège-Paris, 1942), especially 178 f.

93. *Stromata* V, 5 (29, 1), *GCS, Clemens Alex.*, II, 344. For Eurytus-Eurysus, cf. E. Wellmann, in Pauly-Wissowa, *Realencyclopädie der classischen Altertumswissenschaft, Neue Bearbeitung*, VI (Stuttgart, 1909) 1363; H. Diels and W. Kranz, *Fragmente der Vorsokratiker* I (Berlin, 1951) 419; for the genuine Eurytus, H. Cherniss, *Aristotle's Criticism of Presocratic Philosophy* (Baltimore, 1935) 37, n. 139; 239. On the relationship between Eurysus, Clement, and the Neo-Pythagorean Ecphantus, cf. Delatte, *op. cit.*, 177 ff., and see note 158 below.

94. *De vita pythagorica* 18, 86 f., and 28, 137, ed. L. Deubner (Leipzig, 1937) 50 f., 77. For Jamblichus' source, cf. E. Rohde, "Die Quellen des Jamblichus in seiner Biographie des Pythagoras," *Rheinisches Museum für Philologie, Neue Folge*, XXVII (1872) 45 f.

95. *Pro imaginibus* 28.

96. In the following century, Diogenes Laertius (VIII, 1, 19, VI, 2, 5) was to attribute a similar doctrine to Diogenes of Sinope.

97. See *Ambiguorum Liber*, PG XCI, 1084 A. Cf. H. U. v. Balthasar, S.J., *Liturgie cosmique: Maxime le Confesseur* (Paris, 1947) 87.

98. Cf. J. M. Mercati, "Stephani Bostreni nova de sacris imaginibus fragmenta e libro deperdito κατὰ Ἰουδαίων," *Theologische Quartalschrift* LXXVII (1895) 663 ff.

99. Cf. Sirarpie Der Nersessian, "Une Apologie des images du 7ᵐᵉ siècle," *Byzantion* XVII (1944–45) 58 ff.; Norman H. Baynes, "The Icons before Iconoclasm," *Harvard Theological Review* XLIV (1951) 93 ff.; Paul J. Alexander, "Hypatius of Ephesus: A Note on Image Worship in the Sixth Century," *ibid.* XLV (1952) 177 ff.

100. Cf. Mansi, *Concil.* XIII, 160 D ff. There also survives a fragment of a *Sermon on the Images* by Symeon (PG LXXXVI, 3219 f.; cf. O. Bardenhewer, *Geschichte der altkirchlichen Literatur* V [Freiburg i.B., 1932] 71 f.), quoted by John Damascene, *De imaginibus, oratio* III (PG XCIV, 1409 C f.).

101. Cf. Miss Der Nersessian's article quoted above; also J.-B. Frey, "La Question des images chez les Juifs," *Biblica* XV (1934), 298 ff.

102. Cf. S. Der Nersessian, *op. cit.*, 79 ff.; F. Vernet, in *Dictionnaire de théologie catholique* VIII/2 (Paris, 1925) 1876 ff., *s.v. Juifs* (*Controverses avec les*); also *Les Trophées de Damas: Controverse judéo-chrétienne du 7ᵐᵉ siècle*, ed. G. Bardy, *Patrologia Orientalis* XV (1927).

103. PG XCIV, 1376 B ff.

104. Edited in the article quoted in note 98.

105. Cf. Mansi, *Concil.* XII, 1069 A.

106. Mercati, *op. cit.*, 666, 668. The nature of the pagan idol could also be characterized by its unreality, its being based on fiction; for orthodox Byzantine argumentation on these lines, see P. Lucas Koch, "Zur Theologie der Christusikone," *Benediktin. Monatsschrift* XX (1938) 33, n. 1.

107. Cf. J. Geffcken, "Der Bilderstreit des heidnischen Altertums," *Archiv für Religionswissenschaft* XIX (1916–1919) 286 ff.; A. Grabar, *Martyrium* II (Paris, 1946) 350.

108. It is touched upon only in passing by E. Cassirer, "Eidos und Eidolon," *Vorträge der Bibliothek Warburg* 1922/23, I (1924) 1 ff., and H. Willms, ΕΙΚΩΝ (Münster, 1935) 15 ff.

109. This appears as a pagan point of view in Augustine's *Enarratio in Psalm. CXIII, Sermo II*, 4 f., Migne, *Patrologia Latina* (hereafter PL) XXXVII, 1483 f., and in the late seventh-century fictitious dialogue between a "Greek" and a Christian by John of Salonika, quoted in the *Acts of the Second Nicaenum*, Mansi, *Concil.* XIII, 164 C ff.

110. *Ennead* IV, 3, 11. Cf. A. Grabar, "Plotin et les origines de l'esthétique médiévale," *Cahiers archéologiques* I (1945) 17.

111. See J. Bidez, *Vie de Porphyre . . . avec les fragments des traités* Περὶ ἀγαλμάτων *et De regressu animae* (Gand and Leipzig, 1913), fragment 2, p. 2.° Cf. Geffcken, *op. cit.*,

307, for possible dependence on Poseidonius. See, furthermore, E. Bevan, *Holy Images* (London, 1940) 74 ff., 108 f.

112. Philostratus Major, *Imagines* I, Prooem 1, ed. O. Benndorf, C. Schenkl, etc. (Leipzig, 1843) 3: Ὅστις μὴ ἀσπάζεται τὴν ζωγραφίαν, ἀδικεῖ τὴν ἀλήθειαν, etc. (Cf. Borinski, *op. cit.*, I, 1; Panofsky, *op. cit.*, 6). See also his life of *Apollonius of Tyana*, II, 22: . . . ἐστι τι γραφικὴ; εἰ γε . . . καὶ ἀλήθεια.

113. *Ekphrasis* 10, 2, ed. C. Schenkl and E. Reisch (Leipzig, 1902) 64: the image seen seems to be not a τύπος . . . ἀλλὰ τῆς ἀληθείας πλάσμα . . . ἡ τέχνη . . . ἐνεικονισαμένη τὸν θεὸν εἰς αὐτὸν ἐξίσταται. ὕλη μὲν οὖσα θεοειδὲς ἀναπέμπει νόημα . . .

114. *Fragmentum epistolae*, ed. J. Bidez and F. Cumont, *Imp. Caesaris Flavii Claudii Iuliani Epistolae, Leges* . . . (Paris, London, 1922) no. 89 b (293 f.) pp. 133 f.

115. Cf. Leontius of Neapolis in Cyprus, cited in the *Acts of the Second Nicaenum*, Mansi, *Concil.* XIII, 44.

116. Nicephorus, *Antirrheticus III adversus Constantinum Copronymum* 10, PG C, 392 B–C.

117. *De imaginibus, oratio III*, 20, PG XCIV, 1340 C f.; see above.

118. Theodore of Studion, *Antirrheticus III*, 2, 5, PG XCIX, 420 A.

119. Page 13.

120. Cf. my two articles quoted in note 82; the relevant texts from John Damascene and Theodore of Studion are cited in them.

121. Theodore of Studion, *Antirrheticus III*, 3, 1, PG XCIX, 420 D; also *op. cit.* 3, 9, *ibid.* 424 D; furthermore, *Epist.* . . . *ad Platonem de cultu sacrarum imaginum, ibid.* 501 A f., 504 A.

122. Cf., for instance, Theodore of Studion, *Antirrheticus I*, 12, PG XCIX, 344 B: Οὕτω καὶ ἐν εἰκόνι εἶναι τὴν θεότητα εἰπών τις οὐκ ἂν ἁμάρτῃ τοῦ δέοντος.

123. Mansi, *Concil.* XIII, 244 B.

124. *Antirrheticus III*, 2, 11, PG XCIX, 426 A f. (where it is used for an iconoclast's objection); cf. also *Epist.* . . . *ad Platonem de cultu sacrarum imaginum, ibid.* 501 B ff. See, furthermore, *Nicephorus Antirrheticus III versus Constantinum Copronymum* 21, PG C, 405 D–408, referring to St. Basil. The iconoclasts apparently used the *physis-thesis* antithesis for the distinction of the historical and the eucharistic Body of Christ; cf. P. Lucas Koch, "Zur Theologie der Christusikone," *Benediktin. Monatsschrift* XX (1938) 40.

125. Cf. K. Hansmann, *Ein neuentdeckter Kommentar zum Johannesevangelium* (*Forschungen zur christlichen Literatur- und Dogmengeschichte* XVI/4–5, Paderborn, 1930) 42 ff., 46 ff. See also Grumel, in *Dict. de théol. cath.* VII/1, 792, for Euthymus Zigabenus.

126. *De imaginibus, oratio III*, 18, PG XCIV, 1337 C. Cf. Hansmann, *op. cit.*, 42 f.

127. *De imaginibus, oratio III, loc. cit.* 1337 D–1340 B. Cf. also John Damascene's poem on the Transfiguration of Christ, PG XCVI, 848 ff., esp. 849B: Θέσει οὐ γέγονας, etc.

128. PG XCIV, 641 A.

129. Cf. *Categories* 4, 2a.

130. PG XCIV, 641 A f.

131. *Physics* 193 a.

132. *Ibid.* 199 a.

133. *De Haeresibus* 83, PG XCIV, 744 C ff.

134. *Philoponi in Physicorum octo libros commentaria* (*Commentaria in Aristotelem graeca*, ed. Academia Litterarum Regia Borussica, XVI–XVII, Berlin, 1888).

135. *Op. cit.* 213 (to Aristotle, *Physics*, 193a 14): τὴν θέσει καὶ μὴ φύσει διάθεσιν. It is true that elsewhere in his *Physics*, Aristotle uses the term *thesis* (e.g., 205 b 34), and even *thesis* and *physis* combined (208 b 24 ff.).

136. *Op. cit.* 454 (to Aristotle, *Physics* 205 b 24; cf. *Physics* 205 b 34, 208 b 24).

137. See Plato, *Cratylus* 389 D f., 390 D ff., 430 ff.; *Epist.* 7, 342 f.; cf. Steckerl, *op. cit.*, *Class. Philol.* XXXVII (1942) 288 ff. See also Proclus, *In rem publicam*, ed. W. Kroll, I (Leipzig, 1901) 169 f.; *id.*, *In Cratylum*, c. XLVIII, ed. G. Pasquali (Leipzig, 1908) 16, and, especially, c. XVI, *loc. cit.* 5 f., where the *thesis-physis* antithesis is derived from a divergence of opinion concerning the origin of names between Pythagoras and Democritus (see H. Diels,

Die Fragmente der Vorsokratiker[2] II [Berlin, 1922] 68, 55 B 26). For the relationship, established, it seems, by the Stoics, and elaborated on by Philo, between the antithesis *thesis-physis* and that of *nomos* and *physis*, cf. F. Heinimann, *Nomos und Physis* (Basel, 1945) 162 f., and M. Radin's incidental remarks in his article "Early Statutory Interpretation in England," *Illinois Law Review of North Western University* XXXVIII (1944) 25 f. See above all Stephan Kuttner, "Sur les origines du terme 'droit positif,'" *Revue historique de droit français et étranger*, Serie IV, Année XV (1936) 728 ff., where the antithesis *ius positivum — ius naturale* is traced on the one hand to the pre-Socratic-Platonistic tradition, mentioned above, via Proclus' *Cratylus Commentary* and via Chalcidius and Aulus Gellius, and, on the other hand, to a passage concerning the *locus naturalis aut positivus* from Fortunatianus' *Ars Rhetorica* (*Rhetores latini minores* [ed. Halm, Leipzig, 1863] II, 3), which in my opinion must ultimately depend on the Aristotelian tradition here discussed (Münscher, in Pauly-Wissowa, *Realencyclopädie der classischen Altertumswissenschaft* VII [Stuttgart, 1912] 48, speaks only of a Greek source in general). Carl Langer, "Euhemeros und die Theorie der φύσει und θέσει θέοι," *Angelos* II (1926) 53 ff., was not available to me; see the article of E. Kantorowicz quoted in the following note.

138. See above, p. 3 f. Philo could also be quoted, but hardly influenced John Damascene's antithetical use of the terms *physis* and *thesis* as relating to images, though he quotes Philo repeatedly in the *Sacra Parallela*. While this paper was at the press, there appeared the stimulating article by Ernst H. Kantorowicz, "Deus per Naturam, Deus per Gratiam: A Note on Mediaeval Political Theology," *Harvard Theological Review* XLV (1952) 253 ff., which touches on several points discussed here; see, especially, pp. 261 ff., for the *physis-charis* antithesis and its relation to the *physis-thesis* and the *physis-mimesis* antitheses. For the relationship between grace, image, and truth, cf. also below, p. 19.

139. Eustathius of Antioch quoted by Theodoret of Cyrus, *Dialogus* II (*Inconfusus*), PG LXXXIII, 176 C.

140. *Oratio XXX* (*Theologica IV: De Filio*) 20, PG XXXVI, 129 B f.

141. The Platonistic element is obviously strong in all these speculations. The same line of thought is still evident in St. Augustine when he defines a true image by the fact that it is generated or made by that which it resembles, as a son by his father or the reflection in a mirror by that which is reflected in it (cf. *Quaestion. in Heptateuchum* V, 4, PL XXXIV, 749 f.; *De diversis quaestionibus, quaestio* 51, *ibid.* XL, 32 f.). While from this point of view there is no great difficulty in seeing the image of God in man, it is different with the images of art, since they are not, at first sight at least, generated or made by their prototypes. But already Plotinus had answered this objection by stressing the mere instrumentality of the artist without forgetting the nevertheless merely "thetical" character of the image of art (cf. especially *Ennead* VI, 4, 9 f.).

142. *De imaginibus, oratio III*, PG XCIV, 1368 D.

143. I, 2, 6, GCS, *Origenes*, V, 34. Here it is quite clear that the most "natural" image is that of God Father in Christ, and that the relationship of a son and a father is considered less "natural" than that between *the* Son and the Father, but more natural than that between an art image and its prototype. This hierarchical order of images is still found in the iconoclastic period; cf. the ninth-century *Commentary to the Gospel of St. John*, edited by Hansmann (quoted in note 125), pp. 48 f.

144. See Mansi, *Concil.* IX, 384 C. Cf. also *ibid.* 210 B ff. (*Collatio* IV, c. XVII). Furthermore, Johannes Philoponus, *De opificio mundi* VI, 9 f., especially 10 (end), ed. W. Reichardt (Leipzig, 1897) 244 f.: in his Monophysite polemic against Theodore of Mopsuestia, Philoponus compares the latter's conception of Christ's relation to the Father to the pagan conception of the relation between their idols and their gods; see also Philoponus against Iamblichus, in Photius, *Bibliotheca*, Cod. 215, PG CIII, 708 B ff.

145. *Ibid.* IV, 12. Cf. R. Devreesse, *Essai sur Théodore de Mopsueste* (*Studi e Testi* CXLI, Città del Vaticano, 1948) 246 ff., for the doubtful authenticity of the Theodorian texts used by the Council.

146. The antithesis *adoption-birth* is one of the legal applications of the *thesis-physis* antithesis; cf. Heinimann, *op. cit.*, 163.

147. *De imaginibus, oratio III*, PG XCIV, 1412 C f.

148. *In Exod. homil.* VI, 5, *GCS, Origenes,* VI, 196 f. Similarly, Augustine, *Quaestion. in Heptateuch.* V, 4, *loc. cit.*

149. *In Epist. ad Hebraeos* [10, 1], *homil.* XVII, *PG* LXIII, 130: . . . τουτέστιν οὐκ αὐτὴν τὴν ἀλήθειαν. Ἔως μὲν γὰρ ἄν ὡς ἐν γραφῇ περιάγῃ τις τὰ χαράγματα [this must be the correct reading even though Migne (after Montfaucon) has χρώματα in the text and gives χαράγματα only as a variant; χαράγματα is confirmed by the text from Cyril of Alexandria quoted below, and by the *Acts of the Quinisextum,* cited in note 153] σκιὰ τίς ἐστιν· ὅταν δὲ τὸ ἄνθος ἐπαλείψῃ τις καὶ ἐπιχρίσῃ τὰ χρώματα, τότε εἰκὼν γίνεται. Τοιοῦτόν τι καὶ ὁ νόμος ἦν. ⟨⟨Σκιὰν γὰρ⟩⟩ φησιν, ⟨⟨ἔχων ὁ νόμος τῶν μελλόντων ἀγαθῶν οὐκ αὐτὴν τὴν εἰκόνα τῶν πραγμάτων⟩⟩ (Hebrews 10:1), τουτέστι τῆς θυσίας τῆς ἀφέσεως. See also *In Epist. ad Hebr.* [7, 1 ff.], *homil.* XII, *ibid.* 98: Οὕτω καὶ ἐν ταῖς σκιαγραφουμέναις εἰκόσι γινόμεν ἴδοι τις ἄν· ἐν ἐκείναις γὰρ ἐστι μέν τι καὶ ὅμοιον, ἔστι δὲ καὶ ἀνόμοιον· διὰ μὲν γὰρ τῆς ἁπλῶς γραφῆς ὁμοιότης τίς ἐστι τοῦ χαρακτῆρος· τῶν χρωμάτων δὲ ἐπιτεθέντων τότε φανερῶς δείκνυται ἡ διαφορά, καὶ τὸ ὅμοιον καὶ τὸ ἀνόμοιον. Furthermore *In proditionem Iudae, homil.* I, 4 (end), *ibid.* XLIX, 379 (quoted by John Damascene, *De imaginibus, oratio II, PG* XCIV. 1316 A): Καθάπερ γὰρ οἱ ζωγράφοι ἐν αὐτῷ τῷ πίνακι καὶ τὰς γραμμὰς περιάγουσι καὶ τὴν σκιὰν γράφουσι (John Damascene: σκιαγραφοῦσι) καὶ τότε τὴν ἀλήθειαν τῶν χρωμάτων αὐτῷ ἐπιτιθέασιν, οὕτω καὶ ὁ Χριστὸς ἐποίησεν, when at one and the same table He celebrated the Pascha of the Jews, which was only τυπικόν, and the true one of the New Testament. Cf. also Cyril of Alexandria, *Epist.* 41 (to Bishop Acacius of Melitene), *PG* LXXVII, 217 B f.: Φαμὲν δὲ ὅτι σκιὰ καὶ τύπος ὁ νόμος ἦν καὶ οἷόν τις γραφὴ παρατεθεῖσα πρὸς θέαν τοῖς ὁρῶσι τὰ πράγματα. Αἱ δὲ σκιαὶ τῆς τῶν γραφόντων ἐν πίνακι τέχνης τὰ πρῶτα τῶν χαραγμάτων εἰσίν· αἷς εἴπερ ἐπενεχθεῖεν τῶν χρωμάτων τὰ ἄνθη, τότε δὴ τότε τῆς γραφῆς ἀπαστράπτει τὸ κάλλος; this text was quoted by the *Acts of the Second Nicaenum* (Mansi, *Concil.* XIII, 11 B, where the addressee is called Acacius of Scythopolis). Cyril's somewhat younger contemporary, Diadochus of Photicaea, *De perfectione spirituali* (*Centum Capita*) 89, ed. and trans. E. des Places, S.J. (Paris, Lyon, 1943) 151, used the simile of under-painting and finished picture in a somewhat different way: the former is the image of God in man which is his from creation and is restored in baptism, the second the resemblance with God which must be gained by a virtuous life; for this distinction, see p. 11 above. Concerning *skiagraphia* and related terms, it should be noted — and here I owe valuable suggestions to Professor Erwin Panofsky — that in antiquity they did at first not signify an "underpainting" but the painting of shadows which was the invention of Apollodorus of Athens (late fifth century). The texts, from Plato to Photius, are discussed most thoroughly by E. Pfuhl, "Apollodorus ὁ σκιαγράφος," *Jahrbuch des kaiserl. deutschen archäologischen Instituts* XXV, 1910 (1911) 12 ff., R. Schöne, "Σκιαγραφία," *ibid.* XXVII, 1912 (1912) 19 ff., Pfuhl, "Skiagraphia," *ibid.* 227 ff.; *id.*, *Malerei und Zeichnung der Griechen* II (München, 1923) 674 ff.; P.-M. Schuhl, *Platon et l'art de son temps* (Paris, 1933) 10 ff.; for the relationship between *skiagraphia* and *scenographia,* see also E. Panofsky, "Die Perspektive als symbolische Form," *Vorträge der Bibliothek Warburg* 1924–1925 (1927) 301 ff. Probably it was in Hellenistic times that the term *skiagraphia* first could assume the meaning of a sketch or an underpainting; Vitruvius, *De architectura* I, 2, 2 (Rose; I, 2, 8 Choisy) uses the equivalent *adumbratio* in this sense; see also the late second century *Acta Joannis* 27, edd. Lipsius and Bonnet 165. See, furthermore, Pliny, *Naturalis Historia* XXXV, 3 (5) [15], 12 (43) [151], where the art of painting and molding figures is derived from the tracing of the outline of a man's shadow, and similarly Athenagoras, *Legatio pro christianis* 17, *PG* VI, 924 A, where the word σκιαγραφία is used in this connection; see also Philostratus Major, *Life of Apollonius of Tyana,* II, 22. The terminologies of Chrysostom, Cyril, and the Damascene are clearly related to those of Athenagoras and Philostratus.

150. I was unable to find a printed text of John Chrysostom which would exactly correspond to that of John Damascene; the latter's paraphrase may be his own or originate from a different manuscript tradition of John Chrysostom's commentary or from a catena; cf. R. Devreesse, in *Dictionnaire de la Bible, Supplément,* I (Paris, 1928) 1211 ff., *s.v. Chaînes exégétiques grecques.* John Damascene's own anthology from John Chrysostom's commentaries to St. Paul does not contain any similar text commenting on Hebrews (cf. *PG* XCV. 439 ff.).

151. The term εἰκών is here the equivalent of τύπος in the sense of anticipation; see the following note.

152. De imaginibus, oratio III, PG XCIV, 1361 D f. (also oratio I, ibid. 1269 D f., oratio II, ibid. 1312 D): Καί πως εἰκὼν τοῦ δευτέρου τὸ πρῶτον, ὁ Μελχισεδὲκ τοῦ Χριστοῦ· ὥσπερ ἄν τις εἴποι σκιὰν τῆς γραφῆς τῆς ἐν χρώματι τὸ πρὸ ταύτης σκίασμα τοῦ γράφεως. Διὰ τοῦτον γὰρ ὁ νόμος καλεῖται σκιὰ ἡ δὲ χάρις ἀλήθεια, πράγματα δὲ τὰ μέλλοντα. Ὥστε ὁ μὲν νόμος καὶ ὁ Μελχισεδὲκ: προσκίασμα τῆς ἐν χρώμασι γραφῆς; ἡ δὲ χάρις, ἡ ἀλήθεια: ἡ ἐν χρώμασι γραφή; τὰ πράγματα τὰ μέλλοντος αἰῶνος. Ὡς εἶναι τὴν Παλαιὰν τύπου τύπον, καὶ τὴν Νέαν τῶν πραγμάτων τύπον. For the concept of the image as truth, cf. note 112, quoting Philostratus. The texts of John Chrysostom and John Damascene here discussed are cited by H. Lubac, S.J., Corpus Mysticum (Paris, 1949) 219, n. 55; see also his important remarks and texts concerning veritas, imago, figura, etc., ibid. 210 ff., 248 ff. Cf., for instance, the following text from St. Ambrose which differs significantly from John Damascene and even from John Chrysostom: Umbra in Lege, imago vero in Evangelio, veritas in caelestibus (In Psalm. XXXVIII Enarratio, c. 25, PL XIV, 1051 C; Lubac, op. cit., 219; cf. also Dürig, Imago 31). One might note here briefly the relationship of such conceptions to early Christian and mediaeval "typology" in theology, literature and art and also a remote connection with later Joachimite ideas on the "Third Age" of the Holy Spirit — influenced undoubtedly by Greek thought. For the development of the concept of "figure" (τύπος, figura) above all in the Latin west, but with some remarks also about the corresponding Greek terms such as τύπος, μορφή, εἶδος, σχῆμα, see E. Auerbach, Figura, in Neue Dantestudien (Istanbuler Schriften V, Istanbul, 1944). A detailed investigation of the relevant Greek patristic terms (especially χαρακτήρ) in their relation to the image concept would be rewarding.

153. Cf. Mansi, Concil. XI, 977 E–980 A: Ἐν τισι τῶν σεπτῶν εἰκόνων γραφαῖς ἀμνὸς δακτύλῳ τοῦ προδρόμου δεικνύμενος ἐγχαράττεται . . . Τοὺς οὖν παλαιοὺς τύπους καὶ τὰς σκιὰς ὡς τῆς ἀληθείας συμβολάτε καὶ προχαράγματα παραδεδομένους τῇ ἐκκλησίᾳ κατασπαζόμενοι τὴν χάριν προτιμῶμεν καὶ τὴν ἀλήθειαν ὡς πλήρωμα νόμου ταύτην ὑποδεξάμενοι. Ὡς ἂν οὖν τὸ τέλειον κἂν ταῖς χρωματουργίαις ἐν τε͂ις ἀπάντων ὄψεσιν ὑπογράφηται τὸν τοῦ αἴροντος τὴν ἁμαρτίαν τοῦ κόσμου ἀμνοῦ χριστοῦ τοῦ θεοῦ ἡμῶν κατὰ τὸν ἀνθρώπινον χαρακτῆρα καὶ ἐν ταῖς εἰκόσιν ἀπὸ τοῦ νῦν ἀντὶ τοῦ παλαιοῦ ἀμνοῦ ἀναστηλοῦσθαι ὁρίζομεν. . . This text was repeatedly quoted by the iconophiles; cf., for instance, the Acts of the Second Nicaenum, Mansi, op. cit. XII, 1123 E ff., XIII, 40 E f.

154. E. v. Dobschütz, Christusbilder (Texte und Untersuchungen zur Geschichte der altchristlichen Literatur, XVIII, Neue Folge III, 1899), especially 276 ff.

155. A. Grabar, Martyrium II (Paris, 1946) 351 ff.

156. A striking example of this practice, knowledge of which I owe to Professor Albert M. Friend, Jr., may be found in the Acts of the Eighth Ecumenical Council, held at Constantinople in 869 (Mansi, Concil. XVI, 388 C–D). There, one of the stragglers of the defeated iconoclastic movement was confronted with an imperial coin of Basil I which may well have shown the image of Christ in addition to that of the emperor (see below, note 168), and the iconoclast was admonished in vain to render to the "theandric" image of Our Lord the same honor which he was willing to accord to that of the terrestrial Basileus.

157. Edited by L. Delatte, Les Traités de la royauté d'Ecphante, Diotogène et Sthénidas (Liège-Paris, 1942). Cf. also E. R. Goodenough, "The Political Philosophy of Hellenistic Kingship," Yale Classical Studies I (New Haven, 1928) 53 ff. Delatte rather convincingly argues for the first or second century of our era as the date of these treatises; Goodenough thinks that they date from the Hellenistic period itself, which they certainly reflect in many ways.

158. See, especially, Ecphantus, ed. L. Delatte, loc. cit., 27 f. (272, 9 – 273, 2), and Delatte's commentary, 177 ff., where it is made probable that Ecphantus has here utilized and transferred from man in general to the king the text from Eurysus, quoted by Clement of Alexandria and referred to above p. 14.

159. See, for instance, the famous inscription for Ptolemy V Epiphanes on the Rosetta Stone where the king is called εἰκὼν ζῶσα τοῦ Διός; for the cross-connections between this Hellenistic kingship ideology and certain terms of the Old and New Testaments, cf. W.

Bousset, *Kyrios Christos* (Göttingen, 1921) 150 ff., 200 ff., 244 ff. For the related concept of the king as animate law, cf. A. Steinwenter, "ΝΟΜΟΣ ΕΜΨΥΧΟΣ," *Anzeiger der Akademie der Wissenschaften in Wien*, Philosophisch-Historische Klasse, LXXXIII, 1946 (1947) 250 ff.

160. For instance, *De vita Constantini* I, 5, GCS, *Eusebius* I, 9; *Tricennial Oration* I (end), II, *ibid.*, 199 f. Cf. N. H. Baynes, "Eusebius and the Christian Empire," *Mélanges Bidez* (*Annales de l'Institut de Philologie et d'Histoire Orientale*, II, Bruxelles, 1934) 13 ff.; also K. M. Setton, *Christian Attitude towards the Emperor* . . . (quoted in note 8) 47 ff.

161. See *De regno* IX (9c), rec. N. Terzaghi, *Synesii Cyrenensis Hymni et Opuscula* II/1 (Roma, 1944) 20, where the Emperor Arcadius is called a moving and animate divine image (ἄγαλμα . . . κινούμενον . . . καὶ ἔμπνουν); there is contamination here with the νόμος ἔμψυχος idea, cf. note 158. Cf. Setton, *op. cit.*, 152 ff.

162. For Themistius, see the ample references in L. Delatte, *Les Traités de la royauté* . . . 156 ff.

163. See above p. 10 ff. It must be remembered, however, that in the combined Biblical and Platonistic tradition these two relationships were often merged: on the one hand, perfect man as such is a king (according to the Platonic concept of the kingly philosopher as well as according to the Biblical ideas of Adam's royal character and of the Kingdom of God in every true Christian); on the other, the ruler represents God in a special and leading manner. Thus, for Clement of Alexandria (cf. especially *Stromata* I, 24, GCS, *Clemens Alex.*, II, 99 ff. [158, 1 ff.]) as for Philo before him (cf. *De vita Mosis* II, 1 ff., ed. Cohn and Wendland, *loc. cit.* IV, 200 ff.), Moses was the true paragon of royal philosophy, of the wise man who is a king and of the king who is a wise man. Clement thought it certain, furthermore, that Plato's concept of the king-philosopher had its origin in the Old Testament (see, for instance, *Stromata* I, 25, *loc. cit.* 103 [165, 1], II, 5, *ibid.* 123 ff. [20, 1 ff.]). In Clement, the interest for the royal dignity of man is much stronger than that for rulership in the political sense; the topoi of the *animate image* (ἄγαλμα ἔμψυχος, cf. *Protrepticus* 10, GCS, *Clemens Alex.*, I, 71 [98, 3]), and the *animate law* (νόμος ἔμψυχος, cf. *Stromata* I, 26, II, 4, *ibid.* II, 104 [168, 1], 122 [18, 4 ff.]) are here applied in a genuine Biblical and Platonic sense to man and to Moses, respectively, rather than in the Hellenistic way to the ruler. See, similarly, Gregory of Nyssa, *De opificio hominis*, 4, PG XLIV, 136 C, on man as the ἔμψυχος εἰκών (quoted by John Damascene, *De imaginibus*, oratio I, PG XCIV, 1268 D f.); cf. Setton, *op. cit.*, 201. It is likely, however, that Clement knew the ideology of the Hellenistic monarchy; he uses the typical Hellenistic term of royal beneficence for his true gnostic (see *Stromata* II, 19, *loc. cit.* II, 166 [97, 1 f.]): εὐεργέτων καὶ λόγω καὶ ἔργω; (cf. for instance, the attribute Εὐεργετής of Ptolemy III). See now the study of Ernst H. Kantorowicz, quoted in note 138, for a fuller discussion of the relationship between the concepts of man in general, and of the ruler in particular, as image of God; also F. E. Cranz, "Kingdom and Polity in Eusebius of Caesarea," *Harvard Theological Review* XLV (1952) 47 ff., especially 51–56.

164. Matthew 22:21.

165. Cf. *In Lucam homil.* XXXIX, GCS, *Origenes*, IX, 230: "Quod ergo ait: 'reddite quae sunt Caesaris, Caesari,' hoc dicit: deponite personam 'choici,' abjicite imaginem terrenam, ut possitis vobis personam caelestis imponentes reddere 'quae sunt Dei, Deo.' " Cf. also *In Matthaeum, Tom.* XVII, 27, *ibid.* X, 658 ff.

166. Cf. 1 Corinthians 15:49: "Therefore, as we have borne the image of the earthly, let us bear also the image of the heavenly." The first part of this verse refers to Genesis 2:7: "And the Lord God formed man of the slime of the earth . . ."; the second sentence of Genesis 2:7 is quoted by St. Paul in 1 Corinthians 15:45: "The first man Adam was made into a living soul;" and the Apostle continues, "the last Adam into a quickening spirit." The last Adam, the heavenly, is Christ. See above, note 27.

167. That is the man who lives according to Christ, i.e., who strips himself of "the old man with his deeds" and puts on "the new, him who is renewed unto knowledge according to the image of Him that created him" (Colossians 3:9 f.; Genesis 1:26). Although Origen does not here quote Colossians 3:9 f. or Genesis 1:26, his references to the image of Christ

in man (1 Corinthians 15:49) as well as to man's earthly part (Genesis 2:7) imply those two other verses, that is to say, the creational spiritual image of God in man, according to Genesis 1:26, and its renewal or reform according to the doctrine of St. Paul, also expressed in Romans 12:2, 2 Corinthians 3:18, etc. For Origen's interpretation of Genesis 1:26, see above, p. 12.

168. See W. Wroth, *Catalogue of the Imperial Byzantine Coins in the British Museum*, I (London, 1908) xcii, xciv. For the iconoclast emperors' substitution of their own image for the image of Christ, cf. A. Grabar, *L'Empereur dans l'art byzantin* (*Publications de la Faculté des Lettres de l'Université de Strasbourg*, Fasc. LXXV, Paris, 1936) 167 ff.; P. Lucas Koch, "Christusbild-Kaiserbild," *Benediktinische Monatsschrift* XXI (1939) 85 ff.; also the second of my articles quoted in note 82.

Acknowledgments

Schoedel, William R. "Enclosing, Not Enclosed: The Early Christian Doctrine of God." In William R. Schoedel and Robert L. Wilken, eds., *Early Christian Literature and the Classical Intellectual Tradition: In Honorem Robert M. Grant* (Paris: Éditions Beauchesne, 1979): 75–86. Reprinted with the permission of Éditions Beauchesne. Courtesy of Yale University Sterling Memorial Library.

Wiles, Maurice. "Some Reflections on the Origins of the Doctrine of the Trinity." *Journal of Theological Studies* n.s. 8 (1957): 92–106. Reprinted with the permission of Oxford University Press. Courtesy of Yale University Seeley G. Mudd Library.

Stead, G. Christopher. "The Concept of Divine Substance." *Vigiliae Christianae* 29 (1975): 1–14. Reprinted with the permission of E.J. Brill. Courtesy of Yale University Seeley G. Mudd Library.

Kannengiesser, Charles. "Athanasius of Alexandria and the Foundation of Traditional Christology." *Theological Studies* 34 (1973): 103–13. Reprinted with the permission of *Theological Studies*, Georgetown University. Courtesy of *Theological Studies*.

Christou, Panachiotis. "Uncreated and Created, Unbegotten and Begotten in the Theology of Athanasius of Alexandria." *Augustinianum* 13 (1973): 399–409. Reprinted with the permission of Instituto Patristico Augustinianum. Courtesy of Yale University Divinity Library.

Kannengiesser, Charles. "Arius and the Arians." *Theological Studies* 44 (1983): 456–75. Reprinted with the permission of *Theological Studies*, Georgetown University. Courtesy of *Theological Studies*.

Lienhard, Joseph T. "The 'Arian' Controversy: Some Categories Reconsidered." *Theological Studies* 48 (1987): 415–37. Reprinted with the permission of *Theological Studies*, Georgetown University. Courtesy of Yale University Seeley G. Mudd Library.

Stead, G.C. "'Eusebius' and the Council of Nicaea." *Journal of Theological Studies* n.s. 24 (1973): 85–100. Reprinted with the permission of Oxford University Press. Courtesy of Yale University Seeley G. Mudd Library.

Young, Frances M. "Insight or Incoherence? The Greek Fathers on God and Evil." *Journal of Ecclesiastical History* 24 (1973): 113–26. Reprinted with the permission of Cambridge University Press. Courtesy of Yale University Seeley G. Mudd Library.

Wilken, Robert L. "Tradition, Exegesis, and the Christological Controversies." *Church History* 34 (1965): 123–45. Reprinted with the permission of the American Society of Church History. Courtesy of Yale University Seeley G. Mudd Library.

Young, Frances M. "A Reconsideration of Alexandrian Christology." *Journal of Ecclesiastical History* 22 (1971): 103–14. Reprinted with the permission of Cambridge University Press. Courtesy of Yale University Seeley G. Mudd Library.

Greer, Rowan A. "The Antiochene Christology of Diodore of Tarsus." *Journal of Theological Studies* n.s. 17 (1966): 327–41. Reprinted with the permission of Oxford University Press. Courtesy of Yale University Seeley G. Mudd Library.

Anastos, Milton V. "Nestorius Was Orthodox." *Dumbarton Oaks Papers* 16 (1962): 117–40. Reprinted with the permission of Dumbarton Oaks. Courtesy of Yale University Sterling Memorial Library.

Constantelos, Demetrios J. "Justinian and the Three Chapters Controversy." *Greek Orthodox Theological Review* 8 (1962): 71–94. Courtesy of Yale University Divinity Library.

Vööbus, Arthur. "The Origin of the Monophysite Church in Syria and Mesopotamia." *Church History* 42 (1973): 17–26. Reprinted with the permission of the American Society of Church History. Courtesy of Yale University Seeley G. Mudd Library.

Heron, Alasdair. "The Holy Spirit in Origen and Didymus the Blind: A Shift in Perspective from the Third to the Fourth Century." In Adolf Martin Ritter, ed., *Kerygma und Logos* (Gottingen: Vandenhoeck & Ruprecht, 1979): 298–310. Reprinted with the permission of Vandenhoeck und Reprecht. Courtesy of Vandenhoeck und Reprecht.

Baynes, Norman H. "The Icons Before Iconoclasm." *Harvard Theological Review* 44 (1951): 93–106. Copyright 1951 by the President and Fellows of Harvard College. Reprinted by permission. Courtesy of the *Harvard Theological Review.*

Ladner, Gerhart B. "The Concept of the Image in the Greek Fathers and the Byzantine Iconoclastic Controversy." *Dumbarton Oaks Papers* 7 (1953): 1–34. Reprinted with the permission of Dumbarton Oaks. Courtesy of Yale University Sterling Memorial Library.